PARADIGM
CHANGE IN
THEOLOGY

PARADIGM CHANGE IN THEOLOGY

A Symposium for the Future

Edited by

Hans Küng and David Tracy

Translated by
Margaret Köhl

T. & T. CLARK LTD
59 George Street, Edinburgh

Authorised English Translation of *Theologie – Wohin?* and
Das Neue Paradigma von Theologie © T & T Clark Ltd, 1989
Original German Edition © Benziger Verlag Zürich-Köln and Gütersloher
Verlagshaus Gerd Mohn, Gütersloh

Typeset by Bookworm Typesetting Ltd, 9A Gayfield Square, Edinburgh
Printed and bound in Great Britain by Billings & Sons Ltd, Worcester

for

T & T Clark Ltd, Edinburgh
First printed in the U.K. 1989

British Library Cataloguing in Publication Data
Küng, Hans, *1928-*
paradigm change in theology
1. Theology
I. Title   II. Tracy, David
230

ISBN 0 567 09494 4

PARADIGM CHANGE IN THEOLOGY

A Symposium for the Future

Directors:

Professor Hans Küng, Tübingen
Professor David Tracy, Chicago

Co-directors:

Professor Jerald Brauer, Chicago
Professor Norbert Greinacher, Tübingen
Professor Jürgen Moltmann, Tübingen

Programme Co-ordination Tübingen:

Dr. Karl-Josef Kuschel
Dr. Urs Baumann

Staff:

Dr. Bernadette Brooten
Anne Jensen
Karl-Heinz Rauch

Secretariat:

Annegret Dinkel
Eleonore Henn

SPONSORS

Institute for the Advanced Study of Religion,
University of Chicago

Divinity School Institute für ökumenische Forschung,
University of Tübingen

Concilium, International Review of Theology,
Nijmegen

Financial Sponsors

Deutsche Forschungsgemeinschaft
Rockefeller Foundation
University of Tübingen

THE PARTICIPANTS

Gregory Baum, Toronto
Urs Baumann, Tübingen
Oswald Bayer, Tübingen
Hans-Dieter Betz, Chicago
Josef Blank, Saarbrücken
Leonardo Boff, Petropolis, Brazil
Anton van den Boogaard, Nijmegen
P. Brand, Ankeveen
Jerald Brauer, Chicago
Bernadette Brooten, Tübingen/Claremont
Rüdiger Bubner, Tübingen
Anne Carr, Chicago
John Cobb, Claremont
John Coleman, Berkeley
M. Collins, Washington
Ingolf Dalferth, Tübingen
Mariasusai Dhavamony, Rome
Charles Duquoc, Lyons
Enrique Dussel, Mexico
V. Elizondo, San Antonio, Texas
Franklin Gamwell, Chicago
Claude Geffré, Paris
Brian Gerrish, Chicago
Rosino Gibellini, Brescia
Langdon Gilkey, Chicago
Norbert Greinacher, Tübingen
Werner Gross, Tübingen
Jürgen Habermas, Frankfurt
Hermann Häring, Nijmegen
P. Huizing, Nijmegen
Peter Hünermann, Tübingen

Gerfried Hunold, Tübingen
Jens Walter, Tübingen
Werner Jeanrond, Dublin
Jean-Pierre Jossua, Paris
Eberhard Jüngel, Tübingen
Charles Kannengiesser, Paris/Notre Dame, Ind.
Hans Küng, Tübingen
Karl-Josef Kuschel, Tübingen
Matthew Lamb, Milwaukee
Nicholas Lash, Cambridge
René Laurentin, Evry
Marcus Lefébure, Edinburgh
R. Lovin, Chicago
Martin Marty, Chicago
Bernard McGinn, Chicago
Johann Baptist Metz, Münster
Dietmar Mieth, Tübingen
Jürgen Moltmann, Tübingen
R. Murphy, Durham, N.C.
Schubert Ogden, Dallas
Stephan Pfürtner, Marburg
Jacques Pohier, Paris
D. Power, Washington
Paul Ricoeur, Chicago
Edward Schillebeeckx, Nijmegen
Elisabeth Schüssler-Fiorenza, Notre Dame, Ind.
H. Snijdewind, Nijmegen
Leonard Swidler, Philadelphia
Stephen Toulmin, Chicago
David Tracy, Chicago
K. Walf, Nijmegen
A. Weiler, Nijmegen
Michael Welker, Tübingen

TRANSLATOR'S PREFACE

In offering readers the papers presented to this international, ecumenical and interdisciplinary symposium we wished to do more than to present a volume of essays. Our purpose was to convey the living voice of the symposium itself, and to allow those who now read what was said there, to participate in the preparatory work and in the meetings themselves.

This explains the arrangement of the present book. After the roster of participants, the reader is offered the preparatory papers which were distributed before the symposium. Then the reader is invited to listen to the introductions to the symposium, to the papers read, and to the answers presented. The symposium closed with an ecumenical service conducted by Norbert Greinacher and Jürgen Moltmann, at which the sermon was preached by Walter Jens, Professor of Rhetoric at the University of Tübingen.

We felt that this arrangement would best allow the reader to enter into the atmosphere of the discussion. Inevitably, it leaves some loose ends. Papers occasionally refer to comment by other participants (perhaps made in discussion, perhaps in a moderator's remarks) for which the reader will look in vain. Here we can only ask for indulgence, hoping that the vitality which was our aim may compensate for any rough edges which it was impossible to eliminate.

Hans Küng's preparatory paper 'Paradigm Change in Theology' was made available to us in English. All other papers distributed and presented in German have been translated by the undersigned. Some papers were furnished with notes; others were provided with bibliographies instead. Here we have not sought to impose consistency.

Biblical quotations in the papers translated from German are taken from the Revised Standard Version, except where changes of wording were necessary to bring out the author's point.

Margaret Kohl

CONTENTS

THE PREPARATORY PAPERS

I. The Problems

II. Historical Analyses

THE SYMPOSIUM

I. Introductory Perspectives

II. Scientific Theory and the New Paradigm

III. Biblical Theology and Philosophy in the New Paradigm

IV. The Role of History in the New Paradigm

V. The Political Dimension of Theology in the New Paradigm

VI. Particular and Global Aspects of the New Paradigm

VII. Retrospects and Prospects

The Ecumenical Service

ABBREVIATIONS

AJT	*American Journal of Theology*
Chr. Sitte	Schleiermacher, *Die christliche Sitte*, 1843
Chr. Gl	A. Schweizer, *Christliche Glaubenslehre*, 1863-72
Gl	Schleiermacher, *Die christliche Glaube nach den Grundsätzen der evangelischen kirche*, 2nd ed. 1830/31
GS	Troeltsch, *Gesammelte Schriften*, 4 vols, 1912-25
KD	Schleiermacher, *Kurze Darstellung des theologischen Studiums zum Behuf einleitender Vorlesungen*, 1830
KS	Schleiermacher, *Kleine schriften und Predigten*, ed. H. Gerdes and E. Hirsch, 3 vols. Berlin 1969/70
LW	M. Luther, *Works*, ET ed. J. Pelikan and H. Lehmann, 54 vols, Philadelphia and St. Louis, 1955-
RGG	*Die Religion in Geschichte und Gegenwart*, 3rd ed., 1957-65
Sendschr.	Schleiermacher, *Sendschreiben* (1829)
STh Ia IIae	Thomas Aquinas, *Summa Theologiae*
SW	Sämtliche Werke
ThK	*Zeitschrift für Theologie und Kirche*
WA	M. Luther, *Werke*, Weimarer Ausgabe, 1833ff. (See bibliog. to previous contribution by S. Pfürtner)

INTRODUCTION

Is there a basic consensus in Christian theology today, in spite of all our differences? This question was the subject of an international ecumenical symposium held in the University of Tübingen, and attended by 70 men and women from all over the world – theologians, most of them, both Catholic and Protestant, but representatives of other disciplines as well – sociologists of religion, for example, and philosophers.

What drew us all together, from so far afield, on this occasion? Perhaps it was an awareness which ran right through the papers and discussions, the sense that we are living in 'a time of troubles', a time when old certainties are breaking up, a post-modern era, an era post-Auschwitz and post-Hiroshima. How does this affect the proclamation? How can theology be 'contemporary', and yet true to its identity? Are the doubts and crises also an opportunity, and if so, for what? New natural and humane sciences, democratically pluralistic societies, liberation movements of every kind – all these have consequences for theology especially. These consequences have as yet hardly been clearly seen let alone absorbed. Are we at the mercy of all these tensions, diverging systems and fashionable trends? Or can we trace the emergence of a new, different, basic pattern of theology – a 'new paradigm', to use the phrase which we took as *leitmotif* for our symposium? Thomas S. Kuhn defines a paradigm as 'an entire constellation of beliefs, values, techniques, and so on shared by the members of a given community'. Do we find ourselves in a new paradigm in this sense? Does this new paradigm – if it exists – display constants, in spite of all the differing theories, methods and structures which make up the pattern? What are these constants, which the different Christian theologies have to presuppose if they wish to give a scientifically responsible account of the Christian faith for our time?

It is our hope that readers will be stimulated by the range of opinion represented here to enter critically and creatively into the problems that confront us all; but also into the new, painful, hopeful, beginnings.

The symposium was sponsored by the Tübingen Institut für ökumenische Forschung, the Institute for the Advanced Study of Religion in the University of Chicago, and the international theological periodical *Concilium*. It would not have been possible without the generous financial support of the Deutsche Forschungsgemeinschaft, the Rockefeller Foundation, and the University of Tübingen. In the name of all the participants, We would like to express to all these institutions our sincere thanks.

Hans Küng, Tübingen
David Tracy, Chicago
January 1989

THE PREPARATORY PAPERS

I. THE PROBLEMS

PARADIGM CHANGE IN THEOLOGY: A PROPOSAL FOR DISCUSSION

Hans Küng

In the following paper I try to apply the theory of paradigm change to the whole of Christian theology. I am well aware of the difficulties and the limitations of such an attempt. I consider this paper not as a fully worked out theory but as a proposal which – together with the other two preparatory papers – can serve as a foundation for a comprehensive and concentrated discussion.

In this context it has not been possible to work out in detail the complex technical developments in the history of theology in the perspective of the changing of paradigms (specialists in the different periods of the history of theology will provide supplements and corrections. I hope that these will be capable of interpretation in the general framework of this paper). The *hermeneutical and political implications* will be more fully developed in the two other papers. This paper was delivered as a public lecture at the University of Tübingen (1980), and developed further while I was a visiting professor at the University of Chicago Divinity School (1981).

1. Innovation in theology and the theory of knowledge

At all times and in all places, traditional *theology* has been extremely suspicious of the category of the *novum*, a category to which the Marxist philosopher Ernst Bloch has given a new respectability for our times. The attitude has maintained that *innovators* were heresiarchs, heretics, enemies of the church and often also of the state; seduced by Satan and their own doubts; stubbornly persisting in their pride and rigid outlook. These 'unbelievers' who had incurred condemnation were to be per-

secuted with every available means, to be defamed and liquidated
– if not physically, at least morally. But I have no desire to enter
here into a 'history of heretics', either of Catholic or – up to a
point – of Protestant origin. I want to turn to the essential
problems in the context of the *theory of knowledge*, which today
amounts to a science of science, a theory of theory. But it will
quickly become clear that we are concerned here, not only with
the *theory*, but with the *practice* of theology; not only with an
innocuous general analysis, but with an extremely dramatic
history of the past and of the present time which we have to
analyze.

How is a new situation reached in *science*? What is involved
when we hear of something new in *theology*? A typical theologians' squabble, as non-theologians sometimes think –
particularly after recent controversies? It is not without reason
that *rabies theologorum* has become proverbial: a clear sign of how
ideological and religious controversies can, in particular, stir up
people's emotions, overwhelm them existentially, enter – so to
speak – into their bloodstream, far more than political or aesthetic
differences. And especially more than the controversies of the
natural sciences, which – as some natural scientists maintain, not
without pride – pursue their course wholly and entirely
rationally. But, is this true? Is the word 'rational' the right one? In
mathematical and natural scientific thought and research – as
distinct from theology – do subjective conditions and
assumptions, standpoints and perspectives, really play no part?
Can they be completely eliminated for the sake of a pure
objectivity?

A comparison between scientific and theological controversies,
in particular, can clarify how much is at stake for theology: how
the great controversies are far more than mere squabbles. Nor is it
a question of tensions involved in the very nature of theology.
What is really happening – as in the far-reaching controversies of
natural science – is that one theological 'paradigm', or model of
understanding, is being replaced by another – a new one. That, at
any rate, is what the situation looks like when considered at the
level of the *present state of epistemological discussion*: a discussion

which – after logical positivism and critical rationalism – has entered on a new, third phase where it is beginning again to become directly interesting and fruitful for the humanities in general and for theology in particular. What at first seems an unusual comparison, particularly with the natural sciences – and especially with their hard core, physics and chemistry – can help us to develop a keener awareness of problems, even in regard to the question of what is new in theology.

Despite all differences in method, today *the natural and the human sciences* must be again seen more in their interconnection: for every natural science has a horizon of understanding, a hermeneutical dimension, as understood by those like Georg Gadamer who are concerned with the hermeneutics of the human sciences. Nowhere – not even in the natural sciences – can absolute objectivity be sought by excluding the human subject, the researcher himself. Even the conclusions of the natural scientist and the technician are hermeneutically established. They are restricted to those points on which an answer is expected, simply because that is how the question is phrased. Modern physics itself, in connection with the theory of relativity and quantum mechanics, has drawn attention to the fact that the conclusions of natural science have no value in themselves, but only under certain clearly defined conditions and not under others. In the experiments of physics the method changes the object – what it reveals is always only one perspective and only one aspect.

All this is particularly relevant to a critical ecumenical theology, if the latter is meant to be something more than a denominational theological controversy.

It was Karl Popper who as early as 1935 analyzed in his book *Logik der Forschung* (*The Logic of Scientific Discovery*) the rules for establishing new hypotheses and theories in natural science. He concluded that new theories in natural science are not established by positive confirmation, by corroboration in experience, by 'verification'. In the 1920s and 1930s this was the thesis of logical positivism upheld by the Vienna Circle associated with Moritz Schlick and Rudolf Carnap, the latter producing (together with the young Ludwig Wittgenstein) his programme of an anti-metaphysical 'scientific theory of the world' which determined the first phase of the modern theory of knowledge. A positive verification of universal scientific propositions – for instance, 'all copper in the universe conducts electricity' – is simply impossible.

Not by verification – says Popper – *but by 'falsification'*, by refutation, can new scientific hypotheses and theories be established. The discovery of black swans in Australia – for instance – refutes, 'falsifies', the universal proposition that 'all' swans are white and permits the deduction of the general (existential) proposition: 'There are non-white swans'. A hypothesis or theory, therefore, can be regarded as true (*wahr*) or – better – as 'corroborated' (*bewahrt*) when it has withstood all attempts at falsification up to the present. Thus, science appears to be a continually ongoing process of 'trial and error', which leads, not to a secure *possession* of the truth, but to a progressive *approach* to the truth: a process of continuous change and development.

The question, of course, which emerges with increasing clarity in the light of Popper's penetrating logical analysis, is: certainly science is not a subjective and irrational enterprise; but is *logic* an *adequate* means of understanding it? Is progress in science adequately explained by this 'logic of scientific discovery', which consists in continual falsification on the basis of strictly rational tests?

That this is not the case, became clear in the *third phase* of the theory of knowledge: logico–critical penetration is not sufficient (those engaged in the human sciences had always known this). Historico–hermeneutical examination (as practised particularly in the history of theology and history of dogma) is also needed; above all, psychologico–sociological investigation (largely absent from theology hitherto) is required. This is an *investigation of knowledge* which represents a combination of *theory* of knowledge, *history* of knowledge and *sociology* of knowledge.

Hence, in the past fifty years the discussion has moved from an abstract, positivistic logic and linguistic analysis through innumerable interim corrections to taking *history*, the *community of inquiry*, and the *human subject*, seriously again. These widespread attempts at an explanation have already achieved results.

2. Paradigm change

Radically new hypotheses and theories even in natural science do not emerge simply by verification (as the Vienna positivists thought) or simply by falsification (as Popper, the critical rationalist, suggested). Both theories are conceived too much as stereotypes. In fact, new hypotheses and theories emerge as a result of a highly complex and generally protracted *replacement of a hitherto accepted model of interpretation or 'paradigm' by a new one.* They arise from a *'paradigm change'* (not a sudden 'paradigm switch'!) in a longer process that is neither completely rational nor completely irrational, and is often more revolutionary than evolutionary.

This is the theory which the American physicist and historian of science, Thomas S. Kuhn, expounded in a book that has become a classic of modern scientific research: *The Structure of Scientific Revolution* (Chicago, 1962; second, enlarged edition 1970). I gladly admit that it was this theory that enabled me to understand more deeply and comprehensively the problems of growth in knowledge, of development, of progress, of the emergence of a new approach and thus, in particular, the present controversies, also with reference to theology.

I would also like to make Kuhn's terminology my own but only up to a point. I do not want to insist on the term 'paradigm' or 'revolution'. For *'paradigm'* in particular – originally understood simply as 'example', 'classic example' or 'pattern' for further experiments – has turned out to be ambiguous. For my own part I am equally happy to speak of *interpretative models, explanatory models, models for understanding (Verstehensmodelle)*. By this I mean what Kuhn meant by the term 'paradigm': 'an entire constellation of beliefs, values, techniques, and so on shared by the members or a given community' (Kuhn, p.175).[1]

Stephen Toulmin, another leading representative of the third phase, remarks in his basic work on *Human Understanding, The Collective Use and Evolution of Concepts* (Princeton 1972, p.106), that the term 'paradigm' (which is more than a 'conceptual system') for certain fundamental patterns of explanation was already used by George Christoph Lichtenberg (Professor of Natural Philosophy at Göttingen in the mid-eighteenth century). Lichtenberg – after the eclipse of German Idealism – had a great influence on Ernst Mach and Wittgenstein, who picked up the term 'paradigm' as a key to understanding how philosophical models or stereotypes act as 'moulds' (*Gussform*) or 'clamps' (*Klammern*), shaping and directing our thought in predetermined and sometimes quite inappropriate directions. In this form the term entered general philosophical discussion and was first analyzed in Britain by Wittgenstein's student W.H. Watson, by N.R. Hanson and by Toulmin himself. Finally, in the early 1950s, the term arrived in the United States.

In his preface, Toulmin formulates his 'central thesis', his 'deeply held conviction': "that in science and philosophy alike, an *exclusive preoccupation with logical systematicity has been destructive of both historical understanding and rational criticism*. Men demonstrate their rationality, not by ordering their concepts and beliefs in tidy formal structures, but by their preparedness to respond to novel situations with open minds – acknowledging the shortcomings of their former procedures and moving beyond them". And Toulmin agrees with Kuhn in re-establishing the neglected link between conceptual changes and their socio-historical contexts (without entirely identifying them!): 'by re-emphasizing the close connections between the socio-historic development of scientific schools, professions, and institutions, and the intellectual development of scientific theories themselves' (p.116). *In toto* a less formalistic but more historical approach (against 'a self-sufficient anti-historical logical empiricism inherited from the Vienna Circle').

To be sure, there is a dispute between Kuhn and Toulmin whether we have to speak about 'revolutionary' or 'evolutionary' changes; I will have to come back to this question. But more important, it seems to me, is the basic agreement of both authors that 'paradigms' or 'models' change. Whatever term we choose for our specific theological purpose, this term must be understood broadly enough in order to include not only concepts and judgments, but 'an entire constellation of beliefs, values, techniques, and so on, shared by the members of a given community'.

Now, I must affirm frankly that I am involved in no slight risk in attempting here and now, in the course of a single paper, to examine the abundantly documented remarks of Kuhn (and Toulmin) hitherto scarcely noticed in the epistemological reflections of theologians, and to give at the same time an account of the highly complex internal developments in theology to which Kuhn himself (in contrast to Toulmin, who is only accidentally interested in the human sciences) has hitherto paid no attention. But the *hermeneutical discussion* alone, about valid modes, methods and the principles of solution, persisting in both Catholic and Protestant theology, should be evidence of the fact that we are in the midst of a theological upheaval on which further reflection is sadly needed. Today this situation in theology points to the need for reflecting upon the new paradigm in terms of the *theory-praxis discussion* in Europe (e.g. Jürgen Habermas, Karl Otto Apel) as well as in America (besides Kuhn and Toulmin, e.g. Richard Bernstein). Both the hermeneutical and the political implications of the paradigm change will be treated in special papers.

I so distinguish between *macro, meso* and *micromodels*. Thus in *physics: macromodels* for scientific global solutions (like the Copernican, the Newtonian, the Einsteinian model); *mesomodels* for the solutions of problems in the intermediate fields (like the wave theory of light, the dynamic theory of heat or Maxwell's electro-magnetic theory); and *micromodels* for detailed scientific solutions (like the discovery of X-rays). Similarly in *theology: macromodels* for global solutions (the Alexandrian, the Augustinian, the Thomist model); *mesomodels* for the solution of problems in the intermediate field (the doctrines of creation and grace, the understanding of the sacraments); *micromodels* for detailed solutions (the doctrine of original sin, the hypostatic union in Christology).

In *physics* – for instance – it is possible to distinguish between a Ptolemaic, a Copernican, a Newtonian and an Einsteinian macromodel. Ought it not to be possible also in *theology* to distinguish – for instance – a *Greek Alexandrian*, a *Latin Augustinian*, a *medieval Thomistic*, a *Reformation*, and a *modern-critical interpretative macromodel*? Kuhn always speaks of 'science' – as frequently in American and English usage – as synonymous with 'natural science'; I use the term here in the European sense of scholarship, or *Wissenschaft*. But Kuhn sees – albeit with some scepticism – that the problems arise also for the human sciences; in fact, he admits that he himself frequently applied to the natural sciences insights more familiar to the historiography of literature, music, the visual arts and politics. On the other hand, the 'harshness' in particular of the problems of the natural sciences reveals completely new aspects to the practitioner of the human sciences and especially the theologian. For my own theological purpose, it may help to use these broad terms 'paradigm' or 'model' interchangeably.

We speak of a *'model'* as 'paradigm' in order to stress also the provisional character of the project, which in fact holds only under certain assumptions and within certain limits; which does not in principle exclude other projects, but always grasps reality only *comparatively* objectively, in a particular perspectivity and variability. For the scientist and theologian alike, facts are never 'naked' and experiences never 'raw', but are always subjectively arranged and interpreted; every 'seeing' takes place from the outset in a (scientific or prescientific) model of understanding. Even the most adequately tested 'classical' theories, like those of Newton or of Aquinas, have turned out to be inadequate and in need of an overhaul. There is no reason therefore to make a method, a project, a model or paradigm absolute: but there is certainly reason for continually starting on a new quest, for permanent criticism and rational control: on the way through pluralism to ever greater truth.

3. Analogies between natural science and theology

All this sounds very abstract, but can now be expressed more concretely in view of our central question: Where are the *parallels* and where are the *differences between progress in knowledge, in natural science, and in theology?* The differences are more obvious. Consequently I am attempting in this paper – and the whole is meant to be an invitation to share my thought – first to bring out clearly certain parallels, similarities and *analogies*, so that afterwards I can deal with what is more properly theological. Here I shall discuss *five main points*:

(a) With reference to natural science Kuhn makes an observation which can serve as our starting-point: in practice, students accept certain models of understanding less as a result of proofs than because of the authority of the textbook they study and of the teacher to whom they listen. In ancient times this function was fulfilled by the famous classics of science: Aristotle's *Physics*, Ptolemy's *Almagest*; in modern times, Newton's *Principia* and *Opticks*, Franklin's *Electricity*, Lavoisier's *Chemistry*, Lyell's *Geology*, and so on.

Christian theology was distinguished from the outset from both mythico-cultic 'theology' (tales and testimonies of the gods) and philosophical 'theology' (doctrine of God), and began in the New Testament itself with Paul and John. For theology, in addition to the original apostolic witnesses, certain great teachers, 'classical writers' so to speak, remain supremely important: Irenaeus, for instance, the most important theologian of the second century, in his resistance to Gnosticism, produced a first survey of Christianity. Then in the third century Tertullian in the West and in the East especially the Alexandrians Clement and Origen produced theology in the course of a comprehensive discussion with the culture of their time. Theology thus has to be understood again and again as what Tracy calls 'a dialectic of challenge *and* response'.

Theological *textbooks* in the strict sense, however, emerged in mediaeval times when theology was established as a *university discipline*. From that time onwards theological paradigms or models of understanding have therefore become more easily conceivable.

In the *East*, of course, at an earlier stage systematic works like the *Pegegnoseos (Fountain of Wisdom)* of John Damascene – and especially its third part, 'An Exposition of the Orthodox Faith' – offered a summary of eastern theology. As one of the few Byzantine systematic theological surveys, this work exercised an influence in both the Greek and the Slavonic East throughout the whole of the Middle Ages and right up to the present time.

In the *West*, Latin theology bearing the imprint of Augustine was brought to the medieval scholastics by the *Sentences* of Peter Lombard (+1160), which consisted for the most part of quotations from Augustine. In this way, Augustine's thought, together with a mainly neoplatonic system of ideas, came to dominate scholastic philosophy and theology in both method and content up to the middle of the thirteenth century.

At this time Thomas Aquinas (+1274) was still an extremely controversial theologian. He was attacked and denounced as a modernist by traditionalist (Augustinian) theologians, recalled from Paris by his own Dominican Order, eventually subjected to a formal condemnation as a representative of a 'new theology' by the competent ecclesiastical authorities in Paris and Oxford, but then given protection by his Order. It was only just before the outbreak of the Reformation that his *Summa Theologiae* won acceptance outside his Order: the first commentary on the whole *Summa* was that of Cardinal Cajetan, classical interpreter of Aquinas and opponent of Luther; and it was only Francisco de Vittoria, Father of Spanish scholasticism, who in 1526 introduced the Thomistic *Summa* as a textbook at the University of Salamanca; Louvain followed later with two professorships in Aquinas' theology and seven-year courses on the *Summa theologiae*. Up to the present century (1924) 90 commentaries on the whole *Summa* had been published and 218 on its first part .

Although they were not on the same scale, it would be possible to speak similarly of the works of the Reformers – Melancthon's *Loci* and Calvin's *Institutio* – and of the Anglican Hooker's *Laws of Ecclesiastical Polity*: all classics and textbooks which made history.

To be sure, in theology as in natural science there is something like a 'normal science': 'research firmly based upon one or more past scientific achievements that some particular scientific community acknowledges for a time as supplying the foundation for its further practice' (Kuhn, p.10). These great theoretical constructions provide 'examplars', 'patterns', 'paradigms', 'models of understanding' for everyday scientific practice. And whether in *physics* it is the Ptolemaic or – later – Copernican astronomy, Aristotelian or – later – Newtonian dynamics, corpuscular or – later – wave-optics; and whether in *theology* it is Alexandrian or – later – Augustinian or Thomistic teaching; whether it is Reformed teaching, orthodox Protestant or a more recent teaching; *anyone* – even a student – who wants to have his say in regard to the particular science must have mastered by intensive study the model of understanding involved, the macromodel and the meso-and micro-models pertaining to it.

And – this is the odd thing – real novelties within the scope of the established model are not really wanted, either in natural science or in theology. Why? They would change, upset, perhaps destroy the existing model. Normal science is wholly concerned by every means to confirm its model of understanding, its paradigm, to make it more precise, to secure it, to extend its scope; it is interested in development by aggregation, accumulation, a slow process of growth in knowledge.

As we see, in practice, in the last resort, normal science is just not interested in falsification, which would only jeopardize the model. It wants to solve the remaining puzzles. Consequently, an attempt is made to confirm the existing model and – if they are not at first simply denied or suppressed – to incorporate new phenomena, counter-examples, anomalies into the established model, and as far as possible to modify the latter or to formulate it in a new way. In this connection the case of Galileo is of equal interest to theology and physics. Not only in theology, but in natural science, discoverers of novelties or anomalies which jeopardize the usual model are at first frequently morally discredited as 'disturbers of the peace', or simply reduced to silence.

Analogies between natural science and theology then emerge,

especially with reference to normal science. Therefore, in regard to our problems of the emergence of the new, we can formulate a (provisional) *first thesis*, into which, as with the other theses, distinctions will have to be introduced at a later stage.

Like natural science, the theological community has a 'normal science' with its classical authors, textbooks and teachers, which is characterized by a cumulative growth of knowledge, by a solution of remaining problems ('puzzles'), and by resistance to everything that might result in a changing or replacement of the established paradigm.

(b) One should not speak too hastily against this normal science. Scholars practise it to a certain extent and depend on it for their own thinking. But does scientific development really mean only that progress is made slowly but inexorably against a multitude of errors? Do the natural scientific disciplines, or even theology, advance only by coming bit by bit a step closer to the truth?

There is no doubt that this far too simple idea of 'organic development' is widespread even among natural scientists. And among theologians, Catholics especially, the theory was established even in the nineteenth century through the efforts of Newman and – under Hegel's influence – particularly through the Catholic Tübingen School. Paradoxically, it also became popular in Rome in order to explain, for example, the Immaculate Conception (1854) and òther dogmas. All this was organic development! I should like, however, to put forward for consideration the following counter-examples which point, not to a simple development, but to *crises*. First of all in *physics*:

In the sixteenth century what was the initial position for Copernicus' astronomical revolution? It was the obvious crisis of Ptolemaic astronomy to which – in addition to other factors – an inability to cope with the increasingly clearly recognized discrepancies and even anomalies had contributed: a persistent incapacity of normal science to solve the puzzles imposed on it, especially that of a long-range forecast of the positions of the planets. And in the eighteenth century what was the precondition for Lavoisier's fundamental breakthrough in chemistry? It was the crisis of the prevailing phlogiston theory which sought to explain the burning of bodies as due to a concentration of phlogiston. But since (in all its varied proliferations) it could not explain the increasingly frequently observed gains in weight in the process of combustion, Lavoisier began eventually to ignore the existence of such a warm energy substance and recognized that combustion was due to the absorption of oxygen. The foundation for a new formulation of chemistry as a whole had been established.

And in the nineteenth and twentieth centuries what preceded Einstein's theory of relativity? It was the crisis especially of the dominant ether theory, unable to explain – despite all the apparatus and experiments – why no movement, no current or conveyance of ether (no sort of 'ether wind') could be observed. Einstein therefore began simply to ignore the idea of such a sustaining medium for gravitational forces and light waves ('light ether'); he was able to assume the velocity of light as constant for all reference-systems moving uniformly towards each other.

I have cited enough examples from natural science. Are there similar processes in *theology? Crises in theology?*

Even in New Testament times various Jewish and Hellenistic models of understanding of the one Christ-event appeared alongside and after one another, reaching a point of intersection especially with Paul, the Apostle of Jews *and* Hellenes. The non-fulfilment of the apocalyptic imminent expectation meant a first critical situation for early Christianity: God's kingdom, expected at an early stage, did not come. This Jewish apocalyptic model of the imminent end (Christ as the *end* of time) was tacitly replaced – especially in the Lucan writings, in the Pastoral Epistles and the Second Epistle of Peter – by an early-Catholic model of interpretation in terms of salvation history, with Jesus Christ as the *centre* of time, and of an obviously longer time during which the church would persist: a *church* incidentally that now increasingly forgot its Jewish origin and became more and more hellenized and institutionalized.

This deep penetration into the Hellenistic world led, however, to a crisis of *identity*, manifested especially in the second century in Gnosticism, which completely disregarded the historical origin of Christianity and moved towards an unhistorical-mythical theology. Several models of theology were successively developed within the church in face of this challenge to its existence. In the second century there was first the mainly philosophical theology of the *Apologists*, who tried to defend both the identity and the universal validity of Christianity rationally with the aid of borrowings from popular philosophy and by invoking the Hellenistic-Johannine Logos active everywhere in the world. Then, at the turn from the second to the third century, there was the biblical theology oriented to salvation history of Irenaeus, who had recourse to Scripture and apostolic tradition against the Gnostic mythologies. Eventually, in the middle of the third century (in addition to Tertullian in the West), in the East there was the theology of the *Alexandrians* Clement and Origen. They boldly assimilated all previous (including Gnostic) attempts and then – in discussion especially with neoplatonic philosophy – developed a first mature and in the long run *largely authoritative macromodel of a theology*. The structural elements of this Greek theology, open to the world yet wholly ecclesial, historically justified, yet based on philosophical reflection, were the biblical canon, the rule of faith and neoplatonic thought. Origen's allegorical, symbolical reinterpretation of the words of Scripture, his spiritual-pneumatic interpretation of Scripture as a whole, came to prevail in theology – even against the opposition of the mainly Aristotelian and historically and grammatically oriented Antiochene School. That is to say, a theology-model was designed here which helped to prepare the way theologically for the Constantinian turning-point. In the fourth century it was corrected and developed further, particularly by Athanasius and the Cappadocians (Basil, Gregory Narianzen and Gregory of Nyssa) and became the model of Greek Orthodoxy (John Damascene).

In the West, despite all solidarity (particularly in scriptural interpretation) with the Greeks, a very different macromodel became authoritative in the long run: the theology of Augustine. In the midst of the crisis of the Roman Empire this emerged first as a result of Augustine's personal crisis: his turning away from dualistic Manichaeism and academic scepticism, and of his turning to the faith of the church, to Neoplatonism, to allegorizing, to Paul, to an ascetic Christianity, and finally to the episcopal office. But what really determined the specific development of Augustine's particular model of theology were two crises in church history and in the history of theology: the *Donatist crisis* which made its mark on Augustine's conception of the Church and the sacraments and then on that of the West as a whole, and the *Pelagian crisis* which decisively shaped the theology of sin and grace right up to the Reformation and Jansenism.

Here is a further example. What led Thomas Aquinas, the most modern theologian of the thirteenth century, to his new revaluation of reason in regard to faith, of the literal sense of Scripture in regard to the allegorical and spiritual, of nature in regard to grace, and of philosophy in regard to theology, and thus to his large-scale new theological synthesis which – as we saw – was to determine both Spanish scholasticism and the neo-scholasticism of the nineteenth and twentieth centuries? It was the *crisis of Augustinianism*, provoked by the general history of Europe and especially by the reception of Aristotle's work as a whole in Christian Europe. It led to a confrontation with an immense accumulation of recent discoveries, especially in the natural sciences, with Arabian philosophy, with its similarly Aristotelian orientation. With theology now established at the university and in a new form as an academic discipline, a *scientia*, 'science', *Wissenschaft*, Aquinas, with methodical strictness and dialectical skill, fitted the Platonic-Augustinian ideas into his new philosophico-theological system, *without ever indulging in polemics*. He did not hesitate to reinterpret them completely or even firmly to leave them aside when they did not suit him.

Again, in the sixteenth century, what was Luther's starting-point for his new understanding of word and faith, of the justice of God and of the justification of man, and so for his new earth-shattering, biblical-christocentric conception of theology as a whole, rejecting allegorizing and based on strict linguistic-grammatical interpretation of Scripture? It was – within the framework of the crisis of the late mediaeval church and society – the *crisis of systematic and speculative scholasticism*. This was becoming increasingly remote from its biblical sources, neglecting both the basic truths and the existential character of faith, while piling up a mass of purely rational conclusions.

And what was the starting-point in the seventeenth-eighteenth century for that *modern critical theology* which made its definitive appearance at the time of the German Enlightenment? It sought to maintain the scientific character of theology against all pietistic biblicism, and the historical character of Christian faith against all deistic natural theology. *In a spirit of strictly modern rationality it sought to give a critical account of biblical faith*: in undogmatic exegesis the doctrine of verbal inspiration was abandoned and replaced both by an assimilation in principle of the biblical writings to other literature and by an unreservedly philological and historical interpretation of Scripture. The starting-point was undoubtedly the *crisis of orthodox Protestantism* which appeared at the end of the confessional period and its wars of religion. Looking again to Aristotle, and to Lutheran and Calvinist Orthodoxy, it had built up and consolidated a Protestant-scholastic model of theology. *This, however, collapsed at the great turning-point to tolerance, to modern thought, and to the modern world-vision, when Aristotelianism ceased to be the standard mode of thought for all science.* The resultant emancipation of the new philosophy, of the individual sciences, and finally of the state and of society at large from the authority of theology and the church then led to continually fresh revolutionary moves in philosophy and the individual sciences, and eventually to a new understanding of theology as a whole: to a new modern critical paradigm.

What I have outlined here – in so to speak an 'ideally typical' way – are of course historical processes in the theological community which are extremely complex in their causation, initiation and development, and which are scarcely ever accomplished by a single individual, and certainly never overnight (no 'switch' of paradigms). It is an irony of history that for the most part – as in natural science, so too in theology –

normal science itself contributed involuntarily to the undermining of the established model. It did so, in so far as, increasingly refined and specialized, it brought to light additional information that did not fit into the traditional model and complicated the theory.

The more – for example – the movements of the stars were studied and corrected in the light of the Ptolemaic system of the universe, the more material was produced for refutation of that system. The more – for instance – orthodox Protestantism adopted a neo-Aristotelian approach to science, so much the more did it provoke on the one hand the unscientific 'simple' biblicism of Pietism, and on the other hand the unhistorical-rational natural theology of the Enlightenment. Or – we could say – the more the neo-scholasticism of the present century attempted to uphold certain speculative theses – for example, with reference to the Church's constitution, papal primacy and infallibility – in the light of historical research, so much the more did it bring out contradictory elements which contributed to their undermining.

As in natural science, in theology the replacement of an explanatory model is generally preceded by a *transitional period of uncertainty* in which faith in the established model is shaken, people see through the existing patterns, ties are loosened, traditional schools are reduced in numbers and an abundance of new initiatives compete for a place. Catholic theology, which had remained far behind modern developments and new Protestant theological trends, was faced with such a transitional situation at the time of Vatican II. The differences between the classical neo-scholastic schools – Thomists and Scotists, Thomists and Molinists, and so on – no longer played any part and in their place there appeared a whole series of competing new theological initiatives which even now continue to make the future of Catholic theology seem very uncertain.

In despite of all the complexity and pluricausality of any kind of theological development, it has become clear that new models of theological interpretation emerge, not simply because individual theologians like to handle hot potatoes or to construct new models in their studies, but because the traditional model of interpretation breaks down, because 'old thinkers', the 'puzzle-solvers' of normal theology in face of the new historical horizon and its new challenge, *can find no satisfactory answer to great new questions and thus 'model-testers', 'new thinkers', set in motion an extra-normal, 'extra-ordinary' theology alongside normal theology.*

Certainly crisis is not an 'absolute prerequisite' for a change of model, as Kuhn first maintained in his book, but, as he expressed it more cautiously in his postscript of 1969, 'crises need only be the usual prelude, supplying, that is, a self-correcting mechanism which ensures that the rigidity of normal science will not forever go unchallenged'. (p.181).

In the light of the above, with reference to the emergence of the new in theology, I would like to formulate a *second* provisional *thesis:*

As in natural science, so also in the theological community, *awareness of a growing crisis* is the starting-point for the advent of a drastic change in certain hitherto prevailing basic assumptions, and eventually causes the breakthrough of a new paradigm or model of understanding. When the available rules and methods break down, they lead to a search for new ones.

(c) Up to now I have explained only the starting-point for the replacement of a paradigm: crisis. But how does the *replacement* itself come about in a community of inquiry? Here too Kuhn's observations based on the history of natural science are helpful. What is needed for a replacement is not merely the critical state of the old but also the *rise of a new paradigm*. This, intuitively perceived, is generally present even earlier than a definite system of common rules for research and results of research. The new astronomy, the new physics, the new chemistry, the new biology, the general theory of relativity, make it clear that the decision to abandon an old model is simultaneous with the decision to accept a new one. The model to be replaced needs a worthy, a credible model to succeed it before it can retire. It needs a new 'paradigm candidate'.

If, however, such a candidate is at hand, the replacement does not take place simply through continuous 'organic' development, only through the usual cumulative process of normal science.

Here it is not a question simply of correcting course, but of a change of course, whether it is called a 'scientific revolution' or not. It is a fundamental re-organization of the science as a whole, of its concepts, methods and criteria, often with considerable socio-political consequences.

There is no need to explain all this further with reference to the great upheavals in *natural science*. Its application to theology is more important here. In theology also – as we saw – from time to time there are drastic changes, not only in the limited micro-or mesosphere, but in the macrosphere. As in the change from the geocentric to the heliocentric theory, from phlogiston to oxygen chemistry, from corpuscular to wave theory, so in the change from one theology to another: fixed and familiar concepts are changed; laws and criteria controlling the admissibility of certain problems and solutions are shifted; theories and methods are upset.

In a word, *the paradigm or model of understanding is changed*, together with the whole complex of different methods, fields of problems and attempted solutions, as these had previously been recognized by the theological community. The theologians get used as it were to a different way of seeing things: to seeing them in the context of a different model. Some things are now perceived that were not seen formerly, and possibly some things are overlooked that were formerly noticed. A new view of man, world and God begins to prevail in the theological community where the whole and its details appear in a different light.

In times of epochal upheavals theology thus acquires a *new shape*, even in its literary expression; we need only compare within the field of comprehensive systematic projects Clement's *Paidagogos* and Origen's *Peri archon* with Augustine's *Enchiridion* or *De doctrina christiana*, or the latter with the medieval *Summae*, and these medieval works finally with Luther's *Sendschreiben* of 1520 or his catechisms.

As we have seen, even in New Testament times a first and radical change took place when that very model of apocalyptic imminent expectation, taken over from Judaism, was itself unobtrusively replaced by a hellenistically conceived idea of Jesus

Christ within salvation history as the centre of time. The latter was the model which acquired its grandiose first completion by *Clement* and *Origen*, who saw the whole history of humankind as a great educational process continually leading upwards (*paideia*): the image of God in the human being is shattered by guilt and sin; it is restored by God's own instruction and brought to its fulfilment. In God's plan (his *oikonomia*) God's becoming man is itself the precondition for humanity's becoming God. Here the primary event of salvation is regarded as the incarnation rather than the cross and resurrection, as in the New Testament.

A drastic theological change of the same kind took place in the West. Here a formerly very worldly man, that intense thinker and acute dialectician, talented psychologist, brilliant stylist and eventually passionate believer, **Aurelius Augustinus**, started to work out theologically his intellectual and spiritual experiences, but also his earlier sexual experiences, and finally his later experiences of high office in the church. Like the Greeks, he wanted to establish a synthesis of Christian faith and neoplatonic thought. But the detail and the whole had been changed because of the development of his personal career, his later anti-Donatist and anti-Pelagian confrontations, and the crisis of the Roman Empire. I may mention only a few characteristics of his theology: a mysterious and sinister double predestination – predestination of some to bliss, of others to damnation; a new sexually-conditioned notion of sin as original sin and concupiscence; a new theology of history, of the city of God and the earthly city; a new psychological definition of the relationship of Father, Son and Spirit, starting out from the one immutable divine nature.

All in all this was an epoch-making new theological macromodel. It was to last almost a millennium. Understandably, this has been viewed by the Greeks with the greatest mistrust even up to the present time, although the comprehensive and thoroughgoing patristic unity of reason and faith, philosophy and theology, remained secure.

A similar epoch-making theological change, involving great struggles, again took place with *Aquinas*, and later on an even greater scale with *Luther*. These examples likewise illustrate how much each of these paradigm changes had particular *socio-political presuppositions* and at the same time considerable socio-political consequences. Admittedly they were very ambivalent consequences: this is true of the Hellenistic-Christian conception of *paideia* for the Byzantine Churches, or Augustine's two cities or two kingdoms theory for the Middle Ages. Aquinas' papalist ecclesiology or Luther's new understanding of justification, Church and sacraments, for the modern age. And, as already indicated, after Luther, or the Lutheran and Reformed orthodoxy, it would be possible to continue to give further examples of drastic theological changes. But for our purposes these examples from the history of theology should be sufficient to enable me to formulate a *third* provisional *thesis*:

As in natural science, so also in the theological community, an older paradigm or model of understanding is replaced when a new one is available.

(*d*) At the same time another aspect has indirectly become clear, an aspect which might have been perceived at the very beginning of this paper: without opposition, without struggle and personal sacrifice – as is evident from the history of all those great theologians – nothing new ever came to prevail even in the theological community (and in the church). But the *subjective circumstances* in particular of this change of model have to be defined more exactly with reference to comprehensive scholarly research. It is taken for granted that a whole mass of diverse factors are involved when theologians – whether as initiators or recipients, in any case generally in a long and complex process – decide in favour of a new explanatory model. This can also be abundantly proved by reference both to Augustine's *Confessions* and letters and to Luther's life-story and self-testimonies, but the fact is well-known also with regard to Origen (from Eusebius' *Church History*) and Aquinas (especially with reference to the significance of the Dominican Order). But the fact that for natural scientists, not only Popper's 'logic of scientific discovery', but numerous other factors are involved, is again proved by Kuhn with a few remarks that are also very consoling for the theologian.

A first observation: In great crises not only the theologian but the natural scientist has *doubts of faith*, when – that is – normal science and its traditional system let him down and he has to look for something new. 'It was as if the ground had been pulled out from under one, with no firm foundation to be seen anywhere upon which one could have built'. This was said, not by a theologian about theology, but by a physicist – Einstein – about physics.

'At the moment physics is again terribly confused. In any case, it is too difficult for me, and I wish I had been a movie actor or something of that sort and had never heard of physics'. Wolfgang Pauli, later Nobel prize-winner for physics, wrote that in the months before Heisenberg's paper on matrix mechanics pointed the way to a new quantum theory (citations in Kuhn, pp.83-84).

It is also well-known that in such critical situations, when no new way was found, not only have theologians lost their faith in theology, but – and histories of science of course scarcely mention this – natural scientists have lost their faith in natural science and chosen a different calling.

A second observation: Not only in theology, but in natural science, when there is a paradigm change, apart from scientific factors, *non-scientific factors also are important*. A mixture of 'objective' and 'subjective', individual and sociological factors: origins, careers and personalities of those involved play a part, but often also the nationality, the reputation and the teachers especially of the innovator and – not least – the perhaps aesthetically conditioned attractiveness of the solution; the consistency, transparency, effectiveness, and the elegance, simplicity and universality of the proposed paradigm.

A third observation: Kuhn did not observe the influence of *religious convictions* on supposedly purely scientific decisions. Yet it is found not only in great theologians, but in the great physicists, in Copernicus, Newton and Einstein. Remarkably little was heard in his last decades of Einstein, the greatest physicist of the present century, because he thought he could not participate, could not permit himself to participate in the new, epoch-making turn that physics had taken with quantum mechanics – an attitude based on religious grounds, as can be seen from his correspondence with Max Born. *His famous statement that the 'old chap' does not play at dice, is not a joke, but the expression of a definite religious conviction.* Einstein believed to the end in the pantheistic-deterministic God of Spinoza, something that evidently remained concealed even from Born in those discussions.

A fourth observation: Not only in theology, but in natural science, a new model of understanding demands something like a *conversion*, which cannot be extorted in a purely rational way. I speak less of the initiator, the person who (because of a sudden intuitive experience or a long and arduous ripening) has suggested a new model, than of the recipients, those who have to decide for or against. The defenders of the old and of the new model – something that must not be underestimated – live in 'different worlds', different worlds of ideas and of language; often they can scarcely understand each other. Translation from the old to the new language is necessary, but at the same time there must be a new conviction, a conversion.

Certainly convincing objective reasons are important for a conversion of this kind. It is not a question here simply of an irrational process. Nevertheless, even good reasons cannot extort conversion; for it is likewise not a question merely of a rational process. In the last resort it is a question of a 'decision of faith' – in the non-religious sense of the term – or, better, of a 'vote of confidence'. Which model copes better with the new problems and at the same time preserves most of the old solutions to problems? Which model has a future? This is not so easy to foresee. *And since here it is ultimately a question of trust, discussions between the two schools of thought and language-worlds often take the form less of rational argumentation than of more or less successful attempts at recruitment, persuasion and conversion.* Both parties have their own lists of problems, priorities, norms and definitions, their ultimately opposite standpoints: the other party is expected to adopt one's own so obvious standpoint; to accept whatever one's own premises happen to be. In the community of inquiry, the acceptance of the new model then depends on the decision of the individual scientist as to whether he wants to agree with this standpoint, with these particular premises. This is not easy; for it is not a purely theoretical question.

A fifth observation: Not only in theology, but in natural science, a new model at first has only a *few* and generally younger advocates: Copernicus was 34 when he worked out the heliocentric system. Newton, the founder of classical physics, formulated the law of gravity when he was 23. Lavoisier, founder of modern chemistry, was 26 when he deposited with the secretary of the Académie Française his famous sealed testimony expressing his doubts about the dominant phlogiston theory. Einstein presented the special theory of relativity at the age of 26.

Among *theologians*: Origen, the first scholar in Christendom to undertake methodical research, at the age of 18 took over successfully the Christian education work among intellectuals in Alexandria, which had been neglected after Clement's departure. Augustine was 32 at the time of his 'last' conversion and Aquinas was not yet 30 when he began in Paris his commentary on the sentences in the spirit of Aristotle. Luther was 34 when he published his theses on indulgences.

But these examples of the achievement of younger men are sufficient. Certainly Kuhn's finding that increasing numbers of scientists are converted to a new paradigm only in the course of time, and then pursue their investigation into this paradigm more intensely holds for natural science *and* theology. It is not only because of the stubbornness of age, but because they are wholly and entirely attached to the old model that it is often the most experienced older investigators of the established model who keep up their resistance for a lifetime. A new generation is then required – and no less a person than Darwin stated this with almost depressing clarity in his preface to the *Origin of Species* – before the great majority of the scientific community eventually adopted the new explanatory model. *Nor does it eventually depend on this or that scholar, but on the scientific community as a whole, whether a new model prevails.* What the great physicist Max Planck said in his *Scientific Autobiography* (1949, pp.33–34) is true perhaps more of theologians than of physicists: 'A new scientific truth does not triumph by convincing its opponents and making them see the light, but rather because its opponents eventually die, and a new generation grows up that is familiar with it'.

Perhaps now I have cited enough material to enable me to formulate a *fourth* provisional *thesis*:

As in natural science, so in the theological community, in the acceptance or rejection of a new paradigm, not only scientific, but extra-scientific factors are involved, so that the transition to a new model cannot be purely rationally extorted, but may be described as a conversion.

(*e*) There remains one last question, which can be answered briefly. Is it so certain that the new theological paradigm, the new model of understanding, will always prevail? What I want to suggest is that in theology as in the great controversies of natural science there are in principle three possible ways out of the crisis.

The first possibility: The new explanatory model is absorbed into the old. Contrary to all appearances, normal science proves to be capable of coping with the problems that produced the crisis; it can assimilate certain new discoveries and improve the existing model without having to give it up. This was the situation with Augustinianism after Aquinas and with Thomism after Luther.

The *Augustinianism* of the Franciscan School, increasingly incorporating Aristotelian ideas, was able to stay alive even after Aquinas, was then absorbed into 'modern' Scotism and eventually came to an end in that Ockhamism to which Luther probably owed the first imprint of his theology.

Thomism was able to continue until well into the modern age (especially in comparatively secluded regions like Spain), admittedly, however – as a result of ignoring modern science and philosophy – ceasing to be the theological vanguard as in the thirteenth century, and becoming the rearguard of the seventeenth century and (in the form of neo-Thomism, promoted by Rome with every means) of the nineteenth and twentieth centuries, losing its predominance in the Catholic Church to a large extent only with Vatican II.

The second possibility: The new explanatory model *prevails* against normal science and replaces the old. This means in fact that scientific books, commonly understood descriptions and comprehensive interpretations, based on the previous model, have to be wholly or partly rewritten. What was once entirely new now becomes old. What began as heretical *innovation* rapidly becomes venerable *tradition*.

All this can be observed with macromodels in both natural science and theology. At the same time it must be noted that the textbooks describe mainly the *results* of the radical change, while tending to conceal the fact itself and the extent of 'revolutions'. To that extent a textbook of physics or chemistry and often a textbook of dogmatics or ethics can give a misleading impression of the progress of science. Textbooks of this kind frequently render the radical change, the upheaval, invisible, and make it simply look like evolution, an extension of traditional knowledge: the appearance – that is – of a cumulative growth of normal physics, of an organic growth of normal dogmatics.

The third possibility: The problems and possibly also the circumstances of the time resist radically new initiatives; for the time being these problems are 'shelved'. The new model is 'put into cold storage'.

Shelving the model in this way can be a purely scientific process. But particularly in theology and in the church it was often done by compulsion, which meant that instead of analogies there arose more differences between natural science and theology. These differences will be the subject of the next section. I shall bring to an end the series of analogies with a *fifth* provisional *thesis*:

In the theological community, as in natural science, it can be predicted only with difficulty, in the midst of great controversies, whether a new paradigm is absorbed into the old, replaces the old or is shelved for a long period. But if it is accepted, innovation is consolidated as tradition.

'Smashing prejudices is more difficult than smashing atoms', said Albert Einstein on one occasion. I would add that, once they are smashed, they release forces that can perhaps move mountains. I think there is now enough material for thought with reference to a structural similarity between natural science and theology in the emergence of the new. Yet the question thrusts itself upon us: *Does not theology, even Christian truth itself, faced by nothing but paradigm changes and new conceptions, become a victim of historical relativism, which makes it impossible any longer to perceive the Christian reality and make every paradigm equally true, equally valid?* Perhaps the natural scientist is not very much concerned with this problem, but it is of the greatest consequence for the Christian theologian. It was not without reason that I described these theses as 'provisional'. A theological counterpoint is overdue. I must discuss the five theses worked out with reference to Kuhn and deal with the function of Christian theology, the Christian understanding of truth and with what today paradigmatically distinguishes what I would like to call a modern critical ecumenical theology. Therefore I pose the question: *Does a paradigm change involve a total break?*

4. The question of continuity

We must remember that in *natural science* also – in all scientific 'revolutions' – there is never any question of a total break. In every paradigm change, despite all discontinuity, there is a *fundamental continuity*. Kuhn stresses the fact that in natural science also it is a question of 'the same bundle of data as before' which however are placed 'in a new system of relations with one another' (Kuhn, p.85). The transition – for example – of Newtonian to Einsteinian mechanics does not 'involve the introduction of additional objects or concepts', but only 'a displacement of the conceptual network through which scientists view the world' (p.102). 'Whatever he may then see, the scientist after a revolution is still looking at the same world. Furthermore, though he may previously have employed them differently, much of his language and most of his laboratory instruments are still the same as they were before' (pp.129-30).

I affirm even more. There is a common language for theoretical discussion and a procedure for comparing results; thus the 'conversion', not necessarily an irrational event, is not without arguments sanctioning the change of the standpoint, is never an absolute break with the past. *Toulmin* is right: 'We must face the fact that paradigm-switches are never as complete as the fully-fledged definition implies; that rival paradigms never really amount to entire alternative world-views; and that intellectual discontinuities on the theoretical level of science conceal underlying continuities at a deeper, methodological level' (pp.105f).

Indeed, this is my conviction: if we ever want to understand the development of *theology*, we have to avoid the choice not only between an absolutist and a relativist view, but between a radical continuity and a radical discontinuity. Every paradigm change shows at the same time continuity and discontinuity, rationality and irrationality, conceptual stability and conceptual change, evolutionary and revolutionary elements. And if one does not like to speak about 'revolutionary' changes, then one may speak about *drastic* (not only gradual) and *paradigmatic* (not only conceptual) *changes*, which of course include gradual and conceptual changes.

In theology (and in the historical sciences) much more than in the basically unhistorical natural sciences, which mention their fathers and heroes only in introductions and in the margin, *there is no question of the rediscovery of tradition*. It is a question of a new *formulation of tradition*, admittedly in the light of a new paradigm. 'Novelty for its own sake is not a desideratum in the sciences as it is in so many other creative fields' (Kuhn, p.169). Consequently, new models of understanding, even though they 'seldom or never possess all the capabilities of their predecessors', should 'usually preserve a great deal of the most concrete parts of past achievement and always permit additional concrete problem-solutions besides' (p.169).

For theology, the problem of *continuity* appears at a much deeper level. What is involved here is 'truth' (p.170) – Kuhn avoids mentioning even the word before the very last pages. It is a question indeed of the *truth of life* or – as Wittgenstein says – of the *problems of life*. For the natural scientist generally starts out less directly from the problems of life: 'Unlike the engineer, and many doctors, and most theologians, the (natural) scientist need not choose problems because they urgently need solution' (p.164). And because the theologian is more directly concerned with the problems of life, he must also be more concerned about recognition, not only by the 'experts' but by the wider public. Even 'the most abstract of theologians is far more concerned than the scientist with approbation in general' (p.164). Even as a scientist, Kuhn has no answer to the very obvious vital question of the *whither* of the vast process of development of both science and the world as a whole: 'Inevitably that lacuna will have disturbed many readers' (p.171). But neither has he any answer to the vital *question of the whence*: 'Anyone who has followed the argument thus far will nevertheless feel the need to ask why the evolutionary process should work' (p.173).

Here we come to the *frontiers of natural science*, which remains and seeks to remain tied in its judgments to the horizon of our experiences in space and time. Possibly we also reach the frontiers of human and social science, and – if Kant is right – even the frontiers of *philosophy* in so far as it is a science of pure reason. Vital questions about the whence and whither of the world and the human, that is, about ultimate and original meanings and standards, values and norms, and thus about an ultimate and original reality as such, are questions of a believing trust – certainly not irrational, but utterly reasonable – or a trusting belief.

The responsibility for dealing with these lies with *theology* as a science (*Wissenschaft*): theology as a rational exposition or account of God (Augustine, *De civitate Dei*, III, 1: *de divinitate ratio sive sermo*). It exercises this responsibility in accordance with its own method. For, like questions of nature, of the psyche and of society, of law, politics, history and aesthetics, questions of morality and religion must be treated in accordance with their own methods and style, appropriate to their object. What does this imply?

5. The differences between natural science and theology

It is typical of *Christian* theology – which is even less than others a 'science without presuppositions' – that its *presupposition* and *object* is the *Christian message*, as attested originally in Scripture, as it was transmitted through the centuries by church communities and as it is proclaimed today. For all its *scientific* character, Christian theology is therefore – and not less than – essentially characterized by *historicity*.

In Christian theology it is a question of a profoundly historical truth. In this respect it is distinguished from the very outset (1) from *un*historico-mythological 'theologies', that is, tales and testimonies of the gods composed as myths by poets and cultic priests (Plato first used and at the same time criticized the term 'theology' in this sense); (2) from the *supra*historico-philosophical 'theologies', that is, the natural doctrine of God produced by the philosophers.

Christian theology is quite decidedly a rational account of the truth of the *Christian* faith: that is, of the faith concerned with the cause of Jesus Christ and thus with the cause of God and at the same time the cause of humanity. *This Jesus Christ is neither an unhistorical myth nor a suprahistorical idea, doctrine or ideology.* He is the historical man Jesus of Nazareth, who as the Christ of God is according to the New Testament writings the standard for believers of all time and of all Churches. The original *testimony of faith of this Christ Jesus* forms the *basis of Christian theology*. Does this exclude a critical scholarly work? Not at all. As, for example, the historian as constitutional lawyer in critical loyalty has to interpret no other history or constitution than that which is given, so the theologian – at any rate if he wants to be and to remain a Christian theological – in critical loyalty must consider no other testimony of faith than that originally recorded in the Old and New Testaments, which was transmitted through the ages by the church community in continually varying linguistic forms and must be continually, freshly translated for people of the present time.

In this sense Christian theology is not only – like natural science

– *related to the present and the future*. Nor is it *only* – like every historical science (history of literature, of art, of philosophy of the world) – *related to tradition*. Over and above all this, it is in a wholly specific sense *related to the origins*. For theology the primordial event in the history of Israel and of Jesus Christ and consequently the primordial testimony, the original record, of the Old and New Testaments, remains not only the historical original of the Christian faith but the point to which it must constantly return.

HERMENEUTICAL REFLECTIONS IN THE NEW PARADIGM

David Tracy

The essay of Hans Küng has articulated the meaning and utility of understanding the present situation in theology in terms of a shift in 'paradigms'. By creatively interpreting our present theological situation in the light of the work in 'paradigm-shifts' in the philosophy of science of Thomas Kuhn and Stephen Toulmin, Küng has illuminated the possible consensus that exists in contemporary theology not in spite of the real differences but through and within those differences. For one important implication of the general and flexible category 'paradigm' is that one not merely tolerates real difference within a basic consensus *but expects real differences and yet promotes consensus.*

In this second essay, I will develop my own reflections on the *constants* within the contemporary paradigm-shift of theology by focusing on the role that interpretation now plays within contemporary theology. Stephen Toulmin's recent work has shown how even philosophy of science has a genuinely hermeneutical character. Hermeneutics is, of course, even more important for the 'human sciences', including theology. It is necessary to recall that, like both Küng and Lamb in their reflections, my concern is not to present my own more particular paradigm for theology. Rather, my concern is simply to highlight the hermeneutical element which occurs in the different theologies.

Hermeneutics is simply one element that occurs within the two 'constants' which Küng locates in contemporary theology. For each of these two 'constants' demands 'interpretation'. In the shift from what Bernard Lonergan has described as the move from 'classical' consciousness to modern 'historical' consciousness, the role and demands of hermeneutics become central. For the fact is that, whatever our more particular theology, each theologian must *interpret* both 'constants' (the 'present world of experience in all its ambivalence, contingency and change' and 'the Judaeo-Christian tradition which is ultimately based on the Christian message, the Gospel of Jesus Christ'). It is appropriate, therefore, to reflect on what hermeneutics *is* and how hermeneutics actually functions in contemporary theologies.

Accordingly, the present essay is divided into three sections. First, a section describing the *status quaestionis* of hermeneutical theory. Second, the application of hermeneutics to the interpretation of religion. Third, the application to theology itself in the new paradigm. The aim of this paper – as a 'transition' paper between the analysis of the basic 'paradigm-shift' in theology of Hans Küng's essay and the analysis of the theory-praxis relationship in the essay of Matthew Lamb – is, therefore, a modest one: *viz.*, to analyze in properly general terms the *status quaestionis* of contemporary hermeneutics and the import of hermeneutics for the emerging new paradigm in theology.

For if Christian theology is, in fact, the attempt to establish mutually critical correlations between an interpretation of the Christian tradition and an interpretation of contemporary experience, then it becomes vital to reflect on what interpretation itself is and how this affects every interpretation of religion and especially every theology within the new historically conscious paradigm.

I. The turn to interpretation theory in the new paradigm

Christianity, like any religion, is extraordinarily difficult to interpret inasmuch as a religion radicalizes, intensifies, and often transgresses the boundaries of those other central human phenomena to which religion is necessarily related (art, science, metaphysics, ethics-politics). To interpret any religion one must also, consciously or unconsciously, end up interpreting these other phenomena in order to understand the difference which is specifically religious. To read the creative theologians in the modern period alone is to find a pluralism that suggests a seemingly indeterminate creativity of interpretation. To read contemporary work in theology (or even to read one issue of one of the major journals or attend one session of one of the major conferences of scholars in the field) is to recognize a radical pluralism, indeed an intense conflict of interpretations, from which there can often seem no honourable exit.

The clearest expression of that creativity is the pluralism of interpretation itself. Within that pluralism, how is it possible for the wider community of inquiry to agree which are the better and the worse, the truly creative and the mere 'bright ideas' among the various contenders?

Here I simply suggest that the turn to interpretation theory among some scholars in theology provides one way to encourage creativity in interpretation *without forfeiting the need for criteria of adequacy for interpretation.*

Interpretation as a problem or even as an explicit issue becomes a central issue in cultural periods of crisis. So it was for the Stoics and their reinterpretation of the Greek and Roman myths. So it was for the development of allegory in Christian theologies. So it has been for Jews and Christians since the emergence of historical consciousness. The sense of distance that any contemporary Westerner feels in relationship to the classics of western culture impels but need not determine the contemporary interest in the process of interpretation. But if we focus only on our sense of historical distance from the classics of our culture or our western sense of parochialism disclosing our cultural distance from the classics of other cultures, *we are likely to formulate the problem of interpretation as primarily a problem of avoiding misunderstanding.* Even *Schleiermacher*, justly credited as the 'founder' of modern hermeneutics, often tended to formulate the problem of hermeneutics in this manner. One aspect of Schleiermacher's mixed discourse in hermeneutics (his emphasis on *empathy and divination*) tended to encourage the development of Romantic hermeneutics. The other aspect of Schleiermacher's hermeneutics (his emphasis on *developing methodical controls to avoid misunderstanding*) tended to encourage the development of strictly methodological (first historicist, then formalist) controls.

The fruits of the *impasse* occasioned by that mixed discourse remain with us. For many theories of interpretation, the central insight is into the actuality of historical and cultural distance (and hence our 'alienation' from the classics). The central problem is the need to avoid misunderstanding, and our central hope is in the controls afforded by some methodology to keep us from forcing these alien texts of alien cultures or earlier periods of our own culture into the alien and alienating horizon of our present self-understanding.

With some notable exceptions, most contemporary interpreters not only accept but demand the controls and the clear gains which historical methods have allowed contemporary interpreters. *Clearly, the acceptance and use of historico-critical methods is one defining characteristic of the new paradigm in theology.*

It is impossible in so short a space to develop the complex and still ongoing debates on hermeneutics in the modern period. For the purposes of this present analysis of the *status quaestionis* of hermeneutics within the new paradigm, I can presently hope only to clarify my own position and the hermeneutical tradition within which I stand. As my previous remarks suggest, and as I have maintained in written work elsewhere, I do not believe that either of the two principal strands of thought on hermeneutics bequeathed to us by Schleiermacher's creative and, indeed, classic reflections on interpretation is adequate. More exactly, the interpreter as empathizing, divinizing virtuoso (or genius) is a Romantic legacy that has yielded some fruit. Yet basically Romantic notions of creativity and imagination can yield the kind of intellectual havoc that has given creativity a bad name in many circles. Ultimately, the hope for methodological controls (either historicist or formalist) that will 'guarantee' correct understanding seems seriously misplaced. Of course we need historico-critical methods in theology. Those controls do help all interpreters to avoid serious (e.g., anachronistic) misunderstandings of ancient texts, and often help us to reconstruct the authentic text needing interpretation (e.g., the present parabolic texts reconstructed into the parables of Jesus). Modern historical consciousness, moreover, rouses our consciousness of both the text's and our own historicity. But the belief that, by avoiding a-historicist misunderstanding, we also somehow achieve an adequate theological understanding of the questions and responses of the classic text seems mistaken.

At exactly this point in the dialectic on interpretation-theory in the modern period, the contribution of *Hans-Georg Gadamer* becomes notable. Bear with me, therefore, as I shift (and thereby, of course, translate-interpret) Gadamer's own German onto-logical vocabulary into my own Anglo-American experiential, *de facto* language. My basic warrant for this shift is in fact warranted by Gadamer's own claim. His basic claim, after all, is not to provide a *de jure* set of rules for interpretation after the manner of the neo-Kantians. His claim is the quite distinct one of articulating the *de facto* process of interpretation operative in any interpreter of any text.

What, as a matter of fact, happens when we interpret and thereby understand a text is a logically distinct issue from the issue of what ought to happen (i.e., what methodological controls will allow us to avoid misunderstanding).

In the broader spectrum of contemporary hermeneutics, one can speak of three basic steps (not rules!) for interpretation and two correctives to Gadamer's own formulations of those steps.

In a first step, every interpreter enters the task of interpretation with some pre-understanding of the subject-matter of the text. Historical consciousness (and its contemporary correlate, a sociological imagination) helps to clarify the complex reality of the interpreter's pre-understanding. Historical consciousness is, after all, a post-Enlightenment and, in some ways, even an anti-Enlightenment phenomenon. More exactly, the Enlightenment belief (still alive in many 'methodologies') that the interpreter can in principle and should in fact eliminate all 'pre-judgments' was at best a half-truth. The half-truth in the Enlightenment's 'prejudice against pre-judgments', I admit I hold in higher esteem than Gadamer does. For the truth of the Enlightenment is nothing less than the liberating demand classically expressed by Kant as *aude sapere*: i.e., dare to think for yourself and free yourself from the mystifications and obscurantisms inevitably present in all the traditions. Indeed, the emancipatory thrust of critical and practical reason released anew by the Enlightenment was and is a liberating moment that forms part of the horizon (the pre-understanding) of the modern mind.

Yet the reason why this creative truth is only a half-truth can be clarified for any post-historically conscious mind. If the expression 'historicity' is not merely an ontological abstraction, if the phrases 'socialization' or 'enculturation' are other than disciplinary jargon, they all bespeak the other *de facto* truth missed by Enlightenment polemics against 'pre-judgments' and 'trad-itions'. The fact is that no interpreter enters into the attempt to understand any text without pre-judgments formed by the history of the effects of his or her culture. No interpreter, in fact, is as purely autonomous as the Enlightenment model promised. The recognition of tradition means that every interpreter enters into the act of interpretation bearing with her or him the history of the effects, both conscious and unconscious, of the traditions to which we ineluctably belong. We belong to the history of these effects of the traditions – i.e., we belong to history far more than history belongs to us. This truth any theologian attempting to interpret the Christian tradition will surely recognize.

Any thinker (however personally alienated from the dominant traditions of the culture) can recognize the *de facto* presence of the history of the effects of tradition in one's pre-understanding. We can do so best by reflecting upon our own language-use. For the language each of us uses carries with it the history of the effects, the traditions of that language. The very word 'religion', for example, carries with it in the English language the history of the effects of the Roman notions of 'civil religion' and of Jewish and Christian notions of 'faith' and Enlightenment notions of 'natural' and 'positive' religion. No one who thinks in and through a particular language (and who does not?) escapes the history of the effects – the tradition inevitably present in that language. We are left, therefore, with our first matter of fact for every interpreter: no interpreter enters the process of inter-pretation without some pre-judgments. Included in those pre-judgments through the very language we use is the history of the effects of the traditions forming that language.

Yet the fact that we say that the interpreter 'enters' the process of interpretation also allows us to recognize a second step in that process. The clearest way to see this second step is to consider the reality of our actual experience of any classic text, image, symbol, event, ritual or person.

When interpreting any *classic* text in the western traditions, for example, we may note that these texts bear a certain permanence and excess of meaning that resists a 'definitive' interpretation. Our actual experience of the classic texts vexes, provokes, elicits a claim to serious attention. And just this claim to attention from the classic text provokes our own pre-understanding into a dual recognition: a recognition at once of how 'formed' our own pre-understanding is and, at the same time, a recognition of the 'vexing', or 'provocation' elicited by the claim to attention of this text. In sum, the interpreter is now willing to interpret in order to understand. The actual experience of that claim to attention may range from a tentative sense of resonance with the question posed by the text through senses of import or even shock of recognition or repugnance elicited by this classic text.

At this point, the interpreter may search for some heuristic model by means of which better to understand the complex process of interaction between text and interpreter now set in motion by the claim to attention of the text. This search for a heuristic model for the *de facto* process of interpretation provides the third step of interpretation. Gadamer's now famous and controversial suggestion of the model of the 'game' of conversation for this process of interpretation seems appropriate here. For the model of conversation is not imposed upon our actual experience of interpretation as some new *de jure* method, norm, or rule. Rather, the phenomenon of conversation aptly describes anyone's *de facto* experience of interpreting any classic text. To understand how this is the case, first recall the more general phenomenon of the 'game' itself before describing the specific 'game of conversation'. The key to any game is not the self-consciousness of the players in the game, but rather *the release of self-consciousness into a consciousness of the phenomenon of the to-and-fro, the back-and-forth movement which constitutes the game.* The attitude of the players of the game is a phenomenon dependent above all upon this natural back-and-forth movement of the game itself. When we really play any game it is not so much we who play it as the game which plays us. If we cannot release ourselves to the back-and-forth movement of the game, then we cannot play. But if we can play, then we experience ourselves as caught up in the movement of the game itself. We realize that our usual self-consciousness cannot be the key to playing. Rather, we may even find, however temporarily, a new sense of self given in, by and through our actual playing, our release to the to-and-fro movements of the game.

This common human experience of playing a game can become the key to the basic model of conversation for the 'game' of interpretation. For what is authentic conversation (as distinct from mere good feeling or debate, gossip or confrontation) other than the ability to become caught up in the to-and-fro movement of the logic of question and response? Just as the subject in any game releases herself/himself from self-consciousness in order to play, so, too, in every authentic conversation the subject is released by the to-and-fro movement of the question and response of the subject-matter under discussion. It is true, of course, that conversation is ordinarily a phenomenon between two living subjects or even one subject reflecting on a question.

Yet the model of conversation, as Gadamer correctly insists, is also applicable to our experience of the interpretation of texts. For if we allow the claim to serious attention of the text to provoke our questioning, then we enter into the logic of question and response of the subject-matter exposed in the text. This model of the conversation allows us to understand a more general model of an interaction between our pre-understanding and the claim to attention of the text as the peculiar kind of interaction it is. If we cannot converse, if we cannot allow for the demands of any subject-matter in any classic, any process of questioning provoked by the claim to attention of the text to take over, then, but only then, we cannot interpret. But if we have even once entered into any genuine conversation, then we are well prepared to recognize how fruitful that model is for the process of interpretation itself.

We need not retreat into the false hopes for our ultimate control over that subject-matter promised by the methodologies of control. We need not retreat into Romantic notions of the interpreter-as-virtuoso intuiting the meaning of the text by empathizing with the mind of the author or by reconstructing the original audience or questions with responses to the text. Insofar as it is we ourselves who are conversing with this classic text, moreover, we will also recognize the inevitable presence of our own pre-understanding and pre-judgments in the conversation. For the claim to serious attention provoked by the text is a claim for *our* attention. It is not the case that we attempt simply to lose ourselves in the 'autonomy' of the text. Rather, we attempt primarily to gain ourselves by losing ourselves in the logic of questioning the subject-matter disclosed by the text. Interpretation is inevitably creative. The meaning of the text does not lie 'behind' it (in the mind of the author, the original social setting, the original audience), nor even 'in' the text itself. Rather, the meaning of the text lies in front of the text – in the now common question, the now common subject-matter of both text and interpreter. We do not seek simply to repeat, to reproduce the original meaning of the text in order to understand its (and now our) questions. Rather, creativity must be involved as we seek to mediate, translate, interpret its meaning – the meaning in front of the text – into our own horizon. We seek, in Gadamer's often misunderstood phrase, *to fuse the horizon (the horizon of meaning in front of the text) with our own horizon.* More basically, we seek to converse with the subject-matter found and expressed in the classic text. (In theology, recall this hermeneutical principle at work in Barth, Bultmann and Rahner.) We seek, in sum, to interpret in order to understand.

By recognizing the actual experience of the interaction of interpreter and text as an experience of conversation, moreover, we also recognize both the creativity and the inevitable finitude and historicity of even our best acts of interpretation. For we recognize the fate of all interpretation of all classics as a fate that can become, when embraced as a conversation, a destiny. That destiny – present in all the classic conversations, especially the Platonic dialogues, and all the creative interpreters – is the recognition that we live in and by our finitude and historicity with the liberating insight that 'Insofar as we understand at all we understand differently (from the original author).'

In my judgment, two remaining crucial difficulties in Gadamer's interpretation of the process of interpretation demand correction. The first difficulty is Gadamer's too sanguine notion of tradition. One need not retreat to Enlightenment polemics against the inevitable presence of tradition in all understanding in order to share the insistence of several of Gadamer's critics (especially Jürgen Habermas) that Gadamer's notion of tradition bears its own dangers.

One way of clarifying that danger is to restate, as I did above, the liberating truth of the Enlightenment itself: *viz.*, its belief in the emancipatory thrust of critical and practical reason. Yet this will not suffice as a charge against Gadamer's own general programme of interpretation, but only against his particular interpretation of the Enlightenment itself. For whatever the truth of Gadamer's interpretation of the Enlightenment (for myself, it is the partial truth of the corrective of naive Enlightenment polemics against 'tradition': in sum, a kind of conservative humanist exposure of the 'dialectic of the enlightenment' analogous to the left-wing critique of Adorno and Horkheimer), his position on interpretation does not stand or fall on the truth of that particular interpretation. As much as his critics, like Habermas, Gadamer too allows for, indeed demands, moments of creativity (including critical reflection) as intrinsic to the very process of interpretation. The fact that his position is grounded in the conversation between text and interpreter (and not simply the 'text') should be sufficient to indicate this. The kind of creative 'critical reflection' which Gadamer characteristically endorses, to be sure, is that paradigmatically expressed (for him) in the dialogues of Plato and phenomenology of Aristotle rather than in modern critical theory. I grant that these notions of 'critical reflection' are different in several crucial respects.

However, even those differences should not allow interpreters to assume that Gadamer is simply a traditionalist opposed to creativity and unconcerned with the need for critical reflection in any process of interpretation. The real difficulty, in my judgment, lies elsewhere. *Gadamer's retrieval of the enrichment to our preunderstanding provided by the inevitable presence of tradition in all language does demand those forms of critical reflection that can undo error and falsity in the conversation.* Yet it remains an open question whether Gadamer's understanding of the kind of critical reflection available to the interpreter can really allow for the kinds of critical theories demanded to undo not error, but *illusion*, not normal cognitive and moral ambiguity, but *systematic distortions*. Here is where Gadamer's anti-Enlightenment polemic severely damages his case. His apprehension is that any move to critical theory will inevitably become yet another futile attempt to provide a mythical 'presuppositionless' interpreter. Because of that apprehension he seems to discount the occasional necessity of some critical theory in some conversations – including conversations with the classics. The basic development in the post-modern hermeneutic tradition have in fact been developments in interpretation – theories that are explicitly geared to formulating various critical theories forged to expose the latent meanings of texts – especially those latent meanings that enforce not mere error but illusion, not occasional difficulties but systematic distortions.

But Gadamer's own position does not really allow these necessarily suspicious moves (and their attendant critical theories) to play their limited but proper role in the dialectic of interpretation. Yet the very experience of interpretation-as-conversation should alert us to this occasional need for critical theory. To return for the moment to the model of conversation on the inter-personal level: in the course of any conversation, if any one of us begins to suspect (the verb here is apt) that our conversation-partner is psychotic, we would be justified in suspending the conversation for the moment. In sum, the need for suspicion and the need for critical theories (like psychoanalytic theory) to spot and heal systematic distortions in our personal – and, beyond that, our cultural and social – lives has become an indispensable aspect of any modern interpreter's horizon of pre-understanding and possibility for creative interpretation. It is true, of course, that this kind of interpretation of latent, hidden, repressed meanings unconsciously operative as systematic distortions is easier to employ (thanks to psychoanalysis) on the personal and interpersonal levels than on the social, cultural and historical levels. However, even on those levels, various forms of Marxist 'ideology-critique' and, more recently, with thinkers like *Foucault*, various forms of Nietzschean 'genealogical methods' exist, like their theological analogues in liberation and political theologies, as hermeneutic aids to try to locate and undo the illusions, the hidden, repressed, unconscious distortions, present in the pre-understanding of the interpreter and in the classic texts and traditions. Every one of these 'hermeneutics of suspicion', moreover, cannot rest simply on the model of conversation, but needs critical theories to warrant its operation.

If any interpreter so much as suspects that illusions, or repressed systematic distortions, may be present in any particular tradition, the need to develop this sense of suspicion becomes imperative. Whenever we suspect systematic distortion, the model of conversation becomes inadequate to describe the broader process of interpretation. The analyst and the analysand are not engaged in a conversation *tout simple*. Rather, they are engaged in a process of interpretation whereby 'one conversation-partner' (the analyst) employs a critical theory (psychoanalytic theory) to aid the other partner to interpret her or his experience and to emancipate that other partner from the systematic distortions repressed but operative in experience. Only after that kind of emancipation is conversation possible again. Yet not to face that demand or suspicion as part of the demand for interpreting any tradition seems to leave us, unwittingly, without the hermeneutic resource which our post-modern era renders available and which genuine creativity in interpretation now demands.

My first difficulty with Gadamer's position has occasioned a basic acceptance of his model for interpretation system, but has also forced me to insist on a corrective of his critique of the role of 'critical theory' in the interpretative process as a whole. The second difficulty I wish to address is related not so much to the model of conversation as to the notion of the 'text and its subject-matter' as formulated by Gadamer.

The crucial issue here is this: *the subject-matter which becomes the common subject-matter of both interpreter and text in the process of interpretation is a subject-matter whose claim to attention is one expressed in the form of a text.* The point is worth emphasizing in order to understand the broader process of interpretation.

Once again, however, it is not that Gadamer is simply unaware of the importance of form and structure for expressing the subject-matter and thereby, on his terms, for providing the claim to serious attention of the meaning in front of the text.

However, Gadamer's corrective truth (here against methodologism) is in danger of exaggeration and polemic (here against all method). Insofar as we recognize that the text produces its claim to attention by structuring and forming the subject-matter into a work, an ordered whole, *a text*, we must also recognize the legitimacy, even necessity, of the use of some explanatory methods in the process of interpretation. As Paul Ricoeur insists, along with Gadamer, 'understanding' (*Verstehen*) 'envelops' the entire process of interpretation. Yet, as Ricoeur correctly insists against Gadamer, explanatory methods (*Erklären*) can 'develop' our understanding of how the meaning is produced through the very form and structure of the text.

A more appropriate model of conversation thereby suggests itself: *viz*, that the entire process of interpretation encompasses the arc of some initial understanding yielding to an explanation of how the sense and referent (the world of meaning in front of the text) is produced through the meanings-in-form-and-structures *in* the text. After those explanatory moments, the reader has a better understanding of the subject-matter (as an *in-formed* subject-matter) than any interpreter without them. Indeed, without the use of explanatory methods like the methods of literary criticism, the analyses of what constitutes a text, or semiotic and structuralist methods, it is difficult to see how, *contra*

Gadamer's own manifest intentions, the interpreter is not in danger of simply extracting 'messages' (under the rubric 'subject-matter') from the complex, structured, formed subject-matter which is the text.

Every text is a structured whole. Every subject-matter comes to us with its claim to serious attention in and through its form and structure. To resist explanatory methods which can show how such expression occurs from the semiotic level of the word, through the semantics of the sentence, through the structured whole of the work as an ordered whole in the text (achieved principally through composition and genre) to the individuating power of style, is ultimately to resist both understanding and creativity (Ricoeur). Yet just this seems to occur in Gadamer's polemic against method. So apprehensive is he about how explanation (or *Erklären*) can become a means to undo conversation between text and interpreter on a common subject-matter (and, therefore, undo authentic hermeneutical understanding or *Verstehen*) that he is tempted to discount the necessity of explanatory methods in order to interpret.

More exactly, all explanatory methods can be used by any interpreter committed to the kind of process of interpretation which Gadamer himself outlines. Explanatory methods develop or challenge, even confront one's initial understanding of how the subject-matter comes to be expressed in and through its structure and form. *In Riceour's formulation, this may be restated as the ability of these explanatory methods to show how the structured meanings and sense produce the referent of the work.* Understanding and explanation (like truth and method) need not be implacable enemies. For any interpreter they can become allies – albeit wary and uneasy allies. The wider conversation of the contemporary conflict over interpretation-theory need not yield to the spectacle of armed camps shooting over the walls of the one encampment. Rather, creative possibilities exist for the entire community of interpreters in any discipline to engage in conversation on the relative adequacy of any interpretation.

II. Interpretation theory and the interpretation of religion

Before proceeding directly to the role of interpretation-theory in theology, let us look at its role in *any* interpretation of religion. It is important to make this 'detour' by way of the interpretation of religion in order to ensure that the theologian's interpretations of her or his religious tradition for the contemporary situation are not divorced from all interpretations of religion in the 'new paradigm'. On the contrary, the theologian performs one vital kind of interpretation of a particular religion which, precisely *as interpretation*, is intrinsically related to all other interpretations of religion. *Let us see, therefore, how the 'five steps' of interpretation analyzed above are applicable to the interpretation of that puzzling, pluralistic and ambiguous phenomenon called religion.* Once that is clarified, we can then turn to the particular hermeneutical character of Christian theology itself.

The first choice any interpreter, including the theologian, of any religion must make is that of which phenomenon to interpret. The prospective interpreter may believe either that religion is one of the great creative forces of the human spirit or a deadly confusion. Whatever one's predilections on religion, interpreters must be sure that the phenomenon to be interpreted is a genuinely religious one. One way to ensure that the phenomenon will be religious is to choose for one's interpretation one of the religious classics of a particular religion. By choosing a recognized religious classic (text, symbol, myth, ritual, person, event or doctrine), the interpreter will make two gains: first, the phenomenon, whatever else it is, will be religious; second, the phenomenon as a classic religious *expression* will lend itself to an interpretation-theory designed to deal with *expressions* of experience and not directly with claims to purely unexpressed experiences.

With the choice of a single religious classic from among the pluralistic ways of being religious and the plurality of religious classics expressive of those many ways, the interpretation will begin. Then the three 'steps' argued earlier as constitutive of the process of interpretation of expression could be used to interpret this classic expression *as* as religious classic.

The interpreter is likely to note that the religious classic, like any classic, will provoke, vex, and elicit a claim to serious attention. With that provocation, two further steps will occur. *First, if the phenomenon is religious it will ordinarily provoke some fundamental existential question for the human spirit* (e.g. the question of finitude or fault; the question of fundamental trust or meaning) as well as some initial comprehension of a particular response to that question articulated in this particular religious text. As soon as the interpreter recognizes any provocation as present, then the second step of the interpretation process occurs. Not only are we provoked by the classic as by an other (even, sometimes, an alien other). *We are also alerted by that otherness to a recognition of our own pre-understanding.* The otherness, even alienness of the religious classic, heightens the interpreter's consciousness of her or his pre-understanding of religion. The history of the effects of our cultural traditions on religion, along with the history of the effects of our own participation or non-participation in a particular religious community or particular cultural traditions which have been influenced, for good and ill, by particular religious traditions, now becomes clearer to us. The history of effects does not become, *contra* Hegel, fully conscious, but more conscious than the partly unconscious, partly conscious history of effects prior to provocation by the religious classic itself.

This initial form of interaction of the claim to attention provoked by the religious text and the pre-understanding (including the pre-judgments) of the interpreter becomes a genuine interpretation when the initial interaction takes the more specific form of a conversation. In that interaction-game, the interpreter is willing to enter into the to-and-fro movement of the questions and responses of this classic text. *When those questions become the interpreter's own questions, then we too, as interpreters, find ourselves in a conversation with the now common subject-matter of both text and interpreter.* As in the interpretation of any other classic, this does *not* mean that the interpreter must give up her or his own powers of critical reflection on these now common questions. It does mean, however, that if interpreters are to interpret the religious phenomenon as a religious phenomenon, they cannot simply impose their prior value-judgments upon the phenomenon through such strategies as a claim to autonomy and neutrality that is literally unreal, or through such strategies as the claim that these kinds of questions are unintelligble and therefore not open to interpretation. These *de jure* moves crash against the fact that, once the provocation of the text has elicited the interpreter to ask its kind of question and to consider its kind of response to that question, the process of interpretation-as-conversation has already begun.

The spectrum of responses of the interpreter throughout the entire process of interpretation may range from some interest or resonance through a sense that, in Dorothy van Ghent's apt words, 'something else may be the case', to a more negative repugnance or positive 'shock' of recognition. (In theology this latter response is recognized as the gift of 'faith'). In every case along the whole pluralistic spectrum of possible responses, as long as any claim to attention is allowed at all, the process of interpretation-as-conversation between the constantly shifting identities-in-difference of both text and interpreter occasioned by the to-and-fro movement of the conversation, guided by the eventually common questions of the common subject-matter, continues. *Neither interpreter nor text, but the common subject-matter, takes over in genuine conversation.* Interpretation as conversation will not occur, however, if the prospective interpreter allows no provocation from the religious text because she or he already 'knows' that this conversation is hopeless. Nor will a conversation occur if it is decided that the 'text' is so autonomous that the interpreter cannot consider her or his own responses as part of the conversation which is the interpretation. Nor will interpretation as conversation occur if the interpreter decides that the real meaning of the text cannot be found through the text itself but must be found 'behind' the text – in the mind of the author, the socio-historical conditions of the text, or the response of the original audience to the text.

Yet, as this last 'textual' factor indicates, there is also a need for the two 'correctives' analyzed above to ensure that the full arc of interpretation occurs and that a full use of explanatory methods is allowed. When interpreting a religious classic, we are interpreting an *expression* (especially, but not exclusively, a written text); therefore we are interpreting a structured whole which expresses its claim to our attention through such productive strategies as composition, genre and style. *As a work, the text produces its world of meaning in front of the text as a possible way-of-being-in-the-world.* Thus the text produces a genuine possibility for our imagination. As that claim provokes our attention and pre-understanding to the point where a conversation on a now common subject-matter occurs, the interpreter will also recognize that the subject-matter is always-already a formed subject-matter. The subject-matter comes as an expression (whether in written texts, actions, styles of life, images or symbols). As expression (in that general sense of 'structured whole', as 'text'), the interpreter finds the need to employ the explanatory methods to develop his or her initial understanding, and to check, correct, or even confront that initial understanding with explanatory methods. All such methods – whether historico-critical, semiotic, structuralist or literary-critical – may serve as developments, checks and correctives of, and challenges to, the initial understanding. On this hermeneutic model, these methods serve such functions best by showing how the claim to attention provoked by the text is in fact produced as a world of meaning (a referent) in front of the text through the text itself.

On this reading, therefore, there is no reason to hold that a hermeneutics of religion should disallow such semiotic explanations as Louis Marin's analysis of the parables of the New Testament or such structuralist analyses as Claude Lévi-Strauss's analysis of mythic structures. It is true that a hermeneutics of religion of the kind described above will not agree that these interpretations are fully adequate. Yet it will not only agree but insist that such interpretations are legitimate moments of explanation in the full process of interpretation. Any explanatory method that helps to show how the text produces its sense and referent is entirely appropriate to a hermeneutics of religion. As

Schleiermacher's insistence on grammatical methods shows, as Gadamer's own recognition of the roles of structure and form demonstrates, and as Joachim Wach's attention to classic religious *expressions* indicates, there is no reason in principle for the hermeneutical tradition to disallow the use of explanatory methods to develop, check, correct and challenge one's initial interpretation. Creativity in interpretation is not opposed to explanation and method. The very pluralism intrinsic to the religious phenomenon itself, moreover, should encourage the use of the plurality of explanatory methods within the broader process of interpretation. These methods may also serve to show how the religious use of *any* form – any genre or style – is a limit-use that produces the referent of the religious classic as a religious-as-limit-mode-of-being-in-the-world.

The second corrective which I analyzed earlier should also be operative in a hermeneutics of religion. Insofar as there is plurality and cognitive ambiguity in every classic religious text, and insofar as every classic religious text and tradition includes in the history of its effects a moral ambiguity that can become a repressed systematic distortion, there is also a need to develop various hermeneutics of suspicion (and their attendant critical theories), and to apply them to religious classics.

In harmony with the earlier analysis of interpretation theory, and in harmony with a recognition of the plurality and ambiguity internal to the religious phenomenon itself, we may affirm the need for this second corrective as well. All the great hermeneutics of suspicion (Marx, Freud, Nietzsche) remain relevant methods of interpretation. Each develops a critical theory (psychoanalytic theory, ideology-critique, genealogical method) to inform its hermeneutics of suspicion. The critical theories are employed to spot and emancipate the repressed, unconscious distortions that also operate in the classic religious texts and in their history of effects through the classic religious traditions. Not only this general interpretation theory, but the nature of the religious phenomenon itself, allows – indeed demands – this need for a hermeneutics of suspicion, and a hermeneutics of retrieval.

It is sometimes claimed that the various hermeneutics of

suspicion are simply taken from the secular classics and then used by interpreters of the religious classics to interpret religion. To a large extent, of course, this is historically true insofar as such methods of suspicion as Freudian psychoanalysis, Marxist ideology-critique or Nietzschean genealogical methods were first developed outside (indeed usually against) the religious traditions before they were employed within them. Yet, as modern political, liberation and feminist theologians correctly insist, these methods of suspicion are entirely appropriate on inner-religious grounds. The reason for this, I believe, is clearly demonstrated in the Jewish and Christian traditions. Both major strands of these traditions – generically the prophetic and the mystical – include explicitly religious hermeneutics of suspicion that demand constant self-reformation and self-suspicion by the tradition on the tradition's own religious grounds.

Bultmann is correct, on purely hermeneutical grounds, to insist that the prophetic-eschatological strand of Christianity (not merely the problematic of 'modernity') demands a demythologizing of Christianity by Christianity. At the heart of every prophetic tradition is an opening and a demand for any critical theory that helps to uncover repressed illusions – including the repressed illusion (not mere errors) of sexism, racism, classism, and so on, that are also operative in the Jewish and Christian religious classics.

Nor is it the case that the mystical strand of the religious traditions is lacking in its own form of hermeneutics of suspicion. The great developments of spirituality in all the traditions, including the Jewish and Christian, were developed to find not mere errors but systematic unconscious illusions. The very use of the word 'discernment' in the Christian traditions of spirituality, like the development of kabbalistic methods of interpretation in Jewish mysticism or the use of the word 'enlightenment' in Buddhist traditions, are clues that the mystical traditions also include great methods of suspicion to be applied, above all, to such 'religious' experiences as 'ecstasy' and 'vision'. In short, explicitly religious hermeneutics of suspicion already exist in both the mystical and the prophetic strands of the religious traditions. These methods of interpretation of the pluralistic and ambiguous phenomenon of religion empower an internal religious hermeneutics of suspicion and encourage the incorporation (now on inner-religious grounds) of any other 'external' hermeneutics of suspicion and attendant critical theories. As a pluralistic and ambiguous phenomenon, religion not merely allows but demands both hermeneutics of retrieval and suspicion.

III. The new paradigm and hermeneutics in theology

If we grant the description of modern hermeneutics outlined above and grant, as well, the special difficulties and possibilities of interpreting that ambiguous and pluralistic phenomenon named religion, we may note the relevance of all this to the role of hermeneutics in theology proper. As Eduard Schillebeeckx among others has suggested, it is possible to speak of modern theology in general terms as the attempt to develop mutually critical correlations between contemporary experience and the Christian tradition.

It is useful to note how each of these realities – these 'constants', as Hans Küng's paper describes them, necessarily includes hermeneutical elements. Indeed, theology is a deliberately hermeneutical enterprise from beginning to end. Each of the two 'constants' is not available immediately but is understood only by being interpreted. Moreover, in interpreting either of these constants, the other is always already present: theologians, as theological interpreters of contemporary experience and of the Christian tradition, to greater and lesser degrees inevitably interpret each reality in the light of the other.

To speak of theology as the development of mutually critical correlations of contemporary experience and the Christian tradition, therefore, is simply to render *explicit* and *deliberate* the intrinsically hermeneutical character of theology at every stage of its development.

It is not the case, of course, that theology only becomes

hermeneutical in the modern period (see H. de Lubac and G. Ebeling). It is the case, however – as we saw above in the section on hermeneutics – that the explicit concern with hermeneutics since Schleiermacher is occasioned by the crisis of the sense of cultural distance from the religious tradition caused by the seventeenth-century scientific revolution and the eighteenth-century Enlightenment. This sense was intensified by the nineteenth-century emergence of historical consciousness (see E. Troeltsch and B. Lonergan). This same sense has been further intensified in the twentieth century by the emergence of the great liberation movements and their attendant hermeneutics of suspicion (in regard to sexism, racism, classism, and so on). This sense has been further intensified by the western sense of cultural parochialism occasioned by an emerging global culture (and thereby the reality of the other world religions) as well as the tensions, conflicts and possibilities present in the north-south and east-west relationships.

All these epoch-making events have caused a need for explicit reflection on the character of hermeneutics in all the disciplines (even philosophy of science). This is especially the case in theology. We can note this most clearly by returning to Hans Küng's analysis of the two constants.

The first constant is 'our present world of experience in all its ambivalence, contingency and change' (Küng). In order to understand this world – indeed even to experience it – we must interpret it. *Interpretation is not something added to experience and understanding but is always-already present as intrinsic to understanding itself.* This is especially the case for any theological interpretations of our contemporary experience. For theology attempts to discern and interpret those fundamental questions (finitude, estrangement, alienation, oppression, fundamental trust or mistrust, loyalty, anxiety, mortality, and so on) which disclose a genuinely religious dimension in our contemporary experience and language.

With Tillich, we may speak of this hermeneutical task of theology as an analysis of the 'situation': that is, those creative interpretations of our experience which disclose a religious dimension. It is possible to distinguish, but not to separate, the theologian's analysis of this 'first constant' from her or his analysis of the 'second constant' (the Christian message itself). We cannot simply separate these analyses for, like *any other interpreter of our contemporary experience and like any other* interpreter of the religious dimensions of that experience, the theologian too is influenced by the history of effects of her or his tradition, *viz.*, the Christian tradition. The recent retrievals of the eschatological symbols by the liberation and political theologians, for example, are not occasioned merely by the fundamental questions of a sense of alienation and/or oppression. They are also caused by the history of the effects of the Jewish and Christian eschatological symbols themselves upon the Christian sensibilities of the theologian *as interpreter* of these contemporary experiences of alienation and oppression.

In that sense, every theological act of interpretation of the 'first constant' is always-already a hermeneutical act attempting to establish 'mutually critical correlations' between contemporary experience and the Christian message.

Moreover, as the broader spectrum of the principal fundamental questions chosen for a theological analysis of that experience in the different theologies of our period testify, real differences and really different theologies are and will continue to be occasioned by those different interpretations. Consider, for example, the different kinds of theology that emerge when a profound sense of oppression and/or alienation, as distinct from a profound sense of fundamental trust, is explicated as *the* hermeneutical key to contemporary experience. Or note how, in the modern period of theology, the crisis of cognitive claims occasioned by the scientific revolution, the Enlightenment, and the emergence of historical consciousness led to several reformulations of the doctrine of revelation. Contrast these efforts to reformulate the doctrine of revelation with the more recent efforts to retrieve not revelation but eschatology in liberation and political theologies. The later theologies ordinarily interpret our contemporary experience not in the light of the crisis of cognitive claims (as do most earlier theologies of revelation) but rather in the light of the crisis of the 'counter-experience' of massive global suffering.

The differences (even the conflicts) in these interpretations remain real differences of interpretation of contemporary experience. The kinds of real differences which we saw were operative in hermeneutical theory itself are inevitably present in theology as well. The interpretations of the 'first constant', therefore, will yield a 'conflict of interpretations' of the religious dimension (and hence the 'fundamental questions') of *our present world of experience in all its ambivalence, contingency and change*. The unity of theology will be not the unity of a particular interpretation but the unity of a common, deliberate and explicit need to *interpret* this first constant, and to defend any interpretation *vis-à-vis* alternative interpretations, within the entire community of theological inquiry.

To recognize this inevitably hermeneutical character of all theology, therefore, is not to impose some single model of theology (as in some formulations of the 'New Hermeneutic'). It is, rather, to recognize the *common* need to recognize how all theology involves the interpretation of this first constant. Thus the modern paradigm of theology renders explicit what is implicit in all traditional theology as well. One of the most basic *continuities* (Toulmin) operative throughout theological paradigm-shifts is the reality of an interpretation of the two constants.

This same need for explicitly hermeneutical reflection emerges when we turn to an analysis of the 'second constant' of theology. That constant, too, is well formulated, in properly general terms, by Hans Küng as 'the Judaeo-Christian tradition which is ultimately based on the Christian message, the Gospel of Jesus Christ'.

In the light of the outline of the hermeneutical process (section one) and in the context of recalling how any religion is inevitably pluralistic and ambiguous (section two), it becomes imperative for every theologian to render explicit her or his understanding of the ultimate norm of the Christian tradition. This hermeneutical enterprise discloses the common unity of the theological task as a common agreement on the need for each theologian to interpret the two constants.

Since the emergence of historical consciousness and the recognition of the priority of praxis, there have been, for example, various candidates for interpreting the Christian message as norm (e.g., 'the historical Jesus', 'the original apostolic kerygma', 'the Christ-kerygma of Paul and John', the entire tradition, the praxis of *imitatio Christi*, and so on; 'canons within the canon', 'canons outside the canon', 'working canons', 'discrimina', the whole history of effects as tradition, and so on). *As in the case of the interpretation of contemporary experience, it is unlikely that there will be a unity based on any particular interpretation of the Christian message.* Yet there remains a communal recognition of the need to *interpret* this second constant and to make one's interpretation available to the entire community of theological inquiry for assessment. The emphasis on the *common* hermeneutical enterprise of all interpretations of this second constant can provide for some clarifications of the real differences and similarities among modern theologies.

For example, the theological community of inquiry could agree in principle that the often confusing phrase 'the historical Jesus' refers to that 'Jesus who lived *insofar as he is known or knowable today by way of empirico-historical methods*'. On that reading, the 'historical Jesus' can serve as a corrective of christologies (along with such other correctives as the 'original apostolic witness') *but not as the hermeneutical foundation of this second constant.* That foundation would prove to be some particular interpretation of 'the Christian message, the Gospel of Jesus Christ' which would employ this and other correctives.

An explicit hermeneutical concern with this second constant not merely allows for but demands that the entire theological community of inquiry discuss their different interpretations with shared hermeneutical concerns. Then community-wide arguments for the relative adequacy of any particular interpretation would be both encouraged and warranted. *Conflict among various proposals may be our actuality. Yet conversation is our hope.* Hermeneutics itself is grounded in conversation and thereby in a genuine community of inquiry, and thus aids the possible consensus and adjudication of the real differences among particular theologies within the shared new paradigm.

As interpretation, the articulation of this second crucial constant is also an implicit use of a method of developing mutually critical correlations between both constants. As we saw above, insofar as we interpret contemporary experience theologically, we also interpret the history of effects of the Christian message which has formed us as theological interpreters. And insofar as we interpret the Christian message theologically we also apply it to contemporary experience. Insofar as we perform both these interpretations deliberately we correlate these two distinct but, as we have seen, not separate interpretations. We are, in short, performing the distinctly theological task of an interpretation of Christian religion: that is, developing mutually critical correlations between an interpretation of contemporary experience and an interpretation of the Christian message. This formulation, in fact, provides a relatively adequate way to describe the general hermeneutical task of all theologies in the new paradigm.

Schillebeeckx's choice of the phrase, *mutually critical correlations*, is a useful one for the new paradigm. As we saw above in the analysis of the inevitably hermeneutical character of any theological appropriation of either constant, every theological act of interpretation already involves some correlation of the two constants. It remains methodologically helpful to distinguish these two distinct acts of interpretation as distinct. At the same time, the interpreter cannot existentially separate the two acts. Whenever we interpret contemporary experience theologically, the history of effects of the Christian tradition is present in the interpretation itself. Whenever we interpret the Christian message theologically, we inevitably apply it to our contemporary experience precisely in order to understand it.

To call theology a hermeneutical enterprise, therefore, is to recognize that such correlations of these two acts of interpretation are always occurring in order to produce the single act of a given theological interpretation. To add the qualifying phrase 'mutually critical' to the word 'correlation' highlights the hermeneutical reality that the subject-matter itself and not any methodology must ultimately reign in every interpretation. In any concrete case of interpretation of any particular subject-matter (such as christology), the ultimate decision for the kind of correlation between the two constants must be decided not by methodological rules but by the subject-matter itself. The five 'steps' of the hermeneutical process illuminate the possibilities available (e.g., retrieval and/or critique, suspicion; explanation and understanding). But the above-mentioned concrete subject-matter can decide the actual kind of correlation needed in any particular case.

The word 'correlation', therefore, is intended to indicate the full spectrum of logical possibilities available: *viz.*, that the actual interpretation of the particular subject-matter may prove a confrontation between the two constants (from either side); or a claim to identity between the two constants in this particular subject; or a claim to similarities between the two constants or to those similarities-in-difference named *analogies*.

Theological interpretation as developing mutually critical correlations between the two constants remains a deliberately hermeneutical interpretation of that puzzling and ambiguous phenomenon, religion. Precisely because he or she is deliberately hermeneutical in that way, the theologian cannot avoid the claims to meaning and truth operative in an attempt to establish the proper correlation for the concrete subject-matter being interpreted. Sometimes an analysis of contemporary experience will confront earlier theological interpretations of the meaning and truth of the Christian message (e.g., the confrontation of literalist and fundamentalist readings of *Genesis* by the development of evolutionary theory, or the confrontation of traditional theological formulations of christology by a use of the correctives provided by modern historico-critical or socio-scientific methods). At other times, the analysis of the Christian message will confront reigning understandings of contemporary experience (e.g., the confrontation of secularism by theologies of secularity, or the confrontation of developmental theories by the retrieval of apocalyptic in liberation and political theologians, or the confrontation of sexism and anti-semitism operative in the tradition by the appropriation of modern movements of liberating praxis and modern critical theories of ideology-critique.

In every case of genuinely theological interpretation, therefore, the questions of meaning *and* truth must be faced squarely as the theologian attempts to establish the particular form of correlation appropriate to the relationship between the two constants in regard to any particular subject-matter. Hermeneutical method informs the process, yet *the concrete subject-matter rules the interpretation*.

This hermeneutical understanding of the task of theology in the new paradigm, moreover, should increase the understanding of theology as a community of inquiry grounded in a community of commitment. In any authentic community of inquiry, pluralism is not merely tolerated but encouraged. But if that pluralism is not to decay into the mindless geniality or even 'repressive tolerance' of a mere 'let a thousand flowers bloom', then a conversing, responsible theological community of inquiry where all are expected to provide plausible theological warrants for their proposals becomes urgent.

The explicitly hermeneutical moment in modern theology in the new paradigm is one way to assure the existence of a responsible pluralism in the entire theological community of inquiry. The understanding of theology as the development of mutually critical correlations between the two constants, therefore, is one way to render explicit the genuine consensus that in fact exists in spite of the many differences in contemporary theology. A retreat from hermeneutics is ultimately a retreat into a fundamentalism grounded in serious misinterpretations of both constants. The move into hermeneutical reflection in theology as in the other modern disciplines as the new paradigm emerges is not another imperialist declaration of a *de jure* methodology levelling the pluralism of contemporary theology. On the contrary, hermeneutical reflection in theology as in the other modern disciplines renders explicit the *de facto* basic consensus that already exists in spite of the real differences among modern theologies.

But if theology, in its new circumstances, is to remain a genuine community of inquiry and not a mere chaos of fads, fashions and virtuosi, then the need to reflect upon the *de facto* hermeneutical character operative throughout this pluralistic community of inquiry becomes imperative for us all. In both praxis and theory, theology in the new paradigm has become a genuine conversation among the different particular proposals for establishing mutually critical correlations between the Christian message and contemporary experience.

The modern paradigm-shift is both new and momentous. But, as I have tried to suggest throughout this essay, this modern shift is not discontinuous with the great and implicitly hermeneutical tradition of Christian theology. Indeed, without a common commitment to the new general paradigm in spite of our other real differences, we may well find ourselves divorced from both that great tradition and from one another. Our options, fortunately, are not exhausted by the unwelcome alternatives of chaos or fundamentalism. Rather, we find ourselves in a theological community of inquiry and commitment. In that community, we attempt, individually and communally, to work out the most relatively adequate mutually critical correlations between the Christian message and contemporary experience in regard to the pressing theological questions of our day. In every such attempt, explicit reflection on hermeneutics, like explicit reflection on its natural correlate, theory and praxis (Lamb), cannot but aid the enterprise.

THE DIALECTICS OF THEORY AND PRAXIS WITHIN PARADIGM ANALYSIS

Matthew L. Lamb

Hans Küng perceptively sketches several analogies between paradigm changes in natural sciences and those occurring in theology, suggesting possibilities of reconstructing the history of theology in terms of paradigmatic macromodels. David Tracy explores some of the important hermeneutical presuppositions of paradigm analysis; he shows creatively how a hermeneutical transposition of paradigm analysis might provide categories to promote a contemporary theological consensus which takes into account the genuine differences among the dialoguing theologians.

The task of relating paradigm analysis to the various ways in which praxis interests contemporary philosophers of science and theologians is more problematic. It involves shifting from hermeneutics to dialectics and to the critique of ideology: from the primarily interpretative concerns of historical consciousness to the primarily social and emancipatory concerns of dialectical consciousness. Tracy touched on these questions in terms of the critical corrective which Habermas and Ricoeur offer to Gadamer's hermeneutical philosophy.

The problematic is compounded by just what is meant by ideology. Dialectical thinkers tend to use this term with all the protean indefiniteness that hermeneutical thinkers reserve for the term 'myth'. Philosophers of science strongly influenced by Karl Popper, for example, tend to see in the very applicability of paradigm analysis to theology evidence of the 'ideological' or 'irrational' character of Thomas Kuhn's discoveries (*cf.* Agassi, 1981; 457 ff.; Lakatos, 1970: 91-3; 1978: 241; Popper, 1970: 57; Watkins, 1970: 31-7; 1978: 344). Indeed, Kuhn himself was 'puzzled' by the wide applicability of paradigm analysis to fields other than the history of the natural sciences (1970a: 208). And Richard Bernstein wonders whether Kuhn's work really helps us to distinguish scientific paradigms from ideological paradigms (1976: 105).

For their part, theologians interested in relating philosophies of science to theological methods tend either to complement paradigm analysis with philosophical hermeneutics (e.g., Pannenberg, Tracy), or to sublate theories of science into theories of communicative interaction which are then intensified to become limit questions of anamnestic solidarity with the victims of history (e.g., Peukert, Lamb).

Such theologians might well wonder who is being 'ideological' when they see so distinguished a philosopher of science as the late Imre Lakatos state that in his view 'science, as such, has no social responsibility', and that the defence of liberty requires us to maintain 'the high social prestige of applied nuclear scientists working for the army' (1978: 258).

Although liberation theologians have not yet related their concerns to Anglo-American philosophies of science, they would probably ask how science and technology can function as ideology, not just in a Popperian 'Third World', but in terms of the very real economic and political controls First and Second World countries exercise over Third World countries. Such questions recall Marx's and Engels's *The German Ideology* in which, over a hundred years ago, they satirized the 'unparalleled revolutions' occurring in the realm of 'pure philosophy', beside which political revolutions seemed no more than 'child's play'. Such questions concerning the supposed primacy of science in modern liberal societies are beginning to prompt, as Langdon Gilkey points out, a new 'nervousness and uncertainty' in scientific establishments (1981: 75-89).

My task is to present an all too brief overview of the *status quaestionis* and of the dialectic of theory and praxis within the contemporary post-empiricist philosophies of science after paradigm analysis, and to indicate how this might shed some light on possibly analogous developments in the shifts to praxis and dialectics in contemporary theology.

My first section attempts an admittedly incomplete overview of the turn to praxis and dialectics in what Küng and Tracy refer to as 'the new paradigm'. Whereas their tasks could presuppose a familiarity with post-empiricist philosophies of science, I judged it important for mine to hazard an overview. Whereas Kuhn's paradigm analysis definitively introduced historical consciousness into the philosophy of science, it is only by tracing the further developments in the field that I could indicate how the dialectics of theory and praxis operates in it. Kuhn's hermeneutical breakthrough has to be complemented by the efforts of continental and Anglo-American philosophers of science, in order to appreciate the dialectical intensifications of his achievements in the emerging attention given to praxis and the critique of ideology. These developments call into question the fundamental self-understanding of modernity with its illusory dichotomy between science and ideology. These post-modern advances, however, do not lead to the epistemological anarchy propounded by Paul Feyerabend.

My second section loosely traces analogous developments in contemporary theology. There I argue that neither the hermeneutical theologies nor the political and liberation theologies can be adequately understood as long as one is fixated on the typically modern dichotomy between conservative and liberal theological orientations. Post-empiricist philosophies of science are moving beyond the basic assumptions of modernity; as are hermeneutical and dialectical theologies. This becomes especially evident in the dialectical criticisms by political and liberation theologians of the distortions in the historical traditions of Christianity and in so much of contemporary human experience. Any symbol-system or idea-system may become ideological to the degree that it legitimates dominative power.

I. The turn to praxis and dialectics in the new paradigm

A central feature of the new paradigm in theology suggested by

Küng and Tracy is, of course, paradigm analysis itself. In articulating analogies between paradigm or disciplinary matrix shifts in the natural sciences and in theology, Küng sketches a succession of macromodels in the history of theology which he designates as the Greek Alexandrians, Latin Augustinian, medieval Thomistic, Reformation, Protestant Orthodox, and modern interpretative macromodels respectively. His essay acknowledges that the formal presuppositions of the new paradigm – truthful, free, critical, ecumenical – are indeed normative, but not in such a way that they could guarantee or predict the fate of any new paradigm. A new paradigm could be absorbed into a previous one, accepted, or shelved. Küng's essay, therefore, exemplifies how paradigm analysis could provide heuristic categories for contemporary theology as an *interpretative* enterprise.

Tracy intensifies this interpretative orientation by complementing paradigm analysis with categories from hermeneutical philosophy. Drawing upon Gadamer's work, Tracy indicates how interpretation is unavoidable in any theological enterprise, especially in the pluralistic context of contemporary theologies. Paradigm analysis participates in the give-and-take of a 'conversational game' with ongoing mutually corrective exchanges between the interpreter's pre-judgments and classic texts, images, symbols, events, rituals, or persons. Tracy acknowledges the need to modify such a hermeneutical enterprise in the light of both Habermas's emphasis on the need to suspect both traditions and modernity of systematically distorted communication (Marx, Freud, Nietzsche), and in the light of Ricoeur's emphasis on the need to complement hermeneutical understanding with structural explanations of textual communication. Tracy points out how critiques of ideology as hermeneutics of suspicion still involve disclosive criteria of hermeneutics. Transformative concerns of praxis cannot dispense with *interpretative* heuristics, yet, as Tracy also implies, neither can such transformative praxis be reduced to interpretative heuristics.

Both Küng and Tracy recognize that paradigm analysis, even

when used for historical interpretations, is more than just a descriptive enterprise. As Kuhn came to realize, paradigm analysis is not a value-free exercise but involves mediations of objectivity and subjectivity through judgments of value which heuristically anticipate criteria of adequacy in the choice of theories (1977: 320-39). Kuhn describes these criteria as 'accuracy, consistency, scope, simplicity, and fruitfulness'. Like Michael Polanyi (1962), Kuhn rejects any wooden application of such criteria, as though they were logical techniques which could be applied in a purely formalistic manner. Instead, they are invariant *only* in their heuristic (Polanyi's term) anticipations of meaningful intelligibilities; historically they vary greatly (1977: 325). Hence Kuhn rejects the criticism that paradigm analysis must succumb to a complete relativism. Rather, he sees it as involving an ongoing interplay between subjective and objective components in which judgments of fact and of value are continually called to account by the ongoing dialogue of questions and answers in which 'scientists may always be asked to explain their choices, to exhibit the bases for their judgments. Such judgments are eminently discussable, and the man who refuses to discuss his own cannot expect to be taken seriously' (1977: 337).

Thus Kuhn admits that 'hermeneutic method' profoundly influenced his views on normal and extraordinary science (1977: xiii). Admittedly, his views on how to relate histories of science, with their empirically descriptive concerns, to philosophies of science, with their normative concerns, are tentative. Here he recognizes the need 'to bridge the long-standing divide between Continental and English-language philosophical traditions (1977: xv).

Now such bridge-building efforts have been started from both sides of the divide. Tracy's essay directed attention to some of the main hermeneutical efforts in this regard. But I should like to call attention to another 'divide' or fundamental dichotomy which cuts across language differences and seems to affect all highly-industrialized modern societies. As an 'outsider', I was interested to see how the debates in the philosophy of science occasioned by the works of Kuhn, Polanyi, or Stephen Toulmin exhibited some of the general features of this dichotomy. I would suggest that their works – along with those of many other contemporary theorists of science from both sides of the language divide – provide elements for dialectically going beyond or transcending this fundamental dichotomy.

As it impinges upon the debates in the philosophy of science, the dichotomy might be designated as a conception of value-free scientific rationality, on the one hand, and a conception of value decisions as basically pre-rational, a-rational, or irrational on the other hand. This dichotomy has deep roots. It survived the by now widely recognized demise of both the positivism of the Vienna Circle and the local empiricism of the received view (e.g., Carnap, Hempel, Nagel). When Kuhn, Polanyi, and Toulmin proposed their respective views of paradigm analysis, of the tacit dimensions of knowledge, and of the ecological analysis of scientific praxis, they found their views criticized from two apparently contradictory directions. From the side of Popper and those scholars he strongly influenced – sometimes referred to as critical rationalists – their concerns with the philosophical importance of history, value commitments, and the praxis of science were criticized as 'irrational', 'woolly and confused', supportive of 'mob rule', and so on (*cf.* Lakatos, 1978: 107 ff., 224 ff.). From the side of Paul Feyerabend, however, whose position might be designated critical anarchist, their views were criticized as too 'rationalist' and still too supportive of 'elitism' and a false 'absolutism' (*cf.* 1981: 24 ff., 131 ff.).

Both these apparently contradictory sets of criticisms can be traced to a common acceptance of the fundamental dichotomy. Popper admits that the decision to be rational is a moral or value decision and so may be 'described . . . as an irrational faith in reason' (1962: 231). Feyerabend rejects moral evaluations regarding all traditions, including science, and thus also rejects what he considers the unfounded 'moralizing' about supposed 'irrationality': the basic principle of his epistemological anarchism is 'Anything goes!' (1975; 1978; 1981: 21 ff., 202 ff.). By failing to advert to their common acceptance of the fundamental dichotomy, both critical rationalism and critical anarchism commit what Karl-Otto Apel terms the 'conventionalist-liberalistic fallacy of confusing freedom of moral conscience with private arbitrariness of decision' (1979: 312).

The contemporary crisis in the philosophy of science or *Wissenschaftstheorie* occasioned by paradigm analysis, concern for the tacit dimension of value commitments, or attention to the historical praxis of science, consists in how these movements or trends simply go beyond or transcend the fundamental dichotomy. As Apel (*ibid.*) and Jürgen Habermas (1981: 25-71, 504 ff.) indicate, the dichotomy between conceptions of value-free scientific rationality and irrational value decisions is deeply rooted in the modern dichotomy between objectivity and subjectivity. Ordinary discourse tends to ascribe objectivity to such generalities as reason, truth, criticism, science, while subjectivity is ascribed to such generalities as myth, opinion, dogma, religion. Philosophically, the dichotomy could be traced from the Cartesian *res extensa* and *res cogitans*, through the Kantian separation of phenomenal and noumenal, to many general trends which, even in their very diverse efforts to overcome the dichotomy between object and subject, still can be represented as generically exemplifying it: empiricism *versus* idealism, naturalism *versus* pragmatism, logical or linguistic analyticism *versus* existentialism, structuralism *versus* phenomenology, scientific Marxism *versus* critical Marxism, etc. Trends in the human sciences also bear the traces of the dichotomy, as one can see in such generic differences as behaviourism *versus* humanism, functionalism *versus* symbolic interactionism, sociobiologism *versus* anthropologism, and so on. More specifically, as Anthony Giddens (1977: 29-134; 1979: 145 ff.) and others indicate, Max Weber replicated the dichotomy in his analysis of social action, where *Zweckrationalität* had primacy in defining rationality so that *Wertrationalität* could be viewed as irrational and, in his analysis of authority, as either bureaucratic (rational) or charismatic (arational).

An underlying presupposition which fostered this dichotomy between objectivity and subjectivity was a desire to reconstruct the methods of the natural sciences into formally logical, ahistorical procedures of 'pure objectivity' or 'pure reason' cut off from any trace of subjectivity. After the collapse of positivism and logical empiricism, Popper's 'cognitional theory without a knowing subject' was the latest effort to retrieve elements of this presupposition (1972). Yet even here the presupposition is in retreat. Popper himself attempted to give extensive reasons for his supposedly irrational faith in reason (1962: 231-80), and so had to admit decisions could be rational (1962: 380). Feyerabend's strictures against reason and method are admittedly directed against what he considers the too objectivistic conceptions of reason and method in Popper and Lakatos (1975: 165-294), and his very own cognitive performance, by his own admission, passes moral judgments on certain traditions (1978: 13-31, 154 ff.).

Within the extensive debate and disagreements among philosophers of science, it seems to me that there is an emerging consensus about the illusory character of this underlying presupposition of a logically pure objectivism in natural science. Both the positivism of the Vienna Circle and the logical empiricism of the received view are now generally recognized as dead-ends (*cf.* F. Suppe, 1977: 6-118, 617-730). The question is no longer how to modify the scientistic objectivism of positivism or logical empiricism, but what paradigms will eventually take their place. Given the pervasive influence of scientistic objectivism and the consequent dichotomies in philosophy and culture, it is not surprising that it is difficult to delineate just how the philosophy of science will develop (*cf.* Habermas, 1981: 504; and especially, Toulmin, 1977: 600-14).

Nevertheless, there seem to be two generally accepted judgments on the direction of such developments: 1. rationality can no longer be defined solely with reference to the procedures of mathematics, logics, or the natural sciences; and: 2. even in these domains – and *a fortiori* in others – attention is shifting from theories of theories to the heuristic performance or praxis of theorizing. The deductivist ideals of theory *qua* theory providing coherent and complete criteria for rationality are gone, even in mathematics. Theories as formally logical systems are, to paraphrase Kurt Gödel, either incomplete and consistent or complete and inconsistent. Rationality cannot be identified with ideals appealing to non-existent and impossible complete and consistent foundations in theory *qua* theory. There is, I suggest, a shift from scientistic objectivism to the questioning procedures or praxis of communities of inquirers.

This shift is clearly visible in Kuhn and Toulmin. Kuhn transforms Polanyi's concerns with the tacit dimensions in personal knowledge into an analysis of the communal and historical processes by which scientists acquire and augment knowledge. Kuhn indicates how, despite Popper's criticisms, both he and Popper are more concerned 'with the dynamic process by which scientific knowledge is acquired rather than with the logical structure of the products of scientific research' (1977: 267). Similarly, Toulmin takes issue with the *a priori* conceptualism of Kant and emphasizes how reason is a multi-dimensional series of practices or enterprises in which reason is *not yet* ever fully realized (1972: 370 ff., 412 ff.) He is able to pin down how both relativism and absolutism ignore the ongoing praxis of raising ever further relevant questions and, instead, mistakenly presuppose that 'rationality is a sub-species of logicality' (1972: 486). Relative to Popper, Kuhn indicates how his own position on the historiography of science can account for objectivity and the uses of logic without falling into the false objectivism of Popper's naive falsificationalism (1977: 268-92). Relative to Lakatos, Toulmin uncovers the ambiguity of Lakatos's theory of methodology in the atemporal conception of Popper's 'third world'. 'But, once procedures and other elements of praxis are allowed into the "third world", its *temporal* or historical character can no longer be concealed' (1976: 674). Indeed, one could make the point that Toulmin's attention to the linguistic and non-linguistic praxis of science undermines the dichotomy Popper set up between objectivity (world 1 of physical objects and world 3 of cultural products) and subjectivity (world 2 of mental states and acts) (*cf.* Toulmin, 1976: 655-75, 1976a).

The shift from objectivism to the questioning praxis of communities of inquirers can also be substantiated among the critics of Kuhn, Polanyi, and Toulmin. Popper's naive falsificationalism or fallibilism rests upon his distinctions between physical objects (world 1), mental states and acts (world 2), and the products or objectifications of the latter in cultural and linguistic objects (world 3). Where he initially treated these as 'worlds', he now understands them as dimensions of one world. Moreover, where he until recently tended to define 'reality' only in reference to world 1 – 'I propose to say that something exists, or is real, if and only if it can interact with . . . hard physical bodies' (1973: 23) – he now admits that reality and objectivity are also the result of interaction between world 2 and world 3 (*cf.* Popper & Eccles, 1981: 47 ff., 451 f.). If world 2 is real and, in interaction with world 3, the source of ongoing questions and criticisms, as Popper admits, then why not follow the suggestions of Toulmin regarding the 'linguistic and non-linguistic praxis' of knowing and acting? I.C. Jarvie's 'hidden structures of logic' (he does not tell us where they are hidden) might well be hidden in such linguistic and non-linguistic praxis and hence can scarcely be used to impugn Toulmin's account (Jarvie, 1976: 311-33). Otherwise, as Habermas points out in regard to both Popper and Jarvie, there is no possibility of distinguishing adequately between an authentic praxis of questioning and evaluating, so essential to ongoing criticism, and the already thematized and institutionalized world 3 products (1981: 114-26).

Similarly, Lakatos's sophisticated methodological fallibilism rejects objectivism in favour of the praxis of ever further relevant questioning. In dealing with the problem of infinite regress and the foundations of mathematics, he reviews the efforts to stop infinite regress by logical empirical and meta-theoretical means, only to conclude that if there are any foundations they are 'admittedly subjective'. There are no foundations of knowledge in the sense of theoretical proofs or definitions. Lakatos replaces the infinite regress of proofs and definitions with one of guesses: 'There is nothing wrong with an infinite regress of guesses' (1978: 3-23). The only way to avoid the sceptical and dogmatist horns of this dilemma is to recognize how guesses are conjectures responding to ever further relevant questions. This is also brought out in Lakatos's methodology of scientific research programmes. Central features of his methodology are negative and positive heuristics. The negative heuristics are the 'hard cores' of the programmes articulated in the basic laws or intelligible correlations constituting the method of the specific research programme. The positive heuristics are 'partially articulated sets' of suggestions or hints and suggestions on how to change, develop the "refutable variants" of the research programme' (1978a: 50). Insofar as these heuristics are only 'partially articulated', the methodology of such research programmes implies an interaction between world 2 and world 3, i.e., the hints and suggestions are responding to ever further relevant questions. Insofar as the progressive theoretical shifts involve 'more empirical content', the methodology implies that the questions are about world 1. Lakatos developed the methodology of scientific research programmes in order to take into account the insights of Kuhn and Polanyi in a critical fashion, so it is not surprising to see Lakatos's demarcation theory of rationality refer to 'the basic value judgments of scientific communities', and to at least admit that his methodology of research programmes would also apply to the normative aspects of ethics or aesthetics (1978a: 139-67). The recognition of positive heuristics subverts the artificial dichotomies erected in the philosophy of science between objectivity (world 1 and world 3) and subjectivity (world 2), with the consequence that scientific judgments are no longer so seriously dichotomized in terms of contexts of discovery *versus* contexts of justification (*cf.* Wartofsky, 1980: 1-20; Nickles, 1977, 1980).

The shift from scientistic objectivism to the questioning praxis of scientific communities among Anglo-American philosophers of science finds many parallels among continental colleagues with their shifts from theories of science to theories of communicative action (Apel, Habermas, Peukert). Yet Anglo-American philosophers of science are not so burdened as their continental counterparts with the legacies of transcendental idealism and its philosophical objectivism, whereby any 'turn to the subject' is immediately objectivized into conceptualist 'conditions of the possibility' (Kant), 'mediations of absolute knowledge' (Hegel), or 'infinitely regressive reifications of the ego' (Fichte). Where continental philosophers of science tend to overload any discussion of rationality as praxis with such philosophical objectivism or conceptualism (*cf.* Apel, 1979; Habermas, 1981: 518-34; Heinrich, 1976; Tugendhat, 1979), their Anglo-American colleagues tend to display much greater flexibility in the interplay between conscious praxis and thematized knowledge. This flexible interplay between conscious praxis is evident in the mutual interactions between the three dimensions of Popper's 'world', in Polanyi's tacit dimensions, in Kuhn's hermeneutical criteria for paradigms, in Lakatos's partially articulated positive heuristics, in Toulmin's attention to linguistic and non-linguistic praxis of science, in Bernard Lonergan's notion of generalized empirical method (1977, 1978), and in Marx Wartofsky's ongoing representations of human cognitive praxis and metaphysics as heuristics for science (1979).

As a result, Anglo-American philosophers of science are by and large not so ready to understand the natural sciences as *necessarily* informed by 'quasi-transcendental interests in technical control' (Habermas) or by 'transcendental-pragmatic rationality as instrumental and manipulative' (Apel). This concedes far too much to positivism and logical empiricism, tending to lock the natural sciences and technology into the economic and cultural deformations attendant upon the modern dichotomies between objectivity and subjectivity, whereby the natural sciences and technologies are pressed into the service of monopolies and nation-states to exploit nature and increase the dominative power of militarism (*cf.* Capra, 1982; Noble, 1977). Thus the post-empiricists criticize continental philosophers of science for being too caught up in false dichotomies between *Natur- und Geisteswissenschaften* (Anthony Giddens, 1977: 148 ff.; Mary Hesse, 1980: 167-86). These Anglo-Americans are more inclined to understand the rationality operative in the natural sciences as disciplinary matrices where intersubjective communities of investigators pose questions to nature by means of the observational procedures of experimental measurements. The heuristic and asymptotic advances toward agreement about the explanatory results of the empirical knowledge thus gained are mediated by the praxis of argumentative discourse among the investigators. Hence objectivity is attained *neither* through observational techniques *per se* (*contra* positivism and logical empiricism), *nor* through successful manipulation or control (*contra* Apel and Habermas), but through ongoing networks (*cf.* Hesse, 1974) of disciplined questioning and discourse which are the foundations or principles *in praxis* generating and selecting all empirically verifiable or falsifiable intelligibilities or laws in nature (*cf.* Patrick Byrne, 1981; Patrick Heelan, 1965, 1977, 1979). Such an understanding of the natural sciences and technology offer ways out of the alienated and alienating dominative uses to which they are put in modern societies, with the consequent ecological destruction and militarism, by calling attention to the dialogical relations between science and nature (science does not command so much as listen), and by beginning to envisage technologies informed by the mimetic values of praxis–poesis (Gabor, 1970; Ihde, 1979; Wartofsky, 1979: 338-69).

Hermeneutics, therefore, is intrinsic to the natural sciences insofar as it poses questions to nature (Heelan, 1977), and a significant portion of the impact of Kuhn's paradigm analysis is attributable to its initial establishment of this. As an historian *of natural science*, Kuhn's analysis of paradigms brings out both the interplay between the observational measurement-languages and the explanatory theoretical languages, as well as the succeeding interpretations of this interplay in the various scientific paradigms. The *referent* of natural scientific methods (i.e., ways of posing questions) is nature, no matter how theory-laden the data are because of the observational measuring procedures mediating those methods. As an *historian* of natural science, however, the primary referent of Kuhn's paradigm analysis is not nature or the theory-laden data *per se* but the succession of descriptive or explanatory theories interpreting the variations in data. In this respect Kuhn's paradigm analysis shares in what Giddens terms the 'double hermeneutics' operative in the human sciences and scholarly disciplines (1976: 158), i.e., as historical paradigm analysis is posing questions to 'pre-interpreted meaning-frames'. This distinction, it seems to me, helps to clarify the misunderstandings between the so-called critical rationalists (Popper, Lakatos, and so on) and such philosophers of science as Kuhn, Polanyi, or Toulmin; it also explains why paradigm analysis has proved so protean in so many other disciplines besides the history of natural science.

When the referent of inquiry is not nature or theory-laden empirical data, but the historical traditions of pre-interpreted meaning-frames, the distinctions between 'internalist' and 'externalist' histories of science, that is, between the internal theoretical developments of sciences and the external socio-economic or cultural or psychological influences on the developments of research, become less relevant (cf. Toulmin, 1972: 300-18, 504 ff.). Indeed, as Grattan-Guinness points out, this applies also to the history of mathematical analysis (1970: ix-xi). For the *historical* developments of knowledge do not occur in some Platonic realm of 'pure ideas', 'pure objectivity' or 'pure reason'. They are human achievements and, as such, are never beyond question or criticism.

It is not too difficult to understand why the post-empiricists' introduction of hermeneutics with its historical consciousness into the philosophy of science has occasioned such sharp debates and misunderstandings. The first phase of the Enlightenment separated itself from the religious and metaphysical traditions of the past by emphasizing how positive sciences offer true knowledge as distinct from false ideologies. In August Comte's positivism this separation of science from ideology was complete. So deeply did this penetrate into the self-understanding of modernity that subsequent forms of positivism and logical empiricism still viewed science and technology as paradigms of ideology-free objectivity. This process was part of the ongoing dichotomies between subjectivity and objectivity in modern cultures and societies. Traces of this science/ideology separation can still be found in those critical rationalists who, as pointed out at the beginning of this essay, criticize paradigm analysis for confusing science and theology.

Whereas hermeneutics, as Tracy's essay elaborated in reference to Gadamer, exposes this Enlightenment 'prejudice against all prejudice', it does not fall into an historicist relativism which would compromise the quest for truth. Analogous to the trends in post-empiricist philosophies of science, hermeneutics shifts our understanding of the criteria for objectivity and truth from deductivist ideals of theories *qua* theories to the ongoing traditions or contexts of praxis raising ever further relevant questions. Traditions as ongoing contexts of praxis, with their continued inter-subjective dialogues of questions and answers and more questions, are indicative of how the hermeneutic dimensions of rationality are operative in all realms of discourse both in the 'life-worlds' of everyday living and in the more theoretical worlds of scientific and scholarly reflection. Far from being abandoned, the objectivity of truth is appropriated within the ongoing 'logics' and 'dialectics' of human knowing and acting subjects genuinely engaged in the constant exchange of questions and answers (Gadamer, 1981: 44-8). Tracy's elaboration of hermeneutics in the new paradigm, with the three hermeneutical steps or dimensions, is important to understand this process.

As Alasdair MacIntyre has shown, hermeneutics with its emphasis upon tradition and narrative is foundational or central to the philosophy of science now cognizant of the false dichotomies engendered by the Enlightenment (1980: 54-74; 1981). As sciences and technologies arise out of and return to the life-worlds of everyday living, so the logical and theoretical methods of argumentative discourse arise out of and return to the participatory 'fusions of horizons' in the 'mutual agreements' of historical narrative praxis (Gadamer, 1981: 69-138). However, as Tracy's discussion of 'two crucial difficulties in Gadamer's interpretation of the process of interpretation' implies, the hermeneutical and historical dimensions of rationality are not sufficient to answer all further relevant questions posed within them. There is a series of analogies or sublations here. Just as it is important, in order to do justice to the praxis of reason operative in the empirical sciences, to complement their observations and explanatory heuristics with hermeneutical and historical analyses, so it is important, in order to do justice to the praxis of reason operative in exegetical and reconstructive disciplinary matrices of hermeneutics and of history, to complement their interpretative and reconstructive heuristics with *dialectics*.

For the praxis of reason is an ongoing series of human achievements constituted by the raising of ever further relevant questions. As such, it is always bounded or limited and thus also open to further relevant questions and criticisms. The tension between limitation and openness means that the praxis of reason is not an automatically guaranteed process. Truth and freedom are both intrinsic to rational praxis: truth insofar as all further questions and criticisms are *relevant* to, or raised in regard to, what is known; freedom insofar as what is known is continually related to the far vaster unknown constitutive of ever further questions. The praxis of reason is always threatened by what might be termed tempting myths of success. Whether in the everyday life-world of social interaction, or in the theoretic realms of cultural and scientific or scholarly reflections, successful life-forms, or traditions, or paradigms become established, only too often to succumb to the tendency to evaluate their success as powerful enough to answer adequately all further relevant questions or criticisms. Particular successes become ideologically universalized.

Kuhn's paradigm analysis has begun to expose this process in regard to the history of the natural sciences in his notions of normal scientific paradigms and revolutionary or extraordinary paradigm shifts. Within the perspectives of the empirical sciences, which question empirical data via observational and explanatory methods, and the hermeneutical or historical disciplines, which question texts and other expressions of historical traditions via interpretative and reconstructive methods, it could be argued that often successive paradigms are *incommensurable* (Kuhn, 1970: 92-173, 198 ff.; 1970a: 259-77; 1977: 206 ff.). This has led to a host of criticisms and allegations of irrationalism and relativism (*cf.* Lakatos & Musgrave, 1970; Suppe, 1977). Feyerabend's epistemological anarchism relentlessly complicates such criticisms by indicating what he considers empirical and historical incommensurablities, and concluding that the 'authority of reason' and the 'greatness of science' have to be radically criticized and relativized (1975, 1978, 1981).

Insofar as hermeneutics presupposes praxis to be 'conducting oneself and acting in solidarity' (Gadamer, 1981: 87) and 'contexts of mutual agreement' (*ibid.*, 137), it also requires a shift beyond hermeneutics to dialectics. Richard Rorty's recent work indicates how a self-enclosed hermeneutical philosophy, which identifies foundational or epistemological questions (wrongly, I would argue) with transcendental-idealist conceptualisms, can result only in what I would term a hermeneutical fideism sustained by an admittedly 'Whiggish hope and belief ' that the 'conversation of the West' will continue (1979). It is true that dialectics without hermeneutics can be (and too often has been) seduced by the myths of success into universalizing or totalizing particular life-forms or traditions as *the* answer to all questions (*cf.* Enrique Dussel, 1974; Toulmin, 1972: 328-40). But hermeneutics without dialectics cannot engage in the heuristic questioning of *latent value-conflicts and power-complexes* whereby the very raising of further relevant questions itself is individually and socially repressed or oppressed. As a result, hermeneutics can only raise the 'ideals' of 'free and leisured conversation' in the face of oppression and repression (*cf.* Rorty, 1979: 388 ff.).

Continental philosophers of science who do attend to dialectics, but do so in terms of either modifications of transcendental-idealist reflection on the conditions of possibility, or suppositions about science and technology totally objectifying in manipulative methods whatever they investigate, do not get much further One could argue, for instance, that Apel's ethic of 'ideal communication communities' as only a 'regulative idea' is at best a more formalized version of Gadamer's 'dialectic of question and answer' (Apel, 1979: 329-40; and Gadamer's queries, *ibid.*, 348 ff.). Similarly, Habermas's brilliant efforts to distinguish the *Zweckrationalität* of empirically scientific and technological orientations from that of communicative action structures still remains, despite insightful explorations into Kohlberg, Mead, Durkheim, and Piaget, captive to the basic dichotomies of Weber's theory of rationality. Thus the various 'resistance movements' are interpreted as divergent critical reactions to 'the inner colonization of the life-world' by elitist cultural experts and forms of economic and administrative rationality (*cf.* 1981a: 447-593, esp. 488, 518-47, 587 ff.). Habermas's critique of functionalist reason still concedes far too much to Weber's *Zweckrationalität*, with the result that Habermas's interpretation of modernity and post- or anti-modernity movements has many shades of Weber's charismatic or traditional or effective value options *versus* the irresistible advance of monetary-bureaucratic institutionalization. Giddens's criticism of Habermas's earlier work, that it provides 'no general mode of connection between social transformation and power' (1977: 161), is further extended by Seyla Benhabib's insights into how Weber's theory of rationality has tended to derail Habermas's critical theory, imbuing it with a conceptualism in which no 'concrete dialectics' between emancipatory ideals and liberating praxis of social subjects is articulated (1981). As Benhabib concludes: 'It is not clear why a new socialization of the individual beyond the patriarchal family, school and culture, and a new mode of material interaction with nature, beyond the industrial mode of production, would be impossible. No theory can define the limits of future possibility, although it can enlighten us about it. For this possibility is posterior and not prior to actuality – as Aristotle long ago said of praxis' (1981: 59).

If, as suggested above, the Anglo-American post-empiricist philosophers of science provide perspectives on the empirical and historical praxis of science which go beyond positivist and instrumentalist-functionalist pre-judgments, nevertheless these perspectives are still fragmentary. As with hermeneutics (as indeed with positivism, logical empiricism, and linguistic analysis in former decades!), so the development of a more adequate dialectics is going to require extensive dialogue and debate with continental philosophers of science, such as, among many others, Apel and Habermas. The call, for example, by Abner Shimony for 'a dialectics' open to the full range of 'the apriori and the aposteriori' in the evaluation of science (1976: 584

ff.), finds a much fuller articulation in Apel's efforts to explicate
the latent self-differentiation of reason from natural science to
ethics (1979, 1980). Wartofsky's outlines of 'a critique of impure
reason' (1978, 1980), emphasize the importance of engaging in
dialogue and debate with continental traditions. In these
exchanges, as Wartofsky indicates, the Anglo-American post-
empiricists should insist that 'neither the hermeneutic school nor
the critical theorists have come to grips with the natural sciences
in any serious way, tending to lump them in some caricature of
"positivism" ' (1980: 18).

The difference in respect of the social sciences and social theory
made by a debate with continental traditions and by a recognition
of their limitations regarding natural sciences is clearly seen in
Anthony Giddens's work. Like Habermas's, Giddens's works
assay a broad retrieval of all the major figures in social theory,
with special attention to Marx and Weber, for the sake of a 1.
'hermeneutic explication and mediation of divergent forms of life
within descriptive metalanguages of social science', and of a 2.
dialectical 'explication of the production and reproduction of
society as the outcome of human agency' (1976: 162). But where
Habermas has not taken seriously enough the radical critiques of
positivism offered by the post-empiricists, and so tends to remain
locked within the dichotomies underlying Weber's theories of
bureaucratic rationality, Giddens has seen the significance of the
former (1977), therefore provides a radical critique of both the
functionalist deformations of reason and Weberian notions of
Zweckrationalität (1977, 1979), and draws the consequences of this
for a dialectical critique of historical materialism (1981).

Central to Giddens's analyses are his notions of agency and
structuration. Agency is prior to the subject-object split (1979:
92), thereby sublating the prior alternatives of intentionality
analysis and structural analysis. The production and reproduction
of societies is constituted 'by the active doings of subjects' whose
agency as skilled performance is also bounded within structures.
'To enquire into the structuration of social practices is to seek to
explain how it comes about that structures are constituted
through action, and reciprocally how action is constituted

structurally' (1976: 160 f.). This means that there is a dialectical 'duality of structure', participating in both subjects–actors and objects–societies (1979: 70), so that social integration and system integration provide resources and sanctions for interactive power-complexes which are either dominative or transformative (76-95). Institutional reproduction through the modes of signification, domination, and legitimation has to be freed 'from the subject–object dualisms that . . . have dogged most areas of the social sciences' (96-130). Contradictions, therefore, are embedded in power and domination whereby it is impossible to negate fully subjects as knowers and actors. Bureaucracy and autonomy cannot be counterposed, as Weberian theories maintain is possible, for, as empirical studies on bureaucracy and social action seem to indicate, there is a 'dialectic of control' whereby the dominative power of bureaucratization, or objectivistic one-dimensionality, is distanced and delegitimated by active social subjects (131-64). Neither late capitalism nor state socialism is as pessimistically under the sway of bureaucratic rationality or functionalist reason as Weberian theory would suppose (146 ff.; 1982).

Accordingly, the contradictions which Habermas sees between social systems of rationality and the value-orientations of everyday life-worlds are to be located not only at such 'seams between system and life-world' but within the very systems of rationality themselves. Whereas the post-empiricists uncover structure and agency in the praxis of the natural sciences and technology, theorists like Giddens articulate them in the hermeneutics and dialectics of the social sciences. As Giddens indicates, causal regularities are latently operative in human social activity in ways often neglected by hermeneutic philosophies (1979: 196). The dialectical duality of structure and human agency emphasizes the ongoing interplay between the known cognitive performance of social subjects and the limitations or 'bounds' of that performance in unconscious elements and unintended consequences of actions (250). Dialectics, therefore, must complement hermeneutics with an explication of causal regularities in human action provided by psychotherapeutic questioning of latent value-conflicts, and a critique of ideologically distorted power-complexes. Giddens's notions of structuration and agency would also allow Habermas's incorporation of Piaget's genetic epistemology and Kohlberg's stages of moral development to articulate normative interaction of subjects in ways that would subvert the Weberian illusions of objectivistic rationality.

The dichotomies between 'traditional societies' and 'industrialized societies' which have dominated social theory until recently are now being radically revised. Giddens analyzes the correlation of this process with the dichotomy between science and ideology originating in the Comtean 'laws of the three stages' and its continuance into the by now dismantled 'orthodox consensus' in social theory (234 ff.). Parallels between the latter and the received view in the philosophy of science could easily be drawn (238). Giddens criticizes a tendency in Habermas to identify religion with traditional societies, and adopts elements from Marx and Habermas in his revision of the notion of ideology. *Any* symbol-system or idea-system may become ideological, including science and technology, inasmuch as 'structures of signification are mobilized to legitimate the sectional interests of hegemonic groups whereby 'domination is concealed as domination' (184-93). This occurs mainly in three ways: 1. by representing sectional interests as though they were universal; 2. by techniques of denying or transmuting contradictions; and 3. by reifying mutable, historical conditions as though they were embedded in nature (193-97).

Such a critique of ideology can resolve the issues raised by Feyerabend's epistemological anarchism. He saw that post-empiricist philosophies of science were definitely dismantling the science-ideology dichotomy, and concluded that since all interests, including the interest in reason, are sectional, any universalization must be ideological. I believe this is the thrust of his critique of scientific reason (1981: 202-30). Such anarchistic relativism, however, is not radical enough. It fails to criticize the ideological reifications whereby incommensurable paradigms (structures) are identified with rational agency itself, as though the 'nature' of scientific reason were fully embedded in paradigmatic structures. Refute them and you refute reason. Against this, Giddens's dialectics of structure and agency establishes ongoing ideology-critiques in which the opposites are not absolutism *versus* anarchism, but both these alternatives *and* a dialectics of theory and praxis which transcends the subject-object dualisms that have so bedevilled modernity.

The dialectics of theory and praxis within post-empiricist philosophies of science is extending the frontiers of metascience far beyond the false securities of positivisms and idealisms with their variant distortions of the sectional interests of scientific communities. Reason is constituted by the praxis of raising ever further relevant questions, so that reason itself demands a responsibility for reason which cannot be ideologically projected away from the concretely existing communities of inquirers into either observational techniques of theories *qua* theories. Any idea-system and symbol-system may become ideological. If the present nuclear age has a future, there are good reasons to conjecture that its science and technology will be accused of quite massive ideological distortions. As Wartofsky points out, the last illusions of scientific innocence were blown away in the radioactive winds over Hiroshima and Nagasaki (1980: 5). The philosophy of science, or metascience, is confronted with the immense tasks of fostering the collaborative praxis of communicative interaction not only between all the science and scholarly disciplines, but between these and all other forms of rational praxis operative in the human life-worlds. 'No reconstruction of contemporary scientific rationality can be adequate if it fails to take the facts and structures of contemporary scientific practice and its social applications into account', including the political and economic corporate contexts funding and directing scientific research programmes (1980: 21).

Intellectual disciplines and professions (Toulmin, 1972) are continually exposed to ideological distortions by value-conflicts and power-complexes which repress or oppress further very relevant questions. Paradigm analysis and post-empiricist philosophies of science themselves increasingly demand a 'conversion' or 'gestalt-switch' whereby the ideological distortions resulting from subject-object dualisms can be unmasked for what they are. Evolutionary adaptation alone is scarcely adequate to articulate this dialectical practice of reason (*cf.* Giddens, 1981: 20-4, 90-1). The very power delivered by contemporary sciences and technologies is pressing metascience to move from the latent 'cunning of reason' in human history (Toulmin, 1972: 478 ff.) into ever more explicit collaborative commitments attuned to heuristic structures and agencies capable of mediating between our socio-cultural matrices and the significance or role of the sciences in those matrices (*cf.* Lamb, 1978: 195 ff.; Lonergan, 1978: 530-633; Wartofsky, 1979: 40-89, 119-39; 1980).

This incomplete overview of the *status quaestionis* regarding paradigm analysis and post-empiricist philosophies of science has three major conclusions: 1. This meta-level reflection excludes the possibility of arriving at a complete and coherent theoretical articulation of 'the new paradigm', as though it could be a monistic metatheoretical absolute, deductively or inductively articulating rationality fully. 2. Also excluded is the adequacy of inferring from this radical incompleteness that 'the new paradigm' heads toward the incoherence of an arational or irrational relativism or anarchism, since such an inference is premised on a similarly mistaken assumption that if rationality exists it must be capable of complete and coherent metatheoretic articulation. 3. Instead, this meta-level reflection tends to the praxis of theorizing within communities engaged in empirical, hermeneutical, and/or dialectical inquiry in order to articulate coherently – yet always incompletely – the heuristic relationships within and among these communities of inquiry, as well as the relations between the ongoing praxis of theorizing and all other forms of rational praxis (e.g., common sense, aesthetic, moral, religious). Insofar as 'the new paradigm' emerging in metascience attends to the fundamental importance of praxis, an inference is that the crises attendant upon the pluralism of reason are primarily crises of the subjects and institutions of reason. To the degree that these subjects and institutions do not facilitate the praxis of reason as the raising of ever more relevant questions regarding either normal or extraordinary research programmes, they are caught in the ideological distortions fostered by the dichotomies between objectivity and subjectivity, system and life-world, bureaucracy and autonomy, analysis and narrative, technology and art, industry and environment, science and morality, truth and freedom.

II. Religious praxis and theological dialectics in the new paradigm

Many parallels could be drawn between developments in the philosophies of science and those in modern and contemporary theologies. Kuhn's *The Structure of Scientific Revolutions* tended to focus on the unease with the types of reflection dependent upon classical positivism and the logical empiricism of the received view. It articulated, however tentatively, the fundamental import of history for the philosophy of science. The walls which positivism and logical empiricism had erected between subject and object, history and logic, value and fact, ideology and science, and so on, began to crumble at an increasing rate. With this collapse of the 'orthodox consensus' there emerged the series of orientations outlined above, from the radically liberal celebrations of Feyerabend on the death of the authority of reason, through the critical rationalist and hermeneutical efforts at reconstructing the heuristic meaning-frames of scientific rationality, to more dialectical concerns with the heuristics of value-conflicts and power-complexes as they impinge upon the historical praxis of science.

This process has many analogous parallels in modern and contemporary developments within theology as these have attempted to cope with the fundamental import of historical scholarship and other empirically oriented disciplines (e.g., psychology of religion, sociology of religion, comparative histories of religion) on the interactions between *fidem et rationem*, or, in the more inclusive designations of Küng and Tracy, the interactions between Christian religious traditions and human experience. These are 'constants' in a heuristic sense, insofar as they are neither reducible to nor separable from one another, and their constancy is implicitly relational in ongoing matrices such as the macromodels suggested by Küng. Since he and Tracy have outlined historical, ecumenical, and hermeneutical aspects of these interactions, I shall concentrate on the more praxis-oriented and dialectical dimensions.

'The much discussed identity-crisis of Christianity is not primarily a crisis of its message, but a crisis of its subjects and institutions' – this judgment of Johann B. Metz (1977: xi) is central to the project of political theology. It appears to contradict the massive hermeneutics of suspicion in modernity (Marx, Freud, Nietzsche) based upon the dichotomy of science and ideology. Similarly, the emancipatory praxis grounding the many forms of liberation theology whereby the poor, oppressed, and victimized 'non-persons' appropriate the Christian message in order to struggle transformatively against their oppression, also seems to contradict modernity with its claims that emancipation is inseparably bound to processes of secularization (Comte, Mills, Marx). These religious and theological movements do indeed contradict much of modernity, but they do so dialectically – or 'analectically', if one understands dialectics as no more than closed, totalizing techniques (cf. E. Dussel, 1974; J.C. Scannone, 1977). These developments do not 'fall behind' the advances in critical reflection and political freedoms initiated in the Enlightenment, as though they promoted utopian or fideistic collapses of reason into religious witness (cf. H. Maier, 1972; S. Ogden, 1979). The further very relevant questions these movements pose to *both* the Christian traditions *and* forms of contemporary human experience involve them in what might be called a 'double dialectic'. In very radical ways, political and liberation theologians recognize how *any* symbol-, idea-, or social-system may become ideological. Hence they are developing genuine (as opposed to closed) dialectical critiques of the ideological distortions of sacralism in Christianity, and of the ideological distortions of secularism in modernity. I hope that the above sketch of developments in the turn to praxis and dialectics in post-empiricist philosophies of science indicates how these theological developments intensify the concerns for reason as reason yet to be realized more fully in history and society. It should also be noted how Helmut Peukert, in order to articulate this intensification of rational praxis to the point of anamnetic solidarity with the victims of history, had to push critical reflection far beyond the Weberian dichotomies still present in Habermas, and to correlate the insights of the more classic representatives of the Frankfurt School and of Anglo-American developments in theories of science (1978: 248-310).

Political and liberation theologies are able to reap the benefits of the largely unintended consequences of modern historical criticism and of empirical studies of religion, as well as more contemporary hermeneutical reflections on science and life-world. The former – from the German historical school to the works of Marx and Freud – were largely undertaken under the aegis of the science-ideology dichotomy. Studies poured forth on all aspects of Christian traditions, often demonstrating just how Christian symbol and other systems were distorted into ideological legitimations of dominative clerical and/or political élites as Christianity became Christendom. Sacralism, in the form of this ideological distortion, was criticized in historical, sociological, and psychological studies. These also influenced Northern industrialized societies and cultures, leading to a secularism in which religion was either privatized or declared a leftover of pre-historical traditional societies (when history is dated from the revolution).

In this situation theologians tended to face the dichotomy of either a *conservative* preservation of orthodoxy, or a *liberal* embrace of modernity, by leaning towards either an identification of the Christian faith with past forms of its articulation (e.g., Catholic and Protestant scholasticism), or an identification of the faith with the moral and cultural values of secular societies (e.g., Protestant liberalism, Catholic modernism). The conservative response to modern charges of unscientific ideology was to emphasize the primacy of logic and logically derived metaphysics in articulating the intelligibility of faith traditions (e.g., the manualist theologies). While this sometimes led to efforts at reconciling modern science and past conceptions of the primacy of theory, as in Jacques Maritain's hierarchical degrees of knowing, it produced more lasting benefits by stimulating serious historical studies which undermined manualist monotheoretic pretensions, demonstrating as they did the rich pluralisms of medieval theologies. The liberal responses to modern charges of unscientific ideology tended to repudiate the past, and often deformed logical and metaphysical conceptualities in favour of showing the relevance of Christian faith to modern aspirations for meaning and value by forging new hermeneutical and ethical frameworks for interpreting the sources of tradition (e.g., Schleiermacher, the Ritschlians). These frameworks, and the scholarship they promoted, contributed enormously to modern knowledge of Christian origins and history. Insofar as liberal scholarship tended to emphasize those meanings and values which accentuated the primacy of pure practical reason, it not surprisingly seemed sometimes to interpret the manifold expressions of traditions by identifying their meanings and values with those of the cultural matrices in which they emerged (e.g., the 'hellenization' of Christianity in von Harnack); or to project back into the past those meanings and values the investigators cherished (e.g., reconstructions of the historical Jesus or early Christianity with strong Kantian or Hegelian hues). Troeltsch's socio-historical reconstructions of history exemplified the church-sect dichotomies in ways perhaps too dependent upon Weberian bureaucratic-charismatic dichotomies. There were the social gospel efforts to develop ethical complementarity between the churches and middle-class reformism and between theology and modern social science (cf. J. Fishburn, 1981). By and large, liberal theologies have not only set the agenda for modern theology, but have also supported historical research programmes and methods of ethical reflection capable of adjusting any one-sided emphasis by means of their ongoing self-correcting processes of research and learning.

The events of the twentieth century began rather quickly to

dismantle confidence in the inevitability of scientific and technological progress. The science *versus* ideology dichotomy began to crumble as world wars, and ever more refined techniques of manipulation and control, showed how the sciences and technologies themselves could conceal domination ideologically. Psychological studies began to show how religious symbol-systems could promote psychic integration, and need not serve only ideologically distorted neurotic functions legitimating latent value-conflicts (e.g., Adler, Jung, Frankl, Fromm). Sociological studies began to unmask the distorted interests in domination embedded within the subject-object dualisms of modernity, and to articulate elements of communicative interaction (Mead) capable of exposing the power-complexes distorting modern industrialized societies (Ross, Veblen, Horkheimer, Mannheim, Mills). Dialectical methods were gradually assembled which, in conjunction with more radical hermeneutical critiques of subject-object dualisms, began to break down objectivistic illusions regarding ideology. If *any* symbol-system may become ideological, then the dehumanizing tendencies to domination cannot be met adequately by replacing one system judged ideological by another which would guarantee freedom from domination and ideology. This had been the underlying fault in the fateful transitions from feudal-sacralist-hierarchical authoritarian systems to modern-secularist-bureaucratic authoritarian systems. Systems as such cannot exist or be understood adequately apart from the practices of the human subjects reproducing the systems (Giddens, 1979: 49–130). If science, as well as religion, can be ideologically distorted, and if secularism has become as rife with dehumanizing domination as sacralism, then truly radical critiques of ideology have to differentiate between sacred and secular in terms of the contradictions between genuine as opposed to dominative interactions of institutions and subjects within both religious and scientific systems (Giddens, 1971: 205–42; Gilkey, 1981).

As I mentioned in the previous section, post-empiricist philosophies of science are increasingly engaging in these tasks, especially since the acknowledgment that complete and coherent metatheoretical mediations of rational praxis are illusions. Hegel had tried and failed from the side of 'the concept'; positivism and logical empiricism tried and failed from the side of 'the data'. Analogous developments can be found in theology. Kierkegaard's explorations of Christian subjectivity began articulating categories critical of both sacralist Christendom and secularist scientism. Newman's descriptive heuristics of cognitive and religious judgments and decisions provided very fruitful alternatives to the sterile logicism of neo-scholastic manualist theologies. Though these theologians were not heard in their own times, the first world war and its aftermath began to awaken theological communities from their conservative-dogmatic and liberal-progressive slumber.

The *crisis theology* of Karl Barth was able to draw upon the recovery of eschatology in New Testament studies (e.g., Weiss, A. Schweitzer) in order to emphasize the transcendence of the Word of God. Barth's neo-orthodoxy provided an option beyond the conservative *versus* liberal dichotomy. Barth's thematization of God's transcendence highlighted the paradoxical non-identity of Christian faith relative to human, historical experience. He criticized both conservative and liberal tendencies to identify the Christian message with either past or present cultural meanings and values. History and common human experience recorded the meaningless succession of domination and exploitation of the powerful over the lowly. The revelation of God in the Old and New Testaments is the revelation of God's 'taking sides' with the poor and lowly, not with the powerful: 'God is indeed a God of the Jews *and* the heathen, but not a God of the exalted *and* the lowly. He is one-sidedly a God of the lowly . . . Where idols are worshipped, I am not allowed to take part. Rather, against all those who want to be great in this world, I must espouse the standpoint of those little people with whom God makes his beginning' (1919: 366; G. Hunsinger, 1976).

There are curious parallels between Barth's faith-orientation and Popper's critical rationalist orientation. Popper also saw history as meaningless. There is no 'history of mankind' but only the 'history of power politics', which 'is nothing but the history of international crime and mass murder'. A concrete history of mankind would have to be histories of suffering: 'The life of the forgotten, of the unknown individual man; his sorrows and joys, his suffering and death, this is the real content of human experience down the ages'. Popper referred to Kierkegaard and Barth, pointing out how their understandings of Christian faith were congruent with his view of history (1966: 269-76). If sacralist and secularist ideologies of political power 'idolize' the successes and rewards of the 'heroes on the Stage of History', if 'history has no meaning, we can give it meaning' by promoting forms of education and ethical action fostering freedom and responsibility so that 'one day perhaps we may succeed in getting power under control' (1966: 276-80). History, Popper acknowledged, 'badly needs a justification' (*ibid*). While Barth would agree that human beings in history need justification, the only meaning which could truly redeem the countless dead and forgotten, and those living and struggling, was in the gift of God's Word and Spirit calling us to faith in the death and resurrection of Jesus. If the early Barth's 'dialectic' was really more paradoxical, inasmuch as the totally other God only tangentially touches the world of history in Christ, still his articulation of the reality of God and divine revelation posed two major sets of issues for contemporary theologies as distinct from modern theology with its conservative *versus* liberal dichotomy.

The first major set of issues might be designated hermeneutical. If the gift of religious faith transcends the achievements of human reason in history, is this faith in the redemptive revelation of Divine Mystery, with its narrative manifestations and proclamations, extrinsic or intrinsic to the human quest for meaning and hopes for realizing reason in history? The second major set of issues might be designated dialectical. The very posing of the hermeneutical set of issues acknowledges the impossibility of complete and coherent metatheoretical mediations of faith and reason, since only the transcendentally Divine Mystery in itself is that completeness and coherence. Hence the importance of the turn to praxis is recognized inasmuch as the meanings and values of God's revelation in history are incarnated in the dialectics of discipleship, whereby the subjects and institutions mediating faith are called to turn away continually from the ideological distortions of dominative power and towards solidarity with and among those whom God has revealed as chosen, the poor and lowly victims of history.

Hermeneutical issues have been raised and continue to be addressed; by a series of theologians committed to articulating the complementarities and conflicts of interpretation between the heuristic 'constants' of the Christian traditions and contemporary human experiences. By and large, these theologies might be termed *hermeneutical* or *mediational* to the extent that they accept the transcendent non-identity of Christian faith and love emphasized by such neo-orthodox theologians as Barth and von Balthasar, yet also see the importance of mediating this non-identity within the cultural matrices of ongoing human experiences. Bultmann sought the complementarity between historical-critical methods of interpretation with the existential demands of decision-in-faith by several creative adaptations from Hermann, the law-gospel distinctions, and Heideggerian categories. Tillich tried to correlate Christianity and contemporary culture critically through an ontology of human finitude open to the question of God, and thus capable of overcoming the dichotomies between heteronomous and autonomous reason through the appropriation of the theonomous dimensions of reason-as-questioning answered symbolically by means of the narratives and events of Christian revelation. Karl Rahner assayed a *quasi*-Heideggerian transcendental retrieval of Aquinas which, against the idealism of Kant and Hegel, ontologically mediates primordially originating experience and conceptualization through an existential thematization of the prior unthematic existential aspect of transcending experience; thereby he was able to range over the manifold questions confronting contemporary Christianity, seeking to shift the *status quaestionis* from the ontic categories of a cosmological metaphysics to the ontological categories of cognitive metaphysics. Teilhard de Chardin and process theologians sought metaphorical and metaphysical correlations between the advances in the sciences and the symbols of Christian revelation. Other achievements, such as those of the Niebuhrs, Congar, de Lubac, Ebeling, and so on, also contribute to these vast projects of articulating the hermeneutical and historical unity-in-difference of the meanings informing Christian faith and ongoing human experience in history.

Though these hermeneutical and mediational efforts of contemporary theologies sought to overcome the subject-object dualisms threatening modernity, and systematically moved beyond the typically modern problematic of conservative *versus* liberal tendencies, these systematic achievements are not yet fully recognized in the post-systematic communications and interactions of ecclesial and cultural life-worlds. This is all too clear from typically conservative *versus* liberal reactions to these hermeneutical and mediational theologies. Illustrations of conservative reactions are the 'No-other-gospel movement', such papal encyclicals as *Humani Generis* and *Humanae Vitae*, and the harassments of Schillebeeckx and Küng. Liberal reactions can be found in such phenomena as some aspects of secularization theologies and the death-of-God theologies. Insofar as both types of reaction tend to fall back into the modern oppositions between the meanings of faith in Christian traditions and the meanings relevant to contemporary human experience, it is not surprising that contemporary hermeneutical or mediational theologians are emphasizing how the sources of Christian faith transform meanings and questions raised within contemporary human experience. This generally involves greater hermeneutical attention to the subjects and institutions mediating faith. Such theologians as Pannenberg and Barbour engage in detailed dialogues with contemporary philosophies of science in order to explicate more exactly the hermeneutical *Wissenschaftlichkeit* or scholarly heuristics of theology. Jüngel recovers and advances Bonhoeffer's faith-mediation of the death of God by differentiating the modern metaphysical context from the biblical and reformation contexts which interpret the death of God in the sufferings and pains of the Crucified who, as the coming God manifested in the resurrection, calls us through the negativities of reason to faith in the Three-in-One mystery of God as a knowledge born of love. Küng indicates how the atheistic masters of suspicion (Marx, Freud, Nietzsche) and their more contemporary counterparts tend to identify rejection of religion with the rejection of its institutions, rejection of Christianity with rejection of Christendom, and rejection of God with rejection of the churches, so that an adequate response to their critiques must acknowledge the distortions of the institutions and the subjects they uncovered and actively transform those institutions and subjects in the light of the gospel. Gilkey retrieves the symbol of providence, christology and eschatology in order to articulate an interpretative unity of theory and praxis wherein history is understood and creatively realized in relation to God. Schillebeeckx has offered a major integration of the results of exegetical and historical research into a systematic christology which indicates how the pluralism within the sources of Christian faith do not lead to anarchism but to the challenge of discipleship. Tracy elaborates complementarities and conflicts among theologies engaged in trajectories of manifestation, proclamation, and praxis, in order to spell out how the very real differences do not support claims that pluralism is, or leads to, a complacent relativism or anarchism.

The very important differences and conflicts of interpretation among these and other theologians engaged in hermeneutical mediations of faith and contemporary human experience *cannot* be adequately situated within the framework of modern dichotomies between conservative or liberal orientations. The hermeneutical turn in the post–empiricist philosophies of science indicated how the ongoing projects of science imply a dialectics of questions and answers in which the heuristics of research programmes encourages pluralism without falling into the epistemological anarchism claimed by Feyerabend. Analogously, the pluralistic orientations of these post-modern hermeneutical theologies refute the claims of, for example, Peter Berger insofar as he attempts to force their results into the typically modern dichotomy between either resisting conservatively or capitulating liberally (1977; and the responses of Ogden, Gilkey &

Tracy, 1978). These theologians are attuned to how both faith and science may become ideologically distorted. To acknowledge ideological distortions does not imply a total rejection of either faith or science in order to find some other 'pure' realm of meaning, nor any lapse into anarchistic incoherence; instead it demands attention to an interpretative heuristics open to dialectical criticism.

Political and *liberation* theologies are addressing these dialectical issues. They articulate most emphatically the fact that there are limits to pluralism. God is the God of the Jews and of the heathen, but *not* the God of the exalted and of the lowly, as Barth put it. The revelation of God's 'taking sides' with the suffering victims of history in the events and narratives of the Passover-Exodus and the death and resurrection of Jesus is the foundational summons to faith as conversion, whereby the dominative histories of political powers are 'interrupted' and judged by the crucified and risen Lord of history. As Metz, Moltmann, Sölle, Gutiérrez, Sobrino and Boff all indicate in various ways, this revelation of the lordship of Christ redemptively transcends and transforms all the ways in which humans lord it over one another. Divine lordship does not coerce human freedom but liberates that freedom by revealing the dead-ends of dominative power and beckoning humankind to love and worship Divine Mystery freely, in and through love for the least of their sisters and brothers. The histories of the Old and New Covenants, as well as the ongoing histories of the Jewish and Christian peoples, are replete with ideological distortions in which their religious symbol-systems were twisted into legitimations of dominative powers. Covenants were broken, sinned against, religious conversions are never pure and automatically guaranteed events. The kingdom of God prophetically announced in God's option for the poor and powerless was not the revelation of the best of all possible worlds. Rather, it announced the need for *metanoia* as the continual praxis of repenting for sin by withdrawing from the alienations wrought by dominative failures to love.

Political and, perhaps even more emphatically, liberation theologians are not under any illusions that faith reveals some realm of 'pure religion' within history. If one reads, for instance, the various black, feminist, Latin American, African, Asian or native American liberation theologians, one finds an acute dialectical awareness of how Christianity time and again has been distorted into ideologies of oppression and exploitation. Why not simply identify the distortions with the message and reject Christian traditions? Because these theologians clearly recognize how the institutions and subjects of faith are not locked into objectivistic structures of domination and control. They see that they are within what Giddens refers to as the dialectical interactions of subjects and structures, whereby both are continually called to ever more genuine religious solidarity with the poor and the lowly in the Mystery of Christ. As above, the typically modern option of fleeing the impurity of religion for the supposedly pure realm of reason or theory is illusory. Any idea-system or symbol-system can become ideological. From the perspectives of Christian faith, if, as Moltmann shows, 'the truth of freedom is love' (1981), and, as Lonergan explains, genuine faith 'is a knowledge born of love' (1972), then these theologians' task is a post-modern one: dialectically to discern the latent and manifest value-conflicts and power-complexes which historically and personally thwart that love and distort the knowledge it can generate. This, as Metz shows, means encouraging new subject-empowering ways of doing theology attentive to both the subversive memories informing past traditions and the eschatological or apocalyptic hopes for God's reign of justice and love which break or interrupt all efforts to identify the Gospel with conservative-paternalistic or liberal-bourgeois mediations (1977).

The narrative-praxis orientations of political and liberation theologies, as Metz (1977), Peukert (1978), and Clodovis Boff (1978) among others have demonstrated, are not irrational retreats into fideism, but efforts to understand how faith as narrative knowledge born of love, revealing the Divine anamnestic solidarity with all the lowly, redeems human reason and experience from the irrationalities of instrumentalist and other deformations of reason which have distorted rational praxis into modern forms of scientism, wherein knowledge becomes dominative power generated by fear. I have shown in the previous section how post-empiricist philosophies of science are moving beyond such Cartesian subject-object dualisms. Alasdair MacIntyre, for example, has described how the incommensurability of successive paradigms is overcome in narrative praxis, indicating how all scientific theories are embedded within ongoing historical theories and methods (1980). Similarly, Scannone and others draw upon the categories of Ricoeur, Levinas, Heidegger, Karl Rahner, as well as of Dussel and Freire, in order to articulate how the mediations of theory and praxis in liberation theologies can move beyond the dichotomies of conservative *versus* liberal elitist uses of theories, aimed at manipulating the masses from above, by integrating scientific and scholarly pursuits, via the critique of ideology, with the many values informing the narratives and traditions – the popular wisdom – of the multitude of the poor in Latin America (Scannone, 1976, 1977).

Regarding biblical narratives, I believe the new directions now emerging in social-critical reconstructive interpretations in the works of such scholars as Gottwald, Elliott, Schüssler Fiorenza, Theissen and Trible are proleptic. As Giddens, among others, has shown, interpretation theories have to move beyond the dichotomies of romanticist reductions of textual meanings to the author's intentions, and of the more liberal techniques of totally dispensing with intentionality by reducing meaning to synchronic objectivist traces. Like Ricoeur, Giddens articulates 'a recovery of the subject without subjectivism'; by adverting to how texts are embedded within ongoing social practices of cultural production and reproduction in which texts enable distanciated interaction. The meanings and values are not 'contained' in the texts as such (marks on paper), but are enmeshed in ongoing histories of social praxis as communicative interactions constituted by both intended and unintended significations (1979: 9-48, 198-233). By turning their attention to the value-conflicts and power-complexes dialectically informing processes of domination and liberation, contemporary biblical scholars sublate the liberal projects of historical criticism. The more dialectical and social-critical methods of interpretation do not simply reduce the meanings of texts to the plausibility structures of the cultures in which the texts were produced. Instead they go on to articulate the conflicts within *and* against which the faith communities produced and reproduced biblical narratives. As Dussel points out, these more dialectical and socially critical methods have to be further refined and extended to our reconstructions of church history and doctrines as well (1981: 3-20; also Lamb, 1982: 134-42).

The 'double dialectics' referred to above involve political and liberation theologians in open and mutually critical collaboration with those seeking to understand and overcome alienations and ideological distortions in widely differing social, academic and ecclesial contexts. The differences between political and liberation theologies stem from their different cultural matrices and also from their diverse contexts of origin. In recent years it has been generally recognized that the differences are complementary rather than contradictory. Latin American and Black liberation theologies originated as critical reflections on and engagement in those ecclesial communities committed to religious and moral struggles against classism and racism. From within these contexts the theologians began to collaborate critically with complementary perspectives and values in social and academic contexts (*cf.* S. Torres, 1981; R. Gibellini, 1979; J. Cone, 1979). Feminist and ecological liberation theologies originated as efforts to mediate to ecclesial and academic contexts th transformative values within the social struggles against sexism and androcentrism. In doing this they engaged in re-evaluations of both Christian traditions and contemporary experiences in the light of those values and dis-values (*cf.* R. Ruether, 1979, 1981; J. Cobb, 1981, 1982). European and North American critical theologies emerged within primarily academic contexts in order to articulate the dialectical and critical potential of social, moral, religious and intellectual contradictions increasingly uncovered by empirical, hermeneutical, historical and philosophical investigations of ongoing Christian traditions and modern histories of freedom and suffering. In such academic contexts, these theologians realized the fundamental importance of initiating new forms of interdisciplinary collaboration within those contexts (*cf.* Metz, 1971; Peukert, 1978; Lamb, 1978), and of collaborating with a wide variety of ecclesial and social movements committed to the transformative values of humanization and evangelization (*cf.* G. Baum, 1979, 1980, 1982; J. Coleman, 1982; L. Cormie, 1978, 1980; F. Schüssler Fiorenza, 1977, 1982; Metz, 1977, 1980, 1981; Moltmann, 1979, 1981; S. Torres, 1976).

These ongoing developments within liberation and political theologies led me to suggest that they are in a position to harvest the results of continuing empirical, hermeneutical and historical methods of inquiry. Their concerns with value-conflicts and power-complexes are capable of critically thematizing the dialectical differences which are at the roots of divergent and often contradictory historical reconstructions, hermeneutical interpretations and empirical research programmes (*cf.* Lonergan, 1972: 128-30, 235-66). Such post-modern dialectical tasks, like the hermeneutical ones mentioned above, are not exempt from typically modern misunderstandings in terms of conservative and liberal reactions. Conservative and liberal, however, are increasingly unmasked as at bottom identity systems committed to preserving the modern *status quo*. Compare, for instance, the so-called 'neo-conservative' and historical-materialist criticisms of political and liberation theologies. Both have tended to argue for the identification of Christian faith with the modern science-ideology dichotomy. Whereas the neo-conservatives argue for the importance of Christianity for supporting and legitimating late capitalist science and social organization (e.g., Edward Norman, 1979; Michael Novak, 1982), and criticize political and liberation theologies for 'de-spiritualizing' the faith in the direction of state socialism, the historical-materialists argue for the importance of faith legitimating Marxist science – if not state socialist practice – and criticize these theologians for 'de-materializing' the values of solidarity with the poor and oppressed victims (*cf.* Alfredo Fierro, 1977). Such conservative *versus* liberal criticisms find strange parallels in the contemporary rhetorics of the superpowers. Whereas the US media tend to praise the critical influence of the churches in the Soviet block countries, they excoriate the critical influences of the churches in Latin America. USSR media simply reverse the praise and blame.

These criticisms and rhetoric overlook the way in which political and liberation theologies radically transcend both the sacralist faith-ideology and the secularist science-ideology dichotomies. As the institutions and subjects of faith enter into modern histories of freedom and contemporary histories of suffering, they provide possibilities of solidarity and collaboration within social, ecclesial and academic contexts which will go beyond the fateful modern transitions from sacralist-hierarchic to secularist-bureaucratic forms of domination and control in those contexts. If, like Karl Barth, they appropriate the values in socialist traditions of solidarity with the victims of exploitation, they are keenly aware of how those values have been betrayed by precisely those fateful modern transitions. Late capitalism is an ideological materialization of idealism, whereas state socialism is an ideological idealization of materialism. By dialectically engaging in the struggles against racism, sexism, economic exploitation, militarism and environmental pollution, political and liberation theologians are committed by their faith, as a knowledge born of love, to criticize radically the social, ecclesial and academic alienations generated by fear and domination.

Ecclesially, the many basic community churches developing throughout the world are initiating what Metz calls 'a second reformation' in which these liberating basic community churches can transcend the alienations of conservative-paternalistic and liberal-bourgeois ways of bureaucratically institutionalizing the subjects of faith. This new ecumenical movement 'from below' provides paradigms for collaborative dialogues and actions within Christianity and among the world religions. It renounces the use of dominative power, the betrayals of the Cross by the sword which have so deeply alienated Christians from one another and from their brothers and sisters in other religious traditions. Such a renunciation would require, however, profound conversions within all religious institutions and subjects away from the idols of power to which countless humans have been and are being sacrificed, and towards the Divine Mystery transcendentally immanent in all being. Academically, the many efforts to overcome the subject–object dichotomies which have artificially severed tradition and innovation, science and morality, theory and narrative, order and autonomy, technology and art, industry and environment, economic accumulation and social distribution, systems and life-worlds – all these efforts at truly post-modern intellectual transformations have to be encouraged. For only in such processes of intellectual transformation, conversion, or 'gestalt-switch' can these dichotomies be overcome to reveal their dynamic differentiated interactions which are the foundations of intersubjective creativity in communal quests for truth and freedom. In this context of differentiation and interaction the post-empiricist shifts toward praxis and dialectics are very important for complementary shifts in theology, and *vice versa*. Paradigm analysis in metascience and in theology exposes the illusions of monistic metatheoretical absolutism and dichotomous multitheoretical anarchism. Intellectual and religious praxis transcends those illusory alternatives towards the many forms of collaborative hermeneutics and dialectics.

The new paradigm analysis in theology, with its dialectics of theory and praxis, is not meant to be an esoteric exercise in itself. Human history now is clouded by very real threats to what Moltmann describes as 'freedom toward the future'. As the twentieth century draws to a close, humankind on this planet faces challenges of unprecedented gravity. For the first time on this stage of world history, we humans can envisage the possibility – some would say the probability – of a self-inflicted abrupt and almost apocalyptic nuclear end of the human drama as we have known it until now. The drama must change if it is even to continue. Till now it has been rent by wars and conflicts in which some emerged as victors, and most were destroyed or enslaved as victims. The human drama has been marked by pell-mell successions of roles which could be designated as winners *versus* losers, victors *versus* victims, masters *versus* slaves, empires *versus* colonies, superpowers *versus* underdeveloped countries. The titanic irony of the nuclear arms race is that it discloses the lethal potential of dominative power as death. If science and technology are ever to escape tutelage to the dominating superpowers of history, if the drama is to be 'interrupted' redemptively rather than destructively, then Christian theology, which has itself been enticed time and again to legitimate dominative power, can contribute to that future by mediating more dialectically to the present the subversive memories of God's identification with the struggles of victims everywhere in the mystery and message of Christ Jesus.

Bibliography

Agassi, Joseph, *Science and Society: Studies in the Sociology of Science* (Boston, 1981)

Apel, Karl-Otto, 'Types of Rationality Today: The Continuum of Reason between Science and Ethics', in T.F. Geraets (ed.), *Rationality Today* (Ottawa, 1979); *Towards a Transformation of Philosophy* (Boston, 1980)

Barbour, Ian, *Myths, Models, and Paradigms* (New York, 1974)

Barth, Karl, *Der Römerbrief* (Berne, 1919)

Baum, Gregory, *The Social Imperative* (New York, 1970); *Catholics and Canadian Socialism* (N.Y,, 1980); *The Priority of Labor: Commentary on Laborem Exercens* (N.Y., 1982)

Benhabib, Seyla, 'Modernity and the Aporias of Critical Theory', *Telos* (St Louis, Mo., 1981)

Berger, Peter, 'Secular Theology and the Rejection of the Supernatural', *Theological Studies* (Baltimore, Md., 1977)

Bernstein, Richard, *The Restructuring of Social and Political Theory* (New York, 1976)

Boff, Clodovis, *Teologia e Prática: Teologia do Político e suas Mediações* (Petrópolis, 1978)

Boff, Leonardo, *Jesus Christ Liberator* (Maryknoll, N,Y,, 1978)

Byrne, Patrick, 'Lonergan on the Foundations of the Theories of

Relativity', in M. Lamb (ed.), *Creativity and Method* (Milwaukee, Wi., 1981)

Capra, Fritjof, *The Turning Point: Science, Society and the Rising Culture* (N.Y., 1982)

Cobb, John, *The Liberation of Life: From the Cell to the Community*, with L. Charles Birch (N.Y., 1981); *Process Theology as Political Theology* (Philadelphia, Pa., 1982)

Coleman, John, *An American Strategic Theology* (N.Y., 1982)

Cone, James, *Black Theology*, with G.S Wilmore (Maryknoll, N.Y., 1979)

Cormie, Lee, 'The Hermeneutical Privilege of the Oppressed', *Proceedings of the Catholic Theological Society of America* (Bronx, N.Y., 1978); 'The Sociology of National Development and Salvation History', in G. Baum (ed.), *Sociology and Human Destiny* (N.Y., 1980)

Dussel, Enrique, *Método para una filsofía de la liberaciòn* (Salamanca, 1971); *A History of the Church in Latin America: Colonialism to Liberation* (Grand Rapids, Mi., 1981)

Feyerabend, Paul, *Against Method* (London, 1975); *Science in a Free Society* (London, 1978); *Problems of Empiricism*, Vol. 2, (N.Y., 1981)

Fierro, Alfredo, *The Militant Gospel* (Maryknoll, N.Y., 1977)

Fishburn, Janet, *The Fatherhood of God and the Victorian Family: The Social Gospel in America* (Philadelphia, Pa., 1981)

Fiorenza, Frank, 'Political Theology as Foundational Theology', *Proceedings of the Catholic Theological Society of America* (Bronx, N.Y., 1977); 'The Church's Religious Identity and Its Social and Political Mission', *Theological Studies* (Baltimore, Md., 1982)

Gabor, Dennis, *Innovations: Scientific, Technological and Social* (N.Y., 1970)

Gadamer, Hans–Georg, *Reason in the Age of Science* (Boston, 1981)

Gibellini, Rosino, *Frontiers of Theology in Latin America* (Maryknoll, N.Y., 1979)

Giddens, Anthony, *Capitalism and Modern Social Theory* (N.Y., 1971); *New Rules of Sociological Method* (N.Y., 1976); *Studies in Social & Political Theory* (1977); *Central Problems in Social*

Theory (Berkeley, Ca., 1979); *A Contemporary Critique of Historical Materialism* (Berkeley, Ca., 1981); *Classes, Power, & Conflict*, with D. Held (Berkeley, Ca., 1982)

Gilkey, Langdon, *Reaping the Whirlwind* (New York, 1976); *Society and the Sacred* (N.Y., 1981)

Grattan-Guinness, Ivor, *The Development of the Foundations of Mathematical Analysis from Euler to Riemann* (Cambridge, Ma., 1970)

Gutiérrez, Gustavo, *Liberation and Change*, with R. Shaull (Atlanta, Ga., 1977)

Habermas, Jürgen, *Theorie des kommunitätiven Handelns*, Vol.I, & Vol.II (Frankfurt, 1981 and 1981)

Heinrich, D., 'Die Grundstruktur der modernen Philosophie', in H. Ebeling (ed.), *Subjektivität und Selbsterhaltung* (Frankfurt, 1976).

Heelan, Patrick, *Quantum Mechanics and Objectivity* (The Hague, 1965); 'Hermeneutic of Experimental Science', *Interdisciplinary Phenomenology*, Vol. 6, (The Hague, 1977) pp. 1-51; 'The Lattice of Growth in Knowledge', in G. Radnitzky & G. Andersson (eds.), *The Structure of Development of Science* (Boston, 1979)

Hesse, Mary, *The Structure of Scientific Inference* (London, 1974); *Revolutions and Reconstructions in the Philosophy of Science* (London, 1974)

Hunsinger, George, *Karl Barth and Radical Politics* (Philadelphia, Pa., 1976)

Ihde, Don, *Technics and Praxis* (Boston, Ma., 1979)

Jarvie, I.C., 'Toulmin and the Rationality of Science', in R. Cohen, P. Feyerabend & M. Wartofsky (eds.), *Essays in Memory of Imre Lakatos* (Boston, Ma., 1976)

Jüngel, Eberhard, *Gott als Geheimnis der Welt* (Tübingen, 1977)

Kuhn, Thomas, *The Structure of Scientific Revolutions* (Chicago, Il., 1970); 'Reflections on My Critics', in I. Lakatos & A. Musgrave (eds.) *Criticism and the Growth of Knowledge* (New York, 1970a); *The Essential Tension* (Chicago, Il., 1977).

Küng, Hans, *On Being a Christian* (New York, 1976); *Does God Exist? An Answer for Today* (New York, 1976)

Lakatos, Imre, *Criticism and the Growth of Knowledge*, ed. with A. Musgrave (New York, 1970); *The Hethodology of Scientific Research Programmes*, (New York, 1978); *Mathematics, Science and Epistemology* (New York, 1978)

Lamb, Matthew, *History, Method and Theology* (Missoula, 1978); *Solidarity with Victims: Toward a Theology of Social Transformation* (N.Y., 1982)

Lonergan, Bernard, *Method in Theology* (New York, 1972); 'The Ongoing Genesis of Methods', *Studies in Religion*, Vol.6., n.4 (Canada), pp.341-55 (1977); *Insight: A Study of Human Understanding* (N.Y., 1978)

MacIntyre, Alasdair, 'Epistemological Crises, Dramatic Narrative, and the Philosophy of Science', in G. Gutting (ed.), *Paradigms and Revolutions* (Notre Dame, Ind., 1980); *After Virtue: A Study in Moral Theory* (Notre Dame, Ind., 1981)

McCarthy, Thomas, *The Critical Theory of J. Habermas* (Cambridge. Ma., 1979)

Maier, Hans, *Kirche und Gesellschaft* (Munich, 1972).

Marx, Karl, *The German Ideology*, with F. Engels, in *Collected Works*, Vol.5 (New York, 1976)

Metz, Johann, *Die Theologie in der interdisciplinären Forschung*, with T. Rendtorff (Düsseldorf, 1971); *Glaube in Geschichte und Gesellschaft* (Mainz, 1977); *The Emergent Church: The Future of Christianity in a Postbourgeois World* (N.Y., London 1980); *Unterbrechungen: Theologisch-politische Perspektiven und Profile* (Gütersloh, 1981)

Moltmann, Jürgen, *The Future of Creation* (London, Philadelphia, Pa., 1979); *The Trinity and the Kingdom* (London, N.Y., 1981)

Nickles, Thomas, 'Heuristics and Justification in Scientific Research', in F. Suppe (ed.), *The Structure of Scientific Theories* (1977)

Noble, David, *America by Design: Science, Technology & the Rise of Corporate Capitalism* (N.Y., 1977)

Norman, Edward, *Christianity and the World Order* (N.Y., 1979)

Novak, Michael, *The Spirit of Democratic Capitalism* (N.Y., 1982)

Ogden, Schubert, 'Responses to P. Berger', with L. Gilkey & D. Tracy, *Theological Studies* (Baltimore, Md., 1978, pp.486 ff.);

Faith and Freedom: Toward a Theology of Liberation (Nashville, Tn., 1979)

Pannenberg, Wolfhart, *Theology and the Philosophy of Science* (Philadelphia, Pa., 1976); *Ethics* (Philadelphia, Pa., 1981)

Peukert, Helmut, *Wissenschaftstheorie, Handlungstheorie, Fundamentale Theologie* (Frankfurt, 1978)

Polanyi, Michael, *Personal Knowledge: Towards a Post-Critical Philosophy* (N.Y., 1962)

Popper, Karl, *The Open Society and Its Enemies*, Vol.2, 5th revised ed. Princeton, N.J., 1966); 'Normal Science and Its Dangers', in I. Lakatos & A. Musgrave (eds.), *Criticism and the Growth of Knowledge* (n.p., 1970); *Objective Knowledge: An Evolutionary Approach* (New York, 1973); *The Self and Its Brain*, with J. Eccles (N.Y., 1981)

Radnitzky, Gerard, *Progress and Rationality in Science*, ed. with G. Andersson (Boston, Ma., 1978); *The Structure and Development of Science*, ed. with G. Andersson (Boston, Ma., 1979)

Rahner, Karl, *The Shape of the Church to Come* (New York, 1974); *Foundations of Christian Faith: An Introduction to the Idea of Christianity* (N.Y., 1978)

Rorty, Richard, *Philosophy and the Mirror of Nature* (Princeton, N.J., 1979)

Ruether, Rosemary, *Women of Spirit: Female Leadership in the Jewish and Christian Traditions*, with E. McLaughlin (N.Y., 1979); *To Change the World: Christology and Cultural Criticism* (N.Y., 1981)

Scannone, Juan, *Teología de la liberación y praxis popular* (Salamanca, 1978); 'Das Theorie-Praxis Verhältnis in der Theologie der Befreiung', in K. Rahner (ed.), *Befreiende Theologie* (Stuttgart, 1977)

Schillebeeckx, Edward, *Jesus: An Experiment in Christology* (New York, 1979); *Christ: The Experience of Jesus as Lord* (N.Y., 1980)

Segundo, Juan, *The Liberation of Theology* (Maryknoll, N.Y., 1976)

Shapere, Dudley, 'Scientific Theories and Their Domains', in F. Suppe (ed.), *The Structure of Scientific Theories* (1977); 'The Structure of Scientific Revolutions', in G. Gutting (ed.),

Paradigms and Revolutions (N.Y., 1980)

Shimony, Abner, 'Comments on Two Epistemological Theses of Thomas Kuhn', in R.S. Cohen, *et al.*, *Essays in Memory of I. Lakatos* (Boston, 1976)

Sobrino, Jon, *Christology at the Crossroads* (Maryknoll, N.Y., 1978; 'Current Problems in Christology in Latin America', in W. Kelly (ed.), *Theology and Discovery* (Milwaukee, Wis., 1980)

Suppe, Frederick, *The Structure of Scientific Theories*, 2nd enlarged edition (Chicago, Il., 1977)

Torres, Sergio, *Theology in the Americas*, ed. with J. Eagleson (Maryknoll, N.Y., 1976); *The Challenge of Basic Christian Communities*, ed. with J. Eagleson (Maryknoll, N.Y., 1981).

Toulmin, Stephen, *Human Understanding: The Collective Use and Evolution of Concepts* (Princeton, N.J., 1972); 'History, Praxis and the "Third World". Ambiguities in Lakatos' Theory of Methodology', in R.S. Cohen, *et al.*, *Essays in Memory of Imre Lakatos* (Boston, Ma., 1976, pp.655-76); *Knowing and Acting: An Invitation to Philosophy* (New York, 1976a); 'The Structure of Scientific Theories', in F. Suppe (ed.), *The Structure of Scientific Theories* (N.Y., 1977) pp.600-14

Tracy, David, *Blessed Rage for Order* (N.Y., 1975); *The Analogical Imagination: Christian Theology and the Culture of Pluralism* (N.Y., 1981)

Tugendhat, Ernst, *Selbstbewusztsein und Selbstbestimmung* (Frankfurt, 1979)

Wartofsky, Marx, 'Is Science Contemporary Rationality? Historical Epistemology and the Critique of Impure Reason', in *Proceedings of the XVI International Congress of Philosophy* (Düsseldorf, 1978); *Models: Representation and Scientific Understanding* (Boston, Ma., 1979); 'The Critique of Impure Reason II: Sin, Science, and Society', in *Science, Technology and Human Values*, No.33 (Cambridge, Ma., 1980, pp.5-23); 'Scientific Judgment: Creativity and Discovery in Scientific Thought', in Thomas Nickles (ed.), *Scientific Discovery Case Studies* (Boston, Ma., 1980) pp.1-49

Watkins, John, 'Against "Normal Science"', in I. Lakatos & A. Musgrave (eds.), *Criticism and the Growth of Knowledge* (N.Y.,

1970); 'The Popperian Approach to Scientific Knowledge', and 'Corroboration and the Problem of Content-Comparison', in G. Radnitzky & G. Andersson (eds.), *Progress & Rationality in Science* (n.p., 1978)

II

HISTORICAL ANALYSIS

ORIGEN, AUGUSTINE, AND PARADIGM CHANGES IN THEOLOGY

Charles Kannengiesser, SJ

Introduction

In order to discuss the notion of paradigm changes in theology, it may be worthwhile to test this entire notion against the most paradigmatic thinkers in the early church, Origen of Alexandria and Augustine. These two men have always been celebrated in eastern and western Christian traditions as outstanding creators of intellectual forms, who made possible a deeply renewed approach to what Christian faith meant in their world of human experience. The information we have concerning their lives and theological careers allows us to examine the inner process of their creative motivation with some accuracy. We need not consider only the influence they exercised on later generations in the churches, according to a strictly *wirkungsgeschichtliche* view of their paradigmatic significance. We must study them in themselves, with their gifts, their unpredictable destinies, and the social setting in and outside the church which gave them their peculiar meaning in the eyes of their contemporary fellow Christians. Only when modern biography encounters historical theology can we discern, in line with our own concerns, the role played by people like Origen and Augustine in the always changing, living tradition of the church.

We have Peter Brown's *Augustine of Hippo*[1] and Pierre Nautin's *Origène. Sa vie et son oeuvre*[2]. It would certainly be a challenging task to distinguish critically what is clear and sure from what is

---

[1] (Berkeley & Los Angeles, California, 1969. First published in 1967).
[2] Vol.I (*Christianisme antique*, I) (Paris, 1977).

still obscure and speculative in these recent biographical interpretations starting, for instance, by collecting the major reviews of these books. My purpose is different. I try to show how Origen and Augustine are truly paradigmatic figures in the tradition of Christian doctrines, taking into account Küng's essay on 'Paradigm Change in Theology'.

As a fact, the paradigmatic nature of Origen's and Augustine's role in this tradition needs no substantiation here. But it needs to be articulated on the basis and in terms of the proposed theory of paradigm changes in theology and church. What makes such a reappraisal easy in this case is the traditional ground on which Küng is firmly established as a (Roman-) Catholic theologian, when he speaks about church tradition as a whole. What makes it more difficult is the problematic 'structure of scientific revolution', brilliantly demonstrated during the last decade by Kuhn, and now applied by Küng to the complex history of Christian doctrines. There is no doubt that Origen and Augustine are witnesses to the most vital dynamics of the Christian traditions to which they belonged. And it is also beyond doubt whether one should consider their achievements when building a new theory of church traditions and their different forms of theology. In doing so, one does not pay a merely conventional tribute to the Augustinian past of the western churches, or remind the reader of the broad influence of Origenian exegesis and spirituality in the East. One would test one's idea of a Christian tradition by comparing it with the relevant experience and the message about this issue that can be deduced from what remains of Origen's and Augustine's writings. This comparative form of self-criticism seems to be suitable especially when formulating basic notions concerning the permanent structure of church traditions and inquiries into the biases and the limits of a new theory. Such a structure must have at least been experienced, if not critically explored, by the most outstanding theologians of the ancient church.

Faced with the powerful initiatives by which exceptional individuals reshaped theology in the ancient church, cleared spiritual space for a new kind of Christian self-consciousness, and opened it up for coming generations of believers, what are we to make of the proposed theory of 'paradigm changes in theology'? If we return to the dogmatic foundations of any Christian tradition in order to articulate a new view of its dynamics and structures, we are obliged to admit that our own theoretical view remains exposed to the interrogation of the meaningful people we have addressed in the ancient church. We cannot ask them *our* questions without being answered by them in *their* terms. If they are asked in the right way, they may convey to us the best of themselves. If we listen only to what seems to echo our questions in the answers they give us, they may suffer abuse in a more or less anachronistic way. A theory or a judgment based on such a confrontation between past and present needs always to be 'ecumenical'. Striking differences in the mentalities, in cultural and social settings, or in means of communication, from one period of Christian tradition to another, have never dissuaded the most representative Christian theologians. Their response has always been to the urgent need for a global readjustment of the whole past of these traditions in regard to their contemporary experience. Only by listening to answers from a long past, marked by unavoidable doctrinal and institutional differences, and only by catching the essential message of those answers in their own contexts, have generations of believers and churches of many different types built up a continuous tradition of Christianity. It would betoken a complete lack of historical ecumenism in regard to what Christian tradition means, if someone attempted to elaborate a theory of paradigm changes in Christian theology without rooting the key notions of that theory in an active dialogue with the main representatives of the ancient church.

I should like to engage in such a dialogue by introducing Origen of Alexandria as a qualified respondent to Hans Küng's proposal. With only a few references to Augustine, I shall try (I)to illustrate the notion of 'paradigm change ' with an historical sketch of Origen's life and career as a theologian who invented a new paradigm; and (II) to question this same notion by giving Origen a chance to express his own intentions in creating a new 'paradigm' for the church of his time and for so many future generations of Christians.

I. Origen, as an inventor of a new paradigm

If Ignatius of Antioch deserves to be honoured as the creator of theological lyricism for his epistolary celebration of Christian martyrdom, considered by him as the ultimate ministry in the church and the perfect gift in favour of its mystical unity; if Irenaeus and Tertullian in the West, and Clement of Alexandria in the East, deserve, each in his own right, to be recognized as the inventors of the anti-Gnostic Christian synthesis: then historians of Christian dogma in the early church and patristic scholars ought unanimously to acknowledge Origen as the inventor of scientific theology.[3] He invented the appropriate *praxis* for this kind of theology, and the methodological *theory* which it needed. One wonders only if inventing a new paradigm need always entail as much innovation as Origen's creativity required.

Praxis in Origen's case means establishing for the first time the rules of a systematic inquiry in the traditional realm of Christian beliefs. It means a project which he conceived entirely at the outset of a lifetime's work, in order to bring under philological control the entire Greek text of the Hebrew Scriptures. The combined subjection of these hellenized Jewish Scriptures to textual criticism, and of Judaeo-Christian and Hellenistic-Christian beliefs, as inherited by Origen, to metaphysical hermeneutics, was embodied forever in his treatise *On Principles* (*Peri archon*) and in the *Hexapla*, the six-fold critical edition of biblical writings, on which Origen worked so devotedly for more than twenty years. This praxis of theological scholarship, based first on personal dedication to Scripture, was evident in commentary upon these Scriptures more than in any other form

---

[3] A complete bibliographical survey is given by Henri Crouzel, *Bibliographie critique d'Origène* (*Instrumenta Patristica*, VIII) (The Hague, 1971). A complementary volume was published in 1982. See also: Ulrich Berner, *Origenes* (*Erträge der Forschung*) (Darmstadt, 1981).

of teaching. The *Commentary on John* and *On Principles* look somehow like companion works, dictated more or less at the same time by Origen, around 220-230 AD, in his late thirties or early forties. More than the theoretical, and sometimes fragmentary or elliptical statements of the *Peri archon*, his biblical commentaries reveal Origen's heart and soul.

A decisive aspect of this praxis is that Origen, like most of the non-Christian heads of philosophical and/or religious circles of his time, taught his audience in a rather private and primarily oral way. He did this for about twenty years before he decided to dictate books for publication. He was a layman, appointed at the age of eighteen by the bishop of Alexandria to govern his catechetical school under dramatic circumstances: a persecution prescribed by the emperor Septimus Severus. Three decades later, after he had been ordained by a presbyter out of his local Church by a Palestinian bishop, and banished for that reason (among others) by his bishop, he had not changed his theological praxis. In Caesarea of Palestine he again became, for two decades more, a successful teacher and a prolific writer. He now combined his usual scholarship with regular preaching, several times a week,[4] and he allowed, as Eusebius tells us,[5] his sermons to be taken down in shorthand by the so-called 'tachygraphs' (stenographers) for later revision and publication.[6] It is important to keep in mind all these forms of pastoral and scholarly praxis, if the great Alexandrian is to be seen as an inventor of a new theological paradigm.

Theory, even more closely bound up with paradigm change, shows very distinctive features in Origen's case:

1. Divine revelation is absolute of itself. It does not admit any limitation imposed by the cosmos or inherent in the Godhead.

---

[4] P. Nautin, *op.cit.*, pp.389-408.
[5] *Church History*, VI, p.36.
[6] Thanks to de Lubac's initial recommendation the series *Sources Chrétiennes* presents, translated into French with introduction and notes, Origen's *Homilies* on *Genesis, Exodus, Numbers, Joshua, The Song of Songs, Jeremiah* and *Luke*. A worthy German edition of the *Homilies on Jeremiah* has been published recently by Erwin Schadel.

2. Any being that is not God derives from him: the fulness of the Godhead includes the 'first principles' of every thing.

3. Our created mind, illuminated by divine revelation, reflects this fulness even in the limited capacity of its createdness. With the help of its own rational principles, it understands everything according to the divine principles, which ultimately structure both its being and its activity.

4. A logical articulation of these principles gives us some access to the inner (triadic) structure of God, and allows us to develop the complete systematic interpretation of the divine economy of creation and salvation.

5. Developed by us, such a system necessarily becomes *anthropo*centric, but only insofar as we conceive ourselves as part of the 'spiritual' cosmos, inhabited also by myriads of human souls which do not exist presently on earth, by innumerable kinds of angels, and by divine powers.

6. The common nature of the inhabitants of the 'noetic' or 'spiritual' cosmos, even if they live with their bodily components for a short time in the material world, is called *psyche*. Thus, for instance, *anthropological* concerns try to focus on *psycho*logical issues. The *psyche* becomes a key issue also when speaking about other 'spiritual' beings, angels or stars in heaven. This perspective is consistently followed when Origen is discussing metaphysical or ethical questions, or interpreting Scriptures, or quarrelling with non-Christian arguments.

7. Based on a broad range of intuitive or well-defined presuppositions taken over from a very religious middle-Platonic background and from some contemporary schools of Christian-Gnostic doctrines, such a theory must undergo continual scriptural verification, whereas the biblical language needs the mediation of this theory in order to influence the common Christian dogma.

8. The basic theological attitude proper to a rich and coherent theory of this sort is that of a systematic interpreter of God and of all the mysteries related to God's creation and salvation economy, an interpreter who begins as an exegete of divine Scriptures.

This précis of Origen's paradigm, though summarized briefly, may help us to refine our perception of what 'paradigm change' means in the tradition of the church as exemplified by Origen of Alexandria. In particular, I shall return more explicitly to the methodological implications of Origen's theory, and give him a chance to say *why* he engaged himself in such an innovative enterprise as a teacher of Christian doctrine, and *how* he experienced the 'paradigm change' resulting from it.

II. Origen's experience of a 'paradigm change'

1. A sublimate martyrdom

Born into a well-to-do Christian family, Origen was patronized by wealthier friends after he had witnessed his father's martyrdom. In his impetuous teens, his mother prevented him from becoming a martyr himself. He was given access to higher education by his friends. His destiny was sealed by this first episode of his public life. A martyr *manqué* from this very first step, he missed martyrdom when finally jailed under the persecution of Decius, in 250-251.[7] But this failure became Origen's mystical source of motivation for five decades. As Hans Count von Campenhausen has shown on a larger scale,[8] in the case of this young Christian Alexandrian, the ideal of a rigorous ascetism was recognised as the only adequate substitute for the radical sacrifice of martyrdom. Origen's cultivation of mostly intellectual gifts was probably not so much a result of his own decision, as of events. From the patronage of rich friends, who were known as members of a small Christian sect – and there were many sects of that sort in the turbulent and highly diversified Church of Alexandria – Origen came under the direct governance of his bishop, and was made a teacher while he was still a student. Eventually he completed his philosophical training at the

---

[7] '*Il en subit les souffrances sous Dèce, mais il n'en eut pas la gloire aux yeux de la postérité*', P. Nautin, *op.cit.*, p.441.

[8] *Die Idee des Martyriums in der alten Kirche* (Göttingen, 1964).

Academy of Alexandria, in 205-210, after having directed the
bishop's catechetical school for several years. The important
episode in Origen's philosophical training at the time of his début
in Christian scholarship was imposed on him by the pressing
questions of non-Christians and of Gnostic-Christian people
among his packed audiences, as Eusebius tells us.[9] It would be a
waste of time to try to detect in extant Origenian writings some
hidden traces of their author's infatuation with contemporary
philosophers.[10] Neither the sectarian piety in his friends'
households, nor his eclectic introduction to different classical and
post-classical schools of philosophy, was decisive for Origen as a
Christian thinker. His only innovation in the years of his
apprenticeship as a catechetical teacher was a communitarian and
strictly ascetical life, similar to the practice of Neo-Pythagorean
circles. In continuity with this remarkable initiative, which
anticipated the beginnings of monasticism in the region of
Alexandria a few decades later, the older Origen complained
about the loss of the martyr's enthusiasm in the Christian
Church.[11]

There are enough signs in Origen's works of a first, and
probably the central, characteristic in his experience of a
'paradigm change' under way in the church of his generation.
Origen was aware of local or general persecutions of the church
that were only spasmodic. The norms of perfect identification
with Jesus in his passion and death, he concluded, do not
necessarily require the spilling of blood. They demand the
surrogate sacrifice of self on ethical and spiritual levels. Therefore
*the most fundamental paradigmatic certitude, governing Origen's tireless
activity in the service of the church community, points to the idea of a
sublimated form of martyrdom.* Such an idealistic need, as
experienced by the community at large, later produced many
forms of Christian asceticism in worldly milieus, and much more
in monastic structures, in Egypt, Palestine, Syria, Cappadocia, as

---

[9] *Church Hist.*, VI, p.19.
[10] Henri Crouzel, *Origène et la philosophie* (*Théologie*, 52) (Paris, 1962).
[11] In *Homilies on Jeremiah*.

well as in the West. These surrogate forms of martyrdom not infrequently coincided with Origenian revivals. *The 'theologian' Origen of Alexandria developed the themes and structured the mystical dynamics of his personal theory on the ground of this new paradigm on the whole contemporary Church.* He acted in his teaching office as a witness and, at the same time, as a prophet of that sort of 'paradigm change' under way in the church.

2. The acceptance of modernity

Hoisted in less than two years – before he was eighteen or nineteen years old – from the anti-Christian violence in the streets of Alexandria to the study, and to the chairman's office in the catechetical school of his church, Origen succeeded in restructuring completely this place of teaching and of shared doctrinal concerns. His decisions in the initial period of his academic venture are highly significant. We do not need to examine procedures or content, even if we could reconstruct them reliably. Origen's entire *corpus*, between 220 and 250, is full of the same spirit. In opening his classroom to Gnostics and to non-Christian inquirers, as well as in introducing a distinction between an elementary course and a kind of graduate programme in his catechetical school, Origen applied to this school the same methodological criteria he kept in mind later in his literary works.

A prime criterion was a rational, easy and available presentation of the Christian doctrine. No secretive seclusion in matters of faith, but open discussion. Origen liked to discuss textual questions in the Scriptures with Jews. He never missed the opportunity to express his thanks to the rabbis who helped him in his painful struggle with the *veritas hebraica* of the Septuagint. Most of all he liked to clarify his own thoughts. In a simple style, without rhetorical ornament or scholarly stiffness, he announced his topics and expounded the texts with detailed justification. He tried to speak *simultaneously to the educated and to the uneducated.*

A second criterion paradoxically laid a more elitist stress on

Origen's creative behaviour. As he separated the beginners in Christian catechesis from more advanced students, and directed his own lectures to the latter, he constantly adverted in his writings to a lower level of Christian consciousness, his purpose being to help readers at that simpler plane advance into the higher views of his own systematic theology. Many recent studies have been devoted to Origen's pedagogical methods and to his doctrinal achievements, in the form of new critical editions of his main works and of monographs.[12] Guided by the two above-mentioned criteria, I shall only make a few remarks on the 'interpretative model' (Küng, 'Paradigm Change in Theology', p.3) that seems to have determined Origen's behaviour as a theologian.

The living and loving community, in which he considered himself to exist as a believer and a most responsible adult, was the church. Origen did not doubt this in the least. Any now fashionable jargon about an 'identity crisis' would be irrelevant in his case. He spoke from the centre of his ecclesiastical experience, and only to the church.[13] He used the pastoral 'we' in his sermons and commentaries, when identifying himself with anyone engaged in the structures of the church.

But he spoke to this church in his own voice, with a free speech framed by himself, alone, full of the richness of his biblical meditations, structured by the genuine intuitions of his philosophically educated mind. As a man of doctrine, Origen could not be more Alexandrian than he was, and as an original thinker he could not have had more cultural freedom than he did. The local type of education gave him access to sources of inspiration like the literary legacy of Philo, or the many works of his master and predecessor Clement. It also gave him techniques of exegesis, hermeneutical rules, argumentative rhetoric, and so on. But Origen would never have become of such paradigmatic value to the Christian theological tradition had he not invested all

---

[12] In recent years, *On Principles*, for instance, has appeared in two French editions, and in one Italian and one German.

[13] H. de Lubac, *Histoire et Esprit. L'intelligence de l'Écriture d'après Origène* (*Théologie*, 16) (Paris, 1950).

his knowledge and his scientific aptitudes in the common, daily service of the Church community and in the very remarkable free way in which he acted.

Exemplifying as an individual the unfettered access of Christian faith to the universal culture to which be belonged, Origen experienced, with the unique capacities of his genius, what was to become a paradigm for the whole church of future generations: *the acceptance of modernity in Christian theology*.

He almost never discussed the past of his church's traditions, except when mentioning old-fashioned opinions about the meaning of biblical quotations. He never anticipated the problematic future of Christianity in his time. His ecclesiology was not historically oriented like ours today; it was based on more or less Platonist metaphysics. We encounter in Origen *a theologian speaking in the church and to the church with the full strength of the culture of his age*. His message responded to one of the fundamental needs of this church, the need to overcome the more particularistic and literalistic past of Jewish-Christian catechetical exegesis, rooted in the obscure communities of the second century and going back to an even older past.

This message claimed freedom and newness in offering to the church a profoundly transformed interpretation of the divine Scriptures, and thereby a strikingly new image of itself. In a theological language reborn through its integration of contemporary culture, Origen could speak of the Christian God in the terms of this vivid modernity. He brought this God nearer to the minds of non-Christians, and he brought into his Christian comprehension a sense of classical transcendency, and with it a whole world of Greek concepts needed by the church. *Origen's paradigmatic experience of modernity made him, as a theologian, a cultural intermediary*. He symbolized and embodied the project of the whole church community in his own endeavour. For this reason, he delivered his message only on behalf of, and for the good of, the church. But he also pushed the church into an innovative form of interpreting God's mystery or the church's own reality; an unexpected acculturation in non-Christian modernity.

3. The Origenian 'paradigm change'

My very sketchy profile of Origen's 'paradigmatic' experience
may have suggested that one cannot speak of a 'paradigm change'
in the Alexandrian's case, at least as described by Kuhn in regard
to the history of science: 'A paradigm is what the members of a
scientific community, and they alone, share'. (*The Essential
Tension: Selected Studies in Scientific Tradition and Change*;
Chicago, 1977, p.294). There was no scientific community of any
sort behind or around Origen. Nor around Augustine, nor
around the other first-rank contributors to dogmatic foundations
in the ancient church. Thus one cannot speak of a 'paradigm
change' experienced by Origen in the sense of Kuhn's theory, as
a *'replacement of a hitherto accepted model of interpretation or
"paradigm" by a new one'* (Küng, p.3). For no precisely formalized
'model of interpretation' had been 'accepted' in the church before
Origen by 'scientific communities . . . having an independent
existence' (Kuhn, *The Essential Tension*, p.295). Even in regard to
the Jewish-Christian, more literalistic type of exegesis, or the
typological techniques of some early Christian exegetes, or the
allegorical interpretation of sacred texts favoured in the traditions
of Alexandrian schools, all of them older than Origen, it would be
misleading to present his contributions as a 'replacement of a
hitherto accepted model'.

As I argued in my introduction, we cannot avoid being
questioned in return by Origen, if we ask him to endorse our own
theories. A more cautious pace in applying Kuhn's 'structure of
scientific revolutions' to the Christian theological tradition up to
the church of the first millennium is recommended by Kuhn
himself, in his *Second Thoughts on Paradigms* (1974): 'Part of the
reason for its (*The Structure of Scientific Revolution*, 1962) success
is, I regretfully conclude, that it can be too nearly all things to all
people' (in *The Essential Tension*, p.293).

This rather cautionary observation should not exempt us from
listening carefully to Origen's positive answer, which may
contribute to a more critical treatment of the 'paradigm change'
theory in contemporary theology.

First, there was, of course, a real 'interpretative model' invented by Origen, building up 'an entire constellation of beliefs values, techniques' (Küng, p.3, quoting Kuhn. p.175). Origen's burning sublimation of martyrdom,[14] consuming itself in a metaphysical quest of the 'first principles' as revealed by Christ in all the Scriptures and in the universe, opened for him the way to an unprecedented experience of the radical newness of Christian faith. Since the apostle Paul, no one had gone so far in the renewal of his self-consciousness as a believer in the Jewish-Christian tradition.[15] The personal creativity nourished in Origen by such an innovative experience was extremely powerful. The final result was Origen's broad influence for centuries on the exegetical and spiritual traditions of the church.

This mystical inventor of a 'paradigm' could not help being well aware of his modernity. He was open to the great middle-Platonist tradition, and christianized without restraint the essential values of its metaphysical religiosity. He was open to the latest forms of Gnostic mysticism, and he sometimes came very close to the exegesis of *John* by Heracleon, the Valentinian Christian-Gnostic whom he refuted in his own *Commentary on John*. In his scholarly encounters with Jews, he behaved as an open-minded and well-educated Christian of his time. Origen created a new model of a theologian; he did not simply speculate about it.

The 'invention' of a new paradigm was identical in Origen's, as well as in Augustine's, case with the most spontaneous and existential experience of their being theologians in the Christian Church of their time. In third-century Christian Alexandria or Caesarea, the master of catechesis and biblical exegesis concentrates in himself the ideal of a Christian intellectual ascetic, or a 'Christian gnostic' in the 'orthodox' sense of the phrase at that time. By the common experience of church life, which he shared with lay people and with members of the clerical hierarchy, he

---

[14] Illustrated by texts quoted in Hans Urs von Balthasar, *Origenes: Geist und Feuer: Ein Aufbau aus seinen Schriften* (Salzburg-Leipzig, 1938, 1952).

[15] Charles Kannengiesser, *La nouveauté chrétienne selon Origène*, in J. Doré (ed.), *L'Ancien et le Nouveau* (Paris, 1981).

was attentive to the full range of the mystical needs experienced by this community of believers. He responded with his extremely personal logic and lifelong dedication to these same needs. Finally, he set into systematic order the paradigmatic structure of theology, called forth somehow by the needs of his fellow Christians. He formulated its essential principles and made them work, in opening new ways for Christian apologetics, biblical textual criticism, biblical exegesis and systematic inquiry. Not least, he invented the appropriate language for communicating the Christian mystical experience as such.

The 'community' in which Origenian paradigm came to life was not, strictly speaking, a 'theological' one (Küng, p.12), not even 'a community of inquiry' (Küng, p.11). For there were no 'theologians', as 'members of a given community' (Küng, p.3, quoting Kuhn, p.175), with an 'esoteric' and normative type of science, which gave them an 'independent existence', as Kuhn stresses elsewhere. The same would be true, of course, in Augustine's case.

In approaching my conclusions by observing that the confrontation between the founders of Christian dogmatics in the ancient church and the 'paradigm change' theory, taken over from Kuhn and applied by Küng to the theological traditions of Christianity, highlights the value of this theory in a very peculiar way. Not only does it seem to invite us to confine any possible adaptation of Kuhn's theory to the scientific establishment of theology in contemporary universities, but it leads us to a more fundamental statement concerning this establishment, as it is unavoidably challenged by Origenian or Augustinian 'paradigm changes'.

What I call Origenian or Augustinian 'paradigm change' is not deduced from a textbook patrology, which may indeed drastically simplify Augustine's or Origen's figure and the evaluation of their role, in considering their doctrinal contribution only from a very general, and often flattening, *wirkungsgeschichtlich* point of view. The importance of textbooks in normative science has been well underlined by Kuhn, followed by Küng. It should be less decisive in imposing the 'paradigm-change' hypothesis on the global tradition of Christian theology.

I shall conclude this section with eight propositions:

1. In the ancient church, theological creativeness is bound up with *the vital needs of the pastoral church community* in a non-academic way.

2. The invention of new 'paradigms' in the ancient church results from the initiatives of the most creative *theologians acting individually as witnesses and as prophets* in regard to the mystical and doctrinal needs shared by them with the whole church of their time.

3. What becomes 'paradigmatic' in these cases is *a basic attitude before God,* marked by the reason and the passion of these theologians, not by their system or their techniques.

4. From one generation to another, from one local church to another, at the time of Christian dogmatic foundations from the third to the sixth century, 'changing paradigms' always assert and exemplify deeply *innovative interrelations between Christian self-consciousness and contemporary culture.*

5. In their creative assumption of 'the present world as horizon' (Küng, p.25) and of 'the Christian message as standard' (Küng, p.26), ancient theologians kept the Christian notion of *God* as *the formal focus of their paradigmatic invention.*

6. The ancient dynamics of Christian theological traditions with their complexities, inner crises and spiritual renewal, being concentrated to the extreme in the creation of new paradigms by people like Origen or Augustine, *question the very legitimacy of a separate and esoteric* (because 'scientific' in Kuhn's sense) *'community of theologians'* in the churches of today.

7. As in the ancient church, (one may add: as in the church of Aquinas or Luther), a 'paradigm change' today would require first *a renewed commitment to the pastoral service of the church community as a whole.*

8. A reconsideration of the *academic establishment of contemporary Christian theology* seems destined to become, sooner or later, part of a new 'paradigm' creation in our churches.

III. Augustine of Hippo and the contemporary quest for a theological 'change of paradigm'

Even more than in the case of Origen, *individual* creativity, the isolated quest for spiritual perfection, is one of the two most striking aspects of Augustine. The other is his immediate and essential *dedication to the whole local church*, which he served as a bishop for thirty-five years (395-430). More explicitly than Origen, Augustine shows how the apprehension of modernity impinges upon the spiritual odyssey of a Christian theologian, and shows the vital moments of such in innovative spiritual journey. His example also reveals all the elements of Christian theology.

Augustine returned to the origins of his own quest in his *Confessions*. He went back to the biblical myth of the origins of the world and of humankind in his commentaries on *Genesis*, then to the origins and the mystical foundations of the church in the *City of God* and in many of his *Sermons*. Finally, he returned to the elements, the ultimate metaphysical principles of the Christian idea of God, in *De Trinitate*. In all these different directions Augustine exercised the theological dynamics of his diverse encounters with modernity. Aware of the tense religious needs of his time after his nine years as a 'hearer' among the Manichees (374-383), and deeply impressed by the neo-Platonist philosophy which he shared with his best friends as a gift of divine wisdom during his stage in Milan, he was eventually faced with the modernity of the church itself and of its message, when he was attracted by the sermons of Ambrose, bishop of Milan.

Augustine invented a new 'paradigm' in the Latin Church, because he turned each of these fundamental experiences of modernity into passionate research into the first elements, or principles of his beliefs. From the point of his conversion on, this inner dialogue never ceased.

If 'paradigm' is the appropriate word for speaking about Augustine's contribution to Christian theology, then:

1. A theological 'paradigm' presupposes a correlative assumption of contemporary non-Christian culture on the one

hand, and of the specific origins and foundations of the tradition to which one belongs as a believer on the other.

2. A theological 'paradigm' needs to be applied to the common body of the church community, which validates or invalidates its reliability, in accordance with the pastoral ministry assumed in this community by the 'paradigm'-inventor.

3. Like Origen, Augustine shows clearly that 'paradigm' itself, and thus 'change of paradigm', are notions taken over from the history of science, as interpreted by Kuhn, in a very analogical sense.

4. As an inventor of 'paradigm', a theologian experiences non-Christian modernity in a non-theological way. He responds to this modernity as a spiritual witness, reborn to Christianity through his demanding openness to modernity.

5. What becomes a 'paradigm' for later generations is at first in its primary expression the paradoxical experience of a prophet. Theology becomes an empty ideology among others, if it is no longer the creative 'adventure of reason and grace' exemplified by Augustine.

6. The form of creativity needed for a theological 'paradigm change' rests on mystical ground. The experience of the individual theologian acquires a transcendent meaning through its pastoral validation by the non-theological community of the church.

Again, as with Origen, any contemporary theory of 'paradigm change' in the theological tradition of the church seems to be challenged by Augustine. In Kuhnian terms, one is normally led to consider the possibility of a theological 'paradigm change' only in regard to the 'scientific' community of theologians. But what about the church? In Augustine's terms, one would rather expect a 'change of paradigm' inspired and validated by the non-scientific church community. But what about the 'theologians', concerned only with the ideological interests of their 'community of inquiry'? This challenge is experienced today on a broad scale in the church. The most remarkable benefit of Kuhn's theory, introduced into the theological discussion of today, is to stress the urgent need of a decisive reappraisal of Christian foundations and of their dogmatic tradition.

THE PARADIGMS OF THOMAS AQUINAS AND MARTIN LUTHER: DID LUTHER'S MESSAGE OF JUSTIFICATION MEAN A PARADIGM CHANGE?

Stephan Pfürtner

1. The contemporary relevance of the question

(a) When the confrontations of controversial theology changed into an ecumenical encounter between Catholicism and Protestantism, this change was due not least to a new evaluation of the Protestant doctrine of justification. The new viewpoint in theology was introduced by Hans Küng (*Justification*, 1957-1964). It was developed in the light of particular aspects – for example by Albert Brandenburg (*Gericht und Evangelium*, 1960), Stephan Pfürtner (*Luther und Thomas*, 1961; ET 1964), Ulrich Kühn (*Via Caritatis*, 1965) and Hans Vorster (*Freiheitsverständnis*, 1965); and received a more comprehensive treatment from Otto Hermann Pesch (*Rechtfertigung bei Luther und Thomas*, 1967). The degree of convergence meanwhile arrived at can be seen in the joint article by Gerhard Müller and Vinzenz Pfnür on *Rechtfertigung – Glaube – Wer* (1980) or in the joint work on *Gnade und Rechtfertigung* by O.H. Pesch and Albrecht Peters (1981). Owing to these theological efforts, a consensus of opinion has meanwhile increasingly come to prevail in the churches concerned. This is the view that the Protestant doctrine of justification can no longer be termed a source of division. On the contrary, it actually constitutes something like the central foundation of the faith linking the divided churches.

On the Catholic side, this may be said to have been endorsed in the highest official quarter by John Paul II during his visit to West

Germany in 1980. The ecumenical relevance of his address in Mainz has surely been insufficiently grasped. Its importance is that for the first time in history a pope cited Martin Luther as a witness whose message of faith and justification should be listened to by us all (John Paul II, *Predigten und Ansprachen*, 1980, p.81; *cf.* Pfürtner, 'Keine Kirche', 1981, p.266). In their declaration on the ministry, the joint Roman Catholic and Evangelical-Lutheran commission stated: 'In the sixteenth century the doctrine of the justification of the sinner was the main point of controversy. "Today extensive agreement about the interpretation of justification has emerged" (Malta Document No.26)' (*Das geistliche Amt*, 1981, p.16).

(*b*) Since the message of justification is – at least in the Protestant view – the *articulus stantis et cadentis ecclesiae*, agreement here ought to mean community of faith among the churches. Yet in recent years ever new 'differences of belief' between Catholics and Protestants have emerged. Are these differences pseudo-theological attempts at resistance, just out to defend the institutional positions of influence achieved? Do they simply aim to stabilize their own systems, or even merely to preserve and promote 'the churches' in the form in which these have grown up, as a matter of plain historical fact? Or are the differences due after all to a 'viewpoint of faith' that is theologically different in kind, with all that this implies? Immediately after Vatican II, Gottfried Maron claimed from the Protestant side that disagreement about 'justification and the church' still persisted (*Kirche und Rechtfertigung*, 1969). On the Catholic side, Pesch took up the subject anew in preparation for the Lutheran jubilee in 1983, substantiating his view that 'the doctrine of justification does not (any longer) divide the churches' (*Gerechtfertigt aus Glauben*, 1982, p.42).

(*c*) The common ground arrived at ecumenically is certainly welcome and encouraging. But theological discussion will get no further if it tries to ignore points that still have to be cleared up, simply declaring that unsettled controversies regarding the doctrine of justification have been overcome. In order to set ecumenical research on the move again, I thought it would be fruitful to apply Kuhn's paradigm theory to Luther's doctrine of justification, and to look at the existing differences in the light of this interpretative theory ('Keine Kirche', pp.267 f.). Hans Küng has suggested that this whole complex should be considered in the framework of a comprehensive historical comparison of theological thought ('Paradigm Change in Theology', manuscript 1982). In my view this proposal deserves great attention and further research.

2. Paradigm change as an interpretative model for the history of theology and church

(a) In applying the concept of the paradigm here, we should see it initially as a working or interpretative hypothesis. Whether this interpretative model can be shown to apply to processes of change in religion and theology, or to historical transformations in corporate awareness, or in whole cultures, must be considered a matter for investigation. The discussion that is, as to whether Kuhn's interpretation of history can be transferred from the natural sciences to the history of ideology has to be pursued further.

(b) If we are to discover whether the Protestant message of justification was a new paradigm that put its impression on a whole era, certain points should be stressed in the light of Kuhn's exposition.

(i) A new paradigm becomes necessary because freshly acquired recognitions about the conditions of life as a whole show that the old paradigm is no longer adequate (cf. Kuhn, *Structure*, pp.5 f.). The pressure for change builds up when people come to experience numerous anomalies in the old paradigm. An example from the history of science is the change from the Ptolemaic to the Copernican world picture (cf. Kuhn, *ibid.*, pp.6, 10 and *passim*).

(ii) To interpret epoch-making processes with the help of the concept of paradigm change presupposes the view that our history shows ongoing developments from less good interpretative models, or patterns of understanding, to better ones. It also implies that in developments of this kind there is simultaneously continuity and discontinuity.

(iii) The continuity of the process must not be interpreted to mean that the new paradigm comes into being solely through an accumulation of new insights, so that the addition of a final new component is a coping stone that signalizes the actual paradigm change. It is rather that the paradigmatically new recognition brings a change of perspective, and hence a qualitative change, in the former viewpoint. In so far it must count as revolutionary process in the formation of theories: 'Its assimilation requires the reconstruction of prior theory and the re-evaluation of prior fact' (Kuhn, *ibid.*, p.7).

(iv) On the level of scientific theory, the achievement of the ongoing paradigm must be 'sufficiently unprecedented to attract an enduring group of adherents away from competing modes of scientific activity' (Kuhn, *ibid.*, p.10).

(v) At the same time this paradigm must be 'sufficiently open-ended to leave all sorts of problems for the redefined group of practitioners to resolve' (*ibid.*). What is true of the history of science can be transferred correspondingly to the understanding of life in its practical aspects, and accordingly to the development of 'ideological awareness'.

(vi) An understanding of the underlying paradigm is the most important precondition for membership of the community sharing the language determined by that paradigm. This understanding is essential if a person is to understand correctly what is being said, make himself or herself understood, and exert any influence (*ibid.*, pp. 19 ff.); for the paradigm influences the whole complex of understanding and interpretation under discussion. Every part is affected.

(vii) If this were true of the Protestant doctrine of justification, that doctrine would affect all talk about God, the self-understanding of human beings, the interpretation of the church, and relationships between the church and society. An ecclesiastical tradition which – like the Roman Catholic one – is bound up with a pre-Reformation tradition of words and concepts, would therefore mean something substantially different from the Protestant tradition, even when using the same terms (God, grace, conscience, freedom, church, ministry, and so on).

(viii) The emergence of a new paradigm in people's view of the world and their practice of living ('ideological paradigm change') leads to phenomena similar to those which, according to Kuhn, occur in corresponding breakthroughs in the history of science. Every scientific revolution, he says, 'necessitated the community's rejection of one time-honoured theory in favour of another incompatible with it' (*ibid.*, p.6). This means that conflicts arise in the community that had earlier been united by a common intellectual language. 'The invention of other new theories regularly, and appropriately, evokes the same response [i.e., resistance] from some of the specialists on whose area of special competence they impinge. For these men the new theory implies a change in the rules governing the prior practice of normal science' (*ibid.*, p.7). Since in Luther's case it was a question, not merely of a theological theory, but also of a new doctrine about an institution, and a theory about the church's political practice, the theologians were joined by the ecclesiastical and political upholders of the institution as well.

3. Luther's message of justification as the breakthrough insight of a new paradigm

I have already briefly indicated that the main criteria for the concept of a new paradigm may have some bearing on the breakthrough insight which initiated Luther's Protestant thinking. This may be stimulus enough for us to examine the relationship more closely. For purposes of comparison I shall draw on Aquinas, with the community of shared language and concepts to which he belonged; for Aquinas articulated the medieval era (high scholasticism) to a pre-eminent degree. Moreover, his influence on the history of Catholicism was substantial.

(*a*) Was Luther's doctrine of justification really something new in the history of the Christian faith? This has been a matter of frequent discussion in Luther research ever since the turn of the century (*cf.* Lohse, *Durchbruch*). The Lutheran paradigm exerted such an attraction for other Reformers that it finally became the common foundation of Protestant Christianity; and the position or importance assigned to the Protestant doctrine of justification already makes the paradigm a new one. As Denifle showed, even at the beginning of the century, though in an unpleasantly polemical way (*Luther*, p.424 ff.), Luther undoubtedly draws on a complex of words and concepts that were familiar and in continuity with the theological tradition of his time. Aquinas, for example, includes the treatise *de justificatione* in his theological system as a matter of course (*Summa Theologiae* I-II 113). But for him this treatise is one among many. The justification of the sinner is viewed as one of the operations of divine grace in the human being. Throughout the entire first part of the *Summa Theologiae*, as well as the first part of the second section (I and I-II pars), the theme is God first and then human beings, with their moral capabilities and limitations. For Luther, on the other hand, the article about God's justification of the sinner is the centre of Christian faith and life. In the *Apologia Confessionis Augustanae* Melanchthon could therefore call this the *praecipuus locus doctrinae christianae* – 'the first and highest Article of all Christian doctrine'; and he could then go on: 'so that much doth hang on this Article, which also serves pre-eminently for the clear and true understanding of the whole of Holy Scripture and alone pointeth to the ineffable treasure and true knowledge of Christ. Moreover this alone openeth the door to the whole Bible. For without the said Article no miserable conscience may have a true, perpetual and sure consolation, or may perceive the riches of Christ's grace' (BSLK, p.159). The key position of the doctrine of justification had hitherto never been made so explicitly plain in the church's tradition. Pesch rightly says that it was 'a novelty' in the history of Christian doctrine (*Rechtfertigung*, p.154).

(*b*) This means that the further criterion of a new paradigm is also met: Luther's doctrine of justification affects the whole Christian understanding of God, the world and human beings (*cf.*

Härle-Herms, *Rechtfertigung*). It requires a reworking of the traditional terms and rules in the light of the new paradigm. For according to the Protestant interpretation, the article about justification is no longer one tenet of faith among others. It has become the angle from which all theological theory is to be regarded. It affects the whole in all its parts, through a totally refashioning viewpoint. Luther himself says: 'The Article about justification is the master and prince, the lord, the pilot and judge of all the diverse kinds of doctrine. It preserves and governs every doctrine of the church, consoling and heartening our consciences before God. Without this Article the world is death and darkness through and through' (WA 39/I, p.205). In the *Schmalkaldic Articles* Luther once again stresses that the doctrine of justification is the substantial centre: 'On this Article dependeth everything we teach and live, contrary to the Pope, the Devil and the World' (BSLK, p.416). To proclaim the doctrine of justification means confessing faith in Jesus, maintaining that the new righteousness becomes ours only in him. Pesch rightly stresses this, contrary to the purely formal interpretation of the doctrine, with the specialist disputes about precise emphases as regards imputation, forensic interpretation and so forth. This centre is what Luther was concerned about in his paradigm, as he stresses in the passage quoted, appealing to Acts 4.12: 'From this article we may not swerve or yield, though heaven and earth fall, and all that will not endure. "For there is none other name under heaven given among men, whereby we must be saved" saith St. Peter. "And with his stripes we are healed" Isa. 53.5.' "The doctrine of justification" is therefore an abbreviation for the total connection of all theological statements with the article about Christ which sustains them all' (Pesch, *Gerechtfertigt*, p.266). A correct understanding of justification mediates the critical concept of theology which provides the touchstone by which fundamentally correct language in the Church may be distinguished from language that is fundamentally incorrect.

(*c*) The critical concept of theology acquired through the new paradigm also determines the argumentative framework in which theology can work as a scholarly discipline. Kuhn has underlined this point as it applies to all the sciences, suggesting that we here have to arrive at a definition of mythology. For according to what he says, views deemed obsolete from the standpoint of the new paradigm would have to be termed myths (Kuhn, *ibid.*, p.2). Another criterion to be applied according to Kuhn's views is that of 'maximum internal coherence' (p.3) which the new paradigm can offer for the varying aspects and content of all the insights that have meanwhile accumulated. Conversely, statements and principles derived from the obsolete paradigm would, on the basis of the newly developed complexity, display their mutual incompatibility through incoherence.

Let me here propound a thesis which will have to be substantiated in what follows. The new epoch-making paradigm – the Protestant doctrine of justification – constituted a development towards an inward coherence in the whole Christian understanding of life which was greater than that of previous epochs. Moreover, the complexity of the whole experience of life that had begun to impinge on people could no longer be adequately explained by the earlier paradigms. At the same time the new paradigm required the exclusion of numerous elements of shared language, because these had now to be viewed as pre-theological or mythical, even though in the previous epochs these elements undoubtedly still exhibited a certain inward coherence.

(*d*) The new greater coherence can already be found in the doctrine of God, as well as in the newly formulated understanding of the human being – i.e., theological anthropology – and not least because of the inner link between the two. It is part of the Lutheran understanding of justification to show that in theology and the church we can no longer talk about God and his righteousness, his power, wisdom, goodness and liberty *per se*. We can only speak about these things inasmuch as God counts us righteous in faith for Christ's sake through grace alone, and makes us wise, good and free (*cf.* Luther's *Selbstzeugnis*, 1545, WA 54, pp.186 f.). It then becomes clear that theologically we can only talk about God under the presupposition of this faith – and that means talking about human beings too in a particular way. For on the one hand we can no longer behave as if the human being could know, let alone find, God's righteousness and his freedom through faith in Christ, without God's own commitment to him (*sola gratia, sola fide*). On the other hand, we cannot, either, deal with people as if they were not, through God's Word, creatures who are called to liberty and human dignity (*cf.* Luther's *Von der Freiheit eines Christenmenschen*). The consequence for theological anthropology is, first, that with the unreserved recognition of God's righteousness we must equally unreservedly acknowledge the sinfulness of the human being without this divinely conferred righteousness; and, second, that we should live completely from the promise of his new righteousness. In short, what follows is the description of the human being as *simul iustus et peccator*.

(*e*) For Aquinas too it is an undisputed fact that theologically speaking the doctrine of God can in the real sense only follow from the revelation that has taken place in Christ (*Sum. theol.* I 1,2-3). The same thing may be said about his theological anthropology. Consequently we should not do justice to the coherence of his whole theory if we were to talk about his theology as if he had ultimately surrendered it totally to philosophy – a reproach the substance of which we can already find in Luther, and which was later developed by Wilhelm Link, for example. All the same, the critical concept of theology that has grown up out of the new paradigm means that fundamental questions may justifiably be put to Aquinas, when we investigate the history of theory. Because of the rediscovery of Aristotle, Aquinas' paradigm involves an attempt to integrate that philosopher's doctrine of being and life into Christian thinking. Aquinas' efforts to articulate God theologically by way of the Aristotelian concept of being, for example as *actus purus*, permeates his whole work, from his early writing *De ente et essentia* onwards. For him God is the quintessence, the very substance of being (*Sum. theol.* I: 3,4). He is not, like everything else, compounded of act and potentiality. The paradigm of the theological community with its shared language, which Aquinas articulated, was profoundly influenced by this hellenistic understanding of being. 'In its sharply logical, consistent perfecting and development of the Aristotelian doctrine of potentiality and act we see the innermost nature of Thomism', declared Gallus Manser (*Das Wesen des Thomismus*, p.100). Of course true Thomist research has not been content with this interpretation, and has tried to show that the understanding of being is anchored in Aquinas' prior understanding, which was conditioned by faith. But this unclarified intertwining of a philosophical understanding of being and a theological understanding of faith is in itself part of the unique character of the language that provides the framework for Aquinas' paradigm. Here we find as yet no reduction of the complexity in the critical sense of modern theology.

Aquinas' interpretation of what God says about himself to Moses in Exod. 3.11 with reference to the divine Name is significant – though admittedly this interpretation was suggested by the Vulgate's translation of the passage. According to this translation, when the Israelites ask Moses for the name of God, he is to answer: 'Qui est, misit me ad vos'. Aquinas quotes the text and goes on: 'Et hoc nomen "qui est", est maxime proprium nomen Dei' (*Sum. theol.* I 13,11 *sed contra*); that is to say, ' "He who is" is the most appropriate name for God'. Here Aquinas has not slipped into a rationalistic understanding of God. He stresses that God is 'beyond all genus' ('extra omne genus', *ibid.*, 3,5) – that is to say, he is beyond all concepts we can form about being. In saying this, Aquinas adopts the fundamental thesis of negative theology. Yet he tries again and again to discuss the being of God *as it is in itself* – his being as the quintessence of being perfect, being good, true, simple (i.e., uncompounded) and almighty (*ibid.*, Qu4 ff.).

(*f*) The importance of the intellectual comprehension of being in Aquinas corresponds to the importance of the interpretation of

---

[1] Letter of July 21, 1530: 'Primum cum sit certum, duas istas administrationes esse distinctas et diversas, nempe ecclesiasticam et politicam, quas mire confundit et miscuit Satan per papatum, nobis hic acriter vigilandum est, nec committendum, ut denuo confundantur, nec ulli cedendum aut consentiendum, ut confundat' (WA Br 5, p.492).

being in hellenistic thought, and this has the appropriate consequences for his theological method. The principles of Aristotelian logic also have an essential function for the method of arriving at truth in theology. This applies especially to the principle of contradiction. There cannot be any fundamental contradiction between the truth of faith and the truth of reason, for both have God as their common ultimate foundation. Theology is also 'scientia argumentiva' – a probative science (Sum. theol. I 1,8).

In Luther matters are very different. The paradigm determining understanding and language is not God as Supreme Being but the God whom he has experienced in his most profound experience of threat and assailment, the God who has accepted him with endless and unfathomable commitment through his faith in Christ, and who counts him righteous, the God who has revealed himself by acting on him through the promise of justification and has opened to him the gates of heaven in the abyss of his despair (cf. his Selbstzeugnis of 1545). This God is not God as he is in himself; he is God for us. Talk about him is not necessarily subject to the law of non-contradiction. It has its own linguistic laws; for we ultimately experience this God sub contrario, under the contradiction of the cross. This also means that the experience of faith with this God in his history with us – both the common experience of faith and the personal one – becomes the foundation of the perceptions and language of the new paradigm in a wholly new way, if we compare it with the old one. In the face of this, the importance of logical non-contradictoriness diminishes considerably. This makes it quite understandable that, in controversies, specialists belonging to the earlier language community should have continually denied that Luther's doctrine could be described as scholarly theology, citing its lack of logical stringency, or the paradoxical structure of its language.

(g) This also makes it easier to understand why today – beyond all the limits of polemical controversy – fundamental questions have to be put to Aquinas. Apart from the points I have already touched on, questions of this kind have been directed to the plan of the *Summa Theologiae*, for example. This question at the same time involves another about the position of Christ in the whole of Aquinas' theology; for his *Christology* (IIIa pars) would appear to be merely an appendix to an already existing doctrine of God, anthropology and ethics (Ia, Ia-IIae and IIa-IIae pars of the *Summa*). Similarly, it is impossible to ignore the problematical character of his philosophical proofs of God, his doctrine about a 'natural desire' (*desiderium naturale*) of human beings for God, and hence his basic conception of the relation between 'nature and grace'. The theological awareness developed with the new paradigm has made these doctrinal elements irreconcilable with theology's basic presupposition. Aquinas' relationship to all the 'natural' conditions of the human being would in this respect have to be described as still pre-critical or – to use Kuhn's word – as myth. It has not yet been clarified by subjection to scientific or scholarly conditions as these have to be postulated by way of the new paradigm and its critical concept of theology.

(*h*) Aquinas' pre-critical relationship to all the 'natural' conditions of human life meant that there was still an unclarified intertwining of ecclesiastical and political institutions. In Aquinas' paradigm God is the goal (*finis*) of nature and supernature. Consequently society too, with its political power, has to be subservient to the church's own charge. It is not fortuitous, for example, that in the legal theory governing the relations between church and state, the secular arm should have to carry out the sentence imposed by the church's Court of inquisition (*cf.* II-II 11,3 and 39,4.3). In the same way, in accordance with this interpretative model the state is subordinate to the authoritative directives of the church in all matters affecting the supernatural salvation of mankind: that is, in all moral concerns, from matrimonial law down to private and public sexual morality. (This was still maintained from Leo XIII to Pius XII). Here the medieval model of the one *corpus christianum* forms the background for the development of the theory, and this model continued in the state churches of modern times.

(*i*) The experience of justification was part of Luther's biography. In this experience it became evident to him that in

Christ God desires to confer upon us his liberating gospel. He does not wish to keep us captive under the law. Consequently the new paradigm represented by the Protestant doctrine of justification does not merely lend an entirely new emphasis and importance to the Pauline distinction between 'law and promise'. By contrasting 'law and gospel' also, Luther created a new formula which had in this sense never hitherto been established theological terminology, either in the Pauline writings or in later tradition before Luther himself. He made it 'the basic formula of theological understanding' (Ebeling, 'Luther', pp.5–7); and Pesch believes that this was undoubtedly 'a deliberate novelty' (*Gerechtfertigt*, p.58). At all events, for Luther the distinction between 'law and gospel' had a fundamental significance. In his dispute with Erasmus he actually maintained that 'a man knoweth nothing of Holy Scripture' unless he has grasped this distinction (WA 18, p.693), indeed that he can accomplish nothing in theology because he knows nothing of Christ (*ibid.*, p.680). Over against this, the distinction between 'nature and grace' or between 'nature and supernature', which derived from hellenistic tradition and which played a central part in Aquinas, receded entirely into the background.

Above all, this theoretical element in the new paradigm provides the constructively critical principle for the church's task and function. The church has to preach the gospel of God, not to keep men and women under the captivity of the law (*ibid.*, p.624). As we know, Luther's struggles for reform were directed – we might even say were directed above all – to the mind of the Church in this matter: the church and its office-bearers have to proclaim God's kingdom of forgiveness and new liberty, not to act as political potentates, in accordance with political legality. The distinction between law and gospel leads essentially to the distinction between 'worldly rule' and the spiritual charge (of the church). For Luther, this distinction was of such vital importance that from Coburg castle he wrote to Melanchthon at Augsburg, reminding him, as a guideline in drawing up the *Confessio Augustana* (the Augsburg Confession), that in any negotiations about unity he should keep a sharp eye on this differentiation, and should tolerate no relapse into the earlier confusion. 'He regarded it as one of 'the articles pertaining to doctrine . . . on these articles we cannot give way' (WA Br 5, p.590). Aquinas, on the other hand, within the conceptual patterns of medieval thinking, could not as yet find that there was any serious objection if 'prelates of the Church accept temporal office . . .' ('praelati ecclesiarum accipiunt officium principum terrae . . .' *Sum. theol.*, II–II 64, 4, 3). Luther himself did not as yet interpret his own paradigm in today's sense either, so that in the history of Protestantism too the state churches were able to extend their influence. Nevertheless, the paradigm was open enough to provide the theoretical basis for adherents of the modern constitutional body politic, with its separation between church and state.

(j) Luther's experience of justification made his struggle for assurance in the believer of God's justifying grace an essential component in his movement for reform. That consolation of conscience which Luther himself experienced when he realized (especially on reading the Epistle to the Romans) that faith was unshakeable trust in God's promise in Christ, became an important doctrinal tenet among his adherents. The adherents of earlier theological theories rejected this 'new doctrine' as deceptive. What Kuhn said about the introduction of a scientific paradigm and the consequent tensions between the supporters of old paradigm and new can be illustrated in a positively exemplary way by the theological dispute in the Reformation period about the assurance of faith and salvation. The resistance on the part of adherents of the older 'language community' was due not least to the fact that through the new paradigm certain components of their system of ideas and principles had to be reworked and entirely re-evaluated.

It is true that Aquinas had taught both the certitude of faith and the certitude of the hoping person (*Sum. theol.* II–II 1,3: 4,8 and 18,4). Accordingly, it was wrong to postulate a fundamental incompatibility between the old doctrine and the new (see my *Luther und Thomas*, pp.125 ff.). [ET *Luther and Aquinas*]). At the same time, Aquinas also refused to maintain that the believer could possess the certainty of grace (*Sum. theol.* I–II 112,5). The adherents of the old language tradition clung to this perspective and rejected the new one as untenable. In actual fact the paradigm change meant the emergence of two different language communities whose adherents, though using the same words, no longer meant the same thing by them. That is to say, they were no longer using a common language. This made mutual understanding or agreement difficult, if not impossible. (*cf.* Pfürtner, *ibid.*, German ed. p.135 ff).

(*k*) An important element in the new understanding of faith emerges here from Luther's appeal to every individual to trust – by himself and for himself – that God had turned to him in his word of promise. 'For', he explains in the great 1531 commentary on Galatians (in his comment on 4.1) 'it will help thee nothing to believe that Christ hath been delivered up for the sins of the other saints, and to doubt where thine own are concerned. For this is believed even by the godless and by demons. Rather must thou with firm confidence assume that it also counts for thine, and that thou be one of those for whose sins he was delivered up. This faith justifies thee and effects that Christ dwells, lives and reigns in thee' (WA 40 I, p.458). Since in this way faith in justification means the personal relation between the human being and God in his Word, the individual is discovered theologically as a subject of his own, and one who is uniquely affected and valued. In a new phase of awareness, the individual as person becomes part of the church's language.

Of course this cannot be seen in isolation, apart from other processes of social development. We do not need here to accede to the ideologically prompted interpretation of Marxist Luther research, which sees the Reformation as an early bourgeois revolution – an opinion put forward ever since Max Steinmetz ('Die frühbürgerliche Revolution'), even though this assessment has shifted considerably in the meantime (*cf.* Foschepoth, *Reformation und Bauernkrieg*). In his masterly work on 'the genesis and evaluation of the Reformation' (*Werden und Wertung der Reformation*) Heiko Obermann has pointed out, among other things, the way in which economic theory and theology interlocked – and in the development of doctrine of justification especially (*op.cit.*, p.168). Horst Beintker, following investigations by Karl Holl, has also stressed that, as he puts it, 'the notion of personal responsibility and the ringing note proclaiming the right of individuality, as well as the inner thrust towards the self-assertion of the personality' all spring from the Renaissance. 'But', Beintker goes on, 'in Luther all these three things received . . . their ultimate conditioning and their measure through the importance and the weight of the responsibility with which the believer sees himself endowed in the sight of God' ('Das Gewissen', p.122).

Whatever view we may take of the interdependence of religion and society at that period, the new value ascribed to personally and consciously held faith placed the individual in a new light and the liberty of a Christian (*cf.* Luther, *Von der Freiheit eines Christenmenschen,* 1520; Latin 1519) made the individual potentially the subject of civil rights and liberties in a new way. This is true even against the background of the historical fact that Luther himself did not draw the secular conclusions of the new paradigm – for example in relation to the peasants. But in its historical dynamic the new theory fits in admirably with Kuhn's definition of a paradigm. It was sufficiently open to attract new 'specialists' in theory and practice over a period of several centuries, and to present them with new problems. We could not expect Luther himself already to provide, in any direct sense, components for the human rights and democratic constitutions of modern times. Even in the context of specifically scientific paradigms, Kuhn believes that the changes which they open up are 'seldom completed by a single man and never overnight' (Kuhn, *Structure*, p.7).

(*l*) The importance of the Protestant message of justification for the value attributed to the individual as person and subject cannot be described without a reference to the development of *the conscience* in the understanding and language of the new language community. As we know, at the Reichstag at Worms in 1521 Luther appealed to the imperative of his own conscience, as against Emperor and Empire, as well as contrary to his theological opponents, who brought up against him the whole consensus of both tradition and the previous doctrine of the church. Theologically, the appeal to conscience was required of Luther, because in the new paradigm faith in justification always meant personal identity of conscience at the same time. Assurance about God's Word, with its directive power for the personal life, was also a challenge to remain true to oneself in the Word so perceived.

Aquinas had also taught that the conscience was the medium through which a human being received God's directive. He had therefore placed the dictate of conscience above any directive given by a human authority – which meant even an ecclesiastical one (*De Veritate* 17,4–5).In this respect it was a misrepresentation of the Thomist teaching when Emanuel Hirsch wrote 'that wherever Aquinas' view of conscience prevails, the conscience's ability to resist ecclesiastical authority is quite inconceivable' (*Lutherstudien*, Vol.I, p.34). In the historical context, we have only to remember that Albertus Magnus and Aquinas read and commented on the writings of Aristotle in their university teaching, in spite of several prohibitions by church authorities. At the same time, considerable inconsistency is noticeable in Aquinas' teaching at this point. A medieval theologian was not prepared to respect the conscience of a heretic, as the theory we have outlined would have enjoined. He certainly quotes Augustine's original view that in the case of dissidents in the church 'we should deal in words and fight with debate' (*Sum. theol.* II–II 10,8.1); yet he supports the use of force against heretics – even the imposition of the death penalty (*ibid.*, 11,3). How can we explain this?

On the one hand, this view corresponded to the prevailing practice in criminal law, a practice introduced by the Fourth Lateran Council (1215), the popes, and finally Emperor Frederick II, with his heretic laws (*cf.* Bornkamm, 'Toleranz', p.936). With his theory Aquinas is therefore providing practice with a theological legitimation. But why did he not instead adopt a critical stance? As we can see from his writings, he reasons entirely from the standpoint of the common weal of church and state, and its protection: 'Cut off the decayed flesh, expel the mangy sheep from the fold, lest . . . the whole body, the whole flock burn', he writes, quoting Jerome (*ibid.*). But what is behind this stress on the community, and the scant sensitivity towards the rights of the individual? We are familiar with Hegel's profound mistrust of 'the people', which meant that he was able to see the overriding ordering power of mind only in the state. Aquinas had experienced the deficient critical capacity of broad sectors of society (and we must remember the widespread illiteracy of the time). He knew too the selfish machinations of the ruling noble families, with their innumerable feuds. Perhaps for him the church and the papacy filled the place which Hegel later attributed to the state, as mental and cultural, political and moral regulative power?

However that may be, the frequently expressed view would seem to be correct enough: in the mediaeval world, individuals in their personal dignity – and hence human beings in their individuality – did not hold the status in popular awareness which we like to ascribe to them today. It is easy to adduce examples. We need only think of the position of a child in the educational system, where it was largely an object; or what we should consider the appalling disadvantages of the accused in criminal proceedings. We may even remember certain facts about the visual arts: that there is hardly such a thing as portraiture in mediaeval painting while the self-portrait is lacking altogether. This also indicates a lack of concern about individual biography, or the individual features of a particular personality. We have no portraits that can make any genuine claim to be true likenesses even of such outstanding figures as Aquinas, Francis of Assisi or Dominic. Even the painters' own sense of authenticity was not such that it made them sign their works. All this developed to any extent only with the beginning of modern times. In the Middle Ages the individual still lived, largely speaking, in the collective. In terms of developmental psychology, as seen by Piaget or Erikson, we would say that a medieval person was still in a pre-critical stage of rule awareness, in which the community providing the norms was an authority accepted without reservation.

From this angle it is understandable that in theological theory there was so little awareness (according to our way of looking at things) of human beings as subjects in the Holy Spirit, and hence so little stress on their legitimate claim to their own identity of conscience. The collective of faith was everything. Individuals only counted to the extent in which they lived in and from this collective. The individual felt that his or her faith was only safe and in the proper hands within the faith of the church, for 'fides ecclesiae est fides formata' (*Sum. theol.* II–II 1,9.3). The faith of the church was faith formed through the love of God; while the faith of individuals, through their own fault, could be 'deformed' and degenerate into *fides informis*. From the Lutheran standpoint, in the event of justification God's Word and Spirit brings about the *revelatio evangelii* in the individual believer. To the extent in which God's gospel is revealed to him or her, he or she also becomes the prophetic subject for the whole church. Aquinas never sufficiently developed this theological foundation for a critical attitude towards the church, as an expression of the individual's sense of responsibility for the whole; though he might have found an approach for such a development in his teaching about conscience. For him 'heretics' were nothing but malicious evil-doers, worse than counterfeiters and other criminals (*ibid.*, 11,3), when they withdrew themselves from the faith of the church, which was permeated by love. But we must not forget that Luther himself never won through to a theory of religious tolerance and liberty in the modern sense (*cf.* Lecler, *Tolerance*).

Here we still require a critical investigation, which would no longer have to be undertaken under the banner of denominational polemics. Such an investigation would throw light on the growth of a new paradigm in the context of the history of ideas. On the one hand, the new paradigm which Luther introduced into the Christian linguistic community made itself fully evident in his own writings. For example, in writing about worldly authority in 1523, he adopts a standpoint which clearly articulates the new interpretative complex: 'For heresy can no longer be combated by force. Another expedient is required, and this is an altercation and an act other than with the sword. Here God's Word should contend' (*Von weltlicher Obrigkeit*, WA 11, p.268). Yet in 1520, in his comments on Sylvester Prierias's *Epitoma responsionis ad Martinum Lutherum*, he was still preaching the very same pattern of thinking and practice that we found in Aquinas, with the addition of his own hot-headed language: 'If the raging of the Romanists should continue, methinks there remaineth no other instrument than that emperors, kings and princes should proceed with force of arms against this plague of the globe, and that they should settle the dispute, no longer with words but with the sword . . . If we punish thieves with the gallows, robbers with the sword, heretics with fire, why do we not the more defend ourselves against these manipulators of perdition, these cardinals, these popes, this whole dungheap of Roman Sodom, who without intermission destroy the Church of God? Why do we not wash our hands in their blood, as it were to free us and ours from this widespread and most dangerous gangrene?' (WA 6, p.347). Luther's indictment of the peasants five years later, and his attack on the Jews twenty-five years later, both belong to the same basic way of thinking.

Heiko Oberman certainly shows with notable clarity the angle from which all this has to be understood historically. For Luther, the power of the devil in the world was an imaginable reality. In his belief in the devil, he was still a man of the Middle Ages. He thought that it was the Christian duty of all worldly authorities to protect their own people against this chaotic power in the world, even with the sword. The extent to which old and new viewpoints interlocked here is made eminently clear in Oberman's analysis of the Lutheran Reformation: 'The damning of Papists, peasants and Jews' ('Luther', p.307) 'was entangled in a sorry way with the fundamental decision to define the path to reformation as a setting forth to the world. Through his attitude, Luther himself checked this process from being followed through, and checked it in a "damnable way". But he was not able to prevent it.[2]

[2] On the development of the idea of tolerance in Protestantism, see Bornkamm, 'Toleranz', and Hoffmann (ed.), *Toleranz und Reformation* (*cf.* bibliog.)

A new paradigm, therefore, develops something like its own historical dynamic. Under certain circumstances it can even enforce itself against the intention of its own discoverer. It is surely not by chance that the religious and political 'Mayflower' emigrants who founded the new 'civil body politic' in Massachusetts should have been 'pilgrims' from Protestant movements in seventeenth-century England, and that their revolutionary act should have led, by way of the American War of Independence, to the declaration of human rights of 1776 (cf. Strzelewicz, *Menschenrechte*, p.17). Even if human rights as we know them today have often been mediated through religion and philosophy – that is, also through the tradition of natural law – and, not least, through agitation in the sphere of political power – they are inconceivable without the movement towards religious liberty whose foundations were laid in the Reformation (cf. Huber-Tödt, *Menschenrechte*, p.130).

(*m*) Before the message of justification led to secularized results, in the form of human rights and the rights of the individual personality, it had an ecclesiological consequence. If every believer was capable of receiving the revelation of God's gospel through God's Holy Spirit, this was bound to have a revolutionary effect on the understanding of the church's ministry. As we know, it led to the theological theory of the priesthood of all believers. Luther developed this, among other things, in 1523, in a work entitled 'That a Christian assembly or congregation has the right and power to judge all doctrine and to call teachers, install them and depose them. Scriptural ground and reason' (*Das eine christliche Versammlung oder Gemeinde Recht und Macht habe, alle Lehre zu urteilen und Lehrer zu berufen, ein- und abzusetzen. Grund und Ursach aus der Schrift*, WA 11, pp.408-416). This meant that the new paradigm was proving to be irreconcilable with the earlier order in the church, which did not merely distinguish a 'state of perfection' from the rest of the people – the laity – but also postulated an essential difference between 'the consecrated' and 'the unconsecrated', with a corresponding competence with regard to teaching, the worship and ceremonies of the church, and its government. This altered theory had very varying consequences in the different Protestant denominations. In the Lutheran churches it did not lead to the abolition of the ordained ministry of the church. But the old *ordo*, which up to then had meant priestly consecration, understood in a sacramental sense, was in the light of the new paradigm remodelled into *ordination*, as rite of appointment. The division of the church as community of God into 'consecrated' and 'unconsecrated', or into those belonging to the *status perfectionis* ('the state of perfection', which meant the monastic orders) and 'the laity' (the people) proved to be irreconcilable with the new theoretical framework. This division was bound to seem to show lack of faith in God's Word and its justifying power in all who believe. In the light of the new critical concept of theology, and the fundamentally common vocation of all believers which that involved, the old distinction between different members of the church can only be judged a survival from a mythological epoch of archaic, priestly religion, or a relic of religious caste thinking.

(*n*) Finally, the new paradigm no longer permitted an understanding of the church which elevated it into a mystical entity of divine quality, so that it was shielded from the Protestant challenge to reform. The message of justification, with its acknowledgment of the *sola gratia*, did not merely demand the continual conversion of an individual believer who, in spite of being counted righteous, was still bound to discover and acknowledge that he was at the same time a sinner. That same message also demanded the continual conversion of the church, as the fellowship of all believers: it required acknowledgment of the *ecclesia semper reformanda*. The new linguistic community was bound to reject both the earlier concept of the church as a religious myth, and reject also any attempt to project any divine qualities on to its office-bearers. It could anchor its expectation of salvation only in God's Word, given to us in Christ. It was therefore bound, logically and consistently, to acknowledge the church as *creatura verbi*, a creation of the Word. The critical concept of theology involved in the Reformation doctrine of justification had therefore led away from an uncritically mystical attitude towards the church, and in the direction of a critical awareness of it. The purpose was by no means to destroy the church, as the adherents of the old paradigm thought. On the contrary, it was for the church's own sake, and in order to keep it from falling away from its own specific and most individual calling. The new paradigm therefore also demanded that all the church's office-bearers, including the pope, should be open to public criticism.

4. The two paradigms: a summing-up

(a) These comparisons may perhaps have shown sufficiently how fruitful it can be for the history of theological thought to draw on the model which Kuhn developed as a way of interpreting the different phases of scientific history. The process investigated here has touched on a central theoretical element in Reformation history, and the struggles that broke out which the theory was developed and implemented. Kuhn's notion of the paradigm makes this process much more comprehensible. At the same time, features picked out at the beginning have made it possible to arrive at a more precise definition of the sense in which we can properly talk about a paradigm change in the surrounding field of a process belonging to the history of belief. In addition, the results gathered from the investigation would make it seem probable that the paradigm theory could also be extremely valuable as a way of explaining and coming to terms with conflicts in other areas of 'ideological' confrontation – for example in encounters between the higher religions, in the process of arriving at a common world culture or in disputes between major political systems.

(b) What would be more directly affected, however, would be the ecumenical encounter between the churches of the Protestant and Roman Catholic traditions. A definition of the relationship between these two great traditions has of course been a frequent subject of research. In the narrower context of justification, as interpreted by Aquinas and Luther, Otto Hermann Pesch has attempted to arrive at such a definition by contrasting 'sapiential' and 'existential' theology. He sees these two ways of theological thinking and talking as a difference of structure, not merely in the formal outlines of interpretation and the ways in which ideas were expressed, but in the actual way of doing theology in general. He believes that in this way he has 'arrived at the most profound difference and antithesis between Aquinas and Luther', one which 'underpins and conditions all other differences' (*Theologie der Rechtfertigung*, p.941).

This differentiation may well be extremely helpful here and there, but in another respect it is surely hard to maintain. For, as Pesch himself believes, 'the sapiential theology of St. Thomas . . . [is] itself a way of implementing the relationship to God existentially' (*ibid.*, p.946). The same might be said about the wisdom dimension of Luther's existential theology. Pesch has therefore looked for further ways of defining the relationship. He stresses his finding that 'Luther's Protestant theology . . . was a new way of talking about, and understanding, faith in the gospel', and that it was 'new in a special way – epoch-making' (*Gerechtfertigt*, p.44). The proposition that the Lutheran message of justification was a paradigm change would do more than define the nature of this particular novelty more precisely. It would also help to explain why – in spite of its ties with tradition – Luther's theology was considered by those of his contemporaries who held 'the old faith' to be 'a "no" to essential foundations of traditional Christian doctrine – a judgment that was mistaken in fact but was historically (almost) inevitable' (*ibid.*). The section of the church which adhered to tradition lost sight of the continuity in Luther's doctrine because of the discontinuity, whereas the members of the language community of 'the new faith' did not show that their discontinuity was an actualization of what tradition itself had always aimed at – an actualization in accordance with the time and situation.

(c) It is also helpful for us to draw on the paradigm theory in our ecumenical endeavours today. New, clarifying answers can now be found for the question why no further progress is being made in the strivings for unity of the divided churches, in spite of the consensus discovered in the *articulus stantis et cadentis ecclesiae*.

Kuhn pointed out that study of the new paradigm is one of the most important conditions for membership of the language community constituted by that particular paradigm. (Kuhn, *Structure*, pp.10 f.). We might say that the Reformers, with their theologically influential supporters and their communities, pursued a highly intensive 'study' of the new paradigm, in its interpretative framework. This resulted in an interiorization of the new patterns of awareness and thinking out of which the Protestant community of opinion and language crystallized. (Whenever I am in a milieu that takes its colouring from Protestantism, I am struck by the complexes of understanding continually associated – quite as a matter of course – with the headings 'justification by faith', for example, or 'law and gospel'.) The earlier language community had of course never subjected itself to this change of understanding and language. It had at most entered indirectly into the most urgent requirements for reform, within the framework of its own pattern of understanding.

Yet the paradigm penetrated the Catholic sphere too, even there developing its own historical effectivity through its influence on the general awareness. Particularly in Vatican II, the Roman Catholic Church freed itself from the 'anti' mentality of Counter Reformation and anti-modernism, and opened itself up to what other traditions in the church have to offer, with the aim of constructive communication. Various complexes of understanding belonging to the basic Protestant pattern then drew the assent of numerous minds in the Catholic Church. That was made all the easier at points where the Catholic Church's own tradition was able to provide important components for the construction of a new consensus. These were to be found especially in the central problem areas of the article about justification, according to which we achieve 'righteousness before God, not through our merits, works, or any achievements through which God might be reconciled . . . but out of grace, for Christ's sake, through faith', as Article 4 of the Augsburg Confession puts it.

When John Paul II met representatives of the Council of the Evangelical Churches in Germany (EKD) at Mainz on November

17, 1980, he undoubtedly had in mind this fundamental confession of faith when he said (citing a pastoral of the German bishops, and in reference to Luther): 'Let us rejoice that we are able to detect, not merely a partial consensus in some truths, but agreement in central truths of faith' (*Predigten und Ansprachen*, p.81).

In some cases the Catholic tradition of recent centuries did not have to hand any favourable or helpful presuppositions. In some cases it had even spread opposing patterns of thinking (for example, where freedom of religion and conscience were concerned). But even here, as we know, the Catholic theory that developed out of Vatican II entered the orbit of the new paradigm. The same may be said of the Catholic Church's recognition of human rights in the political sphere (*cf.* Pfürtner, *Menschenrechte*), or its fundamental acknowledgment of its own charge, which follows from the distinction between law and gospel, and places the church in the field of the gospel, not in the sphere of the administration and application of political power. Popes and bishops have long since ceased to see themselves as territorial princes.

At the same time, there is still a considerable cleavage between the two communities of the church in their understanding of language and rules. As I have said, there has been a genuine openness in Catholicism for the new paradigm ever since the last Council. But in the face of centuries-long resistance, what can be achieved in so short a time, in the way of study and an intensive absorption of the new complex of understanding? So the disagreement dividing the churches, which continually makes itself felt afresh, can be explained in general tendency by saying that the new paradigm of the Protestant message of justification has been grasped and expressed by leading groups in the Catholic Church only very hesitantly, or really not at all.

But this means that we have to put some radical questions to these groups. The fundamental consensus in essential questions of belief cannot be publicly invoked on the one hand, while on the other there is a continuance of the old resistance to elements that belong essentially to the new paradigm as a dynamic whole.

Anyone who affirms the message of justification, and hence the distinction between law and gospel, cannot make what is a matter of law a matter of the gospel. And this is true right up the scale. It applies to questions of contraception, as well as to the hierarcĥical distribution of offices. It is just this fundamental differentiation which Catholicism finds so difficult – though of course it has to be continually studied and practised afresh in Protestantism too. Kuhn could be a help to all the denominations here, for he points out that the discovery of a new paradigm must not be seen as a process of pure continuity, in which the new pattern develops effortlessly out of what has been passed down by tradition. The new paradigm has to be seen under the insignia of challenging discontinuity, or revolutionary novelty. If Catholicism seriously wishes to apply itself to the central understanding of the Protestant tradition, it must not start from the assumption that this is possible without a fundamental new orientation and change in its own rules and regulative practices. If we transfer the challenge of the paradigm change to theology, then we may say that this attitude is the *metanoia* which requires a new way of thinking called faith by faith; a way of thinking that allows itself truly to be guided by the power of God's Word to open and interpret, and which learns to understand itself afresh in the process.

As I have said, this challenge is not confined to the Roman Catholic tradition of language and rules. In a different way it is directed to the Protestant tradition too. For the result of our brief investigation includes no plea for the Catholic Church to become Protestant. The conclusion is different. There has long been a shared basis in the essential elements of our faith: the doctrine of God and Christology, theological anthropology and ethics. We should now let this common foundation find expression and implementation in the complex of language and interpretation we have been considering here. The body of faith and theory represented by the Protestant doctrine of justification is fundamental. Today no community speaking a Christian language and living the Christian faith can revert to the era before this complex developed, unless it is prepared to betray the gain in understanding which has grown up – under suffering – in history. This means that the paradigm theory does not merely offer better ways of interpreting historical facts in a purely descriptive sense. It also possesses normative functions in providing guidelines and evaluations. To take one example: today the inner coherence of the language itself prevents us from viewing the relationship between the claims of the community (civil or ecclesiastical) and the rights of the individual person in the light of the pattern, or paradigm, of the mediaeval theories. To revert to the mediaeval paradigm here would not only be incompatible with the sustaining foundations of political ethics and the modern sense of human dignity and value; we should also conflict with the understanding of the Bible we have touched upon. We should no longer be able to justify this, in responsible theology.

The Protestant churches surely must have the function, on the one hand, of continually addressing themselves to the task that has been laid on them in the course of history. This task is to keep alive all over the world the awareness that the gospel means faith in God's promise in Jesus Christ; that this is the charge that gives the church its substance and its significance; and that this charge is distorted if it is identified with the preservation of any institutional, cultic or moral regulative traditions, and if these things are secretly turned into the gospel. For ecumenical reasons too, Protestantism must not stand aside from this task, if it wants the paradigm to which it has given expression to remain within the horizons of the Christian faith. On the other hand this new paradigm also forbids the regulative systems that have developed out of it in the denominational traditions of Protestantism from being lent such absolute force that they themselves are made part of the gospel. No ecclesiastical community can make its own denominationally developed traditions the sole measure and standard for the one future church of God. Above all, alertness to the claims of the gospel demands of us that we seek the challenges for an interpretation of the new paradigm with which our own era faces us, the challenges required by the theory of a community of all nations and peoples in solidarity. There can surely be no doubt that here we can see a new form of the paradigm as it has been passed down to us – a form new for the whole of the Christian faith and hence for the unity of the church.

Bibliography

Beintker, Horst, 'Das Gewissen in der Spannung zwischen Gesetz und Evangelium', *Lutherjahrbuch* 48 (1981), pp.115-147

Bornkamm, Heinrich, 'Toleranz, In der Geschichte des Christentums', RGG VI, 933-946 (Tübingen, 1962)

Brandenburg, Albert, *Gericht und Evangelium. Zur Worttheologie in Luthers erster Psalmenvorlesung* (Paderborn, 1960)

BSLK, *Bekenntnisschriften*

Das geistliche Amt in der Kirche, ed. Gemeinsame römisch-katholische/evangelisch-lutherische Kommission (Paderborn & Frankfurt, 1981)

Denifle, Heinrich, *Luther und Luthertum in der ersten Entwicklung*, Vol.1, 2nd ed. (Mainz, 1904/1906); Eng. trans. of Vol.1, pt.1, by R. Volz, *Luther und Lutherdom* (Somerset, O., 1917)

Ebeling, Gerhard, 'Luther. Theologie', RGG IV, 495-520, 3rd ed. (Tübingen, 1960)

Foschepoth, J., *Reformation und Bauernkrieg im Geschichtsbild der DDR. Zur Methodologie eines gewandelten Geschichtsverständnisses* [*Historische Forschungen* 10], (Berlin, 1976)

Härle, Wilfried, and Herms, Eilert, *Rechtfertigung. Das Wirklichkeitsverständnis des christlichen Glaubens* (Göttingen, 1980).

Hirsch, Emanuel, *Lutherstudien*, Vol.1 (Gütersloh, 1954)

Hoffmann, Manfred (ed.), *Toleranz und Reformation. Texte zur Kirchen- und Theologiegeschichte* Vol.24 (Gütersloh, 1979)

Huber, Wolfgang, and Tödt, Heinz Eduard, *Menschenrechte. Perspektiven einer menschlichen Welt* 2nd ed. (Stuttgart & Berlin, 1978)

John Paul II, *Predigten und Ansprachen von Papst Johannes Paul II. bei seinem Pastoralbesuch in Deutschland sowie Begrüssungsworte und Reden, die an den Heiligen Vater gerichtet wurden. 15. bis 19. November 1908. Offizielle Ausgabe. Hrsg. vom Sekretariat der Deutschen Bischöfe*, 3rd rev. ed. (Bonn, 1980)

Kuhn, Thomas S. *The Structure of Scientific Revolutions* (with

'Postscript 1969') 2nd ed. (Chicago, 1970)

Kühn, Ulrich, *Via caritatis. Theologie des Gesetzes bei Thomas von Aquin* (Göttingen, 1965)

Küng, Hans, *Justification. The Doctrine of Karl Barth and a Catholic Reflection*, tr. T. Collins, E.E. Tolk & D. Grandskon (London, 1964)

Küng, Hans, 'Paradigm Change in Theology. A proposal for discussion' (manuscript) (Tübingen, 1982)

Lecler, Joseph, 'Tolerance and Reformation, Eng. tr. (New York & London, 1960)

Lohse, Bernhard (ed.), *Der Durchbruch der reformatorischen Erkenntnis bei Luther,* Wege der Forschung 123 (Darmstadt, 1968)

Luther, Martin, *Werke* (WA – see abbreviations).

Manser, Gallus, *Das Wesen des Thomismus* 3rd ed. (Fribourg, 1949)

Maron, Gottfried, *Kirche und Rechtfertigung. Eine kontrovers-theologische Untersuchung, ausgehend von den Texten des Zweiten Vatikanischen Konzils* (Göttingen, 1969)

Muller, Gerhard, and Pfnür, Vinzenz, 'Rechtfertigung – Glaube – Wer', in *Confessio Augustana. Bekenntnis des einen Glaubens. Gemeinsame Untersuchung lutherischer und katholischer Theologen,* ed. Harding Meyer and Heinz Schütte (Paderborn & Frankfurt, 1980)

Oberman, Heiko Augustinus, *Masters of the Reformation: the emergence of a new intellectual climate in Europe*, tr. D. Martin (New York, 1981)

Oberman, Heiko Augustinus, *Luther. Mensch zwischen Gott und Teufel* (Berlin, 1982)

Pesch, Otto Hermann, *Theologie der Rechtfertigung bei Martin Luther und Thomas von Aquin. Versuch eines systematisch-theologischen Dialogs* (Mainz, 1967)

Pesch, Otto Hermann, *Gerechtfertigt aus Glauben. Luthers Fragen an die Kirche* (Freiburg, Basle & Vienna, 1982)

Pesch, Otto Hermann, *Hinführung zu Luther* (Mainz, 1982)

Pesch, Otto Hermann, and Peters, Albrecht, *Einführung in die Lehre von Gnade und Rechtfertigung* (Darmstadt, 1981)

Pfürtner, Stephan, *Luther and Aquinas – a Conversation. Our*

Salvation, its Certainty and Peril, tr. Edward Quinn (London, 1964; New York, 1965)

Pfürtner, Stephan, 'Die Menschenrechte in der römisch-katholischen Kirche', *Zeitschrift für Evang. Ethik*, 1. Heft 20 (1976), pp.35–63

Pfürtner, Stephan, 'Keine Kirche kann vollkommen sein. Trennt die Rechtfertigungslehre noch die Christen?', *Lutherische Monatshefte*, Heft 5, 20. Jahrgang (1981), pp.264–268; parallel printing in *Orientierung*, 45, No.8 (Zürich, 1981), pp.95–98

Steinmetz, Max, 'Die frühbürgerliche Revolution in Deutschland (1476–1535)', *Zeitschrift für Geschichtswissenshaft* 8 (Berlin, 1960), pp.113–124; reprinted in Rainer Wohlfeil (ed.), *Reformation oder frühbürgerliche Revolution* (Munich, 1972), pp.42–55

Strzelewicz, Willy, *Der Kampf um die Menschenrechte. Von der amerikanischen Unabhängigkeitserklärung bis zur Gegenwart* (Frankfurt, 1968)

Thomas Aquinas, *Summa theologica*, Latin text and Eng. tr. (London & New York, 1964 ff); also *Quaestio disputata 'De veritate', quaest. 17 'De conscientia'*

Vorster, Hans, *Das Freiheitsverständnis bei Thomas von Aquin und Martin Luther* (Göttingen, 1965)

FROM 'DOGMATIK' TO 'GLAUBENSLEHRE': A PARADIGM CHANGE IN MODERN THEOLOGY?

Brian Gerrish

In an early essay on history and metaphysics, Ernst Troeltsch (1865-1923) declared that the historical-critical method, once it gains an entrance, brooks no limits. Developed to deal with natural events, it is bound, if applied to the supernatural, to dissolve it into the natural and to interpret it as analogous to everything else. A separation between the natural and the supernatural, the humanly conditioned and the directly divine, becomes impossible.[1] In another essay, published in the same year, Troeltsch compared the historical-critical method to leaven: it transforms everything and finally bursts the entire mould of previous theological methods.[2] This, clearly, sounds like a promising candidate for the title of a 'paradigm change'. So impressed was Troeltsch with the radical nature of the transformation, that he believed it required a new name for the constructive theological enterprise: no longer *Dogmatik*, but *Glaubenslehre*.

In what follows, I do not claim that *Glaubenslehre* really *is* the new theological paradigm, though I do not deny it either. The claim, or the denial, would require not only a close analysis of the language of paradigm change, but an extensive attempt to locate Troeltsch in the history of modern theology. Instead, I merely sketch (in section 1) what I take to be the heart of the transformation that Troeltsch proclaimed, and then go on to show (in section 2), in agreement with him, that the new by no means severed all continuity with the old, but brought to fruition

---

[1] Troeltsch, 'Geschichte und Metaphysik', *ZThK* 8 (1898): 5-6.
[2] Troeltsch, 'über historische und dogmatische Methode in der Theologie' (1898), *GS* 2:730.

a possibility latent in Reformation theology. I recognize that even on these two themes, or rather sub-themes, a great deal more could be said. But I have attempted to hold on firmly, as far as possible, to the thread of a single argument.[3]

1.

Another Troeltschian aphorism opens up the heart of the matter: the new dogmatics 'is dogmatics no longer, because it knows no dogmas'.[4] The concept of church dogma was an early casualty in the invasion of historical thinking. In Troeltsch's mind, at least, 'dogma' stood for something that historical thought must deny: the possibility of fixed and final points (*Lehrfestsetzungen*) in the ceaseless flux of the history of doctrine. Although the old Protestantism took over the ancient trinitarian and christological dogmas, strictly speaking it had no dogmas; but in their place it put the propositions of the Bible similarly understood as doctrinal definitions. Modern Protestantism, by contrast, discovers in Scripture 'representations of faith', mutable products of the imagination that express a practical religious attitude. The task of *Glaubenslehre* is to reduce both these and subsequent Christian representations to their conceptual content.[5] It is a task that never ends: there is a plasticity to the concepts of faith that makes them always newly adaptable to the natural and historical sciences of the present day.[6] Plainly, this is an understanding of theology as far removed from Protestant orthodoxy as from Roman Catholicism. If we still venture to speak of 'the faith once and for

---

[3] Since my commission was to summarize what I have written elsewhere on the relationship between classical and liberal Protestant theology, I may refer, for more discussion and documentation, in particular to my *The Old Protestantism and the New: Essays on the Reformation Heritage* (Chicago & Edinburgh, 1982), to which I should at least add my essay 'Dr Martin Luther: Subjectivity and Doctrine in the Lutheran Reformation', in *Seven-Headed Luther*, ed. Peter N. Brooks (Oxford, 1983).

[4] Troeltsch, 'Dogmatik', *RGG* 2:109

[5] Troeltsch, 'Dogma', *RGG* 2:105-6

[6] 'Dogmatik', col.108.

all delivered to the saints' (Jude 3), it cannot be any definitive *forms* of faith that we are to contend for.

Troeltsch discovered the pioneer of the new dogmatics in Friedrich Schleiermacher (1768-1834). In this he was undoubtedly correct. 'The Christian church', Schleiermacher had written, ' . . . is a phenomenon of change [*ein Werdendes*], in which at every moment the present must be grasped as the product of the past and the germ of the future'.[7] The concern of theological studies generally is with something in ceaseless motion, an ever-changing community; dogmatics is the part of theological studies that concerns itself with the changing community on its believing, thinking side. In short, a modern dogmatics – that is, a dogmatics that takes historical consciousness in earnest – is, as Schleiermacher put it, a part of *historical* theology, and it can never claim to yield more than an account of 'the doctrine prevalent in a Christian church at a particular time'.[8]

Schleiermacher took the recognition of change to be a defining mark of distinctively Protestant thought. 'The Protestant view of the Christian Church', he said, 'includes this essential characteristic: that we think of it as a totality in movement, as something capable of progress and development'.[9] Hence he claimed the 'right of development' in dogmatics strictly as a Protestant theologian.[10] In the Roman Church, on the other hand, he could see only immutable norms, so that there the question of doctrinal development could not arise. The passage of time may have proved the mutability of this verdict on Roman Catholicism, too. But there remains an apparent difference between Schleiermacher's notion of development and, say, the notion later put forward by John Henry Newman (1801-90), who had no thought of discarding dogmas but only of showing how they came to be. If for Schleiermacher the datum of reflection was *ein Werdendes*, for Newman it was, so to say, *ein Gewordenes*. The

[7] Schleiermacher, *KD* (1811), §33.
[8] *Ibid.*, §97, §195; Gl, (1830-31), §19.
[9] Schleiermacher, *Christliche Sitte* (1884), *SW* 1,12, p.72.
[10] Schleiermacher to F.H. Jacobi, 30 March 1881, Br. 2:351.

cycle of growth in Newman's idea of development achieves its finality – its fruitfulness or maturity – in dogma; in Schleiermacher's idea, the cycle continues to the senility and dissolution of dogma. And this means that the dogmatic task must include the critique of dogmas and, where necessary, the discarding of them as obsolete.[11]

Historical thinking calls for a similar reappraisal of the Reformation confessions. In part, Schleiermacher affirmed the confessions as legitimate protests against errors and abuses that had crept into the Church. What it means to affirm the 'symbolic books' in this way is indicated in the curious formula of subscription that he proposed: 'I declare that I find wholly consonant with the Holy Scripture and the original teaching of the Church everything that is taught in our symbolic books against the errors and abuses of the Roman Church'.[12] From this somewhat negative point of view, the Protestant confessions are an affirmation of the biblical norm only against certain deviations from it. But Schleiermacher also understood them more positively as a distinctive expression of the Christian idea, jointly necessary, with Roman Catholicism, to the historical manifestation of Christianity. The Reformation was a relatively new beginning, and its symbolic books still have their unique value as the first public embodiment of the Protestant spirit. Historical understanding thus provided Schleiermacher with a middle way between confessionalism, which lacked a sense of historical distance between the nineteenth century and the sixteenth, and rationalism, which could see no present usefulness for the documents of another day. No confession of faith, he maintained, has the power of excommunication; and yet, even as products of human authorship in a human context, the symbolic books do have a relative permanence as ecclesiastical norms.[13]

---

[11] KD, [2] (1830), §205: Gl. [2](1834–31), §95, etc. All subsequent references to the Kurze Darstellung and the Glaubenslehre of Schleiermacher are to the second editions.

[12] Schleiermacher, 'über den eigenthümlichen Wert und das bindende Ansehen symbolischer Bücher' (1819), KS 2, p.164.

[13] Schleiermacher, Reden [2](1806), Pünjer, pp.301–2; Gl. §24; Christliche Sitte, p.212; 'Das Ansehen symbolischer Bücher', pp.143–44, 159–62; Gl. §27.

But what of the Holy Scriptures? Schleiermacher did not exempt them from the relativities of history. He denied that reformation could ever mean simply the restitution of the apostolic age: what has once been can never be brought back again at a later time. But, as he pointed out in his remarks on the Protestant confessions, there is a difference between the first decisive moments and the subsequent course of a historical development. And it is this historical principle that makes it possible, and necessary, to take the New Testament as the norm of what is authentically Christian, just as the confessions are the norm of what is authentically Protestant. The parallel is not exact, because the Protestant spirit is not wholly new but rather a new expression of the Christian spirit. The historical point of view, however, is the same. It follows that the scriptural norm is not to be simply identified with the letter of the New Testament, and that no exclusive appeal can be made to the Bible (no *scriptura sola*). The development of doctrine arises out of a critical use of Scripture and constant attention to the current state of knowledge in other fields.[14]

Schleiermacher apparently recognized that the shift in theological method he proposed made a change of name desirable. He did not coin the word *Glaubenslehre*, which is the German equivalent of *doctrina fidei*, an expression that goes all the way back to the Latin fathers. Philipp Jakob Spener (1635-1705) seems to have been the first to use *Glaubenslehre* as the title for a book on Protestant theology (*Evangelische Glaubenslehre*, 1688), but *Dogmatik* was the preferred term throughout the eighteenth century. Schleiermacher never abandoned the dominant term, but he did like to speak of his own great systematic work as his *Glaubenslehre*, notably in the open letters to his friend Friedrich Lücke. Further, he tells us in the introduction to *The Christian Faith* (second edition) that the title, in which the name *Dogmatik* is avoided, contains elements for a definition of the subject. A handwritten note explains: 'Darstellung des Glaubens ist

---

[14] Schleiermacher, *Gl.* §24.1, §27.1; *KD* §83, §103, §167, §177, §181. *Cf.* the letter to Jacobi, p.351.

Glaubenslehre'.[15] One may hazard the guess that Schleiermacher may have been prevented from surrendering the name *Dogmatik* not only by the weight of custom, but by the inflexibility of the other name, *Glaubenslehre*, which lacks usable cognates.

The contrast between *Dogmatik* and *Glaubenslehre*, only hinted at by Schleiermacher, was sharpened by his pupil Alexander Schweizer (1808-88), who chose *Glaubenslehre* as the actual title for his own systematic work and expressed astonishment that his colleague, the speculative theologian A.E. Biedermann (1819-85), would wish to call 'dogmatics' the end product of his ruthless critique of ecclesiastical dogma.[16] At the same time, the recognition that theological studies as a whole, including dogmatics, bear an ineradicably historical stamp – by reason of their historical datum – led to the programmatic historicizing movement in German Protestant thought. In the work of both F.C. Baur (1792-1860) and Adolf Harnack (1851-1930), despite their very different estimates of church dogma, the movement threatened to dissolve dogmatics altogether as an independent discipline. In Troeltsch, on the other hand, at any rate during his Heidelberg period (1894-1914), Schleiermacher's model was followed more closely and avowedly, though it must be admitted that Troeltsch weakened the scientific claims of *Glaubenslehre* even while asserting its place as an independent field of theological study. Still more than Schweizer, Troeltsch stated the antithesis between *Glaubenslehre* and *Dogmatik* in sharply polemical tones;[17] and more than Harnack, though scarcely more than Baur, he presented historical method as a working procedure inextricably interwoven with a comprehensive historical mode of thought, which, he believed, held the key to understanding everything concerned with the products of human existence and culture.

[15] Redeker, 1:9. The full title, *Der christliche Glaube nach den Grundsätzen der evangelischen Kirche im Zusammenhange dargestellt*, was truncated in the English translation.

[16] Schweizer, *Chr. Gl.* (1863-72), 2:v.

[17] Besides the article on 'Dogmatik' (n.4 above), see Troeltsch, *Gl.* (1925) §1 (p.10); 'The Dogmatics of the "Religionsgeschichtliche Schule"', *AJT* 17 (1913):17 (German in *GS* 2:516).

We find in Troeltsch another way of speaking about dogmatics, which also had its roots in Schleiermacher but may seem, at first sight, to diverge from the emphasis on history: the content of *Glaubenslehre* is a 'theology of consciousness' (a *Bewusstseinstheologie*).[18] This, of course, corresponds to Schleiermacher's definition of Christian doctrines (*Glaubenssätze*) as interpretations of the Christian religious affections presented in speech.[19] And there is in fact no disharmony here with the turn to history; for the mutable historical forms are precisely expressions of the Christian consciousness or the specifically Christian way of believing.[20] Schleiermacher could describe his dogmatic method as 'empirical' in the sense that it dealt with actual facts of experience: he proceeded by an interrogation of the Christian consciousness, and what he discovered by this procedure gave him the test for weighing old dogmatic forms.[21] That in Troeltsch's mind, at least, this entire approach combines the historical and the psychological viewpoints in perfect harmony, is strikingly indicated by his use of the compound expression 'the historical-psychological view'.[22] And it was here, in the psychologizing of faith, that he thought he detected a line of continuity going back through Schleiermacher to Martin Luther (1483-1546).

2.

Once again, we can take our point of departure from a Troeltsch quotation: the effect of Luther's *sola fide*, he suggests, is that 'religion is drawn entirely . . . into the domain of the psychologically transparent'. There it becomes the affirmation of a particular way of perceiving God and God's grace.[23] Troeltsch

---

[18] Troeltsch, *Gl.* §11 (p.132).
[19] Schleiermacher, *Gl.* §15.
[20] For the term *Glaubensweise*, see Schleiermacher, *KD* §1.
[21] Schleiermacher, *Sendschr.*, Mulert, pp.20-21, 25; *Gl.* §95, etc.
[22] Troeltsch, *Gl.* §8 (p.103).
[23] Troeltsch, *Die Bedeutung des Protestantismus für die Entstehung der modernen Welt* (Munich & Berlin, 1911), p.96.

goes on to make the interesting remark that, as a consequence of Luther's faith, the new path to the old destination becomes more important than the destination itself. Indeed, the way *contains* the goal: faith, as a way of perceiving God, now *is* redemption, not the way to attain it. The subjective assurance of believing becomes religion itself.[24]

Though always intriguing and illuminating, Troeltsch's formulations are not always self-evidently right. Can one, for instance, really advance as smoothly as he does from Luther to the very modern proposition that the idea of faith has triumphed over the content of faith?[25] But he was right, I believe, when he claimed to discover in Luther's *faith* the crucial link between the old Protestantism and the new; and he never made the mistake of inferring that this link must therefore represent the whole Luther, or even the essential Luther. Neither did he somehow fail to notice the importance of the word of God in Lutheran theology, although he may have failed to appreciate fully the sacramental power of the word. It was, in fact, precisely in Luther's discovery of the word that Troeltsch found the clue to the significance of Luther's faith. In this he was surely on the right lines. In the Lutheran gospel a linguistic change takes place that calls for a reappraisal of the entire religious vocabulary inherited from the Middle Ages. The ripples of change really do, as Troeltsch perceived, radiate out from the concept of the word; and it can be shown that the effect of the change was indeed to move religion towards psychological transparency.

In the Roman Catholic view (or views), justification was held to be effected by the supernatural infusion of sacramental grace. This grace, to be sure, does move the will to accept it in faith, and what is imparted by it is something analogous to a human 'virtue' in the Aristotelian sense: it is a *donum habituale*. To this extent, the gift of grace is made intelligible. The process, however, by which the gift is given and the proper nature of the gift itself are not presented as transparent, but as supernatural; and that the process

[24] *Ibid.*, pp.96, 98.
[25] *Ibid.*, p.99.

happens at all is known only by an authoritative revelation. As Thomas Aquinas (c.1225-74) put it: although justification is not in every respect miraculous, it is utterly mysterious in that it is brought about by a hidden divine power.[26] The movement of the free will is not, in any case, an unconditional requirement, since in the sacrament of baptism justification is normally bestowed on infants, who cannot exercise free will. (The same holds good for the justification of lunatics and morons).[27] And the movement of faith perfected by love, where it does occur, is likewise said to be 'infused': that is, not acquired but imparted supernaturally.[28]

Luther's conception is strikingly different. Once the word of God is identified as the definitive vehicle of grace, it no longer makes sense to describe the efficacy of the means of grace in terms of an *opus operatum*, or to define the corresponding subjectivity as the absence of impediment. A word is a means of communication. Unheard, it is spoken in vain, loses its character as word; it attains its finality only as it awakens attention, discernment, and commitment. For Luther, word and faith are correlative. He who believes, has. As the Augsburg Confession (1530) says: 'The Gospel teaches that we have a gracious God . . . provided we believe it'. (article 5). Here the form of grace as spoken word has changed the meaning of grace. In terms of scholastic theology, the accent has moved from habitual grace to *gratia increata*. In Luther's own terms: 'I take grace in the proper sense of the favour of God – not a quality of the soul'.[29] Not 'entirely', but up to a point, the process of justification has been moved into the domain of the psychologically transparent.

It would be absurd to suggest that the Reformers were out to eliminate the mystery from justification. But they did reduce the mystery by the fundamental thought that faith in God, as trust, is not brought about by a miraculous infusion, but by God's showing himself trustworthy. Philipp Melanchthon (1497-1560) makes the point especially clear in his *Apology of the Augsburg*

[26] *ST* IaIIae, q. 113, a.10.
[27] *Ibid.*, a.3.
[28] *Ibid.*, a.4.
[29] *WA* 8.106.10; *LW* 32:227.

Confession (1531). As long as sinners perceive God as angry, or vengeful, or exacting, they cannot love him. But it takes a sure word of God to convince them that he is not in fact angry; and the perception of God as not angry but merciful in Christ is just what is meant by faith, which hears and heeds the word – and so, which justifies. Grace comes as a word, a promise of mercy, proclaimed in the sermon and depicted in the sacraments; and the form of grace as spoken or visible word determines the form of the response as faith. While, then, faith and love for God are inseparable, faith must precede and love must follow.[30]

The drive towards psychological transparency in Reformation thought could also be illustrated many times over from John Calvin (1509-64), despite the care with which he affirms the mysterious activity of the Spirit as an invariable ingredient in every operation of grace. Take, for instance, his acute analysis of the process of repentance. Whereas Melanchthon spoke of faith as a part of penitence,[31] Calvin reversed the order, asserting that repentance is born of faith; and he gave a psychological reason: because no one can apply himself seriously to repentance unless he knows that he belongs to God, and no one is really persuaded that he belongs to God unless he has first recognized God's grace.[32] But we must dispense with further instances. Recent objections to religious 'subjectivism' require us next to make a distinction.

In making salvation depend on believing that one is saved, Luther, it has been argued, threw the religious subject back upon itself, precluding the self-abandonment to God in which genuine faith consists. This, surely, is a serious misrepresentation of Luther's faith, which was faith precisely in the word – single-minded contemplation of Christ (*intuitus Christi*). But although Luther's *faith* was not anthropocentric, he did present an early type of anthropocentric *theology* insofar as he made the believing subject the object of thought. And this is exactly what Schleiermacher held to be the task of *Glaubenslehre*: dogmatic

---

[30] See esp. *Apol.*, 4.110, 129, 295; 4.262, 337; 4.67, 174, 275-76; 4.141.
[31] *Ibid.*, 4.398.
[32] *Inst.*, 3.3.1-2.

propositions, in his view, arise out of logically ordered reflection on the utterances of the devout self-consciousness.[33] Such a conception of the theological task naturally accompanies, perhaps even is occasioned by, a highly personal variety of faith. But it remains a matter of methodological importance to recognize that one may make the religious subject the object of inquiry without making either the inquiry or the religion 'subjective' (in a pejorative sense). It is just such a theology that is a latent possibility in Luther and becomes an explicit programme in Schleiermacher.

In Schleiermacher's dogmatics, faith turns back upon itself *in reflection*, makes its own believing an object of thought. Christian existence, viewed from the inside, becomes the actual datum of theology; hence the Anselmian admonition on the title page of *The Christian Faith*: 'Unless you believe, you will not understand'. When a disputed point of doctrine lies before him, Schleiermacher can do no more than to appeal to the actual facts of the Christian consciousness – which means, in effect, the consciousness of the reader. At the same time, however, his constant endeavour is to make Christian experience intelligible as a matter of historical existence. Once the redeemer has made his appearance in history, his influence is disseminated in a purely natural way; and this means that his 'work' can be understood through comparison with the psychological impact of one person on another.[34] The supernatural has become a natural fact of history.[35] The entire process of conversion can accordingly be laid out on essentially psychological lines, the 'word' exercising the decisive role, as it did for the Reformers.[36]

The relationship between the old Protestantism and the new remains elusive. On the one hand, the lines of continuity cannot be restricted to the one theme (with two sides) that we have taken up from Troeltsch. Others have urged the kindred point, no less pertinent to the subject of historicizing, that Luther's faith in the

[33] Schleiermacher, *Gl.* §16 (*Zusatz*).
[34] See esp. *ibid.*, §100.2-3.
[35] *Ibid.*, §88.4.
[36] *Ibid.*, §108.5-6.

word of God alone gave him a sovereign freedom over against every attempt to objectivize the Gospel in doctrines and institutions, and so opened the way to historical reappraisals of them as products of time and circumstance. Still other lines of continuity have been missed, I believe, in the common failure to look at Schleiermacher's relationship with Calvin, which is no less interesting and important than his relationship to Luther.

On the other hand, the elements of discontinuity need to be uncovered, too. Perhaps most obvious, as far as theological method is concerned, is the distinction Schleiermacher drew between dogmatics and exegetical theology, which he did not regard as the substance of dogmatics, or even a part of it, but rather as an independent and co-ordinate discipline.[37] For now, however, all these further questions, important though they are, must be set aside and a suitably modest conclusion attempted.

Perhaps the right conclusion should be that the history of Protestantism discloses not one, but two 'paradigm changes' in Western theology: one that enthroned the word, and another that enthroned history. Troeltsch, however, perceived them as fundamentally one. Despite far-reaching changes that he discovered in the transition from *Alt-* to *Neuprotestantismus*, he believed that *Glaubenslehre*, the new dogmatics, could justly appeal to the subjectivizing of the idea of faith and revelation brought about, at least in principle, by Luther.[38] His belief turns out to be by no means fanciful. Schleiermacher himself was already persuaded that, in making dogmatics a matter of reflection on the data of Christian religiousness, he had Luther for his forerunner.[39] But whether or not the pedigree of *Glaubenslehre* can be so written that two changes are seen as one development, the profile of a distinctively modern approach to Christian theology begins to emerge.

Variations of the approach are possible, and distinctions within it are required if dogmatics is to be differentiated from other kinds of theological and religious inquiry. The course of theology in the

[37] *Ibid.*, §19 (*Zusatz*).
[38] 'Dogmatik', col.109.
[39] *Sendschr.*, p.16.

twentieth century has shown up some of its weaknesses or perils. But it no longer belongs to one church or one party. It has become, in some quarters, so much the commonly accepted approach that it is easy to forget how sharply it differs from conceptions of theology before the rise of the historical consciousness. In a word, it is not the explication of authoritative dogmas, nor the exegesis and systematizing of Scripture, but disciplined reflection on a historically given, historically mobile way of believing.

THE SOCIAL CONTEXT OF THE MODERN PARADIGM IN THEOLOGY: A CHURCH HISTORIAN'S VIEW

Martin E. Marty

Three Preliminary Considerations

1. Method

Historians hasten to their proper work, which is telling stories or sorts of stories.[1] Yet they must explain something of what they are about as they tell them. My method will be an historian's analogue to that of the explorer who provides an analogue within and for Edmund Husserl's philosophy. Husserl often saw himself as a wanderer in 'the trackless wilds of a new continent', where he had 'undertaken bits of virgin cultivation'.[2]

The point of comparison is not in pretensions to philosophical or historical discovery on my part. Exactly the opposite is the case. I shall adopt a naive 'common-sense' phenomenological approach to deal with what is familiar, taken for granted, and often overlooked. In a symposium on the modern paradigm in theology, it seems valid to pause here to examine the easily passed-over features. Jacob Burckhardt illumines this interest by reference to the past which is not easily accessible to historians:

---

[1] I employ 'historian' here in the sense which Hegel used it in reference to von Ranke: 'Da ist nur ein gewöhnlicher Historiker'. For preoccupation with 'story', see G.J. Renier, *History: Its Purpose and Method* (Boston, 1950), part one, I, II, 'The Story That Must Be Told' and 'Nothing but a Story'. '. . . If history is less than a story it cannot fulfil its social function, while if it is more it competes unnecessarily with other disciplines, speaks in an uncertain voice, and brings confusion rather than guidance'. (p.8, 36).

[2] Edmund Husserl, *Ideas: General Introduction to Pure Phenomenology* (New York, 1931), p.23.

'Everywhere in the past we encounter things which remain unexplained only because they were completely self-understood in their time and like all daily matters, were thought necessary to write down'.[3]

It is my good fortune to deal with the more recent past and its effects on the contemporary world, which is more nearly accessible. This means that I shall concentrate on features that have little to do with the substance of the modern paradigm; on elements that we take for granted: that theologians write books, that the university is their intellectual home, that they work within disciplines and so forth.

I am not unaware of the perceptual and philosophical difficulties inherent in such an approach. Maurice Natanson reflected on these in his work on Husserl: 'It is not a question of sharpening some special sense, of looking in some extraordinary corner of the mind, or of locating the philosopher's stone. What is called for, above all, is that each one of us examine his style of being in the world at the level of ordinary, common-sense life, so that the philosophical character of that level of experience be clarified . . . What, then, is it that the character of common-sense life is going to reveal which will make being in reality understandable? The direct answer is curious: the mark of common-sense life, the very essence of its style of being, is its failure to make itself an object for its own inspection . . . That common-sense life has a style, has an essential structure, is an insight that necessarily transcends the understanding of common-sense men . . . Yet it is exactly that absolute awareness of the style of our being in common-sense life which must be made an object for inspection if the datum of being in reality is to be gotten. And this is the most difficult of all tasks, largely because what it is that is required of us is exactly the problem. There is a built-in mechanism of protection in the stream of daily life which guards against this awareness; philosophy is an effort to crack this barrier'.[4]

[3] Jacob Burckhardt, *Griechische Kulturgeschichte*, ed. Rudolf Marx (Leipzig, nd), I, p.400. Translated and reproduced in Karl J. Weintraub, *Visions of Culture* (Chicago, 1966), p.270.

[4] Maurice Natanson, 'Existential Categories in Contemporary Literature', in *Literature, Philosophy and the Social Sciences* (The Hague, 1962), p.120.

Discussion of this difficulty will certainly preoccupy many during the symposium. I must leave it here prematurely on the way to the elements of story that I shall speak of as the development of 'the modern' in face of 'post-modern' tendencies.

2. A working definition of 'the modern'

Before a symposium whose participants will constantly be concerned with defining 'the modern', it seems folly to make any preliminary statement. Yet an historian, on the way to telling a sort of story about the modern paradigm, must at least begin to point to something, lest he is left only with 'the trackless wilds of a new continent'. The beginnings of tracks have been cut, and I can at least designate a choice among them.

The simplest and most naive way to do this is to take refuge in the fact that the modern is temporally located most recently in the chronological succession of periods and papers about them at the symposium. In such a case, the analogue is spatial 'mapping'. No one can go far at a symposium inspired by the work of people like Kuhn or Toulmin without reckoning with mapping.[5] In an intentionally ingenuous reminder, two experts on maps, Arthur H. Robinson and Barbara Bartz Petchenik, say: 'Everything is somewhere, and no matter what other characteristics objects do not share, they *always* share relative location, that is, spatiality; hence the desirability of equating knowledge with space, an intellectual space'.[6]

As with space, so with time. Objects like paradigms, books, professors, and disciplines, analogously, we might say, '*always* share relative location in time, that is temporality'. The symposiasts may content themselves therefore with dealing with

---

[5] See T.S. Kuhn, *The Structure of Scientific Revolutions* (Chicago, 1962), p.108; Stephen Toulmin, *The Philosophy of Science: An Introduction* (New York, 1960), pp.105-121, a discussion of 'Theories and Maps' in analogy to one another.

[6] Arthur H. Robinson & Barbara Bartz Petchenik, *The Nature of Maps: Essays Toward Understanding Maps and Mapping* (Chicago, 1976), p.4.

the modern paradigm in the first sense described by the *Oxford English Dictionary*: 'Being at this time; now existing'. They will have to smart over the ironically scourging lexicographical note which follows that definition: '*Obs. rare*'.

The second use is equally safe and less embarrassing: 'Of or pertaining to the present and recent times, as distinguished from the remote past', the past discussed in a preparatory symposium paper by Charles Kannengiesser. The third definition has a slightly more judgmental note: 'Characteristic of the present and recent times; new-fashioned; not antiquated or obsolete'.

To be content with the mere temporal location of the 'modern' could prove frustrating to symposium participants, who will need and may even welcome a number of substantive proposals about the meanings of modernity in religion and theology. The literature on this subject is vast; the schools are competitive; the criticisms of each are searching; and one should speak with considerable timidity and timorousness in selecting a definition. I am aware, for example, of the sometimes cautionary, sometimes devastating qualifications of the term in religious analysis by, for example, Lloyd I. and Susanne Hoeber Rudolph, who believe that modernity and tradition 'infiltrate and transform each other'; and by Mary Douglas, who attacks the assumption that 'moderns are utterly different from everyone else because of modernization'.[7]

Such criticisms are in order, but they may well affect nuances and sound a warning note rather than displace all reasons for designating *something* distinctive in the notion of the 'modern' in the social context of religion, theology, and changes of paradigm.

Rather than write a whole paper on the meaning of the modern and modernization, I shall confine myself to a single proposal. This summarizes one of a number of major alternatives in modernization theory – a strand with a lineage from Max Weber through Talcott Parsons to the generation of Thomas Luckmann,

---

[7] Lloyd I. Rudolph & Susanne Hoeber Rudolph, *The Modernity of Tradition* (Chicago, 1967), p.3 and *passim*; Mary Douglas, 'The Effects of Modernization on Religious Change', in *Daedalus*, III:1 (Winter, 1982), p.2.

Peter Berger, Robert N. Bellah, and others. Each of them offers his own refinements of the theory or protestations against being lumped together by historians who connect them. Though this approach is not a completely defensible definition of the modernization process and its effects, it strikes me as one which helps historians locate events as they go about telling their story.

The very fact that I 'choose' it illustrates an implication of the theory. Peter Berger reminds us that part of modernization is its fateful impulsion towards choice, *haeresis*. There is an 'heretical imperative'. Thus: 'In premodern situations there is a world of religious certainty, occasionally ruptured by heretical deviations. By contrast, the modern situation is a world of religious uncertainty, occasionally staved off by more or less precarious constructions of religious affirmations . . . For premodern man, heresy is a possibility – usually a rather remote one; for modern man, heresy typically becomes a necessity. Or again, modernity creates a new situation in which picking and choosing becomes an imperative'.[8]

Fortunately I am impelled by present circumstances to commit mere intellectual and not profound spiritual or theological heresy by choosing definitions of the modernization process. There is a condensation by John Murray Cuddihy: 'What, then, is this "modernization" process? [Its centre] is differentiation: the differentiation of home from job; the differentiation of political economy (Marx) into politics and economy; differentiation of the culture system from the personality and social systems; differentiation of economy from society (Weber, Parsons and Smelser); differentiation of fact from value, of theory from praxis; differentiation of art from belief.

'Differentiation is the cutting edge of the modernization process, sundering cruelly what tradition has joined. It splits ownership from control (Berle and Means); it separates church from state (the Catholic trauma), ethnicity from religion (the

---

[8] Peter L. Berger, *The Heretical Imperative: Contemporary Possibilities of Religious Affirmation (Garden City, 1974), p.28.*

Jewish trauma); it produces the "separated" or liberal state, a limited state that knows its "place", differentiated from society. Differentiation slices through ancient primordial ties and identities, leaving crisis and "wholeness-hunger" in its wake'.

Intellectually, Cuddihy said, the modernization process could be condensed into 'refinement'. 'Differentiation on the level of the culture system is the power to make *distinctions* between previously fused – *confused* – ideas, values, variables, concepts. Almost all intellectual interchange boils down to pointing out "distinctions" or "aspects" of a topic that have been obscured or neglected.'

I stress Cuddihy's definition in order to locate the modern paradigm between what must provisionally be coded as 'pre-modern' and 'post-modern' alternatives. In the pre-modern situation, there would be less differentiation, more 'wholeness', more 'confusion', less specificity, and less cutting of primordial ties.

In western Christendom the 'wholeness-hunger' characteristically takes two forms of seeking access to tradition. One has recourse to the Bible, particularly to the Hebrew Scriptures, where there is less differentiation on all levels. The other looks to the medieval age, with its presumed organismic society and universities where theology was queen and infuser. That both the Hebrew and medieval worlds and paradigms remain somehow available and accessible as traditions which, if we do not possess them, somehow possess us, shows how paradigms and their contexts remain as sedimentations in complex cultures and in human minds and behaviour.

Awareness of this feature will help prevent development of a sense that there is or can be a radical breach between the contexts of paradigms in a sequence of cultural unfoldings. Eugene Goodheart addressed this theme: 'The *tabula rasa* is a presumption of innocence. It is not the result of genuine discovery, for instance, that the Christian and classical traditions are no longer part of us. The enactments of our personality and character are involuntary, often compulsive. We are not free to choose what we are or even what we will do. [*Pace* Peter Berger and M.E.M.?]

We cannot simply wish away traditions that we have grown to dislike. The very dislike may be conditioned by the fact that they still possess us, if we do not possess them.'[9]

The 'wholeness–hunger' is not satisfied entirely by recovery of tradition through *ressourcement* or its counterfeit, nostalgia. Those weary of differentiation, pluralism, and choice, for a variety of motives project a post–modern, futurist, or ideological alternative. This may apply to the political order, cultural styles, and, as we shall see, religious life and theological expression. Cuddihy anticipates this; he calls it 'the antimodern thrust': "Demodernization, from Marx to Mao, is a dedifferentiation. In the Chinese Cultural Revolution, structural differentiation and the division of labor were denounced violently and explicitly and uprooted *as such* . . . Inward assent to the disciplines of differentiation, and the practice of its rites, may be viewed as the *paideia* of the West. "Ideology" is the name we give to the various resistance movements mounted to stem the onslaught of the differentiation process. Essentially, these movements are demodernizing, dedifferentiating, rebarbative'.[10]

At a conference in Jerusalem in 1974, I spoke of this impulse as '*retro-modern*', because it seeks to go 'backwards, back', but this was judged to be both a linguistic barbarism and an ideological judgment on ideologues who did not see themselves as trying to go backwards to anything; often representing revolutionary, messianic, utopian and millennial movements, they wanted to move forward.

Therefore I shall retreat to a more neutral term and speak of dedifferentiating, 'holistic' cultural or social contexts for paradigm development as being simply '*counter-modern*'. It appears 'against', or 'in return' against the modern as here defined. As such, it may represent the strongest political force in the world, in various socialisms, communisms, and the religious corollaries or justifications for these. Together these challenge what is left of the tenuous modern paradigm.

[9] Eugene Goodheart, *Culture and the Radical Conscience* (Cambridge, 1973), p.9.
[10] John Murray Cuddihy, *The Ordeal of Civility: Freud, Marx, Levi-Strauss, and the Jewish Struggle with Modernity* (New York, 1974) pp.9–11.

The social context of that paradigm has never been stable, of course. Bred into a culture of political freedom – one is 'compelled to be free',[11] or 'forced to be free' in the midst of religious diversity, theological pluralism and personal choice – there is an impulse for more freedom, richer diversity, wider pluralism, almost limitless choice. This tendency has been best documented in the writings of Peter Berger on heresy, Robert N. Bellah on religious evolution[12] and most notably, Thomas Luckmann on 'invisible' (because over-differentiated, over-specified, hence diffused, and utterly 'privatized') religion.[13]

I shall call this tendency to follow through the logic of modernity the *hyper-modern*, because it would go 'over, beyond, and over much, above measure' in respect to the kinetic and unstable modern synthesis. In politics and economics this stresses freedom of choice, as David Apter eloquently insisted in a chapter on Adam Smith and his heirs, 'Modernity as Choice'.[14] In religion there is an anti-communal thrust towards pure individualism and privatism, '*à la carte*' or 'do-it-yourself' religion. Then there would be as many religions as there are citizens. In theology the final logic would be, 'all theologians their own paradigm-makers'; as many paradigms as there are theologians.

The present snippets of a story will indicate several experiments or innovations that developed chronologically between *pre-modern* and *counter-modern* contexts and paradigms in social, ecclesial and intellectual worlds. Its roots may be in Greece and Rome; its development in certain medieval tendencies; and its first burst in Renaissance, and its second in Enlightenment humanism. Then came a flowering during the past two centuries, and almost immediately, a challenge from the de-differentiating post-modern ideologies and organizations of life. While facing this set of challenges, those who follow its story are also

---

[11] The terms are Winston White's and David Little's; see Cuddihy, *op.cit.*, 11.

[12] Robert N. Bellah, *Beyond Belief: Essays on Religion in a Post-Traditional World* (New York, 1970), pp.39-45.

[13] Thomas Luckmann, *The Invisible Religion: The Problem of Religion in Modern Society* (New York, 1967).

[14] David E. Apter, *The Politics of Modernization* (Chicago, 1965), pp.9 ff.

constantly beguiled or threatened by the further logic of its own hyper-modern impulses.

3. Towards a working definition of paradigm

Newcastle has sufficient coal and Tübingen symposia have too many experts on paradigms for an historian to make an original contribution. My story is in any case already too long postponed. In a spirit of not easily assuagable preparatory panic as I face this subject I shall resort to what we may think of as the Gary Gutting-edited, David Hollinger-cited, Margaret Masterman-provoked, T.S. Kuhnian-responsive footnote. I shall reproduce it literally: '10. One ostensibly friendly reader claimed to find twenty-one meanings for [the word paradigm] in *The Structure of Scientific Revolution*: Margaret Masterman. "The Nature of a Paradigm", in Imre Lakatos and Alan Musgrave, eds., *Criticism and the Growth of Knowledge* (Cambridge, 1970), 59–89. Kuhn has subsequently distinguished between two senses of "paradigm": (1) the "disciplinary matrix" consists of "the entire constellation of beliefs, values, techniques, and so on shared by the members of a given community", including (2) exemplars, "the specific, concrete puzzle-solutions which, employed as models or examples, can replace explicit rules on a basis for the solution of the remaining puzzles of normal science" '. See 'Postscript', 175, 182, 187.[15]

Professor Kuhn may have later second thoughts or explanations, but my story is already under way. All I have chosen to do is to comment on the social context of these 'disciplinary matrices' and 'exemplars' in any case.

This preparatory section of a preparatory paper has necessarily communicated in shorthand, and has relied on these condensed

---

[15] David A. Hollinger, 'T.S. Kuhn's Theory of Science and Its Implications for History' in Gary Gutting, ed., *Paradigms and Revolutions: Appraisals and Applications of Thomas Kuhn's Philosophy of Science* (Notre Dame & London, 1980), p.219.

theories. Perhaps it is excessively dependent and footnoted. This is the point for an admission about its genre of a sort once uttered by Nathaniel Micklem: 'I have written nothing learned or original or technical. I am a plagiarist, a popularizer, one of the *epigoni*: *dicitque mihi mea pagina, fur es.* I seem to myself to fall under the condemnation of Tristram Shandy as one of those who "for ever make new books, as apothecaries make new mixtures, by pouring only out of one vessel into another, and who are for ever twisting and untwisting the same rope!" '[16]

In order to compensate for inadequacies in the remainder of this paper, and in order to support its naive, common-sense, story-telling character, I shall try to be a pathfinder in the trackless terrain who relies as little as possible on those who have been before. These pointings and probes are neither fully documented nor fully substantiated.

Four Aspects of the Context: Outlines of the Modern and Post-Modern Stories

1. Theologians and books

If we can repeal our developed consciousness and pretend our way back to 'the trackless wilds' where we come across beings called theologians, one of the first things to notice and recall about moderns is that their paradigms come in the form of *books*.

The few great theologians who write no books but who excel in classroom or pulpit receive honours in the form of banquets or, more significantly, *Festschriften*. These are books by more 'productive' students – people who write books. They are lauded not as theologians but as teachers, prophets and living exemplars. They remain theologians *manqués*. Whoever writes histories of modern theology immediately prepares bibliographies. Those theologians who have extensive listings of books or who have

---

[16] Nathaniel Micklem, *The Theology of Politics* (London, 1941), p.ix.

produced one or more lasting books hold the honoured places.

There is no reason to think about this aspect of their role most of the time. It is one of those elements which we encounter but leave unexplained, as Burckhardt reminded us, 'because they were completely self-understood'. Yet the identification of those who fill theologian-like roles with book-writers, as moderns locate these objects, is ephemeral. Once upon a time there was reflection on the things of God, but there were not yet books. Most of the interpreters of vision and Word in the Hebrew Scriptures and the New Testament were not authors of scrolls or books. As for the great teachers: Socrates and Jesus taught but they did not write anything like books. The Messiah is not a scribe.

One day may come when the book will not continue to play a large part in determining paradigms in theology.

One need not be so abrupt or apocalyptic about the fate of books as the late (Herbert) Marshall McLuhan, author of books. His terse biography in *Encyclopaedia Britannica* climaxes with the line, 'He regrets the book as fated to disappear' because 'electronic disseminators of information upon styles of thinking and thought' are coming to dominate. Nor was would-be paradigm-breaker William Hamilton, a 'death-of-God' theologian precisely on time – he was premature when he described the moment: '. . . Theology . . . is changing its mode of communication. Until quite recently it was a solid, slow moving "book-discipline", and academic discipline in which most of the important material was published in hardcover books. This no longer seems to be the case . . . In this period of rapid theological change no satisfactory means of information-passing has been devised. Communication is by telephone calls, improvised luncheon meetings attended by people who have cut an important conference session, and letter-writing'.[17]

Yet the situation of the book and theology communicated through books is certainly changing. The 'disciplinary matrices'

[17] In Thomas J.J. Altizer & William Hamilton, *Radical Theology and the Death of God* (Indianapolis, 1966), p.4.

and 'exemplars' of recent centuries have ordinarily been conceived at book length. To be a theologian was, by definition, to be someone working on a single book of a multi-volume work on systematic theology or on one of its major problems. Theologians possessed or created the circumstances (leisure?) to read and write books. So long as their work was in the form of a classroom voice, it was the subject of discussion concerning reputations, but did not inspire commitment. So long as the project was conceived at article length, it was regarded only as a 'proposal'. One waited for the book-length development before taking on its implications.

The book and book-like information have not disappeared. Hundreds of thousands of books, thousands of them dealing with theology, appear around the world every year. One might see the book as threatened by the hyper-modernity that has come along with the information explosion. A new generation acquires and appraises data on the basis of electronic and computerized devices. which may or may not issue in 'print-outs'. These are themselves highly disposable and even visually ephemeral in form. Because of the high degree of specialization in the theological disciplines, the market for most books by all but a few seminal figures who take on generic themes, has become too small to remain economically viable. New forms of publishing which take advantage of less expensive technology have developed. Publishers can run off as few as a hundred copies of a book to meet a very limited and temporary demand. There is almost no chance that a work of this sort will be preserved, studied, cherished, and re-read the way in which 'standard' multi-volume books were. Just as general-market magazines have all but disappeared in most western nations, whereas newsletters for, say, left-handed female yacht-manoeuvrers thrive, so the budding theologian can step up to the computer, punch 'Liberation', 'Women', 'Black', and in seconds be made aware of the one article in an American decade that addresses the theme, 'Southern Lay Midwives as Ritual Specialists' by Molly C. Dougherty, in *Women in Ritual and Symbolic Roles*.

Differentiation, specificity, diffusion, refinement – all these characterize the new possibilities in new print technologies or electronic transmission. I bracket for the moment the change in the theologians' own concept of role when they spend their book-writing time on William Hamilton's telephone, at his improvised luncheon meetings, cut conference sessions, writing letters, doing the lecture circuit, or, paradigmatically, attending symposia on paradigms instead of staying home to read and write theology books.

From the opposite side comes not the death of books but a concentration on *The* Book, the *counter-modern* threat to modernity. From a variety of political or ecclesial motives, leadership appeals to the 'wholeness-hunger' of those weary with over-differentiated life, or coerces people (as we find the Maoist cultural revolutionists did) away from the possibilities of choice.

Modern ideology produces bookish societies, but the tendency is away from pluralism and towards the singularity of the one book. In the pseudo-religions that may go with communist political régimes, we have seen such a use of the writings of Marx or, better, the little red book of Chairman Mao. In clerisies and theocracies, for example in much of the Muslim world, the 'book' of an Ayatollah is privileged. Usually it is simply the Koran. In potent subcultures which place a high premium on uniformity, Christian 'fundamentalists', for example, whether in Reformed South Africa or evangelical North America, make claims for the Bible as the only revered book. In extreme cases they speak negatively about all books but the Bible.

Technologically, economically, politically, religiously, and in respect of status, conception, and the use of time, the concept of theology expressed through a moderate diversity of books is called into question by hyper-modern and counter-modern tendencies. This is not the time to speculate what the outcome of the push-and-pull of tensions will be. It is time to say that theological expression was reliant upon the stable, purchasable, book-length literary products of theologians in community within free societies. Those were books written by people whose vocation climaxed in reading and writing them. Now they represent a fragile, endangered species.

What happens to the book will have much to do with the form or cast and eventually, one must speculate, substance of theology.

2. Theological profession in the university

Virtually 'unexplained' and 'self-understood' and 'not . . . necessarily written down', because it was so obvious and taken for granted in 'the trackless wilds' we are pretending to come upon on the theological continent of modernity in the university. It was the normative locale of the professional theologian. Some observer has pointed out that 'who pays for the groceries' has much to do with what theology says and how it speaks. To over-simplify greatly: in the early church the bishops or overseers wrote and defined the 'exemplars'. In the Middle Ages monks developed the 'disciplinary matrices' in the cloister. In the modern world the theological tasks fall to the professors in the university and its corollaries.

The books in codex form began to replace the roll or scroll by around 400 CE. The university was developing by at least the twelfth century in Bologna and elsewhere. The modern book began to develop at the end of the Middle Ages with Johannes Gutenberg (c.1450). In Renaissance times the university moved towards its modern condition, beyond the *studium generale* towards specificity and differentiation of schools, professions and roles. The modern university is a post-Enlightenment development. Theology, proverbially no longer the university's 'queen' – it is hard to see whether anything else has become a queen – has fought for its place among schools, emphases and disciplines.

Of course, by no means all theologians work in universities. It has no formal place in developing societies where the state supports all the higher education and where there was never a great tradition of theology. In *counter-modern* societies where atheistic or non-Christian religious ideologies are privileged, the theological school may survive as a suffered guest and not as a privileged host. In pluralist *hyper-modern* societies where church and state have been highly differentiated, theology may face some difficulties in maintaining its place on legal grounds. Meanwhile, in private universities it is crowded from centrality by other social forces of 'secularization'. The critical mentality nurtured by the modern university in free societies calls into question the university's role in certain historic roles in respect to the community of faith.

For that reason a variety of seminaries, theological schools, underground institutes and the like have developed alongside and sometimes against the university. Yet university modes have remained normative. Most seminary theologians who seek academic respectability know that at scholarly gatherings their endeavours will be judged by the critical norms of the pluralist university or the ideology of the state sponsors more than by the expectations of the various faith communities. Most professors in the seminaries obtain their degree in universities. They send their most intellectually promising students into the universities, either as their true home or for necessary exile. Few theologians are bishops (which may not be the same as saying few bishops are theologians), and most monastics who are theologians studied at, teach in, or receive their norms from the university.

I am not equipped to comment close-up on theologians in the trackless university worlds of Europe, Asia or Africa, but I have data on the locus in North America. In a study completed in the 1970s, only 14 of the 558 professional theologians – 2.51% of the total – served in 'pastoral, executive, or editorial' positions outside the academy. 284, or 50.98%, of the total were employed in 'seminaries and theological schools', but many of the latter were university-based. 258 more, or 46.24%, made their living and pursued their paradigms in 'general college or university contexts', the true home of modern theological norms. If religious disciplines more loosely associated with theology were included, the percentage in 'general college or university contexts' would be much higher.

Thor Hall, sampler and collator, writes: ' . . . systematic theology in North America is considered primarily an academic discipline, the prerogative of scholars; thus, just as the church involvements of active ministers tend to work against their participation in the discipline of systematic theology, the academic preoccupations of systematic theologians tend to prevent them from serious interaction with the ongoing ministry of the churches. The situation is an unhealthy one in several respects . . . '[18]

Hall says that 'the final step and crowning point of the systematic theologian's education', the graduate programme, 'leading to that ultimate distinction which is often referred to by a curiously ghoulish phrase, 'the terminal degree', occurs chiefly in university contexts. Indeed, five programmes (Union-Columbia, Chicago, Pontifical Gregorian, Yale, and Catholic University of America) account for 40.96% of the whole sample. The Gregorian and Catholic University of America may seem, more than a generation ago, to have retained some of the aspects of a seminary because they did not yet represent modern university pluralism. What, then of the Protestants? In the American Protestant world, Union-Columbia, Chicago and Yale, accounted for 46.89% of all Protestant systematic theologians.

The modern university has been challenged from two directions. The *hyper-modern* institution is the natural attraction in democratic technological societies, where differentiation and specificity lead to a diffusion of interest. Theology may be allowed to survive, but it is an arbitrary, individualistic, 'chosen' pursuit which lacks privilege or distinction. The complaint that the modern university has found theology irrelevant has been uttered with wearying frequency. Often this is done against the background of the presumed relevance of other disciplines to each other or to other specialities within additional disciplines, and to still other specialities within still additional disciplines. Many analysts of the modern university or multiversity relish this situation. Others see it as a chaos that breeds 'hunger for wholeness'. A few wail poetically or prophetically. Thus Arthur

---

[18] Thor Hall, *Systematic Theology Today: The State of the Art in North America* (Washington, DC, 1978), pp.37-39, 60.

Cohen: 'Theology need not be a pretentious discipline, it need not usurp the sciences, dismiss natural philosophy, nor overturn logic. It is a modest discipline founded, to be sure, upon an immodest history. Once theologians ruled the sciences and held court in universities, whereas presently they are hidden away in drafty seminaries and muster disciples from the thin readership of lugubrious journals. The unhappy condition of theology has undoubtedly made theologians snappish and defensive, but we can ill afford to forget that whereas theologians are human their object of concern remains God'.[19]

In the *hyper-modern* university setting, the community of faith which provides the language for theology bears no privilege and may even be stigmatized by those who interpret this theology in the academy. The theological voice in each case depends on the character, charisma, eloquence and individual achievements of the private intellectual who does the uttering or, better, the book-writing. Otherwise it is lost among the disciplines that range from animal husbandry to zoology, with intermediate stops at welding, cosmetology, and many variations of preparation for business professions.

The situation has provoked *counter-modern* reactions, where de-differentiation, usually in the form of ideology, has been held at a premium. The university institution still exists. But whether by the choice of revolutionary students, by the régime, or by a prevailing school of thought, pluralism is not permitted. The critical temper which characterized the modern university is devalued. In the twentieth century totalitarian régimes of left and right have permitted universities to live on, but have co-opted, sequestered, harassed or eliminated theologians. Many of these régimes have engendered their own theologies, from 'German Christian' through 'Maoist'. In clerisies, the university itself is downgraded as part of a reaction against technology and pluralism. Yet it may somehow survive and include some curricular equivalent to theology. In such cases privileged

<hr />

[19] Arthur A. Cohen, *The Natural and the Supernatural Jew: An Historical and Theological Introduction* (New York, 1962), p.301.

theology develops in a coerced and monolithic situation. In revolutionary societies, the 'theology' of the university is of a singular character – choice by the winner.

In ultra-conservative Catholicism there have been calls for repeal of the conditions by which modern universities developed, and calls for a new coerced form of coherence. Protestant fundamentalism, in its most suspicious forms long wary of the university and its assumptions and settings, still resists the academy. Sometimes, under counter-modern pressure, this school of thought builds its own institutions of higher learning and then seeks to perpetuate its credal ideology and infuse it into various disciplines.

The modern university, though always fragile and flawed, has long been the matrix for the disciplinary matrices of modern theology, the exemplary base for developing exemplars. To its fate will be tied much of the fate of future paradigms in theology. Its jeopardy, transformation and possible passing can be ignored only with peril by those who concentrate only on the substance of the paradigms, or the cognitive dimensions of theology at the expense of context or setting.

3. Theology located in the humanistic disciplines

The book and the university were not invented in modern times but became more differentiated after the medieval period of rooting and early development. Disciplines are not modern inventions, and the location of theology in the humanistic disciplines is not new. That the liberal arts curriculum in the Middle Ages was already highly differentiated is clear from some charts prepared by G.R. Evans [see illustration][20]

In that period, Christian theology was the queen and putative integrator of the curriculum. It lost that status and something new occurred with the rise of the modern, unintegrated or theologically unintegrated university. Theology itself was

[20] G.K. Evans, *Old Arts and New Theology: The Beginning of Theology as an Academic Discipline* (Oxford, 1980), pp.15–16.

becoming internally more specific (and, paradoxically, more diffuse) and differentiated. Yves Congar pointed this out in a chapter on 'New Specializations' and the collapse of the ancient unity of theology: 'With many, the effort to keep abreast of the new demands works out not in the direction of preserving unity of thought but in that of specialization and division. The fact is general and characteristic of the modern epoch at the end of the sixteenth century. This is the collapse of the medieval synthesis. But not everything is 'collapse' in the advance which we are going to analyze. And the fact of specialization, which is quite manifest, is in great part the normal and beneficial consequence of the new acquisitions which constitute progress'.

In the new period there are new epithets for specializations: 'biblical, Catholic, Christian, dogmatic, fundamental, moral, mystical, natural, polemic, positive, practical, scholastic, speculative . . . etc'.[21]

THE OLD DISCIPLINES

Trees of knowledge

A modification: *aliquando physica large accipitur aequipollens theoricae*

[21] Yves M.J. Congar, OP, *A History of Theology* (Garden City, 1968), p.165.

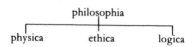

Hugh of St. Victor: *Didascalicon, Epitome Dindimi in Philosophiam*

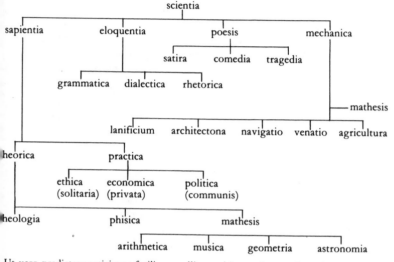

Ut vero predictas particiones facilius recolligas subiectam intuere formulam (p. 72.28–9).
Ysagoge in Theologiam

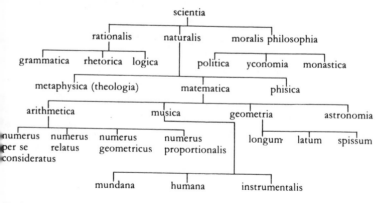

Dialectica Monacensis

Toulmin has reflected philosophically on what disciplines have meant in the development of modern science.[22] Our task is to notice that these disciplines in theology have risen to meet new demands. They have grown more complicated in recent centuries for a variety of reasons. Not the least of these is the growth in numbers of churches and denominations, each of which poses distinctive issues for theological inquiry against the background of different traditions. The larger Christian community has become more aware of national, racial and ethnic differences in the 'ecology' of theology. People speak at times of 'feminist' or 'black' or 'Indian' Christian theologies as separate species of intellectual formulation. There are various philosophical schools and methods. People in the discipline of theology discourse *with* cognates elsewhere in the university: church historians with historians, historians of religion with anthropologists, moral theologians with philosophical ethicists, and the like. This conversation has often contributed to a dispersal of energies and further loss of coherence in theological faculties.

The fundamental shift in the move to the modern occurred when theology was located not only as a discipline among the disciplines but as a humanistic discipline in the humanities. I do not know in detail how this shift translates into all the languages or curricula of the Christian West, but there is an almost fateful play on words in Anglo-American usage, as reflected in an essay that plays on the irony. Thus Ernest Gellner: 'What is "humanist culture?" Essentially, culture based on literacy. All human society and civilization presupposes language as such: but humanist or *literate* culture is not co-extensive with all human civilization. It is distinguishable from illiterate "tribal" culture on the one hand, and from more-than-literate scientific culture on the other. The term "humanist" is of course unfortunate, and survives from the days when a concern with mundane, "human" literature was primarily distinguished, not from either illiteracy or science, but from theological, divine concerns. But for contemporary

---

[22] Stephen Toulmin, *Human Understanding: The Collective Use and Evolution of Concepts* (Princeton, NJ, 1972), chapters 2, 3 on 'Intellectual Discipline', pp.133–260.

purposes, it is the literacy, and not its mundane or extra-mundane orientation, which matters. "Humanist" concerns now embrace the divine. (Both speak the same language.)'[23]

Located as theology came to be in the humanities, it was by 'positive' humanistic criteria – literacy, historical and philosophical – that it came to judge itself and be judged. The newly prevalent style was Cartesian, critical, isolated, individualistic.

Today disciplines become ever more specific, differentiated, and 'refined' in what I have described as a *hyper-modern* situation. The demands and attractions in the field of theology are now so complex and alluring that the conventional disciplines cannot contain them. At my university there have been inventions of 'Religion and Literature', 'Religion and Psychological Studies', 'Ethics and Society', and there have been corollaries to these elsewhere.

The humanities no longer serve as a simple boundary. William Clebsch, an historian, when discussing religion in the university curriculum, sees it not on the continent of the humanities or the social sciences but as a kind of 'isthmus'. Numerous liberation or political theologians, Gregory Baum among them, are frustrated by the character of modern philosophy or by the small social yield from dialogue connected with it. They have begun to argue that sociology and other social sciences provide better partners. Religion and theology in their specificity have become so refined and diffuse they seem to be everywhere and thus, in a way, are 'nowhere'. The definitions of religion as broadened by anthropologists like Clifford Geertz extend so far into the network of general symbol systems that they, too, include few limits. There are almost as many theological disciplines as there are theologians, and these are located all over and beyond the curriculum.

Concurrently, the *counter-modern* trend has developed. It is part of the 'hunger for wholeness' in intellect or spirit, or the drive for

---

[23] Ernest Gellner, 'The Crisis in the Humanities and the Mainstream of Culture', in J.H. Plumb, ed., *Crisis in the Humanities* (Harmondsworth, 1964), p.71.

uniformity in civil or ecclesial order. Its advocates speak with impatience of refined and diffuse disciplines as being luxuries of individualism and pluralism. They are not capable of helping meet the new demands of public or churchly order.

Most of these appeals for a single theology and a single method tend to be calls for the repeal of the Cartesian spirit; a return to a pre-critical stage, but to one enhanced with means of coercing uniformity. The demands come from circles characterized by tribalism, racial or national interest, partisan causes, or ecclesiastical recidivism. Political and Christian revolutionary or fundamentalist factions alike show impatience over differentiation and pluralism. As one example in the political sphere, Robert Heilbroner, a socialist historian, envisages the decline of business civilization. With it has come a wearying but futile impulse by free moderns to protect choice at the expense of inspiring social morale. What would take its place? '. . . I suspect that a major force for the transformation of business civilization will be a new religious orientation, directed against the canons and precepts of our time, and oriented toward a wholly different conception of the meaning of life and a mode of social organization congenial to the encouragement of that life.

'What sort of religious orientation might this be? From our prior argument, a high degree of political authority will be inescapable in the period of extreme exigency we can expect a hundred years hence. This augurs for the cultivation of nationalist, authoritarian attitudes, perhaps today foreshadowed by the kind of religious politicism we find in China. The deification of the state, whatever we may think of it from the standpoint of our still-cherished individualist philosophies, seems therefore the most likely replacement for the deification of materialism that is the unacknowledged religion of our business culture . . . What is crucial in the statist "religion", as I foresee it, is the elevation of the collective and communal destiny of man to the forefront of public consciousness, and the absolute subordination of private interests to public requirements'.[24]

[24] Robert Heilbroner, *Business Civilization in Decline* (New York, 1976), pp.119-20.

Universities and churches would be subsumed in such an arrangement. Demands for uniformity of thought and method would mean the abolition of excessively discrete disciplines of free inquiry.

European scholars may not have experienced the *counter-modern* ecclesial attempt to co-ordinate learning by abolishing most disciplines. On American soil this kind of fundamentalism has expressed itself in the development of 'Bible Institutes' or 'bible colleges' which abolish most of the humanities and social sciences. They permit access to what is left of their disciplines purely instrumentally. One learns language for the practical purpose of reading the Bible, not Goethe or Dante or Shakespeare. Sometimes revanchist post-Vatican II Catholicism speaks in similar tones in defence of 'the scholastic method' and against 'the university approach' in theology.

4. Between privatism and total community

The principle that results from my observation or story is becoming clear. The modern paradigm developed in locations and settings between *hyper-modern* differentiation and *counter-modern* differentiation. There is no point in multiplying examples endlessly. Yet one more illustration or test case is apt because it deals with the specifically Christian communal context in which theology occurs. I shall elaborate on this briefly.

As suggested in a phrase (part 3, above), the variety of confessions and ecclesial communities, particularly after and as a result of the Protestant Reformation but also impelled by proliferating Catholic religious orders, contributed to theological differentiation. The modern discussion of pluralism in theology elaborates on this tendency. It has become especially acute as a problem in Catholicism because of increased freedom for theologians to pursue various paradigms after Vatican II and in all Christianity in an age of inter-religious and ecumenical activity and the stimuli afforded by the mass media.

Modern theology, along with its ancestors, was poised

'between Athens and Jerusalem'. That is, theologians were expected to bring the learning and critical mentality of the academy to the faith community. They also tried to bring the understanding of the faith community's needs and interests into the community of critical inquiry. If this was a tense place to be, there was a long precedent for it. Early Christian theology knew the tension, which is reflected in the Pauline writings in the New Testament, where the Jews are scandalized and the Greeks seek wisdom in the face of the cross.

The Renaissance and the Enlightenment, which were stages in what historians often call 'the secularization of the West', emphasized the tension. Some in both communities despaired of the possibility of a theology located between and in the university and the believing community. Obscurantist movements in the Church counselled a withdrawal from and the shunning of the academy. Much of modern pietism, both Catholic and Protestant, generated such an ethos. Meanwhile, the secular academy tended to rule out all presuppositions of the faith communities. Its advocates, on critical terms in positivist moods, suggested that it could transcend all commitments or assumptions beyond the purely empirical. Modern theological paradigms were worked out near this creative juncture.

As with the other three illustrations, in this case we see opposing pressures at work today in the context and setting where paradigms emerge. On the one hand, to balance the extreme differentiation of the academy to the point where it sees the disintegration of community there, is a final extension of the logic of one kind of Protestant or many kinds of Enlightenment individualism. This may be seen as the *hyper-modern* direction so well chronicled by Luckmann and others who speak of 'privatism' in post-industrial religion. The end result is what Luckmann called *The Invisible Religion*, still present but so diffuse, so unsupported by social forms, that its boundaries are elusive. In effect, there can be as many religions as there are believing or behaving subjects. Berger, an advocate of 'mediating structures' like neighbourhoods, church and school, in effect 'threw in the towel', or counselled making a virtue of necessity, in his post-communal book on modern choice, *The Heretical Imperative*.

This is not the place fully to document the *post-modern* or *hyper-modern* trend towards privatism and autonomous individualism in religion. Suffice it to say that western Catholicism has joined Protestantism in producing an 'alumni association' of people who are selectively and individually responsive to symbols of Christian reminiscence. But just as others who are distanced from community take no part in the communal life of worship, joint activity and the like, so the theologian turns philosopher of religion. If theology by definition works with the language of the believing community, in its emergent form this language is ever more individualized. Theologians take little responsibility for seeing that language is socially revitalized. Each day they, like moderns in literary and other arts, are busy generating a private symbol-system. This is hard on paradigm-development, because paradigms have emerged as exemplars, and in disciplinary matrices not only of the academy but of corollary communities. Among these are political science and the political community, economics and the commercial sector, and so on. Individualism and privatism in religion cause the language of theology, or a language for theology, to be ever more arcane, subjective and 'heretical'.

It would be wrong in this and every other case to see the over-specified or diffuse trend in isolation from the opposite trend, the *counter-modern*. Here the 'hunger for wholeness', whether born of weariness of pluralism, the search for revolutionary or regimented power, or psychological cravings for wholeness, comes into play. We have regularly seen this impulse in various tribalisms, fundamentalisms, revolutionary demands for monolithicity within a cause or, at worst, totalitarianisms.

The 'theologian' within communities as diverse as those marked by Nazi, Soviet, Maoist and Muslim symbol-systems never need ask what are the boundaries of the permissible, or whether he or she dare step over certain methodological bounds or prescriptions. Here all is de-differentiation: The Führer, commissar, party chairman or Ayatollah is the generator of the system and the theologian is the custodian or reinforcer. In any case, the threat to the modern matrix of paradigm-development is as vivid and real, and perhaps numerically stronger, in the *counter-modern* than in the *hyper-modern* script.

Preparatory conclusion

If my elements of a story of the modern resolution and what might follow it have any validity, they can be carried in other directions as we pursue the setting or context of paradigm-development. Clearly, our particular pictures of the book, the university, the discipline and the community, emerge as intensified trends from roots that go back at least to medieval times. *There is no reason to envisage the end of the modern in every aspect and detail: it is likely to leave its sediment. Super-individualists weary of over-specialization adopt moderate de-differentiating stances during voluntary searches for tradition and community. Totalitarian and fundamentalist régimes and sub-cultures may generate itches that new generations scratch:* witness the post-Maoist reactions to the ideologically totalist 'Cultural Revolution', whose height of conformity was in Maoist 'theology'. At this point I am concerned chiefly to notice the datedness, the time-and-place-boundedness of the modern emergence.

To some this function of the historian is comforting. After all, Christian theology antedated the modern forms of book, university, discipline and community, so there is no reason to believe it cannot outlive them as it pursues new settings and paradigms. To others it is disturbing, since it portends the disruption of a context that has become familiar if never wholly congenial. One may attend a symposium on paradigms and find something haunting and hollow about discussions of cognitive and methodological elements which are somehow connected with the forms and ideas that accompany a particular and passing milieu.

In a comment on America which applies to much of the western culture with which Christian theological paradigms have so often been webbed, Langdon Gilkey speaks of a 'myth' as I have of a context for theology. His is a myth of progress, of Enlightenment rationality, of scientific and technological forwardness and democratic increase. 'The sciences, the social sciences, and the humanities understand their role and worth – and large parts of their methods – on its basis; it represents the one common creed of our academic life'. But, Gilkey says, it is this 'myth, and with it much of the substance of our cultural life, [that] has been disintegrating around us. It is,' he goes on to suggest, 'the disintegration of this *secular* myth – not that of the traditional Christian *mythos* – that constitutes the present religious crisis'.[25]

Analogously, the setting for that *mythos*, symbolized here by forms of the book, university, disciplines and community, is disintegrating or developing beyond present forms. Modern Christian theology has expended energy being or becoming 'relevant' to that *mythos* and in that setting. If the *mythos* is disintegrating, so for some similar and more independent reasons, is that context. Awareness of such a change should have much to do with what we say and how we think about 'disciplinary matrices' and 'exemplars' for tomorrow.

[25] Langdon Gilkey, *Society and the Sacred: Toward a Theology of Culture in Decline* (New York, 1981), pp.23-24.

THE SYMPOSIUM

I. INTRODUCTORY PERSPECTIVES

A NEW PARADIGM FOR THEOLOGY?
INTRODUCTORY REMARKS

Jerald Brauer

Our subject for this conference is cast in the form of a question: 'A new paradigm for theology?' That question carries a variety of implications. Undoubtedly each conference participant brings a certain 'pre-understanding' to the question. The adjective 'new' might imply that paradigm has been, in the past, an adequate tool for interpreting the basic shifts that have occurred in Christianity. 'New paradigm' might also imply that the very use of paradigm is something new in an effort to understand what has happened to theology.

Though there is considerable justice in the criticism levelled against Thomas Kuhn for his use of paradigm and paradigm change to account for the basic shifts that have occurred in the history of science, he did open a lively debate that has considerably advanced our understanding of the problem, and he even compelled critics to take account of historical, cultural and social factors. He both broadened the discussion and forced it to become more refined and particularized. It is clear from the conference papers that this group has not literally adopted Kuhn's concept in an attempt to apply it unimaginatively to the modern Christian situation. When Küng and Tracy proposed the topic, it was intended only to provoke discussion and to invite analysis from a fresh and possibly more fruitful perspective.

The conference begins with the assumption that Christianity has undergone a series of especially radical changes in the last century and a half; that it is still in the midst of those changes; and that something new is emerging that is both in continuity with its past and yet is reaching out in new directions. Vast changes have occurred since the Reformation epoch. To contemporaries the sixteenth century seemed a revolutionary age, a massive break with the Christian past, but our present age views it as a period of relative stability and continuity in contrast with today.

Precisely this shift elicits serious efforts at self-interpretation because we do not know where we are going unless we know where we have come from and where we are. Several factors reveal the radical difference between our epoch and that of the Reformation, which demands fruitful modes of interpretation and explanation. I shall focus on only three of those factors, each of which, in its own way, and all together point towards that basic shift.

The first is the massive presence of pluralism in the modern world and in all forms of Christianity today. It is present within each confession, church or denomination of Christendom. Pluralism is the self-conscious recognition within a tradition that though that tradition is shared by all members of a particular community, the way it is interpreted, experienced and analyzed varies even within that group. Some admit that fact grudgingly, and do everything possible to control or even eliminate it. For others, pluralism is truth and practice of a tradition in the face of inevitable finite efforts to understand, appropriate and articulate that tradition.

To a greater or lesser degree, all Christian groups today share the modern situation in which they live and the resources and the methods they use to understand and to articulate that faith. In each Christian group there is a wide spectrum of interpretation and even practice seldom encountered until the last hundred years. Most churches and denominations today have within them representatives who could be classified as fundamentalistic, conservative, moderate, liberal or radical. Vatican II demonstrated how diverse the options of theological interpretation and changing religious practice were within Roman Catholicism. Stereotypes concerning the rigidity of 'the others' as seen from within one's own theological circle have long since broken down. Confessions and denominations still differ profoundly from one another, but all share a common pluralism which they cannot ignore or deny.

If pluralism marks even the inner life of the churches, it also defines the situation between them. Pluralism in the post-Enlightenment period is something new in the history of Christianity both for the inner life of the churches and the relations between them. Christians no longer want to destroy one another in the name of faith, to ignore one another, or to belittle each other. In 1950 nobody believed that within one decade a Roman pontiff would refer to Protestants as separated brethren. In the 1950s Protestant denominational seminaries were reading scholars from all Protestant confessional traditions, but no one was reading Catholic scholars. Today, Lonergan, Schillebeeckx, Rahner and Tracy are all read in Protestant seminaries and Bultmann, Tillich, Barth, Eliade and Ricoeur are all read in Catholic theological institutions. Careful painstaking efforts at dialogue go on without interruption between various Protestant churches, and between them and the Orthodox communities, while Roman Catholicism is engaged in dialogue with Orthodoxy and most major Protestant confessions.

Pluralism is not determined by indifference to important beliefs and practices. It takes seriously the variety and interpretation of basic Christian tradition in an effort to find grounds for mutual respect and acceptance while not excluding differences. Pluralism is encountered at all points – it includes the institutional life as to how the Christian body or bodies are to be organized or administered. It involves both the specific doctrines held by Christians and the methods and ways by which they seek to analyze, interpret and organize those doctrines. It embraces the way Christians should act both in their personal life and in the public order of which they and their churches are a part. Even the very forms in which Christians worship and express their essential piety exhibit this same pluralism.

A second factor that radically sets off the contemporary situation is that Christianity finds itself in a quite new situation in relation to other religions. Christianity has always stood in a special relationship to the Judaism from which it was born. Unfortunately, Christianity has had a deplorable record with regard to its parent. If Judaism was both father and mother to

Christianity, it has sought in an Oedipal way to slay its father and enslave its mother.

Vatican II symbolized the beginning of a new relationship with our Jewish brethren, but it is only just started. The fact that numerous Christians now call into question every effort to missionize Jews reflects a new understanding between Christianity and Judaism. Granted the problems that remain, there is a more serious effort today on the part of each to understand the other than has ever existed in past history.

The relation of Christianity to the world's great religions has also changed drastically. In 1893 the World's Congress of Religions signalled that a new relationship existed, but it was built on Enlightenment principles that sought to deny the historicity and peculiarity of each religion in an effort to affirm a set of abstract ethical principles that all held in common. It exhibited an openness and friendliness of the religions towards each other, but it did not produce serious dialogue between them. With the passing of western imperialism, the rise of new and the rebirth of older national states, the world's other great religions experienced a rebirth. Even Christian missions are undergoing a radical assessment.

In this new situation, Christianity and the other great religions of the world are now open to serious dialogue. Those religions find themselves in a world situation identical with or at least very similar to our own. All are confronted with the powerful forces of the modern world that press relentlessly on them. Within each religion there are groups that absolutely refuse any dialogue: for example, the extreme fundamentalists within Christianity or the Shi'ites within Islam. However, within all religions there are now those who recognize that the moment has come to engage seriously in an effort not only to understand each other but also, through that, to understand themselves better. As the late Paul Tillich stated in his final lecture on the relation of systematic theology to the history of religions, all participants enter this dialogue so that they can be 'open to spiritual freedom both from one's own foundation and for one's own foundation'. The pluralism we face within the various Christian churches and between them also prevails with regard to other religions.

A third factor that marks the radicality of our epoch as against its immediate past is the question of the viability of religion itself. There is probably more awareness of and writing on this issue than in regard to any other problem of our age. Whether one uses the term 'secularization' or 'the impact of modernity', probably no epoch in history has thought more and written more about the demise of religion and the death of God than this one. It is a truism to state that since the Catholic and Protestant Reformation there has been a massive change in people's attitudes to inherited Christian beliefs, practices and institutions. Nowhere has this change been more prevalent than in the attitudes and judgments of the intellectual and cultural élite.

It is difficult to determine if this marks an effort to reaffirm a deeper, more profound religiousness, or if it signifies an effort to kill all the gods, even the sacred itself. In his profound analysis of the nature of religion in *The Sacred and Profane*, Eliade said that modern man would never be satisfied until he had killed the last god. If there are two modes of being in the world, two existential situations, one sacred and one profane, the modern world is marked more by the second mode than the first.

In recent times the way in which the Christian churches and other religions of the world understand themselves and relate themselves to the cosmos has been largely determined by this fact. Perhaps the increasing spread of the profane mode of living in the cosmos is one of the primary factors driving the world's religions towards serious dialogue. However, this must not become a concern to establish a united front to defend the sacred as against the profane. Rather, it ought to be the occasion for serious exploration of what it means for religions to represent the sacred mode in the contemporary world as against a profane mode. Only in that way can religion be honest with itself and its situation, so that it is renewed in respect of the sacred in order to serve humanity. The very presence of this problematic situation is the third factor that sets us off from the age of the Reformation and compels us to seek an interpretation to help us understand ourselves in our situation.

The complexity of this situation and our contemporary efforts to understand it moved Küng and Tracy to suggest experimenting with paradigm analysis as a more satisfactory mode of explanation. It is to be used as a heuristic tool open to modification and even rejection. It represents an effort to combine the intellectual dimensions of the formulation of Christian doctrine with social, historical, cultural and imaginative dimensions. From the planning stages this conference was viewed as a trial balloon to see if the approach works.

If this conference fulfils our expectations, we hope to hold additional international conferences to focus attention on the problem of paradigm or model shift and its consequences for Christianity and for religion today. Perhaps we shall require additional conferences for Christian theologians. It is our hope that this conversation will reflect sufficient mutual understanding of the basic issues confronting Christianity today so that even in our diversity we can work toward a consensus of understanding. Then we shall be ready to take the next step. Each time an appropriate volume should indicate whence we have come, where we are, and what the next step should be.

When we are ready, as quickly as possible we should bring into the discussion representatives of Judaism, and later those of other religions. If we focus on a common issue such as paradigm, or a model in terms of which we can all better interpret our respective situations, we shall probably make greater progress in mutual understanding than if we deliberately set out to focus on the latter.

All religions in the world today face the same context in which they live and understand themselves. They have experienced this differently and at a different pace, but that in itself is part of the discussion. A series of questions awaits us. Great care will have to be exercised in carefully preparing the topics and the limits for discussion. Perhaps a paradigm or model approach would provide the point of departure to enable representatives of the various religions to avoid a fatuous good-will approach or an anti-historical, abstract analysis. The purpose of our discussions is neither to seek unification of the various religions nor to convince other groups of the superiority of our own position. It is to exemplify a mutual search for self-understanding in the midst of a complex world which impinges upon all people, even though in varying ways. With such an approach, religions could learn from one another, discover considerably more about themselves, and genuinely begin to respect other traditions.

Finally, it is our hope and purpose that, as quickly as possible, we will be able to bring into future conferences younger representatives, and men and women of various races and religions with a special responsibility for the future. It is not sufficient for senior scholars alone to dialogue. It is necessary to involve creative, promising younger scholars in their formative stage as they too wrestle with these issues of great import. We hope that this Tübingen conference marks only the beginning of an ongoing process of analysis and construction of religious understanding in confrontation with the modern world.

WHAT DOES A CHANGE OF PARADIGM MEAN?

Hans Küng

It was not originally my intention to speak at the opening of this symposium. But, as one of its initiators – and with the agreement of my colleague Professor David Tracy of the University of Chicago Divinity School – I am glad to have this opportunity of explaining to you, who have come from all over the world, why we have arranged this symposium. I shall try to convey to you the vision of the matter that has, so to speak, impelled us.

Let me put your minds at rest about one possible anxiety. This symposium is not going to develop a rigid, uniform, monolithic, single paradigm of theology and the church. Still less will it force any such paradigm on anybody. On the contrary, we are convinced that today, as in the past, paradigms of theology and the church (always seeing the two as a single whole) inevitably contain a *plurality* of divergent schools, diverging intellectual trends and, indeed, diverging theologies. This has always been an expression of creativity and vitality, though it has also been a source of conflict and strife.

But we have not come here from all over the world mutually to endorse the well-known fact that there are divergencies, differences and dissonances in the sphere of theology. At this symposium we should direct our minds to what is deeper and more fundamental than that, so that we can pierce through the divergent theologies to common ground. This is especially required in view of the critical condition of theology, church and society today. A glance at history will show what I mean. *Historia docet.* If, as Kuhn maintains, this is true even of the natural sciences, then it of course applies even more to theology and the church.

I have learnt a great deal from the preparatory historical papers: Charles Kannengiesser on Origen and Augustine; Stephan Pfürtner on Aquinas and Luther; Brian Gerrish on early Protestant dogmatics and modern Protestant 'representations of faith'; and Martin Marty on the social context of the modern theological paradigm. All this has stimulated me to try to *periodize* the paradigm change in theology and the church. For if we look at church history and the history of theology we shall see the following:

– Although theologians such as Irenaeus, Clement and Origen, Tertullian and Cyprian, Athanasius and the Cappadocians varied greatly in their theological approach, in the solutions they tried to find, and in the conclusions they drew, yet – seen in retrospect – they were nonetheless united by 'an entire constellation of beliefs, values, techniques, and so on, shared by the members of a given community' (community here meaning that of theologians and that of the church). It was the constellation belonging to their own time, totally different from the apocalyptic-eschatological constellation of the earliest Christian community, which consisted originally of Jewish Christians.

– Although (inspired by Augustine) Anselm and Abelard, Aquinas and Bonaventure, Scotus and Ockham took methodologically different paths, and arrived at partly different, indeed irreconcilable, substantial conclusions, yet they all reflected the fundamental interpretative model of their own medieval era; and this model differed essentially, not only from the early Christian apocalyptic model, but also from the interpretative framework of the Greek and early Latin Fathers.

– Although Luther, Zwingli and Calvin were at theological loggerheads, they were united by precisely what was irreconcilable with the typical mediaeval Roman Catholic (as distinct from Eastern) interpretative model of theology and the church.

– And although, with the beginning of modern times, theology split apart into divergent schools, under the impression of the new rationalist and empirical philosophy and science, it was as obvious for Semler as it was for Reimarus, and as clear to

Schleiermacher as to Baur, Ritschl, Harnack and Troeltsch, that theology could no longer be pursued as it had been in the Reformation era, or in the age of Protestant orthodoxy.

Here everywhere – in discontinuity *and* in continuity – what had once been innovation finally became tradition. Of course these great historical processes of change could also be ignored. In that case tradition turned into traditionalism. Then, as now, people tried to conserve their old familiar interpretative model; or they attempted to restore it by plastering over the cracks.

– In the framework of Greek or Russian Orthodoxy there were those who became defenders of the patristic hellenistic model, the keywords being *paradosis, traditio* and *patres*.

– In Catholicism there were neo-scholastic supporters of the medieval (or rather, Counter-Reformation) Roman Catholic system and a Denzinger theology, the keywords being *ecclesia, papa* and *magisterium*.

– On the Protestant side there were defenders of a biblicistic Lutheran or Calvinist orthodoxy and of a Protestant fundamentalism, the keywords here being the Word of God and inerrancy.

– And today we can also talk about a liberal traditionalism which has contrived to ignore the turn to the post-Enlightenment and post-modern situation. In this case the keywords are reason and history.

Following Thomas S. Kuhn, we may give the name of *paradigm* to these major, comprehensive models for understanding theology and the church – models built up in the wake of wide-scale upheavals, marking the turn of an era; and we may call the replacement of an old interpretative pattern by a new paradigm candidate 'a paradigm change'. I should like further to clarify and distinguish these notions by giving the name of *macro*-paradigms to these major paradigms or fundamental models characteristic of whole epochs, because they themselves include a whole series of *meso*-paradigms for different areas of theology (in Christology the doctrine of the two natures, in soteriology the Anselmian doctrine of satisfaction), as well as even more *micro*-paradigms for many individual questions with which the various theologies have to deal.

Our concern here, then, is certainly not to propagate a naively optimistic belief in progress (whether sponsored by idealism or Marxism, by positivism or social Darwinism); but neither is our aim to disseminate a sceptically pessimistic theory of decline and apostasy (a falling away from the gospel). We are concerned with a *dialectical* interpretation of the history of theology and church, which always involves a rise and a fall; an advance in knowledge and perception, and a forgetting; continuity and discontinuity. It involves a relativizing negation, a conserving affirmation and an on-going transcendence.

I know that any all too neatly defined periodization such as I tentatively put forward here is open to highly controversial discussion. But I think the greatest danger to which this symposium is exposed is for every theologian to want to have his own paradigm or paradigm definition. The preliminary work for the symposium concentrated on clarifying the concept paradigm, which – elastic flexible and comprehensive though it is – is by no means arbitrary or open to random definition. The authors of the three systematic preparatory papers and the four historical ones have precisely and consistently used the same definition, which is taken from Kuhn's *Postscriptum* of 1969: 'A paradigm is not a theory or a leading idea. It is an entire constellation of beliefs, values, techniques and so on shared by the members of a given community' (p.175). In other words, *several* theologies are possible within a *single* paradigm.

We do not want to waste a great deal of time on a semantic dispute about terminology. I should therefore like to propose that we take this definition of paradigm as a working hypothesis, since it was used in all the preparatory systematic and historical papers. The initiators of our symposium are not concerned to discuss the numerous individual definitions and problems involved in Kuhn's paradigm theory. Still less are they anxious to sanction or justify Kuhn's theory from the specifically theological side; for the theory itself is problematical in many respects. So do not let us get hung up for too long on an exegesis of Kuhn!

The vision behind our Tübingen enterprise is a different one. We hope to take Kuhn's incontrovertibly correct and important basic ideas about the history and theory of science, and to enquire whether they can be applied within the sphere of the humanities. Coming more particularly to theology, we must also ask whether these ideas can help contemporary theology to illuminate and ascertain its own condition and situation. From the diagram given to you, one thing at least will be clear: in our century we have to do with the rivalry – indeed the conflict-laden dispute – not merely between diverging theologies but between diverging paradigms. This conflict is the result of the historical non-simultaneity of the great interpretative pattern with which theologians and representatives of the churches are working in any given case. I am convinced that in this analysis of the overlapping and superimposition of different major paradigms during one and the same period Kuhn's paradigm theory can be extremely illuminating. In this way contemporary theology can satisfy itself about its origins and its future. In this way too it can do historical justice to the respective paradigms of particular eras. And it is because these are paradigms – slowly-matured, deeply-rooted, ill-influencing, often conscious and often unconscious basic assumptions – that the conflict between the 'progressives' and the 'conservatives' in the different churches is often so severe and apparently irreconcilable.

In the meantime, in our own century, as is evident to us all, new theological approaches have developed in theology and the church, following two world wars. These approaches are attempts to react adequately to the tremendous social and cultural upheavals of our time. So we are again faced with a question. Although Barth, Bultmann and Tillich, Niebuhr and Rauschenbusch differ widely in their approach, methods and conclusions, they nonetheless agree, not only in their criticism of the Roman Catholic system and Protestant orthodoxy, but in their censure of an Enlightenment-fostered credulity about reason and progress, and in their condemnation of cultural Protestantism and historicism. In short, they agree in rejecting nineteenth-century liberalism. They are, in fact, at one in their affirmation of 'an entire constellation of beliefs, values, techniques and so on, shared by the members of a given community'. In spite of all the divergencies, therefore, ought we not to see these great theologians together in the framework of a new paradigm of theology and church – a modern, post-Enlightenment or post-modern paradigm, which seems to determine the intellectual rhythm of our time?

So where do we stand, those of us who have to do theology today, with Auschwitz, Hiroshima and the Gulag Archipelago at our backs? If I am right, we have among us no representatives of any of the paradigms that have become obsolete – the traditional-istic paradigms of Eastern Orthodox, Roman Catholic or Protestant fundamentalist provenance. On the contrary: here ecumenically united, we have pupils of Barth, Bultmann and Tillich, Niebuhr and Rauschenbusch, Whitehead and Teilhard de Chardin, Chénu, Congar, Lonergan, de Lubac and Rahner. Your theological vitality and creativity is a visible expression of the fact that we are in the midst of a struggle for an adequate interpretative model of theology and the church for our time. Just as eastern Orthodox and western Protestant theologians are here thinking in the framework of the *oikoumene*, Catholic theologians are thinking along the lines of the Second Vatican Council which, it seems to me, was forced, in the modern ecumenical spirit, to digest two Protestant paradigm changes at the same time: that of the Reformation *and* that of the Enlightenment.

The subject of this ecumenical symposium is therefore really this:

– What unites such different pupils of such different teachers, all of whom were nonetheless ultimately determined by a single paradigm?

– What, in spite of all the differences, unites the representatives of dialectical and existential theology, hermeneutical and political theology, process theology and feminist, black and non-western liberation theology?

– What, that is to say, are the conditions – the conditions common to us all – which make it possible to do theology today, the conditions which, beneath the surface of all the deviating theologies, hold together post-Enlightenment theology in the *oikoumene*?

That means that what we are seeking here is not a consensus about particular doctrines and dogmas. What we are trying to find is a consensus about a particular theoretical and practical understanding of theology today. Our aim is not a rigid canon of unchangeable truths, but a historically changing canon of fundamental conditions which have to be fulfilled if theology is to take its contemporary character seriously; if it wants to be in accordance both with the time and with the gospel.

With this purpose in mind, what we expect from this symposium is illumination and a deepened insight, a contribution that will be both critical and constructive. We shall have achieved a great deal if the symposium becomes a focus, a burning glass, to draw together the most widely varying theological trends from all over the world, from many cultures and many theological centres, and perhaps to direct them towards a somewhat brighter future. For all of us who have helped to bring the symposium into being – not least the Deutsche Forschungsgemeinschaft and the Rockefeller Foundation, who provided the financial basis – it would be the greatest reward if we were to go home different from what we were when we came. But however that may be: my colleagues and I should like to thank you all most warmly, here and now, for accepting our invitation.

mpt at a periodisation

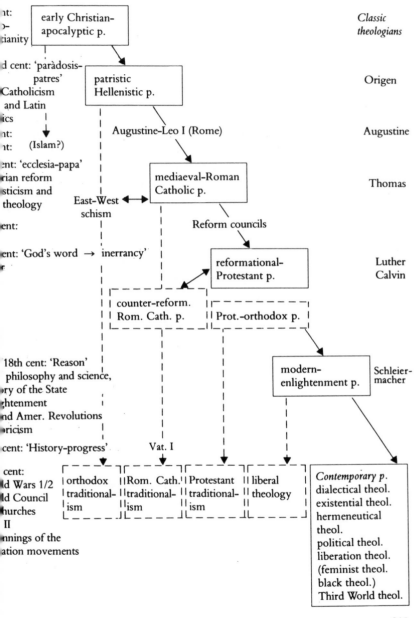

						Classic theologians

nt:
)-
tianity — **early Christian-apocalyptic p.**

d cent: 'paràdosis-patres' — **patristic Hellenistic p.** — Origen
Catholicism and Latin
ics

nt:
nt: (Islam?) — Augustine-Leo I (Rome) — Augustine

ent: 'ecclesia-papa'
rian reform
sticism and — **mediaeval-Roman Catholic p.** — Thomas
theology — East-West schism

ent: — Reform councils

ent: 'God's word → inerrancy' — **reformational-Protestant p.** — Luther Calvin

counter-reform. Rom. Cath. p. **Prot.-orthodox p.**

18th cent: 'Reason'
philosophy and science,
ry of the State — **modern-enlightenment p.** — Schleiermacher
ghtenment
nd Amer. Revolutions
ricism

cent: 'History-progress' — Vat. I

cent:
d Wars 1/2
d Council
hurches
II
nnings of the
ation movements

orthodox traditional-ism	Rom. Cath. traditional-ism	Protestant traditional-ism	liberal theology	*Contemporary p.* dialectical theol. existential theol. hermeneutical theol. political theol. liberation theol. (feminist theol. black theol.) Third World theol.

THEOLOGY IN TRANSITION – TO WHAT?

Jürgen Moltmann

I am delighted that *Concilium* and the University of Chicago should have chosen Tübingen of all places for this interdenominational, international and transatlantic conference. 'If Mohammed won't come to the mountain, then the mountain must simply go to Mohammed'. Tübingen is not precisely one of the major cities of the world; so it gives us all the more pleasure when the world comes to Tübingen, and when Tübingen is drawn into the great transitions of the world today.

As many of you will know, Tübingen has ancient and weighty theological traditions, and some of their high-water marks may be said to belong to times of transition: the transition from the Middle Ages to the Reformation period; the transition from early Protestant orthodoxy to the Enlightenment; the transition from scholastic to historical thinking; and, in the 20th century, the transition from liberalism to dialectical theology. Of course these traditions must be cultivated and cherished. But they must also be translated into the upheavals and innovations of our own time if they are not to become sterile, and are not to moulder away as museum pieces. Tübingen is not a museum, even if looks like one. So in these few introductory remarks I should like to talk about some transitions which are of immediate and challenging importance for the transformations of theology today.

1. Let us begin with what is closest to hand: *theology's transition from the denominational to the ecumenical age.* Here it is quite appropriate to begin with Tübingen: for we have the good fortune to possess two theological faculties. Our seminars are under a single roof – the roof (is this significant?) of a hospital for internal medicine. Our students cross from one faculty to another

to attend lectures, and for the last fifteen years a theological 'working party' from both faculties has tried out and discussed the new ideas that have occurred to us. Earlier, in the ancient study of 'controversial theology', a particular denominational identity was maintained through an account and refutation of the others. This study has long since disappeared. It has not been replaced by a special 'ecumenical theology' because here the ecumenical dimension (even if only the Catholic-Protestant one) is present in all the different theological disciplines. At the same time, we are still standing on the bridge spanning the denominational and the ecumenical eras. We have by no means reached the other side. The speaker who preceded me is himself an accusatory sign of this, though fortunately still a living sign, and one capable of surviving.

We have to take this seriously: the transition to the ecumenical age is replacing the absolutist identity which was hitherto denominationally maintained; and this transition requires us to discover a new identity that is relationally open. That is why every ecumenical spring is apparently followed by a denominational autumn of identity anxiety.

But thinking ecumenically means ending particularist thinking, or rather, gathering it into a universal thinking. It means ceasing to consider one's own part to be the whole, but instead bringing in one's own whole to become part of the whole common to us all. Ecumenical thinking therefore means looking at the theological texts, not for their denominational impress, but for their approximation to the Christian faith, and seeing them as texts we have in common. Finally, ecumenical thinking means no longer staying outside but getting involved, and seeing the theological problems of the other church as our own. The Protestant interpretation of the Lord's Supper is a Catholic problem too, and the Roman doctrine of infallibility is also a Protestant problem.

2. The second theological transition is linked to the first. This is *the transition from the Eurocentric age to the age of humanity as a whole.* Here the abolition, or rather gathering-in, of our own whole, to become part of a coming community, will be more difficult. Ever

since the *corpus christianum* came into being under the Roman empire, with only a few exceptions, the Christian Church and its theology has been centred on Europe. Catholic theology is centred on Rome, whether it likes it or not, as the often disliked expression 'Roman Catholic' suggests. Protestant theology has its determining point in the Reformation, which took place in the Europe of the western Church, and in the 'European' Enlightenment, which was part of modern 'European' times. And up to the present day, Protestant theology in the United States too has taken its bearings from the same determining point.

Today the Christian faith is acquiring new centres of gravity in Africa, Latin America and Asia, and these new centres are accompanied by the development of non-European Christian theologies. The traditional centres of theology are receding into the background and threatening to become marginal. This process is undoubtedly painful for European theologies. It is a demand for transformation. But first of all it evokes a series of highly disturbed reactions. There is the retreat syndrome: 'If they don't want to listen to us any more, let them get on with their theology by themselves'. 'We are simply Europeans and intend to go on being so'. Then there is the bandwaggon syndrome: 'We need a European liberation theology too, or an American Min-jung theology'.

Between these two extremes, as it seems to me, lies the healthy transformation into self–relativity. We are Europeans and think as Europeans, but that does not mean that we have necessarily to be Eurocentrically fixed. We live in the first world, but that does not mean that our theology is inescapably bound to be the ideological expression of that world's domination.

All of us in some way or other assume that our standpoint is absolute. Otherwise where could we stand at all? But if we are seeking encounter and dialogue, we can all put our own stand-points in the context of the common whole. Whatever isolates itself, petrifies; and whatever petrifies, dies. Perhaps this is a European danger, for theology too. Part of the same movement should be the superseding of male theology and patriarchal thinking in the interests of a feminine and masculine theology within the framework of a thinking that will be truly and fully human.

3. As a third point I should like to name *the transition from the age of mechanistic domination of the world to the age of ecological world-wide community*. This is required of us in all the industrial countries. For what people once lauded as the age of enlightenment, secularization and 'the modern world' has after all turned into the era of mechanistic domination of the world, and the technological exploitation of nature. Today we have arrived at the limits of this universal system. The cost-utility sums show that major industrial projects, such as central nuclear power stations, mammoth hospitals in every city, and motorways in every German village, are obsolete. Progress is apparent only if the costs are shuffled off on to coming generations and to nature, so that these are *not* apparent. The security system based on nuclear deterrents has arrived at the zone of apocalyptic insanity. Here too the costs hardly justify the usefulness. In the modern health system as well, we see everywhere the limits of the kind of thinking which has hitherto viewed the body as a mechanism, and defined health and sickness according to the degree to which that body functions effectively. The transition to an outlook on the world which will allow nature and human beings to survive together, confronts Christian theology too with difficult problems. Whereas modern Protestant apologetics particularly had just adjusted itself to 'the secularization of the world' by way of belief in creation and to the modern human domination of nature by way of the subjectivity of belief, today a change of direction is required – an about-turn of almost 180°. What is needed is not the secularization of the world but its sacralization; not the legitimation of human domination of nature but the incorporation of humanity in the universe. What has hitherto often enough been proclaimed as modern theology, and considered to be such is becoming obsolete, while such ancient traditions such as the mystical ones are proving to be sources for the ideas of the future about a spirit of cosmic community and fellowship.

Transitions wherever we look – problems of adjustment and identity wherever we go. *Historia docet?* History may teach, but we never learn from it. In this case history probably teaches merely that fifty years ago Protestant theology was already in a state of upheaval, and saw itself as 'between the times'. But for Christian theology it cannot be solely a question of either acting as the train-bearer for cultural, scientific and political development, or of running ahead of that development, carrying its torch. Christian theology must adapt – must absorb what is new – must prove its relevance. It must be *contemporary* theology, in the positive sense of the word, and must share 'the sufferings of this present time' with the whole creation. But Christian theology must be identifiable *as* Christian. In every age it must find its Christian identity anew. For us there is probably after all no such thing as a continually progressing paradigm change. Instead there is the dialectical process of adjustment and reformation, relevance and identity. The reformation movements typical of Christianity, and the no less typical reaction movements, are to be explained in the light of this dialectic. Both must be taken seriously, at this conference too.

I hope and wish that we may sail through the straits between Scylla and Charybdis into the open sea. The Scylla can be the anxiety-ridden and aggressive insistence on an out-of-date theological paradigm, prompted by a concern to preserve our own identity. But the Charybdis can be the general pluralism of different groups in our civilization. On the one hand there is the danger of being condemned and declared a heretic. On the other, anyone can say what he likes, only nobody takes it seriously.

For that reason I wish this symposium not merely an amicable, peaceable convergence in the sweetness and light of a modern theological consensus. I wish it also friendly but distinct dissension and the discovery of new and worthwhile controversies. I have no immediate doubt about our capacity for consensus. What I am dubious about is our willingness and our capacity for controversy. Could it not well be that it is in its great classical controversies, and not so much in its many feeble unifying formulas, that theology – unlike other studies – reveals the truth that is not its own? So let me wish this esteemed assembly drawn from so many parts of the world, from Chicago and Tübingen, the disputatious spirit – delight in controversy for truth's sake – the good old *rabies theologorum*.

WHAT MUST BE BORNE IN MIND IN
A NEW PARADIGM

Norbert Greinacher

A few hundred yards away from here stands the Bursa – an old, pink-coloured building, which has now been renovated. Ever since the university was founded in 1477, the Bursa has housed the theological faculty. The building still has two outside staircases leading to two separate wings. The one wing, which is called the Pfau, or dove, used to contain the rooms belonging to the realists; the other wing, the Adler, or eagle, was the home of the nominalists. Professors and students lived and studied under a single roof. There was only one faculty, but that faculty's statutes laid down precisely the strict priority between Thomists and Ockhamists.

So you see, for Tübingen the question about a new paradigm in theology is not entirely new. Even at that time there were two different theological paradigms. There was the *via moderna*, represented by a man such as Gabriel Biel, who – by way of Staupitz – became Luther's spiritual grandfather, so to speak (though Eck was also a pupil of Biel's, incidentally). This *via moderna* laid great stress on dialectic, logic and rhetoric, and maintained a resolute scepticism in questions of epistemology. And in the same house and the same faculty there was the *via antiqua* of Summenhart, Heynlin, and others like them, who maintained the real existence of universals.

If we contemplate this coexistence of two theological paradigms, existing side by side, even before the Reformation – a coexistence that has taken form in stone – then we have to ask whether Thomas Kuhn was right, at least where theology is concerned, when he wrote: 'We may now take it for granted that the differences between successive paradigms are both necessary and irreconcilable'.[1] Were, and are, theological paradigms really as antagonistic and irreconcilable as Kuhn postulates? Is there no possibility of an *Aufheben* of theological paradigms, in Hegel's sense of the word: a negation, that is to say, which at the same time gathers in and preserves the thing negated? Was there then, and is there now, really only a *single* paradigm in theology? Is this claim to devise a new theological paradigm not really a crypto-claim on the part of theologians belonging to the western world that their particular paradigm should be binding for the rest of the world?

But this already plunges us right into the subject our symposium is there to discuss. Before we enter into a heated dispute about it, I should like to say something about this city of Tübingen. If you look round the city a little (and I hope you will find time to do so) you will come upon the traces of some great intellects, a fact which has led some people to call Tübingen 'the breeding ground of the Swabian mind'. However that may be, we in Tübingen really are on terms of intimacy, so to speak, with Johannes Kepler (who incidentally could not become a professor here because he did not sign the formulations of the Book of Concord), with Melanchthon and David Friedrich Strauss, with Hegel and Schelling, with Hölderlin and Johann Adam Möhler, with Karl Adam and Romano Guardini. I hope that you will sense something of this liberal and ecumenical atmosphere, begotten of philosophy and theology, as it were, and that it will exert a favourable influence on our symposium.

In 1913, in a lecture on religion and economics, Ernst Troeltsch asked: 'What does the real life of religion show us about an inner and essential influence exerted on the religious life by economic life and by the growth of classes and castes in society, which is largely economically conditioned?'[2] And in 1925 Karl Mannheim wrote: 'In the cultural sciences especially, we are convinced that not every question can be posed – let alone solved – in every

---

[1] Thomas S. Kuhn, *The Structure of Scientific Revolutions* (Chicago & London, 1962), p.102.

[2] E. Troeltsch, *Aufsätze zur Geistesgeschichte und Religionssoziologie* (Tübingen, 1925), p.24.

historical situation, and that problems arise and fade away in a particular rhythm which can be ascertained . . . [that here] problems not foreshadowed by anything immanent to the preceding thought processes emerge abruptly, and other problems are suddenly dropped . . . Here, if anywhere, we see the saying confirmed that nothing can become a problem intellectually if it has not become a problem of practical life beforehand'.[3]

I find it a little surprising that in the whole paradigm discussion since Kuhn practically no notice has been taken of the recognitions of the 1920s and 1930s about the sociology of knowledge. We need only think of the ideas of Max Scheler, Ernst Troeltsch, Max Weber, Karl Mannheim and others. In Kuhn, for instance, we look in vain for any reference of this kind. But the questions and insights of the sociology of knowledge seem to me extraordinarily important in our context – for example, questions like: what was the historical context in which an Alexandrian theology was able to develop? Against what political background do we have to see Aquinas' paradigm? Why and how did theologians in Tübingen come to enter the house they shared by way of two separate staircases – what brought this about? What economic factors influenced Protestant theology? Or – to put it in somewhat abbreviated terms – do we not require a 'materialist history of theology', analogous to a materialist exegesis?

I think it is extremely important for us to ask ourselves about the concern that has brought us to Tübingen. I think that the question about the concern for a paradigm change is very important indeed.

Hans Küng convincingly explained, as it seemed to me, that our contemporary experience of the world is a constitutive element in the new theological paradigm. But this means that, from a Tübingen point of view, we should not forget the following three experiences, at least, in our theological reflections. Fifteen miles away from here, in Grossengstingen, six

---

[3] K. Mannheim, 'The Problem of a Sociology of Knowledge', in *Essays on the Sociology of Knowledge*, trans. & ed. P. Kecskemeti (London, 1952), p.135.

nuclear lance rockets are installed in a bunker. They have a range of about 80 miles, and together they have an explosive power corresponding to 12 Hiroshima bombs. Can we do theology in Tübingen and elsewhere without continually recollecting this fact? Do theologians ask themselves whether they do not share guilty responsibility for it? Or whether they do not at least belong to theological traditions which were partly the cause of today's nuclear insanity? Johann Baptist Metz continually talks about a theology after Auschwitz, and rightly so. Must there not be something like a theology before the nuclear holocaust?

When you look at the beautiful forests round about Tübingen, do not forget that in Baden-Württemberg 99% of the fir trees and 94% of the spruces are sick, in fact dying.[4] What does it mean for a new paradigm of theology when it is confronted by a destruction of nature caused partly by belief in the charge 'subdue the earth'?

Perhaps during the next few days you will be passing through the market which is held every morning in front of the town hall. On this market I have seen potatoes for sale which come from Peru and are being sold as such – as Peruvian potatoes. I should be interested to know what the new paradigm of theology has to say about the fact that here in Tübingen and elsewhere we are eating up the potatoes of the poorest of the poor in Peru. In other words: what does a theology look like which is pursued in a world-wide society where hundreds of millions of people are growing rich at the cost of eight hundred million starving?

But enough of questions: I hope that our symposium will be able to provide us with one or two answers!

[4] *Südwest-Presse* (April 30, 1983).

II. SCIENTIFIC THEORY AND THE NEW PARADIGM

THE HISTORICIZATION OF NATURAL SCIENCE: ITS IMPLICATIONS FOR THEOLOGY

Stephen Toulmin

I shall not here address the question whether Thomas Kuhn's theory of paradigms and conceptual change in science is true, or how far it gives a lifelike account of the manner in which the basic ideas of natural science change and succeed one another. That question quickly becomes scholastic. The first edition of Kuhn's *The Structure of Scientific Revolutions* had a rough rhetorical point, and stated it more effectively than exactly. By now, there is an extensive literature about the ambiguities and assumptions in Kuhn's arguments;[1] and the resulting dispute would distract us here. It is sufficient that basic conceptual changes in fact take place, which transform the theoretical basis of the natural sciences either rapidly or gradually: whether we should call these changes 'paradigm switches', with all the extra implications of that phrase, is not important.

What is more to the point here is another question: why Kuhn's book has been so influential, and what significance attaches to the widespread attention his views have received. The reasons for this attention lie less in the answers Kuhn has given to the fundamental questions about conceptual change in science than they do in the broader background of the questions. By insisting on the radical character of scientific change, Kuhn completed the *historicization* of human thought that had begun in the eighteenth century, and so finally undercut older views about the 'immutable' order of nature and human knowledge. The task for

---

[1] I. Lakatos and A. Musgrave (eds.) *Criticism and the Growth of Knowledge* (Cambridge, 1970). *Cf.* Margaret Masterman's contribution. *Cf.* also Stephen Toulmin, *Human Understanding* Vol 1 (Princeton, 1972).

those who are interested in the theological implications of contemporary natural science is, therefore, not to replace one static but outdated system of doctrine (paradigm) by another, equally static but more up-to-date system: instead, it is to carry further the work of Troeltsch and those other theologians who have reflected on the specific relevance of *Historismus* to the projects of theology and cosmology.[2]

Both in antiquity and after the Renaissance, the philosophy of nature was basically *ahistorical*. Ancient philosophers mainly thought of nature as *cosmos*: as a fixed and 'well-ordered' body of eternal entities and their relationships. From Parmenides and Pythagoras on (most notably, of course, in Plato) the *fixity* of the underlying ('real') entities was treated as a precondition for the intelligibility of the natural world: only *unchanging* structures, it seemed, could be grasped by the human intellect, or understood in the geometrical and timeless terms of Plato's preferred *episteme*.

From the late sixteenth century on, again, mathematical and experimental natural philosophers in western Europe thought of nature as *creation*: as fashioned by divine design, to God's own fixed pattern and specification. How could merely human thinkers decipher the design for such a divinely-created nature? It was, presumably, within God's power to give us the intellects required for that stupendous task. While separating nature from humanity, matter from mind, and causes from reasons, proponents of the new, seventeenth-century science thus preserved the earlier picture of nature as static; and this picture was reinforced by the current scale of historical time, which encompassed the entire life of the world within a few thousand years.[3] Only from 1750 on did the new historical point of view begin to put down serious roots. At first, it made inroads only into the human sciences; but it soon spread into natural sciences: first, into the history of the earth, by way of paleontology and

---

[2] Ernst Troeltsch, *Der Historismus und seine Probleme* (Arnheim: Leyden, 1933).
[3] *Cf.* the more extensive discussion in Stephen Toulmin and June Goodfield, *The Discovery of Time* (N.Y. 1965).

historical geology, and next into biology, with the discovery of organic evolution, which led up to Darwin's theory of variation and natural selection. As a result, the accepted scale of historical time was forcibly expanded from a few thousand years to many million.

For the time being, few philosophers abandoned the ambition which Descartes and Kant had shared: to demonstrate the *uniqueness and permanence* of the structure of nature. Newton's laws of motion merely took a place beside the axioms of Euclidean geometry, as the foundations for any modern *episteme*.[4] Whether those laws reported unchanging features of the material world, or laid down the constitutive patterns of rational understanding, Descartes' faith that God gives us 'clear and distinct' ideas of the basic principles of physics had been fulfilled through the writing of Newton's *Principia Mathematica Philosophiae Naturalis*. Despite their thorough historicization of human affairs, Hegel and Marx too left this basic fabric of physical nature untouched. The development of non-Euclidean geometries might call the full and absolute universality of the Euclidean system in doubt, but the axioms of Newtonian physics went unchallenged until the early twentieth century, when Einstein forced a reconsideration of its basic assumptions about spatial and temporal measurement.

Even this theoretical landslip was quickly overcome. The philosophers of the Vienna Circle, whose concerns Einstein had done much to shape, rewove the fabric of natural science on a new and 'logical' backcloth: the formal marriage of pure mathematics and symbolic logic set out in Russell and Whitehead's *Principia Mathematica*. At the heart of their world picture, too, there lay a permanent formal system, with a fixed and unchanging structure; and this central core was to be extended into new fields of empirical knowledge by building on conceptual annexes for each of the specialized sciences. So, despite their claim to modernity, the scientist-philosophers of the Vienna Circle were, rather, the last spokesmen of the Enlightenment. They aimed to construct a

---

[4] A. Koyre, Newtonian Studies (Cambridge, 1965).

modern 'Encyclopedia' which would do for Einstein's century what the French *Encyclopédie* did for the age of Newton.

By a curious irony, Kuhn's *anti*-positivist theory of 'scientific revolutions' first saw the light as a slim fascicule of the resulting *Encyclopedia of Unified Science*. The irony was, of course, that nobody's writings have done more than Kuhn's to undercut the dreams of the unified science movement. If natural science no longer makes any claim to permanent or fixed ideas – if the sciences are always liable to run into 'crises' that force us to dismantle them and reconstruct them on new foundations – then physical theory, which had for so long remained the last stronghold of intellectual absolutes, is finally engulfed in the same historical flux as the human and social sciences.

From that point of view, human ways of thinking about nature can no longer be the concern of a 'pure reason' that transcends the contingent human situation in (say) the fifth century BC, or the seventeenth century AD. Rather, as Ludvik Fleck had seen in the 1930s,[5] those ways of thinking must be seen against their historical, cultural and social background, as the work of finite beings dealing with particular problems in specific situations. In Popper's terminology, the debate about conceptual change in science thus shifts from the third world (of abstract concepts, entities and relationships) to the second world: i.e., the world of human activities, institutions and judgments.[6] Or, to use a different language: once this lesson is taken to heart, the problems of natural science, too, become *hermeneutic* problems.

What new roads are opened up for theology and cosmology as a result of this change? Our situation calls (I suspect) not for haste but for caution. We may be tempted, for instance, to seek the raw material for new theological 'paradigms' in the theories of late twentieth-century natural science, hoping to use these bricks to construct new and more authoritative conceptions, both of the world and of humanity's place in that world.

[5] L. Fleck, *Genesis and Development of a Scientific Fact* (Chicago, 1979).
[6] Karl Popper, *Conjectures and Refutations: The Growth of Scientific Knowledge* (N.Y. 1965).

That would be a dangerous path to take. Twice already, Christian theologians have committed themselves enthusiastically to the detailed ideas of particular systems of scientific theory. This happened, firstly, when the medieval church 'naturalized' Aristotle, and gave his views about nature an authority beyond their true strength: secondly when, from the 1680s up to the late nineteenth century, Protestant thinkers (especially in Britain) based a new religious cosmology on mechanical ideas about nature borrowed from Descartes and Newton, as interpreted by an edifying reading of the argument from design. In both cases, the results were unfortunate. Having plunged too deep in their original scientific commitments, the theologians concerned failed to foresee the possibility that Aristotle's or Newton's principles might not forever be 'the last word'; and, when radical changes took place in the natural sciences, they were unprepared to deal with them. (For reasons I do not understand, Judaic scholars did not make the same mistake.)

So the call for 'new paradigms' in theology should not ask us to assemble the more up-to-date scientific ideas of a post-Darwin, post-Einstein, post-Freud era into a novel cosmological construction that claims the same fundamental authority and permanence that were claimed for Aristotle and Newton earlier. That will simply lay up fresh trouble for theology a century or two down the road, when scientists have rethought the problems of their own disciplines, to the point of making radical changes for which theologians would once again be ill prepared. It may well be the case, indeed, that theology can hope for no secure and permanently reliable foothold in the natural sciences, at least on the abstract, theoretical level. If that is so, it will be better if theologians heed the sceptics, free themselves from the seduction of 'new paradigms', and become frankly reconciled to being (in that sense) 'paradigmless'. It will be better if they distance themselves from the ideas of science rather than embrace them too systematically and uncritically.

This is not to say that philosophical theologians can afford to *ignore* the natural sciences, or confine themselves (as they have too often done since Kant) to discussing, in transcendental terms, the 'bare possibility' of intellectual coexistence between the fundamental ideas of natural science and religion *überhaupt*. It is to say, rather, that some way must be found to carry on the dialogue between natural science and theology on equal terms. It is no longer sufficient for theology to declare itself 'queen', with authority over the methods of all other sciences. Nor is it sufficient, either, for theologians to surrender to the natural scientists authority over all that concerns the world of nature, without reserving some critical foothold, from which they can comment on the theological significance of scientific theories and discoveries, as seen from a religious point of view.

In particular, now that natural scientists have brought many aspects of human affairs into the scope of their inquiries, they have entered a field where they cannot help encountering rival interpretations of the same human affairs, arrived at from other directions and based on different hermeneutic principles; and they must recognize that their interpretations of those affairs are limited by the presuppositions of their methods of inquiry.

Consider, for example, the methods of 'radical behaviourism'. A strong case can (in my view) be made out for these methods, as a way of discovering important relationships involved in behaviour change; and, to that extent, radical behaviourism can provide us with a defensible hermeneutic for the interpretation of human thought and conduct. But B.F. Skinner's book, *Beyond Freedom and Dignity*, goes far beyond such modest claims, and presents the behaviourist interpretation of human experience as discrediting all other, earlier ('unscientific') interpretations.[7] In this respect, of course, Skinner repeats the same over-extrapolation that Küng rightly criticizes, when he contrasts the modest clinical methods of Freud's psychoanalysis with the imperialistic position that he rejects as 'Freudism': the exaggerated cultural and theological critique to be found in Freud's essay, *The Future of an Illusion*. Skinner thus claims unrestricted authority and scope for his particular set of abstract

---

[7] *Cf.* also B.F. Skinner, *Science and Human Behaviour* (N.Y. 1953).

theoretical concepts, instead of recognizing that they have at best a conditional value (as *topoi*) as throwing light on the relations between behaviour change and the situations in which it occurs.

On the level of concrete practical experience, then, natural scientists and theologians can speak as equals: particularly, in discussing the *topical* significance of their ideas and methods of analysis, as applied in one context or another, for one purpose or another. Such discussions, however, involve something less than the global construction of 'new paradigms'.[8] Instead, they call for a patient, piecemeal examination of the specific ways in which concepts of different kinds contribute, as *topoi*, to the understanding and management of our experience.

The clinical concept of 'wish fulfilment', the scientific idea of 'reinforcement', the moral notion of 'autonomy' and the religious ideal of 'human dignity'; these ideas, rather than being claimants to sovereign authority over the whole field of human conduct, co-exist on the plane of *practical reasoning*.
In what kinds of psychoanalytic situations is the concept of 'wish fulfilment' clinically relevant? On what kinds of behaviour change does the idea of 'reinforcement' throw scientific light?

In what kinds of human interaction does the notion of 'autonomy' have its full moral significance?

From what theological standpoint and demands does the idea of 'dignity' derive its religious power? How far the detailed results of the resulting patient, piecemeal inquiries will 'add up', or fit together into a comprehensive and systematic new 'paradigm', there is no way of knowing in advance. It is unwise to *force* them into any such global form prematurely; and, meanwhile, there is a lot of work to be done.

For a start, we need to show how it is that an *historically developing* religious tradition can both change, and yet maintain its essential continuity, through this historical development. How,

[8] Thomas Kúhn, *The Structure of Scientific Revolutions* (Chicago, 1970).

for example, do new concepts, doctrines and interpretations come to displace earlier ones within the *Lebensformen* (forms of life) (or, if you prefer, the *Lebenswelt* – lived world) of that particular tradition? These questions deserve to be answered with something like the same detail and precision that are available for answering similar questions about conceptual change in the natural sciences. They are (that is) not just *synchronic* questions, about the practical significance of the ideas concerned at a particular time. They are also *diachronic* questions about the manner in which our ideas are refined and improved: specifically, about the criteria by which we recognize that they have been refined and improved.

What theology can learn from the historicization of natural science is, thus, something methodological or topical rather than cosmological or substantive.[9] Both lessons should be congenial to the religious mind. In the first place, conceding that human ideas and conjectures can never claim unchangeable authority or rational finality, but are always open to refinement and revision – the methodological doctrine Popper calls 'fallibilism' – is a proper admission of *human finitude*. And that thesis is, surely, as relevant to our religious forms of thought and life as it is to our scientific understanding of nature. (Even in the case of 'revealed truths', the human *interpretations* of the documents that embody those truths, notoriously display the same historical mutability as all other doctrines.)

In the second place, the topical implications of the present discussion can lead the philosophy of religion back to its own proper territory: to a reflective examination of the religious life *from within* that life. Now, however, this examination must be conducted in terms that recognize the legitimate claims of the human sciences as standpoints from which to illuminate the nature and dynamics of that life. The constraints that were placed on the philosophy of science by the example of Gottlob Frege – constraints which for fifty years kept philosophers in fear of committing the 'genetic' and 'psychologistic' fallacies – have been

[9] *Cf.* Stephen Toulmin, *The Return to Cosmology* (Berkley 1982), 217-275.

removed; so that we are no longer prevented from asking what social, historical and psychological factors play a part in the growth and refinement of scientific understanding.

In a similar way, if our starting-point is an examination of historically developing traditions and conceptions of religion *from within*, we need no longer view the historical sociology of religion, and the psychoanalytical study of religious attitudes, as *threats*: rather, they can be helpful instruments for use in analyzing and refining those conceptions, and the traditions in which they are primarily 'at home'.

PARADIGM CHANGE:
SOME CONTINENTAL PERSPECTIVES

Rüdiger Bubner

It cannot be my function simply to review the debate about paradigm shift which was triggered off by Thomas Kuhn. For that I am not competent, not being a science historian. Moreover, twenty years have passed since the appearance of his unusually provocative book on *The Structure of Scientific Revolutions*, and the fundamental ideas have meanwhile become current coin. In the overwrought hermeneutical atmosphere of German philosophy especially, Kuhn has been greeted with lively assent; and this suggests that he met a latent need reaching far beyond his own original intentions. Kuhn himself was probably astonished at the breadth of the impact made by his doctrine; for the concept of paradigm change was initially no more than a generalization drawn from insights which he had acquired while investigating the Copernican revolution in astronomy a few years previously.[1] Today the moment has perhaps come to ask what fascinated the philosophers so much about Kuhn's catchword. Perhaps, at a distance, certain contours have become plainer than they were in the immanence of the dispute about the theory and history of science which Kuhn provoked. We can probably now say that on the methodological level there has in fact been a paradigm shift of the kind that Kuhn described in the context of scientific research itself.

In what I am about to say, therefore, I shall not be contributing anything to the numerous attempts we find in the literature on the

---

[1] *The Copernican Revolution* (Harvard, 1957), esp. chs.4 & 5. *Cf.* Kuhn's own account of the development of his ideas in the preface to a collection of essays published in German, *Die Entstehung des Neuen* (Frankfurt, 1977).

subject to make Kuhn's revolution analysis more comprehensible and coherent; for the rational reconstruction of the gestalt switch between theories generally tend to explain away the obscurities which Kuhn himself leaves shrouded in metaphorical language and hence to eliminate the philosophical challenge which is inherent especially in the thesis about the *incomparability* and *incommensurability* of paradigms. Nor shall I take the other, more subtle approach which, though it recognizes the irreducible historical element in the paradigm, only does so in order to render it innocuous in a complex conception. The danger of a relativistic historicism that will demolish all the dykes of methodological rationality tempts many people to take refuge in heuristic, strategic or idealizing solutions. These are all endeavours to undermine the doubt Kuhn throws on the identification of science with rationality. Lakatos chooses the *heuristic* solution, with his model of the research programme that combines a hard normative core with a flexible trying-out of historically changing variants.[2] Stegmüller prefers the *strategic* solution, describing revolutionary change as the successful dislodgment of one theory by another.[3] Popper, finally, goes furthest of all in his late work, departing from his earlier dissociation from metaphysics and even rehabilitating *idealism*, so as to abolish the supposed irrationality of history.[4] He postulates an independent sphere of Platonic entities in which – rather like Hegel's objective Mind – ideas, theories and problems (or their formulation) succeed one another on the undeviating path leading to the ultimate, comprehensive and definitively true theory of reality, the paradigm of all paradigms.

What I should like to do, instead of these things, is to take a few quite provisional steps towards defining '*the rational*', especially in

[2] 'Falsification and the Methodology of Research Programmes', in I. Lakatos & A. Musgrave (eds.), *Criticism and the Growth of Knowledge* (Cambridge, 1970). See also Lakatos, 'History of Science and its Rational Reconstructions', in C.C. Buck & R.S. Cohen (eds.), *Boston Studies in the Philosophy of Science*, Vol.8 (1972), pp.91-135.

[3] *The Structuralist View of Theories* (Berlin & New York, 1979).

[4] *Objective Knowledge* (Oxford, 1972).

a paradigm change that is taken seriously, by which I mean one that has not already been blurred and softened by the intervention of logic. The history which has always already outpaced the formation of theory, so that it can neither be planned in advance nor integrated afterwards, confronts science with a finitude which belongs to the nature of all cognition that aims to be scientific. It is therefore not surprising that science, since it here comes up against its limits, is not capable of overcoming these limits by its own efforts. Nor is any help to be found in a methodological discussion which operates on the meta-level but which links its standards of rationality firmly to the 'given' of the scientific process of arriving at knowledge. The logic of research must presuppose the fact of science, as the saying has gone ever since the neo-Kantians. Historical development has made this fact part of modern times; and it is accepted without any further ado or attempt at justification, inasmuch as the standards of rationality are simply derived from the normal assumptions and practice of research.

The same unreflected *a priori* limitations which its subject exhibits then enter into the explanation of fundamentals. Scientific procedures need methodic guidance, and this guidance in its turn derives from a previous *objectification and specialization* of the subject or theme. Through objectification and specialization – i.e., by way of fixing and limiting competence – science binds itself to assumptions for which it does not in itself give a reason, but which are simply enjoined on it with all cogency by the successful history of modern research. The methods which scientists learn to apply and by which they proceed depend on the previous decisions which prevailed when the various disciplines were established. There is nothing to complain about here, nor is there anything we can do about it, since this quite simply constitutes the particular character of science itself.

The reflections of *philosophy*, however, are directed towards the unquestioned limits of rationality in any available knowledge; and it is therefore only philosophy which is in a position to make us aware of what has necessarily been forgotten in the structure and conception of science. Philosophy has to be able to comprehend the underlying principles of what happens to normal science (as Kuhn calls it) on the rare occasions when a historical upheaval turns everything that has hitherto held good upside down. It is true that philosophical reflection cannot wholly cushion professional scientists against the – for them – inexplicable experience that their dealings with knowledge depend on unrecognized assumptions. No philosophical counselling would save the research community from the painful revolutions in which history itself brings to light the systematic limitations of the ruling paradigms. But, whereas these break in upon the scientists as unexpectedly as a natural disaster, an abrupt veering in the winds of mass psychology, or the mysterious factors determining victory in the struggle of dogmas and schools, philosophical observation is nonetheless in a position to discover a rational import in these things. And this rational import consists in *the discovery of those very limits of rationality* to which I have referred. This of course throws open an understanding of rationality which does not equate it with the spread, imitation and logical discussion of scientific methods. The crass alternative between irrational paradigm shifts and rational scientific behaviour which long fanned the flames of the debate now proves to be a phantom.

Let me explain what I mean in three different contexts: 1. modern semantics; 2. the problem of the awareness of historical periods and epochs; 3. the dialectic of knowledge and history.

With regard to the first of these points: we have to remember the development of modern semantics, which runs from Frege to Quine and Davidson by way of Wittgenstein. The old nominalist conviction had been that every linguistic sign has its correspondence in something particular in the world; to this the sign points as a name points to an object. With the development of modern semantics this conviction disappeared. Linguistic expressions mean something different from themselves, but their reference can be explained only in the wider context of language systems, language games or language frameworks. I shall leave on one side the highly important details to which modern semantics devotes its acumen, and shall concentrate solely on the main problem of how the special reference of a sign or expression is to be understood in the total framework of a known and inter-subjectively used language.

The connection cannot be fully explained from within any given language, because all linguistic communication assumes that language can be unproblematically mastered. The hope that the introduction of meta-level would show a way out of the dilemma is threatened either by infinite regress or by circularity. If, however, the problem is tackled from the outside, spontaneous talking, and going on talking, come to a halt. Where linguistic tools cease to function, linguistic explanation is hopeless. How should we still arrive at an understanding about conditions under which language functions, once the self-evidency of these very conditions is suspended? In other words, how can language be explained without damage to the total context? It is only hesitantly that the semantic discussion has admitted that this dilemma conceals the problem already familiar from transcendental philosophy – the problem of reflection about the constitution of our inter-subjective understanding of the world. The cost of a transcendental philosophy seems too high, because it is not thought that we can rely on any pre-language evidence in pure consciousness. The hypostasizing of a supra-individual constitutive principle in the form of the self-consciousness is considered either as an irresponsible relapse into metaphysics, or as a reprehensible solipsism which infringes the rules of communication that unite several subjects in dialogue from the outset.

The usual solution is a pragmatic one. The person who shrinks away from the speculative costs, still believes that he can work with the notion that, according to all previous experience, different languages fulfil the same function, without our being able to trace them back to a prototype from which they may be strictly derived. There is no legitimizing point or 'agency' behind the empirical languages which would explain *a priori* how we can become speakers of different languages. As we know, Chomsky was not content solely with the observation that people can learn different languages. He had recourse to the risky concept of 'innate ideas' (which, according to classical rationalism, precede all empirical experience) in order in this way to anchor the generation rules common to all empirical languages in the psychological equipment of human beings.[5]

In the pragmatic sense, certainly, we have to accept that the same people can apparently talk different languages even though the different linguistic material is not based on identical semantic structures. One language could be translated into another with absolute certainty only if a language-transcendent world of things in themselves (*Dinge an sich*) were available to us, as a single shared vanishing-point. Since this seems doubtful, Quine took the decisive step from 'the indeterminacy of translation' to ontological relativity, according to which every meaningfully used language has behind it a corresponding ontology of referentially denoted components of reality.

Now it is at this point that we have to fit in the real problem for scientific theory, which we find in Hanson, Feyerabend and other of Kuhn's allies under the heading of 'the *theory-ladenness* of empirical terms'. For if there is no world in itself beyond our linguistic forms of referring to it, then we have no contact with empirical experience either, except through language. We must dismiss as naive the earlier view of orthodox positivism, according to which there are pure sense data before the linguistic transformation into the records of observation or basic propositions reshapes this into discussion material for an interacting scientific community. What we observe and describe is initially dependent on the background of a systematically practised terminology, on the intention dominating the investigation, on a body of corroborated hypotheses of law-like status, on commonly held standards of critical research, on the refined techniques of appropriate measuring instruments, and so on. As we know, all this is what Kuhn understands by a 'paradigm'. Transitions from one paradigm to another must no longer be seen as translations from one language to another, since these – though

[5] *Cf.* A.N. Chomsky, H. Putnam & N. Goodman, 'Symposium on Innate Ideas', in J.R. Searle (ed.), *Philosophy of Language* (Oxford, 1971).

pragmatically warrantable – have as their key signature an ineradicable indeterminacy. Transitions between paradigms, on the other hand, are historically irreversible, every paradigm making an absolute claim. These transitions draw their dynamic from their intention to promote unbroken guidance for the research that characterizes the phases of 'normal science'.

The second aspect to which I should like to draw attention affects the mutual delimitation of old and new. The developed awareness of 'the epoch' has always, from the very beginning, worked with this double relational definition. As soon as a phenomenon emerges that can be described as new in relationship to the phenomenon to which people are accustomed, this latter phenomenon moves into historical distance and suddenly seems to be old. It is in the caesura that opens up between the two sides that the awareness of 'the epoch' grows. Among theologians it may be appropriate to point to the medieval controversies about the *via antiqua* and the *via moderna*. The scientific mind of modern times, from Bacon to Vico, has argued with the corresponding comparison between what ancient and modern times have achieved. In the seventeenth and eighteenth centuries, the aesthetic continuation of this line of thought presented the extensive *'querelle des anciens et des modernes'*, which lived on in Schiller, Goethe and Hegel in the form of the distinction between classic and romantic – a distinction still familiar to us today.[6]

We must in general, of course, I must remember the deeply-rooted historicization of our world picture on which this is based. Ever since the decisive turning point when a whole epoch began to define itself as 'modern times', long-existing, firmly confident ways of dealing with the world have been disappearing, giving way to relations over which one can in principle dispose. Our relationship to nature is no longer determined by eternal nature herself. The power of the subject is now beginning to intervene. This releases so many possibilities that historical transformation is given a substantial chance.

[6] See here, e.g., R.F. Jones, *Ancients and Moderns. A Study of the Rise of the Scientific Movement in 17th Century England*, 2nd ed. (Berkeley, 1965), as well as the first two studies in H.R. Jauss, *Literaturgeschichte als Provokation* (Frankfurt, 1970).

The more dominant the change, the more urgently the need for order makes itself felt. Viewed hermeneutically, the ordering patterns which have become established in the course of history itself show that the old, the new, and the transition between them always emerge over against each other, and together with one another. *Epoché* – the ancient term for a sceptical withholding of judgment – means withdrawal from the flux of time, whose current normally carries us along. At decisive points we step back, so as to bring order into the sequence of events; for we need the order, so as to know in each given case where we are, and what we have to hold on to, in the undeviating, undifferentiating flow of time. Time itself does not tell us what the old is, and what the new, because time, in its character of unceasing change, is itself changeless. But if a supra-historical standpoint from which we could definitively judge is not available to human beings, all structuring must take place immanently and relatively. It is true that the definition of old and new *per se* requires an option in favour of, or against, the one or the other. Yet we have to expect that, after a certain phase, what was originally the new will now have become the old. So although revolutionary upheavals repeat themselves, their regular succession does not breed indifference of the kind expressed by the mocking dictum, coined after the French Revolution: *plus ça change, plus ça reste la même chose.*

Such resignation towards the speed of change implies a surrender of the *orientating* effect of division. For an explicitly-made distinction between the old and new identifies paradigms, which offer the patterns or models of scientific, artistic or even political behaviour that have to be pursued, and whose antitheses would accordingly have to be rejected. Where everything is equally valid, all differences are lost. Consequently a division into epochs is made within the homogeneous field of historical continuity according to factually cogent standpoints; but these standpoints themselves derive only from a rational differentiation between what is past and superseded compared with what is present and points towards the future. Paradigms stand above chronology, and are yet chronology's creation. In paradigms, an era comes to comprehend itself as a limited section in the eternal flux.

The third aspect leads on easily from this, for it has to do with the dialectic of knowledge and history. The basic theory about the connection between the two is still to be found in Hegel's *Phenomenology of Mind**. Marx termed it the birthplace of dialectic in general, because it brings together forms of knowledge and historical factors. In our own century the sociology of knowledge has reshaped Marx's way of looking at things into a neutral instrument of investigation, though certainly renouncing the logic of progress and an End-time hope. Since then the intertwined connections of theories and extra-theoretical determinants have often been dealt with by contrasting the internal history of science and knowledge and the external conditions which provide the framework.

Robert Merton and Ludwik Fleck provide two relevant examples which may suffice here. Max Weber's study of Protest-antism[7] (which is an implicit reply to Marx) among other things stood sponsor to the sociologist Merton's now classic analysis of science and technology in Puritan England.[8] Many more recent writers have consciously or unconsciously taken up what Merton said. Parallel to this is the long-forgotten study by the outsider Ludwik Fleck on *The Genesis and Development of a Scientific Fact*, which Kuhn mentions in the preface to his main work. Fleck's interest in 'the style and collective of thinking' goes back to ideas put forward in the sociology of knowledge during the 1920s. Because of the events of the time (before World War II), the medical case study was published in a place where it received no echo. It is only recently that Fleck's book has been re-edited and translated into English;[9] and it is still well worth reading.

* Some recent translations of Hegel's book (e.g. by A.V. Miller, Oxford 1977) choose 'Spirit' as translation for Hegel's 'Geist'. However 'Mind' is still considered by many to be a closer approximation (*translator*).

[7] M. Weber, *The Protestant Ethic and the Spirit of Capitalism*, tr. T. Parsons, foreword R.H. Tawney (London, 1930; reprint 1965).

[8] *Science, Technology and Society in Seventeenth-Century England* (New York, [2]1970).

[9] First published Basle, 1935; *The Genesis and Development of a Scientific Fact*, tr. F. Bradley & T.J. Trenn, ed. T.J. Trenn & R.K. Merton, foreword T.S. Kuhn (Chicago, 1979); new German ed. by L. Schäfer & T. Schnelle (Frankfurt, 1980).

Generally speaking, the weakness of the approach by way of the sociology of knowledge is that what really belongs together is divided into *external* and *internal*. Which circumstances contribute to which scientific theory can be judged, if at all, only in the light of the theory in question. The selection of the relevant factors of social development is always already made, in anticipation of the features which have to be explained in a theory, a successful method, or a world view which has come to prevail. As Marxist scholasticism shows, the simple mechanics of the base/superstructure pattern explains nothing at all, because not all economic upheavals leave recognizable traces in the structure of scientific theory.

The parallels between social development and theory dynamic is completely in the air as long as no conceptual method is available for linking the two so closely that their reciprocal influence in itself becomes the vehicle of the process. Then a self-assured social research would no longer stand over against an evolution of the world picture 'prepared' by the historians of science. Rather, recourse to history becomes necessary in the face of gaps in rationality which cannot be fully closed within the framework of the theory itself. On the other hand, the anomalies that crop up in theories or theory systems compel the research community to depart from the institutional matter-of-course assumptions of the everyday practice of research. Thus to take leave of trust in the further validity of normal science expands the perspective to such a degree that the thematizing of framework conditions for research takes research itself into new paths.

That theories are begotten in the purity of a parthenogenesis is just as illusory as the dependency of science on pre-given conditions for which it is not responsible. For an adequate view of the dialectic of knowledge and history, Hegel's systematic conception is still astonishingly fruitful. One need only cite Stephen Toulmin's great book *Human Understanding*,[10] which at a central point invokes Hegel's 'cunning of reason'.[11] This makes

[10] Princeton, 1972.
[11] See Vol.1, pp.478 ff.

Toulmin still an exception among Anglo-Saxon philosophers (apart from the solitary Collingwood); for in the English-speaking world, the tone is set by those who might be called, in a free adaptation of Schleiermacher, 'the uncultured among the despisers' of Hegel.

If, with Hegel, we relate reciprocally the forms of knowledge that have come into being in any given case and the historical conditions that gave them birth, this offers a key for an investigation of the development. The crystallization of a new form of knowledge becomes possible and necessary at the point when the undetected bond between the preceding form and its external conditions of existence makes itself felt as a restriction of theoretical capacity. This restriction on the part of the precursor form is not merely the contingent factor that triggers off a revolutionary event, at the end of which a successor suddenly emerges. Since the precursor, in its particular claim to knowledge, appears inadequate, a genuine successor is bound to eliminate this reason for the revolution. It is only the abolition of the restricting conditions that permits the successor legitimately to assume the place where a certain form of knowledge had foundered by reason of its own deficiencies.

At the same time, the amendment only applies relatively, in relation to the precursor. It does not do away with all conceivable conditions in general which might crop up historically at some time or other. To that extent the successor too will be faced with a similar fate – the fate of being vanquished by another – as long as science does not succeed in emancipating itself entirely from all history. The shift between historically-conditioned forms of knowledge derives neither from the pure processes of reflection, nor from economic or social upheavals, but can be defined, beyond such one-sided diagnoses, as the need to overcome deficiencies of rationality which run directly counter to the genuine claim to knowledge put forward by theory. The elimination of the deficiencies must include the condition under which, though unrecognized, the deficient theories existed; so the next theory is certainly superior in this respect. But it is still, for its own part, again subject to limitations which go back to unrecognized new conditions. The rationality of the paradigm change consists in the diagnosis and removal of such deficiencies, which undermine the claim of every paradigm, although this does not mean that the whole sequence of all paradigm changes is at the disposal of a higher logic, removed from the dialectic of knowledge and history.[12]

Let me sum up. 1. In the semantic parallelism of linguistic systems, these stand in parity side by side, no ultimate decision between them being possible. With Kuhn's paradigm concept, this state of things moves into a historical perspective, where the succession has on its side more than merely the pragmatic reason of coming to terms with any given alternatives. Even though we are unable to assume any compulsive trend, the succession nonetheless counts initially as irreversible until, with greater distance, a deliberate casting back, for example, also inaugurates renaissances. 2. The imminent epochal distinction between old and new provides a partial definition of position, so that we know how we have to behave in a given situation, until we learn otherwise. The new paradigm can never promise absolute truth, but it can offer an adequate orientation which regulates the absolute relativism of historical awareness. 3. Sociology puts a name to external factors from which something follows, or does not follow. In contrast to this, the dialectical, reciprocal reference of knowledge and history opens up insight into the conditions on which the formation of a certain theory depends, without expressly determining these conditions. No theory is ultimately the master of its conditions, but in the framework of this dialectic it is at least no longer completely at their mercy.

We may say that the lesson to be learnt from the three observations I have indicated is as follows. The interaction of history and theory shows step by step the limitation of the capacity of any given theories. This limitation can never be obliterated once and for all, since it belongs to the nature of science itself. But what

---

[12] See my 'Dialektische Elemente einer Forschungslogik' in *Dialektik und Wissenschaft* (Frankfurt, 1973). ET forthcoming: *Hermeneutics and Critical Theory* (Columbia Univ. Press).

science experiences only as historicity, philosophical reflection can comprehend by interpreting a revolutionary fate as a definition of the limitation. This interpretation will certainly not free us from further experiences with the limitations of rationality, but it does draw a rational profit from the derangement of normal science. [13]

[13] I have meanwhile found the view I have put forward here largely confirmed by Kuhn's still unpublished Thelheimer Lectures, given at Johns Hopkins University in November 1984.

A CRISIS OF THE PARADIGM, OR A CRISIS OF THE SCIENTIFIC NATURE OF THEOLOGY?

Jean-Pierre Jossua

I had to write this paper without the reports which it was supposed to answer, and with only the preliminary papers. I found Stephen Toulmin's paper at the end, and discovered this fascinating statement in it: 'It will be better if theologians heed the sceptics, free themselves from the seduction of "new paradigms", and become frankly reconciled to being "paradigmless"'. In my own life as a theologian, the change of paradigm – by which I mean change in the model of scientific or even cultural reference, or of epistemological outlook – appeared as a profound crisis: not only of a given type of criteriology, but of all claim to scientific status. I think that what I am going to say goes beyond my own particular case, and concerns several others, especially in the Latin areas. This is doubtless a sign of a less academic, more ecclesial contextual influence, and one more closely related to the human sciences.

Given the task of teaching dogmatic theology, from the first I took more seriously than others the destruction of harmony between reason and faith and the constructive possibilities which Greek philosophy, revised and corrected by medieval thinkers, offered theology.. The diversity, difficulty and post-Christian character of modern thought no longer seemed capable of providing an instrument with which to tackle the classic model of the philosophical scientific approach. I must confess that my colleagues' endeavours have often seemed to me to resemble nothing more than a makeshift piece of cobbling, or involuntary absorption by a system whose cohesive power they had underestimated, or a new mode of apologetics. Second, the movement of the ecclesiastical disciplines of exegesis and history towards a truly scientific historical method, seemed to me so radically to question the fixed points on which the detailed dogmatic system was established, that I considered it to be not only circumstantially faulty, but faulty as a project in itself. For their part, exegesis and history as such can never act as Christian theology. Third, the self-transformation by what are the most indisputable and definitive aspects of the 'human sciences' (deceptive and analogical term, if there is one) makes one very suspicious of all systematical discourse; the delusion of its conceptual practice, its irremovable distance from life, its alibis to escape decisions, and its concealment of ideological, socio-ecclesial and socio-political functions. It also makes one realize vividly the present explosion of knowledge. Certainly, theology tells of the coming of God within the whole breadth of human and worldly reality, but is it capable of a single specific statement, one inclusive statement, one organized statement about it? Add to all this some questions I had long been asking myself on the relationship between theology as charism or spiritual experience, and its claims to scientific status, and the measure will be full.

I thus arrived at the conviction that theology had lost and would doubtless never recover the assured illusion of truly scientific status, for instance, the harmonious and constructive relationship between history, faith and reason. Dare I voice my suspicion that only academic impulses or apologetical fanaticism can henceforth sustain the illusion? In this crisis situation I have chosen a starting-point that seems solid enough to me: the description and explanation of Christian experience, of the lived, commentated and interpreted experience of believers, of the fundamentals of faith in the state of radical accomplishment through experience itself. In the context formed by a profession of faith (always a believer's experience expressed in symbols) and present Christian experience (always brought about by a realized profession of faith), this means of access had a real advantage. When expressed in words, it offered the possibility of bringing into cultural existence, and of communicating by testimony, what could no longer be the object of a descending logos, constructed in relation to a scientific paradigm; on condition, however, that this testimony is referred strictly to the origins of faith, and that it is approached critically, using all the resources of modernity. Serious intellectual labour and a mentally responsible life within the faith remained possible, as we are shown by the example of several thinkers from the past who refused the systematic or positivist patterns of theological science: Erasmus, Bayle, Kierkegaard, Newman . . . It was only necessary to remember that this intellectual life could also be conceived as an open debate, or a struggle – Unamuno spoke of its 'agonizing' character – a critical labour, endlessly resumed.

The rest of the road matters less: it is more closely linked to a personal history. Whereas others, reckoning on somewhat similar critical assertations, have theologized on the fringe of their exegesis (like E. Käsemann), have philosophized within the faith or its bounds (P. Ricoeur), have opened up an exacting inner dialogue with one of the major aspects of modernity (J. Pohier), I am oriented towards the expression and quest of experience and the profession of faith through the beauty and precision of writing. In Germany and the USA this is known as narrative theology; in France it would be called literary theology – a term with the advantage of embracing poetry, the narrative, and various types of biography writings; essays – a mixture of theoretical studies and literary writing, open in form and unsystematic, always revealing traces of what led to it. But since the basic theme of our discussion includes a comparison between the status of theology and that of other fields of intellectual endeavour, I shall close by outlining a parallel between the trend I have described and one that exists at present in France in an important area of psychoanalysis.

The same crisis with regard to scientific models (in particular the 'medical' aims of Freud, but also a ratification of psychoanalysis as one of the branches of psychology, and more recently the Lacanian system). The same awareness of the primacy of experience, that is to say, here, of the interpretation of the derivatives of the unconscious. The same reflective reworking: the development within a given space of a discourse or a symbolic exercise. An identical reference to an original corpus and vocabulary. The same mistrust of the unconscious aims and weak power of any theoretical construction. A comparable recourse to a register of testimony intended for an audience which is to be provoked. Often the same commitment to writing with its power to evoke what emerges from ourselves as we seek for words – the experience of analysis and of self-analysis – if one accepts the method's constraints as well as its infinite capacity for offering meaning. The major difference is obviously that in psychoanalysis the totality of the experience remains *in* the interpretation, and not elsewhere. For theology, for faith on the other hand, there is the interpretation of a mysterious but not inaccessible experience, even if I can never be anything more than one of the partners: the advent of God, 'unconscious from above', inexhaustible, but capable of being uttered in true human words.

III. BIBLICAL THEOLOGY AND PHILOSOPHY
IN THE NEW PARADIGM

'ACCORDING TO THE SCRIPTURES': THE NEW TESTAMENT ORIGINS AND STRUCTURE OF THEOLOGICAL HERMENEUTICS

Josef Blank

1. What is the role and significance of biblical studies in the hermeneutical discourse of theology?

This is the first point that needs clarification. What do you expect a biblical exegete's contribution to be? Will he fulfil these expectations or disappoint them? Since there is no Old Testament scholar among us, I have the job of representing Old and New Testaments. This is a tremendous task, for which I cannot possibly consider myself competent. And yet let me say deliberately: I represent the Bible – and not only biblical studies but exegesis as well. In saying this I have already said enough to indicate that in this paper it cannot merely be a matter of agreement. There is bound to be disagreement too: not merely assent, but challenge and criticism as well. The Bible is an unruly book which, if we take it seriously, refuses to be locked up in any systematic cage.

My idea of hermeneutics has of course been moulded by the exegetical tools with which I work, through my dealings with the New Testament texts, and with texts in general. In my view the hermeneutical process includes the whole process of understanding, beginning with textual criticism, of course taking in historical and critical methods, and ending with the working out of an overall theological interpretation. This means that I am bound to understand 'hermeneutics' as a complex happening, which includes a whole series of individual aspects. Among these is certainly a consideration of the interpreter's own stance, and his 'guiding concerns'. What seems to me important here is the distinction between methods or hermeneutical rules on the one hand, and the guiding hermeneutical ideas, principles and paradigms on the other hand.

The aim of my contribution is to show that the hermeneutical problem is one of the basic, primal problems of Christian theology in general. I say this in order to indicate from the outset that I am taking up a counter position to another view, and in order to avoid a possible misunderstanding; for the nature of hermeneutics and the term itself is often narrowed down unduly, as if hermeneutics were merely a modern procedure, a 'new method' or a 'new philosophy', designed to make the 'antiquated' biblical or early Christian texts, with their obsolete, mythical world pictures and notions, comprehensible and acceptable to 'modern thinking'. This view often accords a hermeneutical priority to modern thinking which also, without more ado, simply makes this thinking the ultimate criterion of truth, or – more correctly – the principle determining the selection of what can or cannot allegedly be expected of 'modern people'. In my view this involves the danger that the message of the ancient religious, philosophical or aesthetic texts in its full substance and richness is no longer perceived and can no longer make its proper impact because a particular hermeneutical concept or paradigm acts as a filter that may well exclude from the very outset the most important things the texts have to say, on the grounds that no one can be expected to accept them any more. The modern scientific-positivist concept of science and scholarship continually screens out reality of this kind, so that it cannot make itself felt. In this way, under the false guise of enlightenment, this concept helps to build up an extremely efficacious social prejudice. But in my opinion theology cannot permit itself to be tied down to a concept of science and scholarship like this, or to the paradigm it provides.

Traditional neo-scholastic dogmatics also largely acted as a filter and screen of a similar kind; for in these dogmatics 'the Jesus of history' played as good as no part at all. To put it more generally: as exegete and historian, I take a sceptical view of every 'systematic' concept or paradigm because, with its claim to grasp 'the whole thing' in a new way, it tends to magnify its own importance, often setting up its own position as absolute, and in so doing violating the historical circumstances and facts to a greater or lesser degree. A historical hotch-potch and violation of history constitute a fault too frequently committed in dogmatics for one not to be on one's guard against it. New paradigms are all the less immune to this danger since here solid work on texts and sources is often lacking. I see this as a great and dangerous deficiency in contemporary theology, and I should like to say so quite frankly to the illustrious assembly gathered here. Biblical and historical theology may be inconvenient partners and critics. They may here and there pull down some attractive construction. But without them theology is at the mercy of every kind of illusion, including false views of history (for example, where the historical Jesus is concerned), without possessing the sure criteria with which to defend itself against these same illusions.

However, for me there are no such things as 'settled problems'. In my view it is just as useful for us to turn our attention to the pre-Socratics as to the book of Job, the Gospels, or even Buddhist texts and so forth. For there we find human questions articulated which tell us something about human beings *per se*, and therefore have something to say to us even today. I believe that these questions have still by no means been answered, even though today we like to push them aside. I believe too that a reconsideration of these questions might well contribute to our deliverance. I would therefore make a plea for the independent significance of the past – of history – for the very reason that it often fails to fit in with our contemporary ideas. It is these rights of the past which exegesis, and the whole of historical theology, has to maintain.

But if, as I believe, 'the hermeneutical problem' is already inherent in the biblical and early Christian texts themselves, then we shall no longer be able in a one-sided way to understand the modern notion of hermeneutics as a selective and normative-critical concept. We shall have to see it instead as a 'problematical concept'. It must subject itself to objective criticism of its criteria and must not, either, conceal the concerns that motivate it. Today all the world likes to appeal to hermeneutics, so that the appeal as such really means nothing at all. It is Hegel's 'night in which all cows are black'. But if hermeneutics is grasped as being a problematical concept, this does imply at least the beginnings of self-critical reflection. Then New Testament and early Christian hermeneutics on the one hand, and modern hermeneutics on the other, confront one another as comparable, competing, mutually illuminating and critically enquiring matrices, systems or models, which have to enter into serious dialogue with one another – i.e., have to be understood from the outset as 'open systems' – open for one another. Under these conditions, 'old' and 'new' paradigms never, in my view, confront one another as mutually exclusive alternatives, so that a new paradigm would simply be bound to replace and dislodge the old one. On the contrary, the new paradigm has only established itself once it has discovered its link with the older model – with tradition. Otherwise it would be like an astronaut in space who has lost touch with his spacecraft and wanders about the universe, lost.

If we think it through to the end, hermeneutics in this sense includes the whole history of the theology and interpretation of the biblical texts, and their influence on the history of dogma, liturgy and spirituality in church and world. Let me quote some words of Ebeling's: 'Against this background it is understandable that I should define church history as the history of the interpretation of Holy Scripture. What I find particularly important about this definition is that it includes the category of interpretation. For this category brings out the theological importance of the historicity of the church. As I have said, historicity in general includes the parallelism of persistence and alteration, identity and variability'.[1] I may add that this hermeneutical programme has hardly begun to be implemented. For example, it would be extremely important to know what

---

[1] Cf. G. Ebeling, *Die Geschichtlichkeit der Kirche und ihrer Verkündigung als theologisches Problem* (Tübingen, 1954), p.81.

influence the political conditions of the day had in any given case on the interpretation of the Sermon on the Mount, or on the church's attitude to war and military service, and so on.

2. The model provided by Pauline hermeneutics

The hermeneutical problem in the New Testament presents itself, in a way that is both comprehensive and concentrated, as a question about the relationship between Old and New Testaments, and as the problem of the new eschatological-Christological interpretation of Scripture as a whole. Lack of space unfortunately prevents me from considering this comprehensive background to hermeneutics in fundamental theology. Instead I shall confine myself to a special New Testament paradigm: Pauline hermeneutics.

The New Testament offers various paradigm possibilities from which to choose. I might have traced the development from the proclamation of the historical Jesus to the fixed, written form of the gospel, by way of the church's shaping of the tradition – that is, the problem of tradition and redaction – presenting this as 'the hermeneutical process of early Christianity'. Or there is the question about the picture of Jesus we find in the synoptics and in John. It is surely in John if anywhere that we should have to talk about a 'paradigm shift', 'a new hermeneutical concept' and 'a new interpretation of Jesus'. But I have in the end decided for Paul, because he provides a particularly good illustration of the problems of a theological hermeneutics; for Paul offers more theological reflection. Moreover, I hope that this example may provide a useful link, and an opportunity for comparison, with Stephan Pfürtner's paper, in which this problem also crops up, under another aspect. I should like to make it clear in this connection that I am not primarily concerned here to make yet one more contribution to Pauline research. What I should like to do is to draw Paul into our discussions at this conference. The question that concerns us here is Paul's contribution to theological hermeneutics.

2.1 Now, Paul shows us that it was quite possible to put at the service of the new overall Christian understanding, the exegetical methods and hermeneutical rules which were studied and applied in the Jewish schools.[2] Paul himself had learnt these exegetical methods and ways of arguing in that milieu, and he introduced them into the beginnings of Christian theology. Michel points out that 'Pauline argumentation can largely be explained in the rabbinical context'.[3] But now, after his 'conversion', he put what he had learnt at the service of a completely different overall interpretation – a new paradigm, the paradigm 'gospel'.

Another important gift which Paul brought with him from his rabbinical centre of learning is the concept of tradition or *paradosis*. What is important here is not merely that Paul goes back to tradition, or *paradosis*, or that he is also able to understand the proclamation of the gospel as the further transmission of what had already been passed down. The significant point is that in what he says he also uses the appropriate technical terms (received from – passed on to: παραλαμβάνειν/παραδιδόναι, παράδοσις[4]). I am sure that I need not particularly stress here that the concept of tradition holds an important place in theological hermeneutics. 'It is New Testament doctrine', writes Geiselmann, 'that the tradition, the *paradosis*, is the form in which the faith is transmitted to us.'[5] But modern hermeneutics too has sufficiently stressed the importance of tradition: 'Hermeneutics', says Gadamer, 'must start from the position that a person seeking to understand something has a relation to the object that comes into language in the transmitted text and has, or acquires, a connection with the tradition out of which the text speaks'.[6]

---

[2] *Cf.* H.L. Strack & G. Stemberger, *Einleitung in Talmud und Midrasch*, 7th ed. (Munich, 1982), pp.25–40.

[3] O. Michel, *Paulus und seine Bibel* (1929, reprint Darmstadt 1972), p.102. Also E.E. Ellis, *Paul's Use of the Old Testament* (London, 1957), pp.45 ff.

[4] *Cf.* here J.R. Geiselmann, *Jesus der Christus* (Stuttgart, 1951), pp.54–101 (Eng. tr. of first three chapters by W.J. O'Hara in *The Meaning of Tradition* (London & Freiburg, 1966); also his *Die Heilige Schrift und die Tradition* (Freiburg, 1962).

[5] Geiselmann, *Jesus der Christus*, op.cit., p.54.

[6] H.-G. Gadamer, *Truth and Method*, tr. & ed. G. Barden & J. Cumming, 2nd ed. (London, 1979), p.262; see also index under 'Tradition'.

According to this thesis, whatever has to be understood comes to us only by historical paths, which is to say by way of tradition (the tradition of the church or the Christian faith); and the new understanding of the same thing is again bound to the historical form in which it has been transmitted. According to Paul, tradition has this double aspect: on the one hand the reception – the acceptance of tradition as an already given factor or phenomenon; and, on the other, the further transmission of the gospel as an on-going missionary task. It is under this double aspect that we have to consider the problems with which Christianity in Europe especially is struggling today: the problem of the breach with tradition and – linked with that – the question about how to pass the Christian traditions on. I suspect that this is the specific situation – the *Sitz im Leben* – of the search for new paradigms. Yet I should like to put on record here my doubts as to whether we can really get to the bottom of this problem in a symposium. All the same, it will be legitimate to ask: what must we do, if Christianity is to have a future?

2.2 Second, what does this deliberate link with the traditions of the first Christian congregation mean for Paul? To this we have to answer: for Paul, the link with tradition means in the first instance showing and implementing the unity of the gospel. He introduces the passage I Cor. 15. 1-11, for example, by presenting 'the gospel' as the heart of the tradition, and ends: 'Whether then it was I or they, so *we* preach and so you believed'. Paul never harks back to the experience of his conversion in making his claim for the gospel and what it contains. This is not for him in any way the justification of his theology, nor is it the foundation for that theology. He appeals to the common tradition. For Paul, 'the gospel' involves a basic consensus which was already prior to the apostolic proclamation. And, as the Epistle to the Galatians shows, the question whether a doctrine is in accord with this general testimony to the gospel is an essential criterion. Paul roundly denies that the people who, he believes, preach 'another gospel' are able to offer this consensus. Probably this is what is meant in Rom. 12.6b: 'If anyone has to put forward a prophecy, let it be in agreement with the faith' (κατὰ τὴν ἀναλογίαν τῆς πίστεως; Vulg. *sive prophetiam, secundum rationem fidei*). That is to say, it must be possible for a spontaneous utterance such as 'prophecy' to be brought into line with the gospel and what the gospel contains. And – a further consequence – where this is not the case, the prophecy has no chance. Moreover, it is interesting to see that whenever Paul has reason to expect a misunderstanding, he likes to appeal to pre-Pauline credal formulas – that is, to already existing traditions (*cf.* Gal. 1.4; Rom. 1.3f.). 'Tradition' represents what has been generally received and accepted, and includes too what can in general be tolerated. What is new, on the other hand, must first justify its claim in relation to tradition. It has to be weighed up, and only prevails once it has led to a new consensus.

The conclusion from all this is that the purpose of every hermeneutical innovation is either to prolong the old consensus or to bring about a new one. The formation of a consensus is the real goal. It is really quite normal, and no serious objection, to say that the road to this goal is difficult and dangerous, and involves conflicts and disputes. These things can have a purging or clarifying effect on what is at issue, and on its supporters. It is also the normal function of the church's magisterium, or teaching office, to support the side of tradition. The argument of tradition also has its own weight, as one argument among others. To this surely no objection can be made.

2.3 Paul therefore takes over the new interpretation of Scripture together with what was probably the oldest credal formula passed down to him, I Cor. 15.3-5. This links the event of Christ's death and his resurrection with the phrase 'according to the Scriptures' (κατὰ τὰς γραφάς). Both Christ's death and his resurrection from the dead have their foundation in the promise of 'the Scriptures'. It is interesting that the reference to Scripture here is quite generally formulated. It is not pinpointed to any special scriptural passage. This has led to hot disputes among scholars, down to the present day, as to whether the background is Isaiah 53 or not. In my own view, the phrase 'according to the Scriptures' does two things. On the one hand it is a link, referring the Christ event back to Israel's previous salvation history. It is the 'feedback' to the scriptural promises, as it were. At the same time, this implies the particular quality which has to be attributed to the Christ event: the quality of God's saving End-time act in the history of Jesus of Nazareth, to which the raising of Jesus from the dead essentially belongs. For it is precisely this which is meant to show the eschatological and soteriological reference of the history of Jesus. As a final and consummated saving event, the resurrection is at the same time 'the new beginning' of the new christological hermeneutic. The risen Christ is the key to Scripture. As we shall see, this also implies the distinction between 'the letter and the spirit'.

2.4 I said that Paul employs the methods and basic concepts of rabbinical hermeneutics, which he had acquired in his schooling as a Pharisee. But the direction, the intention and the guiding principles of his scriptural understanding are quite different from those of Jewish interpretation. A Jew cannot subscribe to the statement that 'Christ is the end of the law, that everyone who has faith may be justified' (Rom. 10.4) without ceasing to be a Jew; yet no Christian can dispense with it without thereby renouncing the Christian doctrine of redemption. This again brings us to a problem fundamental to all hermeneutics: that of the hermeneutical approach and principle: the question of 'entry' into *the hermeneutical circle* and the reason behind it. Here we may remember Heidegger's well-known saying: 'What is decisive is not to get out of the circle but to come into it in the right way'.[7] In philosophy, the way into the hermeneutical circle is the conscious discovery of human existence 'in the world' or 'in history'; but in theology the entry is faith. The problem of the way into the hermeneutical circle is of the greatest interest, because this is the point at which the question about the hermeneutical approach and principle is decided; and this is constitutive for every interpretation. The problem cannot be solved merely through hermeneutical reflection, for it also involves the aspect of deliberate decision (*voluntas, liberum arbitrium* – will or free will; it

---

[7] M. Heidegger, *Being and Time*, tr. J. Macquarrie & E. Robinson (London, 1962), p.195. *Cf.* Gadamer, *Truth and Method, op.cit.*, pp.156 ff.

does not seem to me admissible simply to term this factor irrational). If this is correct, then hermeneutics includes a *cum assensione cogitare* – thinking with the assent of the whole person.[8] 'Belief' of this kind is either conditioned by the historical position of the interpreter or, as in theology, it is meant as 'faith', in the strict theological sense (of a *fides divina*). This widens out the problem of entry into the hermeneutical circle once more through the additional aspect of the specific subjective situation of the interpreter. What does the interpreter bring with him? The answer is: his own viewpoint, his approach, his particular concern; but also his prior understanding and his prejudices (*cf.* Nietzsche).

2.5 Paul takes over the congregational confession of faith or kerygma of the first church. (e.g., I Cor. 15.3-8; Rom. 1.3f.; and elsewhere) as well as the new interpretation of the whole of Scripture which this implied. In the preamble to his letter to the Romans he can say that 'the gospel of God' was 'promised beforehand through his prophets in the holy Scriptures' as 'the gospel concerning his Son' Jesus Christ (Rom. 1.2f). But 'righteousness through faith' is also foretold in Scripture. Here Paul can arrive at the dialectical formula: 'But now the righteousness of God to which the law and the prophets bear witness has been manifested apart from the law (χωρὶς νόμου), the righteousness of God through faith in Jesus Christ for all who believe (Rom. 3.21f.).

This brings us to a further hermeneutical problem. Here Paul articulates the new total understanding of gospel and Scripture, which he shares with the first church, in a new, specific way of thinking and terminology: the thinking and terminology of 'the doctrine of justification', the δικαιοσύνη θεοῦ. The Pauline doctrine of justification is undoubtedly one of the most important examples of the emergence of a new model of theological thought, or paradigm, in the earliest period of the church. Compared with earlier paradigms (first, Jesus' proclamation of

---

[8] *Cf.* Thomas Aquinas, *De Ver.* q.14, art. 1; *Summa Theol.* II-II[ae] q.2. art. 1; J.H. Newman, *A Grammar of Assent* (London 1870).

the kingdom of God; and second, the post-Easter kerygma of Jesus as crucified and raised Messiah) this third paradigm of the Pauline doctrine of justification, the δικαιοσύνη θεοῦ, is something new and different, both in language and way of thinking. One indication of this among others is the fact that this paradigm – unlike other New Testament paradigms – was not completely accepted in the patristic church. One might also say that Paul translates the gospel of the primitive church into the language of his code of justification, which was partially moulded by rabbinical thinking. This means that the gospel as it had been received underwent an authoritative linguistic transformation – in surface structure certainly, and perhaps even a transformation at depth as well. The phrase δικαιοσύνη θεοῦ, the right-eousness of God, is balanced by other, corresponding phrases: δικαιοσύνη ἐκ πίστεως – οὐκ ἐξ ἔργων νόμου – righteousness through faith (alone), not through works of the law.

Now, an interesting point is that in Paul we meet the doctrine of justification in full force for the first time in the letter to the Galatians and then, in somewhat more moderate form, in the letter to the Romans. We hardly come across it at all in the other letters. It is certainly not absent altogether but it is not expounded as clearly and trenchantly as in Galatians especially. Why? Has it perhaps something to do with *the new specific situation* in which the letter to the Galatians was written? This seems to be the case. The reason why Paul was moved to formulate the doctrine of justification more radically was the conflict with which he saw himself confronted when he wrote the letter to the Galatians. He felt that his law-free gospel had been called in question by his opponents' demand that Gentile Christians should be circumcized and observe the Torah.

This provides us with a new element in hermeneutics – the specific challenge of a new situation. We know that Paul did not develop his theology in the abstract, or in the meditative tranquillity of a Christian school. It grew up in the framework of his continuous contact with his congregations. The difference in the various congregational situations and the varying pastoral intention of his letters are part of the actual historical conditions of his hermeneutics and theology, which developed in the tension between coherence and contingency, to echo J.C. Beker's phrase.[9] To put it in general terms: the hermeneutical thrust leading to the formulation of a new paradigm does not usually come about without a concrete external reason – without a 'hermeneutical shock' (see, for example, Luther's revolutionary reform, which also came to make a general impact only because of a specific external situation – the sale of indulgences). This hermeneutical shock can be triggered off by personal situations and experiences, but also by general, historical ones. At all events, it is because of it that the hermeneutical process really gets under way.

2.6 Now comes the next question: what is the relation between the old and new paradigms? Paul is quite convinced that with his interpretation of the δικαιοσύνη θεοῦ/δικαιοσύνη ἐκ πίστεως (the righteousness of God and righteousness through faith) he has arrived at and manifested the heart of the gospel. Whether his view was correct has been a matter of dispute down to the present day. The background is the old problem, 'Paul and Jesus' – the often-canvassed thesis that through his 'dogmatics' Paul falsified Jesus' simple gospel. This is by no means my opinion. In the context of paradigm shift, I would certainly say that there is without doubt an enormous difference between the language and thinking of Jesus as we know it from the synoptic gospels, and the language and thinking of the apostle Paul. We get the impression that we have to do with two completely different personalities and characters. But we have to ask whether the difference between Jesus and Paul is a substantial difference also. Is Paul's view a falsification of Jesus' message? Are Jesus and Paul really incompatible? I believe that when we consider the structure in depth we find common ground which the surface structure disguises. It is probably true to say that Jesus promises sinners God's salvation and love without any conditions. In the parable of 'the Pharisee and the tax collector' (Luke 18.9–14) he calls the tax collector 'justified': 'I tell you this man went down to his house

---

[9] J.C. Beker, *Paul the Apostle* (Philadelphia, 1980), p.35.

justified rather than the other'. What, then, one may ask, does Jesus do in this parable except himself to implement the *justificatio impii* – the justification of the sinner? And what difference is there when Paul says that faith alone justifies a person, without the works of the law? I cannot see any distinction of fact here, at least not substantially or in principle. Jesus and Paul are saying the same thing, only in different images (Jesus) and concepts (Paul). There is therefore undoubtedly a factual correspondence even though the wording is different.

Of course Jesus' language 'code' is not exactly the same as Paul's. Jesus thinks and talks much more pictorially. Paul's language is more the abstract, conceptual language of theology. We can also say that the two language codes overlap and are as a whole differently structured. To put it in general terms once again: between the *interpretandum* – the thing to be interpreted – and the *interpretatio* – the result of the interpretation process – there is no flat, simple identity. What we have is rather *a factual correspondence with a different linguistic and conceptual codification*. Anyone who recognizes and affirms this factual correspondence will have no difficulty in recognizing the agreement between the gospel and the doctrine of justification. We know that this was Luther's most profound conviction. And yet the conclusion is not absolutely binding. Biblical scholarship today would have grave doubts about interpreting Matthew's Gospel with Paul's doctrine of justification as paradigm. As we know, Luther had difficulties with the Epistle of James.

2.7 The new paradigm of 'righteousness through faith alone, not through the works of the law' determines Paul's dealings with Scripture, and above all his choice of scriptural quotations. He takes from the Tenach precisely the quotations he needs for what he wants to say, and he shows an astonishing sureness of touch hermeneutically in his choice of what he cites: the passages Gen. 15.6, Lev. 18.5, Deut. 27.26; 21.23 (*cf.* Gal. 3.1-14); and the Abraham midrash in Gal. 3 and Rom. 4. The hermeneutical thread that runs throughout is the idea of righteousness through faith (δικαιοσύνη ἐκ πίστεως). For Paul this problem also includes the calling of the nations to faith (*cf.* Rom. 15) as well as

the question about Israel's new position in salvation history
(Rom. 9-11), which Paul again tries to define with the help of the
antithesis 'righteousness through faith – not through works of the
law'.

Here too we can generalize. In his dealings with Scripture (the
usus scripturae) Paul behaves as a 'systematic theologian', who
picks out from Scripture his *dicta probantia* and *loci theologici* as he
needs them. Texts which would speak against what he wants to
say are neither sought for, admitted, nor even examined. Paul's
procedure here is a thoroughly selective one. We see this best if we
compare the Epistle of James. Whereas Paul claims Abraham as
'the father of all believers', who was justified 'by faith alone,
without works', the Epistle of James maintains the precise
opposite: 'Was not Abraham our father justified by works, when
he offered his son Isaac upon the altar?' (James 2.21). There is no
question but that the two concepts contradict one another and
cannot be harmonized. Two antithetical positions were evidently
maintained in the primitive church. Was there a *coincidentia
oppositorum* from the very beginning? It is certainly true that the
way systematic theologians today deal with the Bible, especially
with modern exegesis, urgently requires a critical exposition and
investigation. Let me say at once that I by no means consider a
'systematic' use of Scripture as inadmissible in principle; but I see
that here, as in every systematic discussion, a choice and
limitation of theme has to be made. The citation of scriptural texts
must not merely document comprehensive learning, or represent
the proper obeisance due to learned colleagues. It can also be the
sign of a productive pondering and assimilation of prior tradition.
Every new paradigm is also a reconstruction, which uses the
bricks of the older building for its own purposes and plans. And
this is the case in Paul, as it is in every innovation that takes us a
step forward.

Of course we must also recognize that every new paradigm is
always at the same time something partial and incomplete. By
shedding a bright light on certain points, it casts others into
shadow. In this way it approximates in some degree to scientific
experiment. At this point there still seems something for

theology to learn. We are still probably encumbered by the 'summa theologica', whose guiding principle was to unite in itself 'the whole' of theology. Progressive specialization in all theological sectors of course makes it obvious that this idea can no longer be maintained. But its traces can still be detected in two attitudes: first of all in the viewpoint of the church's magisterium, which still thinks that it possesses 'the whole', and can exercise control over it; second, when theologians make an absolute claim for their own theories. Contrary to these views, it must be said that every paradigm proceeds selectively. It has its strengths and its weaknesses, and needs other paradigms, perhaps even antithetical ones, if it is not to come to grief because of its own Achilles heel, or the blind spot we all have. Another problem crops up at this point which has probably never yet been properly taken into account in theology: the problem of side-effects. To take an example, what were the undesired side-effects of *Humanae vitae*?

By now you will have gathered where I myself stand in relation to the problem of a new paradigm in theology. I affirm the need for a multiplicity of different paradigms, openly related to one another and in correspondence. But I think that the question about *the* new paradigm, which is supposedly determinant for all the others, is a highly problematical and unanswerable enquiry. After everthing that has been said, I should have to reject anything of the kind, because the absolute claim which is thereby concealed smacks very much of ideology.

2.8 Let me now say a word about the problem of 'the letter and the spirit', the γράμμα and the πνεῦμα, *de spiritu et littera*. This also crops up in Paul for the first time and can never really be ignored in theological hermeneutics. The relationship between the two is the basis for self-relativization, but is is also the real self-justification of theological hermeneutics.

Paul treats the problem in chapter 3 of the second letter to the Corinthians, where he contrasts the ministry of the Old and New Testaments, the ministry of Moses and the ministry of Christ. In this context we find the following statements: 'God . . . has made us able ministers of the new testament; not of the letter, but of the spirit: for the letter killeth, but the spirit giveth life' (II Cor. 3.6 AV). Paul applies the same distinction to the new interpretation of Scripture when he says of the Israelites (v. 14 AV): 'For until this day remaineth the same vail untaken away in the reading of the old testament' (ἐπὶ τῃ αναγνώσει τῆς παλαιᾶς διαθήκης) – this passage incidentally is the first use of the term 'old testament' for the Tenach, and especially for the Torah – 'which vail is done away in Christ'. This means that the veil will only be lifted when the sons of Israel are converted to the Lord Jesus Christ. Paul then goes on: 'Now the Lord is the Spirit, and where the Spirit of the Lord is, there is freedom. And we all, with unveiled face, reflecting the glory of the Lord, are being changed into his likeness from one degree of glory to another; for this comes from the Lord who is the Spirit' (II Cor. 3.12-18).

This text surely touches the profoundest dimensions and ultimate presuppositions of 'the hermeneutical business'. It seems to me that it is in the ineradicable tension between 'the letter and the spirit', 'law and gospel', that the most explosive problems of a theological hermeneutic are to be found. What does this distinction mean? What is at issue in the relation between letter and spirit? 'Letter' is supposed to mean that tradition is viewed so exclusively as tied to fixed fomulations that these must not be deviated from by a hair; for in possessing the fore-given wording one believes one has the thing itself. In extreme cases the question about the meaning, significance and spirit of the thing is considered unimportant. Since theology always has to do with the *intellectus fidei*, it has never been able to accept this view. 'Spirit', on the other hand, means that it is the living, spiritual wrestling with tradition, and its effectuation by way of a fully conscious and assimilated mental appropriation which first constitutes the hermeneutical process.

'The heritage your fathers gave you – that
lay hold upon, in order to possess it',
says Goethe (*Faust* I).
The point is not to pass on sacred traditions and formulas like a closed book with seven seals. The essential is to understand the thing itself and to reformulate it accordingly. It is not the letter we

need but the spirit, the *ratio* or the *spiritus litterae* – although this certainly does not exist without the letter. But have not all the enthusiasts and the heretics appealed to the spirit as against the letter? Is this not the thin end of the wedge, the beginning of unrestricted subjectivism?

First of all, hermeneutics cannot in actual fact get along without the element of subjectivity, subjective understanding and subjective appropriation. I can interpret only what I myself have understood and to the extent to which I have understood it, within the limits of my own reason – '*contemplata aliis tradere*', as Aquinas says: to pass on to others what one has seen oneself. Above all, insofar as the new formulation – the interpretation as such – is also a constructive process leading to the formation of a concept, the interpreter is bound to introduce his subjectivity into the interpretation, rather as a painter has to incorporate his whole view of the world in his picture. The interpreter can only arrive at a sound interpretation by investing his whole intellectual and human capabilities. We all know that in every interpretation the interpreter interprets, not only the object – his text – but himself as well, and most of all in his unquestioned hermeneutical premises. We know too that as a result certain theologians view hermeneutics with reserve; they would like to exclude every 'subjective' aspect. But it must be asked in return: in matters of faith, and in theology generally, can we do without 'the subject' – the human person? Is insistence on the formal letter of tradition not the death of faith, since it involves the expulsion of the Spirit? Of course no hermeneutics can dispose of the Spirit – but even less can it dispense with that Spirit. In matters of faith Kierkegaard was to a certain degree right when he said that 'subjectivity is truth'. Over against a petrified understanding of tradition, 'the subject' can claim more rights still, when he or she tries to discover the vital force of tradition for the present and the future. It is this, after all, that shows our own readiness to answer for tradition towards the society of today and tomorrow.

The Spirit, therefore, is the *sine qua non*, and the Spirit bloweth where it listeth. There is no interpretation without spiritual commitment and without the liberty of the Spirit. But – and this must be said too – every interpretation is a venture and an adventure, which carries its own risk. For it can also founder. Here too one must bear the personal responsibility. But it is useless to try to avoid the risk by falling back on the fixed letter, as a kind of insurance policy. Anyone who enters into hermeneutics must not be afraid of difficulties and conflict. But he needs a tranquil and firm reliance on the Spirit most of all.

3. Some final thoughts

What, then, does all this come down to? Let me, in concluding, say the following.

First, there have been both hermeneutics and paradigm shifts in Christian theology from the beginning. We already find them in the New Testament, as I have tried to show, taking the apostle Paul as example. They are also to be found in the history of theology down to the present day. To say this is to blunt the edge of the question about the new paradigm, for the question is then at once legitimized and relativized. A further insight is this people who are living in history and see themselves in a historical context can only act interpetatively towards tradition; and in the very act of doing so they also carry tradition forward. Hermeneutics – interpretation – is a *signum,* a sign and token of every *theologia viatorum,* or on-going theology. The refusal to interpret, on the other hand, can be motivated only by the self-understanding of a theology which believes that it has finally reached the haven of eternal truth. Today we are more aware of this than we were in the past.

An important task would be to take up more seriously and thoroughly than before the problem of a history of theology and church under the aspect of the interpretation of Scripture, in Gerhard Ebeling's sense; and for this, detailed philological and historical work would be required. The aim would be to understand more clearly the diachronic and synchronic structural problems of this history. In view of our contemporary loss of awareness of the depths of the historical dimension, this would seem to me an urgent requirement. I am thinking here of an approach via social history, of the kind pursued today by French historians in particular. What is at issue here is above all a recognition of the reciprocal influence of different phenomena and institutions; for instance, church and state, Christianity and society. Such carefully worked out cross-sections, both horizontal and vertical, could surely help us to master our contemporary problems; and I would see one important advantage in the opportunity it would give us to compare earlier paradigms with modern ones. It is surely not enough simply to postulate a new paradigm, and to urge its acceptance over against earlier ones. The contrast between old paradigms and new must rather serve to reveal unconscious errors and biases, so that advantages and disadvantages may be weighed up against one another.

Second, I should like a better criticism of criteria whereby to decide whether new paradigms are really helpful and really take us a step further. The distinction between hermeneutical conditions and hermeneutical essentials or principles is important here. In my view feminist interpretation belongs to the hermeneutical conditions, and not to the hermeneutical essentials or principles. And in fact it belongs to the 'unchangeable' conditions. Here there ought to be more interdisciplinary conferences, for example on the question whether or not a 'materialist' or 'depth-psychology' interpretation of the Bible can be maintained, what this whole problem involves, and so forth. We should also honestly admit that not every theological swallow makes a summer, or deserves to be hailed at once as the mighty inspiration and revelation of genius or prophecy. In the last fifty years, many a star has risen and set in theology. Much has been forgotten which today ought to be remembered, especially the pioneer work of French theology in the first half of this century.

Third, I have arrived at the view that the question about new scientific or scholarly paradigms in theology is not really the central problem, but is, in actual fact, an epiphenomenon, a symptom of deeper developments and rock-shifts in theology. It therefore seems to me too hasty and superficial merely to ask about new paradigms without entering into the whole breadth and depth of the new problems. Here developments are much less within our grasp than we imagine.

I should like to illustrate this from three different sectors, although the three are very closely connected.

(a) One essential problem is the relationship between theological thinking and modern science and technology. We can meanwhile skip 'the Galileo case', as well as other defensive assurances that theology has nothing against the independence and immanent objective logic of the natural sciences, and that the contradiction between theology and science is really a misunderstanding. Today we have to do with very different problems, namely with the question of what is going to happen to the tradition of Christian humanism in general? Is technology going to turn human beings into its object (see the problems of human genetics), or will human beings finally come to use technology for their own benefit? Have theologians in the past not thought and written much too uncritically about these things? Today the theology that has urged adaptation to the modern age is especially challenged to say where it stands.

(b) A second problem directly connected with this is the awakening or admission of fear of the threatening self-annihilation of human beings through a nuclear war, the question of the peace movement, and so forth. The problem of modern weapons of annihilation is after all nothing other than the most extreme form of the question about global changes through technology, and human responsibility for them. We need only remember Marx's famous statement: 'The philosophers have merely *interpreted* the world differently; the important thing is *to change* it' (*11th Thesis on Feuerbach*). We must ask whether capitulation in the face of this development would not be the renunciation, not only of reason and liberty, but also of faith, hope and love, right along the line? It was high time that we woke up to this. The option we have to make here as theologians seems to me much more vital than the question about a new theoretical paradigm.

(c) A third and last aspect: I have the impression that we have arrived at a point where the traditional 'Constantinian relationship' between church and state is finally beginning to crumble everywhere, including West Germany. Where nuclear armaments are concerned, Catholic bishops all over the world have brought themselves to break the taboo and to criticize their own governments. A point has evidently been reached where Christians who want to remain true to the gospel, and to the biblical view of God, human beings and the world, feel bound to criticize political and economic practice, and above all arms production, because this can lead only to the self-destruction of humanity and the world in which we live. Parallel to this, a new goal is emerging: the idea of a genuine, world-wide community of peoples, in peace, justice and liberty, in solidarity with one another. I believe that this will not be without consequences. In this connection it has become increasingly clear to me that every theology has its politically conditioned presuppositions, whether it likes to admit it or not. After all, even the pope is still a political question. This, incidentally, is not the same thing as the programme of a political theology. The political presuppositions are to be found in the relationship between church and state in any given case, and in my view these are changing only very slowly. But I ask myself what will happen when the governments of the United States and West Germany, for example, no longer receive moral support from the churches but criticism instead, and if this will make them less certain about their policies? And if this comes about because more and more Christians are taking their bearings from the Sermon on the Mount? These are some of the new 'hermeneutical conditions' to which theology ought to turn its attention.

But most important of all seems to me the question: what has to happen if the saving Word of God is really to penetrate a world which has permanently excluded this particular aspect of things from its interpretation of reality? Let me close with a poem by Friedrich Hölderlin, who began his career here in Tübingen, spent forty years of his life mentally deranged, and is buried in a Tübingen graveyard:

Mnemosyne (Second Version)

A sign we are, but uninterpreted,
Painless we are and almost dumb,
Our language lost to us in foreign land.
For when about us mortal beings
Heaven disputes, and the moons
Sweep through their courses,
The sea speaks too, and rivers
Must seek their paths. Beyond doubt
Is but One. He
Can daily change the course of things, has hardly need
Of law. And the leaf will sound and oak trees sway
Beside the snowfields. For the Heavenly Ones
Are not all-powerful. And mortals
First stand before the abyss. So the echo turns
With these. Long
Is time. But it will come to pass
The True.

So what should we say? What must we say? And whence do we derive our competence?

[10] The original is as follows:

Mnemosyne. Zweite Fassung

Ein Zeichen sind wir, deutungslos
Schmerzlos sind wir und haben fast
Die Sprache in der Fremde verloren.
Wenn nämlich über Menschen
Ein Streit ist an dem Himmel und gewaltig
Die Monde gehn, so redet
Das Meer auch und Ströme müssen
Den Pfad sich suchen. Zweifellos
Ist aber Einer. Der
Kann täglich es ändern. Kaum bedarf er
Gesetz. Und es tönet das Blatt und Eichbäume wehn dann neben
Den Firnen. Denn nicht vermögen
Die Himmlischen alles. Nämlich es reichen
Die Sterblichen eh an den Abgrund. Also wendet es sich, das Echo
Mit diesen. Lang ist
Die Zeit, es ereignet sich aber
Das Wahre.

I am indebted to Dr Jeremy Adler for valuable suggestions on the translation of this poem. He is of course in no way responsible for the inadequacies of the English version (translator).

RESPONSE TO JOSEF BLANK*

Paul Ricoeur

I wish to discuss the main assumption of Blank's paper: that the question of the essence and meaning of hermeneutics is nearly identical with the structure of the subject-matter of the New Testament texts and of their theologies. I agree with the 'soft' version of the previous statement, according to which biblical exegesis *reveals an hermeneutical process already at work within the texts themselves and, accordingly, discloses a first model of paradigm change in theology.* I disagree with the 'hard' version of the basic statement: *that this first model, found within the biblical texts themselves, responds to our modern concern for a new paradigm in theology.* Against any attempt to subordinate theology to exegesis, I want to argue that *there must be, from the very beginning, a mutually supportive and corrective relationship between biblical exegesis and systematic theology, if they both wish to be hermeneutical.*

I. Blank's paper is very convincing in all its duly exegetical aspects. *First*, Blank is right to depict the theologian as making demands of the exegete, to the extent that the former refers his or her discourse to the testimonies in the canonical texts regarding the God of Israel and Jesus. Accordingly, textual criticism must precede theological discourse. *Second*, Blank is very convincing when he shows that a hermeneutical process is already at work in the Christian Bible. Demonstration is the backbone of the paper. *Third*, Blank is very strong when he underscores the plurality of

---

* Josef Blank's paper had to be somewhat shortened for print. Consequently not all the references in the Responses can be followed up in the paper as printed.

interpretations already competing within our texts and, when he consequently concludes that paradigms are selective, and to that extent, limited and relative. *Fourth*, Blank is very helpful when he discerns in the dialectic of the 'letter' and the 'spirit' the starting-point of a self-critical and self-corrective stance (that the 'letter' alone is only a dead deposit; that the 'spirit' alone legitimates the subjectivism of all potential fanatics and heretics; that the interpreter has to interpret himself or herself, is the hermeneutical rule in this stance). *Fifth*, I still follow Blank when he deplores the exegetical weakness of many theological enterprises and, above all, when he denies to philosophical hermeneutics the right to *filter* the meaning of the text in terms of what modern man is supposed to understand and to accept. An exegete is right to be suspicious of this *reductive* hermeneutics. A good hermeneutic, then, is one which lets the voices of the text speak from afar, as alien and disturbing, and overwhelming as they may be. *Finally*, Blank is right when he asks for a *critique of criteria*, directed against any hermeneutical imperialism superimposed on the *subject-matter* itself of the text.

II.   Against the 'strong' thesis that textual criticism could claim to be hermeneutics of itself, and could provide the theologian with paradigms of interpretation without any mutual borrowing between exegesis and theology, I want to stress the following arguments for which I find support in Blank's paper itself.

First, textual criticism becomes hermeneutics, not because of the famous hermeneutical circle which may be found everywhere, even in the natural sciences, but because the *subject-matter* of the text governs the interpretation. But how could the subject-matter of the text be identified, if not with the help of the *logic of question and answer*? (Who is the God of Israel? Who is Jesus Christ?) And how could such questions be raised, if they were not also *our* questions, although in a cultural context different from that of the text? In other words, is it possible to start and to pursue an inquiry into the hermeneutical process going on *within* the text, without any interest in the theological concerns *of the present*? In this respect, the illusion of an autonomous significance of past history is no less dangerous than that of a criteriology unilaterally ruled by some of our present expectations. I doubt that we would be able to speak in respect of Luke-Acts of a theology of salvation history, if this theology had not generated later on a series of effects which help us to identify it, retrospectively, as a 'theology'. Hence my first suggestion: we cannot take a fully-fledged theological paradigm from the canonical texts themselves, without a dialogue – which may be highly conflictual – between the theological concerns of our time and those of the biblical texts.

Second, if we assume this *dialogical* and *bipolar* structure of biblical theology, we have no direct access to the meaning of the text (as distinct from its structure) beyond the history of its effects (in dogmas, liturgies and worship). No text could reach us, if it were not *transmitted*, handed down to us, channelled by a tradition of interpretation. In that respect, temporal distance is not only a gulf which separates, but a productive transmission (*Überlieferung*) which mediates. To that extent, the history of effects (Gadamer) is a part of the potential meaning of the text; this meaning is unfinished, dialectically related to the horizon of expectation (Koselleck) of an endless succession of readers, and to the history of the reception of the text (Jauss). A hermeneutics which was merely *internal* to the text is an impossible requirement.

Third, if we consider the history of effects as a part of the meaning of the text, then the dialectics between text and reader tends to assume the form of *tension*, even of conflict, between the subject-matter of the text, with its alien character, and the concerns of a modern reader, which are themselves the product of all the *crises* through which the history of interpretation has passed (our example of the Septuagint translation receives its full meaning here: it is, as Blank says, the encounter and the clash between two cultures, as the translation of *Exodus* 3, 14 shows it. But translation, as George Steiner has demonstrated in *After Babel*, gives only linguistic visibility to the broader problem of understanding, which is always a transfer of the same into a different medium). Then the major crises of western thought

(Renaissance, Reformation, Enlightenment, Romanticism, Positivism, and so on) are included in the very question that we *now* address to our texts. Then, also, philosophy, epistemology, psychoanalysis and ideology-criticism (*Ideologie-Kritik*) become unavoidable components of our present mode of understanding.

Fourth, if we have to include in our search for the meaning of the text, not only the history of its effects, but the predicament of our modern situation, then the changes of paradigms, as *read in* the text, cannot by themselves provide us with the *new* theological models that the present situation of thought requires.

The hermeneutical rule which I see as the only operable one would be: *our* answers should be to *our* problems what the answers of the biblical writers were to the problems of their time, as we perceive them by means of biblical exegesis. This relation of *analogy* between the question-answer relationship of today and the question-answer relationship of the primitive church seems to me the best approximation to the kind of truthfulness that we expect from a Christian hermeneutical theology. But because this truthfulness relies on an analogical relationship to the interpretation of questions and answers which constitute the hermeneutical process at work in the text, it does not exclude, but rather requires, imagination, boldness and coherence. Such are the qualities that I find in the last pages of Professor Blank's paper, when he addresses three questions: that of the relation between theological thinking and modern science and technology; that of the threat of mankind's self-annihilation in a nuclear war; and that of a complete separation of state and church. These questions are not external to a biblical theology, to the extent that a biblical hermeneutics is not in turn a self-contained enterprise. Between the hermeneutical process that exegesis discloses *within* the biblical texts and our search for new models for theology, the dialogical relationship must never be broken, if it is to fulfil its mutually supportive and corrective task.

RESPONSE TO JOSEF BLANK: BIBLICAL THEOLOGY AND PHILOSOPHY IN THE NEW PARADIGM

Schubert M. Ogden

I

Before responding to Josef Blank's paper, I want to summarize the answer that I would give to what I understand to be the specific question before this session of the symposium. It seems to me all the more important to do this, both because Blank's contribution to our discussion is limited to clarifying only the first part of this specific question, which asks about the role of biblical theology in the new paradigm, and because there is no other paper that undertakes to clarify the second part of the question, which asks about the role of philosophy.

As I understand it, the specific question before us is this: what is the role of biblical theology and philosophy in the new paradigm of theology? I can summarize my answer to this question by asking and briefly answering five still more specific questions.

1. What is properly meant by 'paradigm'?

According to Thomas Kuhn, one may distinguish two senses of the term. In the first, relatively broader sense it refers to a 'disciplinary matrix' which consists in 'an entire constellation of beliefs, values, techniques and so on shared by the members of a given community'. In the second, relatively stricter sense it refers to one of the types of items included in this disciplinary matrix – namely, 'exemplars' or 'concrete puzzle-solutions which, employed as models or examples, can replace explicit rules as a basis for the solution of the remaining puzzles of normal science' (Kuhn: 175, 182, 187). It seems clear that it is primarily the first sense of paradigm that figures in the question before the symposium. At any rate, this question is formulated elsewhere in the preparatory papers for the symposium as follows: 'Is it possible today, in spite of all differences and divergences, to reach a basic hermeneutical consensus in Christian theology on an international and ecumenical foundation?' And in another place, a distinction is carefully made between two types of consensus: 'a consensus (of a hermeneutical kind) about a certain theoretical-practical understanding of theology' and 'a consensus (of a material kind) about particular teachings, doctrines, dogmas'.

2. What is to be understood by 'the new paradigm of theology'?

Assuming the meaning of 'paradigm' just clarified, I would suppose that this phrase is to be understood as referring to a relatively new, recently emergent disciplinary matrix or hermeneutical consensus shared by Christian theologians across national and confessional differences (cf. Küng). Of course, one may well ask about the newness of this new paradigm. I have the distinct impression that what is really new about it is less the constellation of beliefs, values, techniques and so on that go to make it up, than the fact that these beliefs, values, techniques and so on have now come to be far more widely shared, across greater differences between Christian theologians, than ever before. Broadly speaking, I should say that the disciplinary matrix or basic consensus that has now come to be so widely shared is that of the revisionary theology pioneered, above all, by Schleiermacher, if not in its earlier liberal phase, then in its later neo-orthodox or genuinely post-liberal phases. Essential to this new consensus, to be sure, are the concerns of what has been called the second, as well as those of the first, Enlightenment; hence theology's widespread preoccupation today with praxis as well as with self-understanding, and with issues of action and justice as well as with problems of belief and truth. But it is arguable that even in this respect the consensus itself is hardly new – witness Schleiermacher's own insistence that 'what makes a person a Christian can be conceived with equal justification as being originally knowledge and a way of acting' (Schleiermacher: 18). In any case, to ask, as we are asking in this symposium, whether there is a new paradigm of theology, is to ask whether, or to what extent, there is any such relatively new, recently emergent understanding of theology itself now widely shared by Christian theologians. Clearly, the only way to answer this question is to formulate just such an understanding of theology and then to determine whether, or to what extent, theologians today do in fact share it.

3. How, then, should such a new paradigm of theology be formulated?

In the new paradigm, theology is understood as either the process or the product of critical reflection on the validity claims expressed or implied by the Christian witness of faith. More exactly, theology is understood to be either the process or the product of such reflection as is required to validate the claims of this witness to be both *appropriate* to what is normatively Christian and *credible* to men and women in terms of their common human experience (*cf.* Küng). Thus theology is to Christian witness in particular what critical reflection is to self-understanding and praxis in general. This means that, while theology does indeed arise out of Christian self-understanding and praxis, and exists in order to be of service to them, it nevertheless is properly distinguished from them and can be of service to them only indirectly. Using Habermas' terminology, one might express this understanding of theology in its relation to, and difference from, Christian witness by saying that they are related to and different from one another as 'discourse', on the one hand, and 'life-praxis', or 'action', on the other hand. Thus theology, as a form of discourse, is 'unburdened by action and freed from experience' (Habermas, 1973a: 386). In order to do theology, accordingly, 'we must in a certain way step outside of contexts of action and of experience; in this case we do not exchange items of information [or experiences related to action] but, rather, exchange arguments that serve to ground (or to reject) validity claims that have become problematic' (Habermas, 1973b: 214).

4. What is the role of biblical theology in the new paradigm?

The role of biblical theology in the new paradigm is essentially that of historical theology generally: namely, so to mediate the privileged data of the Christian witness, in the language and experience of contemporary men and women, as to make possible theology's validation of the validity claim to appropriateness that is expressed or implied in this witness. Consequently, biblical theology, like historical theology in general, performs an indispensable function in the total process of critical reflection that is theology, insofar as without it systematic theology could not carry out the historical aspect of its task by validating the claim of Christian witness to be appropriate. The methods necessary to systematic theology's carrying out this task are two: *dual interpretation* – namely, of normative Christian witness, on the one hand, and of common human experience, on the other – and *mutual confirmation* – namely, of this same normative witness by this same common human experience, and *vice versa* (Ogden, 1976). But the task of historical theology in general and of biblical theology in particular is to interpret the Christian witness of faith, including the original and originating and, therefore, uniquely normative form of this witness that is properly distinguished as 'apostolic'. Because or insofar as this is so, the role of biblical theology in the new paradigm is irreplaceable.

5. What is the role of philosophy in the new paradigm?

The role of philosophy in the new paradigm is to provide the terms – concepts, methods and so on – whereby philosophical theology can so mediate all the data of human self-understanding and praxis, in the language and experience of men and women today, so as to make possible theology's validation of the validity claim to credibility that is also expressed or implied by the Christian witness of faith. Consequently philosophy also has an indispensable function to perform in the total process of theological reflection, although in this case neither it nor the philosophical theology constituted by it is an integral part of this process, but, rather, is a necessary condition of the systematic theology that is such an integral part. Without philosophy, there could no more be philosophical theology than there could be historical theology without history. But without philosophical theology, systematic theology could not carry out the philosophical aspect of its task by validating the validity claim of the Christian witness to be credible. Neither the dual interpretation nor the mutual confirmation that are the methods necessary to systematic theology's carrying out its task could be followed without the interpretation of human self-understanding and praxis that is the proper business of philosophical theology (Ogden, 1971: 72-82). For this reason, the role of philosophy in the new paradigm is also irreplaceable.

II

So much for my summary answer to our specific question. I now wish to state what I take to be Blank's answer to the first part of the question, and then to make three comments by way of furthering our critical appropriation of his argument.

According to Blank, the task of exegesis, as of historical theology as a whole, is to represent the 'right of the past' over against the legitimate but always limited concerns of the present. The past retains its own independent significance in spite of, or just because of, the fact that it so often fails to fit our highly selective preconceptions. Consequently, the role or function of biblical theology, like that of historical theology generally, is so to contribute to the 'critique of criteria' of our contemporary standards of critical reflection, as to keep the unruly book that is the Bible from ever being locked up in a systematic cage.

This biblical theology does by demonstrating that the 'hermeneutical problem', far from being peculiarly modern, is among the oldest and most basic problems of Christian theology – witness the early church's christological interpretation of the Hebrew Scriptures. Similarly, it shows that there has been 'paradigm change' in theology right from the beginning – as is clear from the vast difference between Jesus' way of picturing the reign of God in concrete images and Paul's way of thinking about the righteousness of God in abstract concepts. Thus biblical theology at once legitimates our concern for new paradigms and relativizes or defuses it, insisting that even such 'old' and 'new' paradigms as New Testament hermeneutics and modern hermeneutics are never mutually exclusive alternatives, but are so related that the new can win out only when it establishes connections with the old. Biblical theology confirms the need for a number of different paradigms that correspond and are open to one another, even while it exposes the question about *the* new paradigm as exceedingly problematic and unanswerable.

Such, as I understand it, is Blank's answer to the part of our question that asks about the role or function of biblical theology. My first critical comment is that I can readily agree with what I take to be the main point of this answer. Certainly, in any new paradigm of theology that I could accept as adequate, biblical theology, like historical theology in general, would have to play its proper role of representing the past – specifically, the past documented by the biblical writings – in its independent significance for the present. But more than this, I also take biblical theology to show that interpreting the Christian witness, and thus the hermeneutical problem, was already a problem for the early church, and that there has been paradigm change in theology right from the outset, in the sense that even from Jesus to Paul there is a vast difference between the images and the concepts through which they bear their witness of faith.

Nevertheless – and this is my second critical comment – I am extremely doubtful whether this is the same sense in which the preparatory papers for the symposium have used the term 'paradigm change' in posing the question of a new paradigm of theology. At any rate, as I noted above, care is taken in formulating the objective of the symposium to distinguish the basic consensus being asked about as 'a consensus (of a hermeneutical kind) about a certain theoretical and practical understanding of theology' from 'a consensus (of a material kind) about particular teachings, doctrines, dogmas'. But then, if one were to employ the terms of this distinction, surely the difference between Jesus and Paul, however vast, would be more appropriately described as 'material' rather than 'hermeneutical', and, therefore, as precisely not involving 'paradigm change' in the proper sense of the words.

Of course, this is not the only difference that Blank takes to involve a change of paradigms. In fact, in one place he expressly uses the distinction between 'old' and 'new' paradigms to refer to the difference between 'New Testament and early Christian hermeneutics' on the one hand, and 'modern hermeneutics' on the other hand. But I fear that this use makes only too clear one of the most serious dangers of our entire symposium – namely, that in using Kuhn's term 'paradigm' we will allow its meaning to expand or contract on demand in something like the way in which theologians have often done in using Wittgenstein's term 'language game'. Clearly, if we are to avoid merely verbal issues, we are going to have to use this and all the other operative terms in our discussion with a certain precision. Considering, then, that talk about 'a new paradigm of theology' was introduced in the first place simply as one way of asking whether there can be a basic hermeneutical consensus today about the nature and task of theology, we have good reason to discipline our use of such talk by continually referring it to this, the real issue before the symposium.

In that event, however, we will have to question whether biblical theology has quite the relativizing or defusing effect that Blank avers. He confesses at one point that for him there are no 'settled problems'. But then one also notes how utterly he takes for granted that the hermeneutical process of which exegesis is a part includes 'the historical-critical method', thereby presuming upon the settlement of at least one problem – namely, whether the interpretative procedures of theology today will or will not be responsibly historical–critical. I submit that there is hardly a clearer case of what is properly meant by 'paradigm change in theology' than the difference between the early church's christological interpretation of the Hebrew Scriptures and the kind of historical–critical exegesis that Blank evidently expects of himself and his colleagues as contemporary biblical theologians. In fact the difference here is so basic that to leave the impression that both kinds of interpretation are ways of dealing with the same hermeneutical problem can scarcely fail to mislead. But then I, for one, simply cannot agree that old and new paradigms are never mutually exclusive alternatives, but must urge, on the contrary, that in this case, at least, the choice between them is clear–cut and cannot be avoided.

My third critical comment also has to do with how biblical theology must be understood in the new paradigm – only in this case it is occasioned not only by what Blank says but what he fails to say. One of the most gratifying things about his argument is the way in which he represents the task of exegesis as one and the same with that of historical theology as a whole. But unless I have somehow missed it, he nowhere explicitly answers the question of the specific difference between biblical theology and historical theology in general. And if we look for an implicit answer to this question, his most relevant statements appear to point in contrary directions. On the one hand, what he has to say about the model of Pauline hermeneutics seems to indicate, surely correctly, that the real canon for Paul is not Scripture, whether Old Testament or New, but rather 'the common tradition' of the 'Gospel' in the sense of 'a basic consensus given prior to the apostolic proclamation'. On the other hand, his anachronistic formulation of the title of Section 2 of his paper, according to which 'the basic problem of theological hermeneutics in the New Testament' is 'the question about the relation of Old and New Testaments', appears to point, rather, to Scripture as the real Christian canon. And he gives the same indication, I believe, when he claims, surely questionably, that 'from the beginning the early Church had its Bible in the form of the 'Old Testament'.

In short, what Blank says and what he does not say raises the question of the nature of the difference of biblical theology from historical theology generally: Is it in the last analysis a difference in principle, because the writings of which biblical theology is the exegesis are themselves the uniquely authoritative canon for all Christian witness and theology? Or is it finally only a difference in fact because the real Christian canon is *prior* to the canon of Scripture, and even New Testament theology may be defined with Ferdinand Christian Baur as simply 'the history of Christian dogma in its course within the New Testament' (Marxsen: 17)?

No doubt, on either answer, the role or function of biblical theology in the process of theological reflection remains secure. For even if one holds, as I do, that in any genuinely new paradigm of theology the real Christian canon must be located in what for us today, given our own historical methods and knowledge, can most reasonably be said to be the original and originating witness of the apostles – even then, the biblical writings remain the indispensable sources both for reconstructing this apostolic witness and for understanding the distinctive form of the religious question to which it presents itself as the answer. Even so, the issue between these answers seems sufficiently clear and basic that we will hardly be able to avoid it if we are to deal adequately with either the specific question before us here or the more general question before the symposium.

Bibliography

Habermas, Jürgen, *Erkenntnis und Interesse, Mit einem neuen Nachwort* (Frankfurt, 1973); also 'Wahrheitstheorien', in *Wirklichkeit und Reflexion, Walter Schulz zum 60. Geburtstag*, ed. Helmut Fahrenbach (Pfullingen, 1973), pp.211-65.

Kuhn, Thomas, *The Structure of Scientific Revolutions*, 2nd ed. (Chicago, 1970).

Küng, Hans 'Paradigm Change in Theology: A Proposal for Discussion' (manuscript, 1981).

Marxsen, Willi, *Einleitung in das Neue Testament, Eine Einführung in ihre Probleme*, 4th ed. (Gütersloh, 1978).

Ogden, Schubert M. 'The Task of Philosophical Theology', in *The Future of Philosophical Theology*, ed. Robert A. Evans (Philadelphia, 1971), pp.55-84; 'Sources of Religious Authority in Liberal Protestantism', *Journal of the American Academy of Religion* 44: (1976), pp.403-416.

Schleiermacher, Friedrich, *Die christliche Sitte nach den Grundsätzen der evangelischen Kirche in Zusammenhange dargestellt*, ed. L. Jonas (Berlin, 1843).

RESPONSE TO JOSEF BLANK

Eberhard Jüngel

A Preliminary Observation. It is of course up-to-date to talk about paradigms and paradigm change in scientific theory; but I do not consider it to be so helpful that theology is *bound* to adopt this terminology. It probably confuses more than it clarifies. However, our symposium has chosen this as its subject, so I have to play my part in the language game. For the moment, therefore, I will set aside my own scepticism, and do what is most appropriate for a symposium – propose a toast: Here's to the *modus loquendi* of a new paradigm in theology! May it only prove useful! As I see it, my function here is to subject the opulent contours of Josef Blank's paper to a slimming cure. So I shall restrict myself to clarifying a few terminological premises, and to selecting systematically some aspects of Blank's paper which seem to me particularly important, modifying them and supplementing them.

1. The expression 'paradigm change' can be used in different ways in the context of Christian theology (πολλαχῶς λέγεται). It is therefore essential to state the sense in which 'paradigm' or 'paradigm change' is being used in any given case.

1.1 The problem of the many different ways in which the terms 'paradigm' and 'paradigm change' are used is certainly pre-theological in kind. But in the context of theology the problem becomes more acute since, by nature of the subject with which it deals, theology has to do with a paradigm change *sui generis*: the existential change in human understanding conveyed in the phrases τὰ τῆς σαρκὸς φρονεῖν and τὰ τοῦ πνεύματος φϱονεῖν (Rom. 8.5) – setting one's mind on the things of the flesh, and setting one's mind on the things of the Spirit. Blank cites, for example, Paul's completely different overall interpretation 'after his "conversion"'.

1.2   A useful starting-point in clarifying the many different ways in which paradigm and paradigm change are used is the trivial recognition that the human mind (*intellectus humanus*), unlike the *intellectus divinus*, is not an *intuitus originarius*, which in the very act of thinking also engenders as a whole Being as such. The mind always merely selects out of the multiplicity of what already exists (either actually or potentially), and achieves orientation for itself on the basis of what has been selected. Or we might say with Hölderlin's later version of *Brot und Wein*:

> . . . at home is the spirit
> Not in the origin, not at the source.

1.3   An intellect which achieves orientation for itself is dependent on *aids towards this orientation*. Paradigms are aids of this kind which prove useful, not merely individually and *ad hoc*, but for a whole series of acts of the *intellectus humanus* and among a group of people.

1.3.1 Paradigms result in the forming of a *consensus*.

1.4   A paradigm in the stricter sense of the term is an exemplary case or *typical example*. That is to say, it is a specific solution to a problem which leads on to μίμησις, a mimesis or imitation, or to analogical procedures (Kuhn's paradigm 2).

1.5   A paradigm in the broader sense of the word is *an orientation framework* which provides guidelines and standards for the activities of the human mind.

1.5.1 Paradigms in both the narrower sense and the broader sense of the word are necessary in the world of living both for *the existential understanding* of world and self, and for *the formation of scientific theory*, with the appropriate acts of cognition that belong to that.

1.5.2 In the context of the formation of scientific theory and the acts of cognition belonging to it, paradigms are made of *what is shared* by individuals working in the scientific field. This makes possible relatively unproblematical professional communication and a relatively unanimous professional judgment on the part of scientists in a particular discipline: 'disciplinary matrix' (Kuhn's paradigm 1).

– Apart from symbolic generalizations, heuristic and ontological models and so on, paradigms in the narrower sense (1.4) are parts of paradigms in the broader sense (1.5).

1.6 In the context of Christian theology, a distinction must be made between:

1.6.1 paradigms which guide scientific or scholarly findings in the wider sense (1.5), where a change remodels the whole of theological knowledge (or the whole of a theological discipline) and promises a general advancement of knowledge;

1.6.2 paradigms in the narrower sense, which determine detailed research and detailed argumentation (1.4), where a change promises to extend the special problem-awareness of the expert in a particular field;

1.6.3 a change of paradigm given with the object of theological studies themselves, a change which has continually to be made anew, or followed up (1.5)

(*a*) either in the sense of a change in tradition, or a breach with tradition, within the biblical material transmitted to us (Blank),

(*b*) or in the sense of a change of argumentation: law and gospel; demand and promise; letter and spirit (Blank),

(*c*) or in the sense of new bearings in the self-understanding of human beings: κατὰ σάρκα – κατὰ πνεῦμα, ἐν ᾽Αδάμ – ἐν χριστῷ (according to the flesh – according to the spirit; in Adam – in Christ).

1.7   In theology there is not merely paradigm *change*; paradigms are also *interwoven*, so that the new paradigm remains permanently related to the old one.

2.   Theology shares with its own time – even if critically – *the general sense of truth* and of what is plausible. To this extent it participates in the overriding paradigms of interpretation, which are pre-eminently formulated in philosophy. It therefore also participates in the paradigm changes which modify the general sense of truth and of what is plausible. But theology must not allow itself to be prevented by any paradigm change from giving effect to the intention of the authors of the biblical texts, who were thinking in 'obsolete' paradigms, even if this intention is not in accord with contemporary ideas (Blank).

2.1   A decisive overriding paradigm change is the transition which has taken place in modern times from *the metaphysics of substance* to *an ontology* which takes its bearings from *event, subject* (ascertaining and ratifying through the subject) and *relation*.[1] To this correspond methods of historical interpretation which are critical of tradition. Let me remind you explicitly that ever since Aristotle, the metaphysics of substance has been *theistically* constituted, whereas the constitution of the new paradigm is neither theistic nor atheistic, but makes a way of thinking possible that is *beyond* both theism and atheism.

2.1.1   One late consequence of this paradigm change is the hermeneutical revaluation (in the positive sense) of metaphorical ways of speaking and of anthromorphism in exegesis and dogmatics; in short, the superseding of the hermeneutics of signification.

---

[1] *deum quaerendum esse non in praedicamento substantiae sed relationis* (God is to be sought, not in what is predicated of substance, but in what is predicated of relation).

2.2 The theological claims to truth once formulated in the 'metaphysics of substance' paradigm must be capable of being *reproduced* in the 'ontology of event, relation and subject' paradigm (Blank); and it must be possible to state them in a fashion that is both more fundamental and more differentiated.

2.2.1 If these claims to truth can be expressed in a more fundamental and more differentiated way in the new paradigm, this will make possible *an experiential increase* of knowledge and hence an increased awareness of the theological problems – but also in the theological power to solve them.

2.2.2 The increased awareness of the problems and the increased power to solve problems in theological perception must prove itself in *practical consequences.*

– The practical consequences deriving from an increased awareness of the theological problems and increased theological power to solve problems will no doubt not least include the exegetical exposure of a false formulation of problems, and hence the systematic abolition of obsolete problems belonging to controversial theology. One problem of this kind has, for example, been institutionalized in the refusal of mutual participation in the Lord's Supper.

2.3 The paradigm constituted by the ontology of event, relation and subject has not only made possible a clearer understanding of *the historicity of the claim to truth of the biblical texts.* It has also enabled us to arrive at a stricter understanding of *the historicity of the God* who (according to these texts) has come to the world.

2.3.1 Only insight into the historicity and worldliness of God reveals the self-interpretation of God as the final and most profound reason for a theological hermeneutics (Blank).

2.3.2 A clearer understanding of the historicity and worldliness of God must be matched by a stricter perception of the rationality of God's Being (as a trinitarian fellowship of mutual Otherness).

    – Without a minimal consensus with regard to the trinitarian idea of God, theology is not capable of consensus at all.

2.4   In the paradigm constituted by an ontology of event, relation and subject, the Being of God, and hence also the relationship between God and human beings, is conceivable as *event*.

2.4.1   Christian theology has to call to remembrance God's coming to the world in the history of Israel and Jesus Christ, as the primal event (revelation) which precedes all paradigms, while requiring paradigms that are adequate (Blank). This primal event faces people with the demand and decision *to believe* its promise and its claim – a decision which no hermeneutics can bring about.

2.4.2   The human being can believe only in the context of his or her experience of the world (and only, it may also be, *in opposition* to that experience). The exegesis of biblical texts therefore purposes to translate their claim to truth out of the experience of the world of their time into present experience of the world, in such a way that faith can become *possible*.

3.   To know that theological paradigms are necessary at the same time relativizes their importance: they are orientation aids serving a better understanding of the truth, but they are not a component part of truth itself. One of the things that certifies a paradigm's usefulness in the pursuit of truth is hence its provisional nature. It must put itself at our disposal, not in the interests of a random and disordered 'wildcat' thinking without paradigms, but in the interests of a paradigm that meets in the best possible way *the situation* of the person who has to respond to the truth of the gospel.

3.1   All the claims to truth formulated in older paradigms have their *criterion of understanding* in the human being who has to respond to the truth of the gospel; whereas they have their *infallible substantial criterion* in the paradigm change of human self-understanding given by christology (1.1 and 1.6.3c).

3.2 The infallible substantial criterion of a new self-understanding ἐν Χριστῷ ('in Christ') is approached most closely by the paradigm of the Pauline *doctrine of justification*, because this is the fundamental paradigm in which theology is most strictly and most radically understood as, and challenged to be, *a theology of liberation*: liberation in the sense of (*a*) the liberation of the sinner from the power of sin (self-realization); (*b*) the liberation of theology from the leading strings of ecclesiastical institutions and tradition; (*c*) the liberation of worldly responsibility from clerical, theocratic tutelage.

3.2.1 The special affinity of this paradigm to the new self-understanding ἐν Χριστῷ (and to the christological paradigm which is its foundation: 1.6.3c) does not exclude factual criticism of the formulations of the Pauline doctrine of justification; it includes such criticism.

3.2.2 Formulations within the same paradigm may be appropriate to a greater or lesser degree; but the paradigm itself can also be formulated in a way that is appropriate to a greater or lesser degree. In our present situation in theology and the church, we are still in need of a better formulation of the paradigm of the doctrine of justification – a formulation which would permit the whole of theology to be built up in a new way. The presupposition of an improved formulation of the fundamental paradigm is a capacity which still has to be learnt: the capacity to concentrate, in a post-atheistic age, on *the essence* of Christianity, and thus to bring out the fact that it is the truth, and only the truth, which makes us free.

4. What has been left out of this list is the following *impasse*: the more strictly scientific theology is, and the more it

investigates and teaches in the framework of paradigms, the greater its distance from the world in which faith lives, which takes its bearings from everyday language: from, that is, the language of faith. Should we therefore dispense with theological scholarship? Surely not! What we need is, rather, a continual mediation between the scientific or scholarly research into truth, and the language of faith, which lives from truth.

IV. THE ROLE OF HISTORY IN THE NEW PARADIGM

THE ROLE OF HISTORY IN WHAT IS CALLED THE NEW PARADIGM

Edward Schillebeeckx

The paradigm vogue in the natural sciences began to fascinate theologians at a moment when the discussion round Thomas S. Kuhn had ebbed away and when almost anything began to be called 'paradigms' (theories, hypotheses, axioms, laws, postulates and basic assumptions), while conversely a more precise understanding and use of models and paradigms was being achieved.

1. The present-day use of models

Apart from what could be called 'methodical models' (for example, the literary-historical method and the structuralist method in exegesis), some clarity has now been reached with respect to 'theoretical models' as used in the empirical sciences. From the literature dealing with the theory of science after Kuhn, a meaningful and operational definition can be distilled, on the basis of which one can verify how far theology also thinks in models. As a result of this discussion, a model appears to be an incomplete and insufficient design, which, on the one hand, *represents empirical observation*, and, on the other hand, *interprets the theory*: (*a*) in order to explain the empirical data; (*b*) in terms of a theory (in the making), and (*c*) in the service of the formation of theory. Consequently, in the empirical sciences theoretical models form a link between empirical observation and theory; for that reason they touch on both empirical observation and theory.

The link between empirical observation and theory is seen as necessary in order to translate the (highly formalized) language of coherence characteristic of theory into a language of correspondence. The researchers themselves through models make the theories refer to empirical observation. But we must not forget that all this takes place in the context of a polemic in the theory of science about the primacy of either theory or the so-called 'hard facts' (or experience, which itself is already 'laden with theory'). In sciences dedicated to the investigation of laws, like the natural sciences, this thinking–in–models was at times even seen as setting a standard for all other sciences. As a result Christian theology, which speaks of the unrepeatable uniqueness of Jesus of Nazareth, confessed as the Christ, and which at the same time was making serious efforts in academic circles to be accepted as a 'science', sometimes got into trouble through this emphasis on a standard model. Meanwhile we were taken by surprise when the so–called structuralistic phenomenology (in particular, as proposed by Roman Jakobson) proffered the thesis that the universal is to be found not only on the side of theory, but on that of experience: the universal is co–experienced, in the sense of 'observed'.

What can theology do with this limited and more sharply defined concept of paradigm and model? It is a fact that on the analogy of this empirical use of the category 'model' too, theology thinks in models. There is for example the Anselmian, Germanic-feudal 'model of a legal order', used to shed light on Christian soteriology. The model originates in feudal punitive practice. As with every model, it allows of alternative models and is essentially incomplete and insufficient. It is better, therefore, not to speak of a 'theory of satisfaction', but rather of a 'model of satisfaction'. In fact this model put paid to a patristic model which saw salvation as a 'ransom from the power of the devil', in which sinful man had been able to find a sort of alibi. If, then, the Council of Trent mentions the word 'satisfecit' (DS 1529), it speaks of real salvation in Christ, but through a model. As a result it is not the model which is 'dogmatized', but only something which has occurred in the history of Jesus' life and which through this model is being put into words. This thinking-in-models is important because it enables us to make a conscious distinction between the substance of faith and the model in which the faith is put into words. Theologians often confuse 'the thought' with 'thinking-in-models'.

In this way we can also speak of the 'two-natures model' in christology which, as a model, is naturally incomplete and insufficient: other models remain possible. Another example is the 'original sin model', and so on. On the analogy of this thinking-in-models in the empirical sciences, theology employs models just as much. To understand this is an advantage, but at the same time it should warn us, for thinking-in-models is not without its own dangers.

All the same, I get the impression that at this congress the problem concerning models and paradigms presents itself at a completely different level from the one just mentioned, in which case we cannot look for any help from the empirical, and in particular the natural sciences.

2. So-called 'epochal ruptures'

Karl Rahner and Bernhard Welte talked a considerable time ago of what they called 'epochal ruptures'. They did not elaborate these categories. In my view the *Annales*-school of French historiography can provide theology with more light on this matter than Kuhn. In addition to a short-term or 'ephemeral' history of facts there is a 'structural' and 'conjunctural' history. The conjunctural history embraces larger periods, branches out further, penetrates deeper, and is more comprehensive; a cultural conjuncture lasts a long time. On the other hand 'structural history', in spite of being history, passes very slowly. It is characterized by an age-long duration which is almost identical with stagnation, and yet it moves.

The conjunctural history (which I compare to what Rahner and Welte have called the 'epochal level') is very important for theological thinking. This cultural conjuncture provides the framework within which the history of facts, which took place in a determined period, can be interpreted. Precisely this conjunctural history shows a resemblance to what at this congress is called 'paradigm'. A conjunctural epoch has its own conjunctural horizon of understanding and gives rise to models of understanding in order to be able to situate and comprehend events. Such was the case in feudal times with the Anselmian model of a 'legal order' in christology. In a particular conjunctural culture this sharpens people's capacity to discern certain problems.

Sometimes the conjunctural epoch changes, as a result of a variety of factors. At first it remains unnoticed, but at last a conscious change is made to a new cultural horizon, with its own new models. People's eyes start to see different problems. In such a case we talk about a 'paradigm shift'.

Nevertheless, it is the 'structural level' of history which is the most fundamental and the least changeable. This structure makes it possible that interpretations from different conjunctural horizons of understanding can still be made accessible once more to people who live in another cultural epoch. This enables us, for example, to understand biblical models, like those of Chalcedon, today too, even if we use other models.

It does mean, however, that if we transfer the Chalcedon model to our own cultural conjuncture, we run a serious risk of misunderstanding such a model from a different cultural conjuncture. Consequently interpretation, when we come down to it, is something of a culture-shock. A particular conjunctural horizon of understanding sees as fundamental certain questions which we, in a different cultural epoch, experience as peripheral. Each epoch also has its blind spots, and this gives rise to 'forgotten truths' which will once more become relevant in a different conjuncture. The emphasis on horizons and models (within the structural and conjunctural history and also within the fluctuations inside cultural conjunctures) provides us indeed with the possibility of re-interpreting, for example, the model of Chalcedon for other times and other places.

3. Theology as a hermeneutical enterprise within a practical-critical intention and as a criticism of ideology

The above-mentioned distinction between structural and conjunctural historical periods is, theologically, all the more important because the specific culture is what Christian faith in fact is modelled on; it is also that through which the Christian faith is assimilated in a living way, and, finally, it is in this that the faith is lived specifically by people here and now. This social and cultural mediation and incorporation of the faith causes problems for believers when the social and cultural patterns and their categories of experience and thought undergo drastic changes.

The Christian faith's tradition of experience and interpretation is a tradition of *meaning* with *liberating force*. It opens a horizon of possible experience for us today also. What we are dealing with here is not primarily a theoretical disclosure of meaning, but first and foremost a *narrative* revelation of meaning, which nevertheless was already being accompanied by at least an initial theological reflection even in the Old and New Testament.

(*a*) A hermeneutical enterprise

We are facing a very delicate problem here. On the one hand, the gospel in its fundamental tendency and power is transcendent and universal and, in that sense, 'transcultural', by which I mean that it is not limited to *one* culture. On the other hand, precisely this universal and 'transcultural gospel, which challenges all people and cultures, can only be found in the forms of *particular cultures* (the Jewish, Judaic-hellenistic, Hellenistic, Carolingian, Celtic, Roman, African, Asian . . . cultures), – never above or outside them; one never comes across a 'peeled substance' of faith; there is no way of stripping off the skin and getting down to the essence of the gospel. Only in the concrete and in the particular can the gospel be the revelation of the universality of God and his salvation. In that sense, the expressions of faith in the Bible and church's traditions depend on context and culture; they are localized and particular, while they nonetheless keep referring to the universal message of the gospel. The point at issue is *the historical identity* of what is permanent, *precisely in* what is *transitory* because of its contingent character.

If, then, we speak of two poles, these must lie in the cultural forms of the past (first pole) and in the present-day cultural forms (second pole) of *the one substance of faith*, which itself is the *source*, both of the past and of the contemporary expressions of the faith. It is not a question of applying a normative Bible to a 'theologically free' situation; in the Christian tradition of faith the *past situation* has already been accounted for; and in the *present-day situation* God's saving presence is just as creative and liberating as in the past. The distinction between, on the one hand, source (the Bible) and, on the other 'situation', which can only be understood as 'context', is inadequate and even misleading.

Cultural forms are constitutive mediations of the explicit message of revelation. God's revelation in Jesus is an event *independent* of men and women and their experiences and history; but it is experienced and put into words in the form of a religious tradition of accumulating experiences and interpretations by human beings. By being experienced and expressed by human beings, this revelation receives a historical seal, *dependent* on the place and time when the discussion takes place. It is this that makes this revelation communicable. For the personal and collective experience of faith and of eschatological salvation in Jesus by the first disciples could be mediated in a communicable way to contemporaries and further generations, because those first disciples described their experiences *by means of a commonly shared* (semiotic) *system of communication* (in conjunctural cultural forms). 'Correlation' cannot really be used to express this adequately. It is better to speak of 'the encounter of cultures', a 'culture-shock', or confrontation of cultures that draw their vitality from the Christian gospel and acclimatize it in their own cultural forms.

As a consequence of this, it will be obvious that for us a 'Christian identity of meaning' cannot be found on the level of the Bible and the Christian tradition, *as such*; and therefore it cannot be found in a material repetition or repristination of the past. But it cannot be found either on the level of the situation, past and present, *as such* (whether in a biblicist or in a modernist direction). This identity of meaning can only be found *on the level of the corresponding relation between the original message (tradition) and the always different situation*, both in the past and in the present. The fundamental identity of meaning between subsequent periods of Christian understanding of the tradition of faith does not concern the corresponding *terms*; it concerns the corresponding *relations* between the terms (message and situation, then and now). So there is a fundamental unity and equality, but this bears no relation to the terms of the hermeneutical equation, but to the *relation* between those terms. The relation of equality between these *relations* carries within itself the Christian identity of meaning. At stake is a proportional equality. Thus we never get a straight look at the Christian identity of meaning; moreover, this identity can never be fixed once and for all. Although in their divergent interpretation of the one gospel all these historical-cultural mediations do not contradict each other, we cannot either harmonize them all on one even level. Their unity is a unity in depth. It is a process of an always new 'cultural incorporation' of the gospel's transcultural substance of faith, which itself can never be found or received outside a particular cultural form. At stake is the Christian identity *in* cultural ruptures or shifts and not an identity through what formerly was called, purely intellectualistically, 'homogeneous continuity' (which for that matter cannot be proved historically). The Christian *perception* of meaning takes place *in* a creative process of *giving* meaning: a re-reading of the tradition from within new situations. Interpretation produces new traditions, in creative faithfulness. This is what it means to hand on the tradition of faith in a living way to future generations.

The 'common Christian element' (Christian identity) in the mediation of different cultural worlds like those of Jesus, Paul, Augustine, Pope Gregory, Thomas Aquinas or Bonaventure, Bellarmine, Luther or Calvin, Teresa of Avila or Bishop Romero, is to be found in one and the same fundamental view of God and humankind in their mutual relation, although that same vision and its corresponding life styles appear in forms which differ from each other historically and culturally, even geographically and psychologically, and also according to social class participation. But these limits (which may give a distorted picture) were always, and still are, crossed and transcended in a specifically Christian manner.

(b) Hermeneutical theology in an anti–ideological perspective
The tradition of faith which discloses meaning is at the same time a call for a clearly determined personal and communal praxis of liberation. In the last analysis it is a question of two stories converging: the story of the Christian tradition of faith, and the personal and communal story of our lives.

Jesus' gospel of the kingdom of God is so much integrated in his acts of communicative and liberating association with human beings, that this preaching and the praxis of his life interpret each other mutually, while together they change the heart and the given situation. In his human existence Jesus affirms, through his liberating human activity, God as saving reality. Consequently, we cannot reduce theology to a purely theoretical interpretation of the Christian past. There is dialectical relation between the past, the present and the future yet to be made. Its relation to praxis ('*sequela Jesu*') is essential to theological theory itself. The purely theoretical approach forgets that there may be ideological elements contained in both the Christian tradition (in the massive way it has been handed down to us), and in the present-day situation in which we live.

By 'ideology', I understand in the first instance something which in itself is positive but which can degenerate. In a positive sense I call ideology a totality of images, representations and symbols which a particular society creates in order to justify its identity. Ideology is the reproduction and confirmation of one's own identity through 'founding symbols'. However, this ideological function of identification and safeguarding of one's own identity can develop into something diseased, resulting in various negative forms of 'ideology', which have been analysed in divergent ways by Karl Marx, Freud and Nietzsche, and after them by many others. The function of ideology becomes 'pathological' especially insofar as that legitimization is distorted, manipulated and monopolized by the ruling or dominating people in society. But because a group cannot provide a false view of itself *unless* it was previously constituted at the level of symbolic structure, the unfavourable meaning of ideology is not the original one. Precisely because every society possesses a symbolic structure, these symbols can also become mendacious and diseased. In this sense, *any* complex of thought can become ideological, in the second and derived sense.

With hermeneutics which is critical of ideology (in the derived sense) I mean to unmask the naive idea that *being* and *language* (= thinking and speaking) are always congruent as far as their contents go, in spite of all the conceptual inadequacy already recognized by the classics. Thinking and speaking are also dependent on all kinds of private and group interests. Very often concepts and theories are used to justify and safeguard systematically certain social interests and positions of power.

Often enough, too, the history of theology is the history of the victors and the powerful, by whom possible alternatives to the gospel have been pushed into the background or even silenced altogether, having suffered defeat at the time (although, this cannot last forever, for forgotten truths do tend to come to the surface again). Without a de-ideologizing intention, every form of theoretical hermeneutical theologizing could miss its proper target in two directions:

(*a*) on the one hand the theologian would in such a case unconsciously adapt the Christian tradition of faith, through a false '*aggiornamento*' or timing with modernity, for example with our western technocratic consumer society, privatized and geared to the a-political individual, and with its modern faith in progress. This theology would deprive the Christian faith of its liberating power, also in respect of the repressive aspects of our modern societies. In such a case Christian faith is adapted to the categories of experience and thought of what is called 'modern men and women', without an attempt to analyse those categories critically;

(b) on the other hand, a theologian would also fail in his mission in respect of past traditions of faith. For these, too, do not come to us in pure evangelical form, but in categories of experience and thought belonging to many cultures and cultural periods, which also should be examined for their ideological elements. The danger lies in this: that under the pretext of the gospel or church's tradition we would posit obsolete and ideologically loaded concepts as normative for the Christian and theological understanding of the faith, thus curtailing Christians unduly in their evangelical freedom.

4. The new paradigm? Or new paradigms?

An analysis of the various – Synoptic, Pauline, Johannine, Petrine, Asia Minor, etc. – traditions in the New Testament makes it clear that, even within what is globally one and the same, albeit varied, conjunctural-cultural period, Christians express their faith within divergent paradigms and models. Striving for one and the same paradigm (in a kind of ideal 'theological consensus') would lead to an impoverishment of the gospel's very message, too rich to be contained within one paradigm. 'Do not extinguish the Spirit!'

On the other hand, history can teach us that a humanism which (in any society) is founded exclusively or at least predominantly on science and technology and on concentrated economic powers (our present-day situation) poses the threat of inhumanity to human beings and their society. If religion here has its irreplaceable word to say, this must be a religion concerned for human beings in the world, a religion which begins from faith in a liberating God who is interested in humanity and its history and, as a consequence of this, in human individuals in their specific historical and social context. Can there be any other humanism than the humanism of God himself, a God concerned for humanity, who wants people to be concerned for humanity as well? A humanism neither dogmatic nor threatening, but more universal and more humanist? But if the religions and the

Christian churches want to proclaim this message with any credibility, they should begin by confessing that they have often obscured and even mutilated the face of God's humanity. Where religion or science is made absolute rather than God himself, not only the image of God but humanity itself is disfigured: the *ecce homo* on the cross and on the many crosses which men have set up and keep setting up. Theology has also played its part here in the past. But whatever one thinks of contemporary theologians, one thing should be granted them: by means of a historical praxis of commitment to mysticism and politics they are trying to discover the human face of God, starting from there in order to revive hope in a society, a humanity with a more humane face.

In the Jewish-Christian tradition God is experienced as a God who is concerned with humanity, as the promoter of good and the enemy of evil – as pure Positivity, albeit non-definable even in his own positiveness by human knowledge. The biblical vision of the coming of God's kingdom or rule envisages a humanity in which there are no more exploiters and no more exploited humanity, no more individual or structural servitude and no more slaves.

Our time imposes on us the task of stressing two things at the same time, both of which we need to realize as an authentic two-in-oneness. Precisely in Jesus Christ the unmistakable two-in-oneness becomes manifest in one indivisible personality. On the one hand Jesus identifies himself with God's concern; spirituality (theology) is concerned with God. On the other hand he identifies himself with humankind's concern; spirituality and theology are concerned with human beings and the life that they live; theology serves humanity. Finally, in Jesus these two concerns seem to be simply one concern: humanity's concern is God's concern and God's concern is also humanity's concern. Precisely because it expresses this through the central idea of Jesus' message, the Kingdom of God among men and women, present-day Christian contextual theology (and spirituality) can be recognized.

If one can speak about 'the new paradigm' (theology after Auschwitz, and theology after a Christian history of domination and victors), it would be this: the recognition that the contemporary context for talking meaningfully about God is the context of humankind's need for liberation, emancipation and redemption. In our times, an authentic faith in God only seems to be possible in the context of a praxis of liberation and of solidarity with the needy. It is in that praxis that the idea develops that God reveals himself as the mystery and the very heart of humanity's striving for liberation, wholeness and soundness. The concept of that mystery, which is at first concealed in the praxis of liberation and of making whole, is only made explicit in the naming of that concept in the statement made in faith that God is the liberator, the promoter of what is good and the opponent of what is evil. The discovery that God himself is the very heart and the mystery of all liberation gives rise to praise and thanksgiving and to liturgical celebration of God the liberator, even before we are completely liberated.

This means that mysticism (understood as an intensive form of prayer) and politics (understood as an intensive form of social-political involvement) are each bound to be at the heart of the other. Critical memory of the past, consciously believing in and belonging to the Christian faith's tradition of experience and interpretation, is not only a liturgical confession but, in two-in-oneness, a political act.

If, therefore, we are able to speak about *the* paradigm in today's situation, *it will be the paradigm of 'humanity'*, the paradigm of the (undefinable) cry for the humane, open to God's future which transcends human history. A religion which in fact has a de-humanizing effect, in whatever way, is either a false religion or a religion which understands itself wrongly. This criterion of humanizing proclaimed by Jesus, this concern for the humanity of humankind, is not a reduction or evacuation of religion; it is the first condition for its human possibility and credibility. It is of this God, and no other, that Jesus Christ is 'the great symbol': 'the image of the invisible God' (Col. 1, 15; see 2 Cor. 4, 3-4).

If living human beings are the fundamental symbol of God (*imago Dei*), then the place where human beings are dishonoured and oppressed, both in the depth of their own hearts and in an oppressive society, is at the same time the privileged place where religious experience becomes possible in a life style which seeks to give form to that symbol, to heal and restore it to itself: to express its deepest truth.

Nevertheless, an active search for the incomprehensible mystery of the ultimate *humanum,* which always takes place within a particular cultural, social and even geographical context, in fact merges into the mystery of 'the suffering righteous messianic prophet', Jesus, 'the Holy and Righteous one' (Acts 3, 14), rightly called 'Son of God'. It is here that the power (*dynamis*) of defenceless and disarming love is revealed: suffering *through* and *for* others as an expression of the unconditional validity of a praxis of doing good and opposing evil and innocent suffering.

That seems to me the new paradigm – the words *of old*: 'I have seen the affliction of my people in Egypt, and I have heard their cry because of their taskmasters; I know their sufferings, and I have come down to deliver my people' (Ex. 3, 7-8).

'He is'; the same and the one God who is concerned with humanity calls us to the same solidarity with suffering humanity (see Ex. 3, 14). The new paradigm is the Newness of the Gospel itself *within* humanity's changed conjunctural culture and situation.

THE INTERLACED TIMES OF HISTORY: SOME NECESSARY DIFFERENTIATIONS AND LIMITATIONS OF HISTORY AS CONCEPT

Jürgen Moltmann

History, as a general concept, and without the addition of any special subject, is undoubtedly one of the fundamental symbols for the world of modern European times. It is also one of the almost untranslatable mysteries of the German mind in particular. It is therefore difficult for a German theologian to decipher this mystery adequately, and it is the counsel of wisdom for me to restrict myself to some dimensions of time and the historical experience of time, as a way of comprehending both the value and the limitations of this modern world symbol.

The modern symbol 'history' is often interpreted through the picture of progress. We human beings take steps and advance, and when we have a clear goal in front of us, our progress is like a straight line. The human being who advances towards a particular goal sees the past as what he leaves behind him with every step, and he sees the future as that which opens up ahead of him in a new way with every fresh step. For the advancing human being, the present is no more than the transition from the past to the future. Through the power of memory he can still hold fast to the past – sometimes and to some degree; but the more the past recedes, the more it escapes him. He anticipates the future with every step that brings him nearer to his goal. But he hardly experiences the present at all, because he knows no rest and can never linger anywhere. There is *one* way and *one* progression and *one* goal. Consequently, for the advancing man or woman there is always merely *one* past and *one* future. Whether it is he himself who 'hastens' through the different modes of time, or whether it is time that 'passes him by', as we say, may remain an open question. We can make this clear to ourselves by considering the 'advancing' person; but the same thing can also be transferred to modern society, inasmuch as it too is involved in a single and common progress and in a process which can be defined in unified terms.

But does this idea fit the community in which we live, or does it violate that community? Does it do justice to the men and women of past generations, and the community we share with them? Does it respect the rights and the dignity of the generations of the future? Isn't history, pictured as progress, always at the same time an instrument of imperialism – the imperialism of one society, one class, and the one, present generation, an instrument used to suppress all the others and take possession of them? And isn't history, pictured as progress, also an instrument for subjecting nature to the will and intentions of human beings?

Today we are coming up against the limits of this modern world symbol at a number of different points. Consequently we have to differentiate within the concept of history itself, and have to integrate that concept into the wider concept of nature. I shall try to do the first by way of a complex modalization of the tenses: past, present and future; and shall then go on to point to the limitations of history through the synchronization of human time with the natural time of the ecosystem 'earth'.

1. The experience of reality as history becomes meaningful and endurable in the eschatological context of 'the future of history'.

2. Historical awareness differentiates between the present past and the past present, and puts us in a position to discover the future in the past, to pick up past possibilities again and to link them with the present future.

3. Awareness of the future differentiates between the present future and the future present, and puts us in a position to distinguish between future past and future future. This then gives rise to the theologically important distinction between *historical* future and *eschatological* future.

4. Present future is aligned towards *the synchronization* of the different historical times or tenses: the different human histories fuse into a single history because, through growing

interdependencies and growing conflicts, either 'a single humanity' will come into being as the subject of a common history, or the hostile groups will all perish together in the one, single catastrophe.

5. Present future is aligned towards *the synchronization* of human historical time with the rhythms of natural time – the rhythms of the ecosystem earth, and the bio-rhythms of the human body. Either human history and the history of nature will arrive at a co-ordinated harmony, or human history will find its irrevocable end in ecological death.

These theses do more than merely describe a function of history, as a paradigm of modern theology. They also indicate certain changes of function which this paradigm has to undergo today.

1. The experience of history against the horizon of its future

The modern experience of reality as history apparently grew up out of the industrial and political revolutions of European and American modern times.[1] The 'philosophy of history', as a genre of its own, began in the eighteenth century, with Bossuet and Voltaire. The nineteenth century then tried to comprehend the crises of the French Revolution and the opportunities of the industrial revolution with continually new outlines of a 'universal history' or 'history of the world'. The development of these ideas has been described often enough. In our present context the following elements are important.

1. Once a human world, made by human beings and modified by human beings, cuts itself off from the world of nature, that human world, to the same degree, loses its orientation towards

---

[1] I have discussed this in more detail in *Theology of Hope*, tr. J.W. Leitch (London, 1967), ch.IV: 'Eschatology and History', pp.230 ff.

the laws of the cosmos and the rhythms of nature.[2] The Becoming of human history no longer corresponds to the Becoming of nature. Human beings now take their bearings, not from nature, but from their own human hopes and purposes. People no longer seek to live 'in accordance with nature', as the Stoics taught. They now live in accordance with their own notions of what they want *to effect through* their actions, and what they can *expect from* the effects of those actions. The more human beings experience themselves as the subject of history, the more they therefore require an answer to Kant's question: What can I hope for?[3] The question about the future of history therefore also becomes the question about the meaning which an event experienced and caused by human beings can have on human hopes and purposes. History is experienced as meaningless when the horizon of hopes and purposes is dark and obscure. On the other hand, the horizon of human hopes and purposes becomes dim and uncertain if the history experienced and caused by human beings can no longer be related to it.

2. As the world of human beings becomes detached from the natural environment, the old ideas about the cycles and rhythms of time are lost. The linear series of points-in-time takes their place. The different experiences and traditions about times of living can be related to their abstract form, into which they can be integrated. Time as it is measured by the clock quantifies everything in exactly the same way. The clock has therefore become the omnipresent and omnipotent time-keeper in modern industrial society.

3. As the human world became detached from the world of nature, 'modern time' began – that experiment which Hegel was will able to welcome as 'the glorious dawn which stands man on

---

[2] L. Landgrebe, 'Das philosophische Problem des Endes der Geschichte', in *Phänomenologie und Geschichte* (Gütersloh, 1967), pp.182-201; J. Moltmann, 'Das Ende der Geschichte', in *Geschichte – Element der Zukunft. Vorträge an den Hochschultagen der Evangelischen Studentengemeinde Tübingen 1965* by R. Wittram, H.-G. Gadamer & J. Moltmann.

[3] *Cf.* here P. Ricoeur, 'Freedom in the Light of Hope', in *The Conflict of Interpretations* (ET, Evanston, 1974), pp.402-424.

his head, that is to say on his own ideas, and forms reality accordingly'.[4] Yet even then, conservative critics branded this 'experiment' as 'the most abominable beast from the abyss'.[5] If scientific and technological civilization is an experiment carried out by human beings, then we must also view it as a human *project*.[6] But a project is only pursued as long as the hopes which prompt it are not fundamentally disappointed by the experiences to which it gives rise. These experiences can interpret the hopes in a new way, and changes of direction within the general orientation can seem called for on the basis of new experiences. But this hermeneutical process still preserves the continuity. It presupposes that there is no alternative to the way which has been chosen. But the visions of the future which accompany the experiment of modern times are so ambivalent that they already display doubt even here. Nor is it by any means certain, even today, how long the chance to turn back will still be open to us, in the crises to which the experiment of modern times is exposed, or when these crises will become the foretokens of the experiment's inexorable catastrophe. So by making history the fundamental symbol of the world, we have not made the world situation progressively better. On the contrary, it has become increasingly critical.

This is already evident from the theoretical contradictions within the actual concept of history. How can history be thought of as a unity, if history does not have a subject – or at least, not a single subject? How can history be thought of as a whole, if the future is unknown, so that the whole is either incomplete or, at least, not yet present? How can the world be conceived of as history at all if we ourselves exist as historical beings *in* history, and do not confront it from outside?

[4] G.W.F. Hegel, *Vorlesungen über die Philosophie der Weltgeschichte, Werke*, XI, p.557. (*Cf.* ET: *Lectures on the Philosophy of History* (London, 1857), p.466. See also trans. by E.S. Haldane, 3 vols., London 1892–96. The present passage has been translated directly from the German.

[5] A. Vilmar, quoted in R. Strunk, *Politische Ekklesiologie im Zeitalter der Revolution* (Mainz & Munich, 1971), p.236.

[6] On the concept of 'project', *cf.* R. Garaudy, *Le projet espérance* (Paris, 1976).

These general problems in the experiment 'history' also emerge in the individual dimensions of time and the experiences of time within this experiment. History means temporal differentiation. It is perceived in the differences between present and future, present and past, and future and past. But the modern linearization of time – in order to reduce these differences to the relationship 'before – after' – has depicted them as lying along a single temporal line, P – Pr – F.

Yet the historical concept of time cannot work with a one-dimensional idea of time like this; for history is not a matter of a single process. The historical concept of time cannot view the past merely as the history preliminary to the present. It must see the past as *a past present*, with its own past and its own future, and must then distinguish between the future of that past present, and the present which has grown out of it. Present present has as its presupposition, not merely past present, but also the future of the past present. What is called present today came into being out of the hopes and multifarious possibilities of the past present. Analogously, we must distinguish between the present future (as an imaginative field of hopes, fears and diverging aims, with a forecourt of already definable and as yet undefinable possibilities) and a future present (which is the reality that develops out of these). The present present is not identical with the future of the past present; nor will the future present be congruent with the present future.

Augustine already thought in this way about the different tenses or modes of time, talking about the present past (PrP) in terms of *memoria*, the present present ((PrPr) in terms of *contuitus*, and the present future (PrF) in terms of *expectatio*.[7] Georg Picht,[8] A.M. Klaus Müller,[9] Arthur Prior,[10] Niklas Luhmann,[11]

---

[7] Augustine, *Confessions*, XI, esp. XI 20, 26.

[8] G. Picht, *Hier und Jetzt: Philosophieren nach Auschwitz und Hiroshima* (Stuttgart, 1980), V, 17: 'Die Zeit und die Modalitäten', pp.362-374.

[9] A.M.K. Müller, *Die präparierte Zeit* (Stuttgart, 1972).

[10] A Prior, *Past, Present and Future* (Oxford, 1967).

[11] N. Luhmann, 'Weltzeit und Systemgeschichte', in *Soziologische Aufklärung* 2 (Opladen, 1975), pp.103-133.

Reinhart Koselleck[12] and Erich Jantzsch[13] have differentiated these modes of time even further. Linear time covers only simple series of events. But if these series of events are woven into a network of interrelations and multiple effects, networks of time have to be developed, in which linear and cyclical temporal concepts are combined. In feedback processes, for example, the present comes back to the past future, in order to make its own future comprehensible.

Linear time: $P \rightarrow Pr \rightarrow F$

Historicization of the times (tenses):
Augustine: $PrP \rightarrow PrPr \leftarrow PF$

Matrix of the times (tenses): $P\,P \leftarrow PrP \leftarrow FP$
$PrP \rightarrow PrPr \leftarrow PF$
$P\,F \rightarrow PrF \rightarrow FF$

The network of the times: $PrP \rightarrow PrPr \leftarrow PrF$
$\downarrow \qquad \downarrow$
$PrP \rightarrow PrPr \leftarrow PrF$
$\downarrow \qquad \downarrow$
$PrP \rightarrow PrPr \leftarrow PrF$

etc. F

What moves in history, therefore, is the temporal present with its past and its future. But what moves it? We can see that the shifts only continue as long as the present in any given case does not fulfil the future of the past present; and we can then perceive that *the future as project* always goes beyond *the future as experience*. The future that transcends all remembered, experienced and still-to-be-experienced presents is what we call *the eschatological future*. We have to understand it, not as future history, but as the future *of*

---

[12] R. Koselleck, 'Geschichte, Geschichten und formale Zeitstrukturen', in R. Koselleck & W.D. Stempel, *Geschichte – Ereignis und Erzählung* (Munich, 1973); D.M. Lowe, 'Intentionality and the Method of History', in M. Natanson (ed.), *Phenomenology and the Social Sciences* (Toronto, 1979), pp.103-130.

[13] E. Jantzsch, *Die Selbstorganisation des Universums* (Munich, 1982), esp. pp.315 ff.

history. As the future of history, it is the future of the past, as well as the future of the present and the future. In this sense it is the source and fountain of historical time. 'The primary phenomenon of primordial and authentic temporality is the future.'[14]

2. The historicization of the present past

History encounters us in two forms: as the event which actually took place, and as the description and reconstruction of that event. German has tried to find a way out of this ambiguity by sometimes using two different words: *Geschichte* for past events; *Historie* for the account of these events. But the ambiguity suggests the further inherent equivocality of history as a concept: it can be the event, the past experience of the event, the actualization of the experienced event through memory, and the scholarly investigation of the past present 'as it really was', to use Leopold von Ranke's words. We are familiar with history in at least four different senses – as event, as experience, as tradition, and as an account of the past.

What is of interest to us in our present context is the connection between tradition and history as historical account; for the historical investigation of the past present has always been, and still is, critically related to the actualization – the re-presentation, in the literal sense – of this past through traditions. Historical criticism breaks through the matter-of-course continuity of past and present, as tradition depicts it, by showing the difference between the past and its 're-presentation', and by making the connections between present and past contingent, and a matter for decision.[15]

---

[14] M. Heidegger, *Being and Time*, tr. J. Macquarrie & E. Robinson (London & New York, 1962), §74; 'The Basic Constitution of Historicality', pp.434 ff.; cit. from p.378.

[15] R. Wittram, *Zukunft in der Geschichte* (Göttingen, 1966); R. Koselleck, *Vergangene Zukunft. Zur Semantik geschichtlicher Zeiten* (Frankfurt, 1979). I myself am taking up and modifying ideas expressed by W. Benjamin, 'Geschichtsphilosophische Thesen', in *Illuminationen* (Frankfurt, 1961), pp.268-280.

Historical criticism began with the investigation of the origins of the legends through which the religious and political powers consolidated their rule, and with the consequent exposure of these legends for what they are. 'The true criticism of dogma is its history.'[16] Through recognition of the historical relativity and contingency of tradition, people living in the present acquire liberty from the traditions of their origins, and the freedom to form their own future. 'The pressure which tradition exerts upon our behaviour, on a preconscious level, is increasingly reduced by the advances made in the historical sciences', said Max Scheler.[17] And in Dilthey's words: 'The historical sense breaks the last chains which philosophy and science were unable to break. Now the human being stands there on his own, completely free'.[18] But if this liberation of men and women from the tutelage of the past and from its prejudices and prejudgments is the concern which at present guides the historically critical attitude to past history, this must not be allowed to lead to an unhistorical understanding of the present.

As we can see from Ernst Troeltsch, historical relativism always has the absolutism of the present subject as its precondition and its consequence. Historical criticism may certainly demolish the absolutist claims of the forces of tradition, but it apparently has difficulty in abolishing the absolutism of the present. Relativism in respect of history and subjective pluralism therefore go hand in hand.

In addition, if historical criticism declares the past things which the different traditions actualize to be 'the past', then this past is assigned to the *one* past of the present present. This implies a kind of imperialism on the part of the present present towards earlier presents. Not least, the vista of the future which is already implicit, or in germ, in the past itself, is lost. But the past is more

---

[16] D.F. Strauss, *Die christliche Glaubenslehre* I (Tübingen & Stuttgart, 1840), p.71.

[17] M. Scheler, *Die Stellung des Menschen im Kosmos* (Munich, 1947), p.31; *cf.* ET *Man's Place in Nature* (Boston, 1961), p.27. The present passage has been translated directly from the German.

[18] W. Dilthey, *Gesammelte Schriften* VIII (Leipzig & Berlin, 1931), p.225.

than merely a prologue to the present and the future.

These deadlocks in modern historicism can be solved to a certain degree if, on the one hand, the present past (tradition, both conscious and unconscious) is confronted critically with the past present, identified – with the help of historical reconstruction – as 'things as they really were'; and if, on the other hand, this present past is compared with its own future and its own possibilities, which were already implicit or in germ in that past present. Then traditions and dogmas can be critically relativized, and the hopes which they preserve and the hopes which they suppress can be taken up again. Then the possibilities of the past present which were cut short or suppressed or merely neglected, can be picked up once more and integrated into the future of the present present.[19]

A good example is the role which Thomas Müntzer and the German Peasants' Revolt of 1525 have played in the German historical consciousness. For three hundred years remembrance of this sombre chapter in the history of the Lutheran Reformation and German feudalism was stifled and repressed. It was only when, with the French Revolution, hope for 'liberty, equality and fraternity' dawned on the horizon of the present future, that Friedrich Schiller wrote his play *Wilhelm Tell*, taking over from the struggle of the Swiss confederates the idea of 'A free people on free land'. When, 'in the Year of Revolutions' (1848), popular sovereignty and democracy became a real possibility in Germany, people remembered the shattered hopes of the peasants in 1525 and took them up again. In 1848-49 Friedrich Engels wrote the

---

[19] 'The future in the past' is something which Ernst Bloch stressed; *cf. Das Prinzip Hoffnung* (Frankfurt, 1959), p.7: 'The rigid divisions between future and past then collapse of themselves, future which has never become future becomes visible in the past; revenged and inherited, mediated and fulfilled past in the future'. *Cf.* ET *The Principle of Hope* (Cambridge, Mass., & Oxford, 1986). The present passage has been translated directly from the German. See also D.M .Lowe, *History of Bourgeois Perception* (Chicago, 1982), pp.174 f., where Lowe draws on Husserl's analysis of the sense of time: 'How is it possible to represent a past without losing sight of its unique prospective reality? This I believe is the crucial problem in historical method. History ought to be the present representation of the prospective reality of a past, within the historian's retrospection'.

first history of the Peasants' Revolt. And in 1921 Ernst Bloch hailed Müntzer – who had for so long been damned as a rebel and agitator – as the first 'theologian of revolution'.

Historical consciousness therefore has at least these two components: historical criticism is critically related to the actualization of the past in traditions and institutions, comparing these with the past present which is open to historical investigation; but historical research also enquires about the future of that past present which was interrupted, suppressed or simply forgotten. The concern prompting the historical criticism of tradition is the liberty of those living in the present. The concern behind the historical investigation of the future in the past is always prompted by questions about the present future. But can then 'the historicism of our modern society' be described as 'a reflection of its future'?[20]

The demolition of the absolute claims of tradition and the abolition of the absolute claims of those living in the present do not necessarily end in a general sceptical relativism. They lead to a living relationism in an intricate fabric of interconnections. The concern that determines these relationships will undoubtedly be stamped by the hopes and fears, the purposes and tasks of the present future. For these will decide the future of the past as well – that is to say, the future of the dead, inasmuch as there is a community of hope between the dead and the living. Eschatological hope for the future always also confers retroactive historical community. The biblical symbol of the eschatological hope for the future is 'the resurrection of the dead'; and this is an expression of hope for those who have gone. The inscription at Yad Vashem in Jerusalem rightly reminds us that

> Forgetfulness leads to exile,
> while remembrance is the secret of redemption.

[20] N. Luhmann, op.cit., p.252, following K. Löwith, Zur Kritik der christlichen Überlieferung (Stuttgart, 1966), p.155.

3. The futurization of the present future

Like history, the future is equivocal. Most European languages have two possible ways of talking about the future. *Futurum*, or its equivalent, is used for what *will be*; *adventus*, or its cognates, for that which *is coming*. But English and German have only one possibility open to them. The English word 'future' comes from the Latin *futurum*, while the German '*Zukunft*' is related to the Latin *adventus* (Greek *parousia*).[21]

If the future is understood in the sense of *futurum*, it means what *will be* out of past and present. It is one form in the process of becoming *physis*. In this sense, the future offers no occasion for a hope which could communicate enduring certainty. For what is *not yet* will sometime or other *no longer* be. In this sense, the future offers nothing but future past. The process is irreversible: the future will become the past, but the past will never again be future. The future of becoming certainly offers a reason and occasion for development and planning, prediction and programmes; but not for enduring hope.

On the other hand, if we understand future as *adventus*, it means what is coming – what is on the way towards the present. What we describe as a 'coming' event is not something that develops out of the present. It confronts the present with *something new*, whether it be good or evil. In Greek, *parousia* means presence or arrival. But in the New Testament the word is never applied to Christ's past or his presence here and now. It is always and exclusively kept for his promised and expected coming in glory. In this way the word 'advent' became the quintessence of the messianic hope. When the word *adventus* was translated into German by *Zukunft*, the German word acquired a messianic, advent note. What is meant is something that is coming and which will never go or pass away; something which remains. It is the moment to which we can say, with Goethe's Faust, 'Tarry

---

[21] For a more detailed exposition *cf.* J. Moltmann, 'The Future as a New Paradigm of Transcendence', in *The Future of Creation*, tr. Margaret Kohl (London & Philadelphia, 1979), pp.1-17.

awhile, thou art so fair'. This is the new, enduring age of the
Jewish and Christian hope.

What happens when this 'coming' takes the place of 'the
future'? Revelation 1.4 does in fact replace the one by the other:
'Peace to you', says the writer, 'from him who is and who was
and who is to come'. We would expect as third term the words
'. . . and who will be'. But the future tense of the verb 'to be' is
replaced by the future of the verb 'to come'. This alters the third
term in the traditional concept of time quite decisively. God's
being is in his coming, not in his *becoming*. So his being does not
pass away when once it comes. If God and the future are linked
together theologically in this way, God's being has to be thought
of eschatologically; and then the future has to be understood
theologically. But if the future is thought of theologically, it
acquires a continual transcendence compared with every present,
and makes of every present a provisional present. In this way the
future becomes the paradigm of transcendence. Of course past
and future can then no longer be reduced to the same linear
temporal concept, for their relation to one another is now one of
qualitative difference. It is the difference between 'old' and
'new'.

This future is not merely the temporal forecourt of any given
present. It is the transcending forecourt of past presents as well.
This, then, means that there is a past future, a present future and a
future future. The eschatological future determines all three
modes of time.

The theoretical distinction between 'the future' and 'the
coming' leads to the distinction between extrapolation and
anticipation in our practical dealings with what is ahead.

There are trends and lines of development in past and present
which we can extrapolate into the future.[22] But these extrapolations turn the future into a prolongation of the present. These
prolongations of the present are always used to stabilize present
conditions of ownership and power; for only the person who has

[22] J. Moltmann, title essay in *Hope and Planning*, tr. Margaret Clarkson (London
& New York, 1971), pp.178–199.

the power to implement his purposes can plan, and has any interest in extrapolation. But the prolongations and extensions of present conditions do not create a real future. On the contrary, they suppress the alternative possibilities the future holds. Extrapolations do not treat the future as an open field of the possible; they see it as a reality already determined by past and present. But this is illusory: it leads to a dangerous blindness to the apocalypse among men and women in the modern system.

On the other hand, the understanding of the future as what is to come corresponds to the anticipation through which men and women attune themselves to something ahead, whether through their fear of something terrible, or through their hope for happiness. These foretastes, search images and attunements are part of every perception of the unknown. Without anticipatory awareness we should not discern something that is in the future at all.[23] But in anticipatory awareness, we always align ourselves to what is last and final – to happiness or unhappiness, life or death. The last thing to penetrate our experience is the first in our expectation.[24] It is in the light of this that we then perceive and judge what can come upon us, and what actually does come.

In actual practice we always combine anticipation and extrapolation in a single act, because we link what we hope for, or fear, with what we consider possible. On the levels of planning and programmes, we also link the future we desire with the future we consider possible and achievable.

The content of the future we hope for and consider desirable, or the future we dread and wish to avoid, always has to do with our fundamental concerns, the things towards which our whole existence is aligned and on which it depends. These are the symbols of the eschatological future.

The traces of this eschatological future can be discerned in the different prospective futures of the present – whether it is one's own past present, or the present of someone or something else.

---

[23] E. Bloch, *Das Prinzip Hoffnung*, Pt.II: *Das antizipierende Bewusstsein* ('The Anticipating Consciousness'), pp.49-394.

[24] F. Rosenzweig, *Der Stern der Erlösung* (Heidelberg, 1954) Pt.II, Book III, p.170.

The reason is apparently that time is itself prophetically a parable of the future-eternal. It is this which puts its impress on human experiences of time. No present prospect of the future is identical or identifiable with 'the future' itself. Eschatological future cannot be reduced to a dogma. The critical distinction between the present future in any given case, and the historically always-future future preserves these differences.

4. The synchronization of historical times

In a limited and provisional way, the present future always determines the hope and the functions or tasks of history. We must look here at two of these tasks, because unless they are implemented in future there will be no more future for human beings at all.

We might call one of them the synchronization of the different historical times in which human beings have lived and are still living. Earlier, the different nations all had their 'histories', in the plural. Every people, every civilization and every religion had its own past and its own future, and it was these that gave their particular present form and colouring. In reality there has never been any such thing as 'universal history' in the singular. Up to now there have only been different human histories in our world. When people talked about 'world history', the idea was always associated with an inclusive claim to power. The notion was an instrument for the imperialism of *one* nation, *one* culture or *one* religion, which tried to bring the rest of the world under the dictatorship of its own time. The concept of 'history' *per se* is also an instrument of European, American and Russian domination.

But apart from this, a singular subject of history is coming into existence today, because of the growing danger that humanity will destroy itself.[25] In the face of the nuclear annihilation of the

---

[25] I mean this in the sense of a 'hermeneutics of danger' (J.B. Metz), which W. Benjamin (*op.cit.*, p.270) expressed thus: 'It is essential to lay hold of a recollection which flashes through the mind in a moment of danger'.

world, the inexorable alternative is 'one world or none'. And if this is so, then we are standing on a cultural threshold of a very special kind. If we are today entering a common world – initially for merely negative reasons, because of the mutual threat of global annihilation – then we shall continue to have plural pasts and traditions, but we shall have hope and future only in the singular. For us human beings there is only a common future, for we can now only survive in peace. World peace is the fundamental condition for the survival of humanity. But what will this community of all humanity look like? And who is going to determine its character?

To say that the threatening danger of mutual nuclear annihilation through the super-powers makes the unity of humanity essential, is a negative way of describing that unity; it shows that a united humanity is necessary, but not that it is possible. Because of the shared peril, humanity is really being described as a common object of annihilation, not yet as a common subject of survival. We therefore have to discover the saving element in the apocalyptic peril. But deliverance can come only from the community of hope for life, and out of the solidarity of the will to build a peaceful world. By virtue of the will which this hope inspires, an ever-denser web of interrelations must be created on all levels, between the political blocks and the nations on earth. Forms of communication must be built up at higher and higher stages, so that one day humanity will be so organized that it can become the author of its own history, and can determine its own future. The category of danger in which the future is perceived here is only the framework for the category of hope in which we have to act.

What interests us in this context is the transition from thinking in terms of one's own history to a consideration of one's own history in terms of the necessary community of humanity. It is the transition from particularist to universal thinking. In the present situation of the world, particularist thinking is merely schismatic thinking, because it refuses the community which is necessary and also possible. Thinking like this is aggressively concerned with determining its own particular identity by way of separation from other and alien traditions. In theology, this profile-neurosis was for centuries represented by 'controversial' theology. The transition from controversial to ecumenical theology is the way from the demarcation line drawn against other people to the distinctive, individual contribution to the common life.

If we choose this path, we no longer read the testimonies of other histories and traditions with an eye for their particularity. We read them with a view to the coming ecumenical community. It is possible to read the testimonies of the different traditions in order to see whether they are Protestant or Catholic or Orthodox. But we shall have to read them in the light of what they contribute to an ecumenical community of the Christian faith. The person who thinks schismatically considers his own part to be the whole. The person who thinks ecumenically considers his own whole to be one part of the coming community. What happens within the ecumenical community of Christians in this way can also have an exemplary effect on the ecumenical community of religions and cultures, and on the economic and political habitability of our globe.

5. The synchronization of historical time and natural time

Ever since the beginning of the experiment we know as modern times, history and nature have continually been defined over against one another. This gave people the impression that nature was static, recurring and cyclical; while the experiences of time, change, contingency and the possible were all reserved for human history. A view of nature without history grew up, and with it a view of history without nature.

In the great modern conceptions of world history, nature plays at most a marginal role . In the sciences nature is encountered as the embodiment or synthesis of the objects which the human subject is capable of knowing methodically. In work and in the technologies, nature is encountered as the embodiment or synthesis of the materials over which the human subject disposes. In law, nature counts as unclaimed property. According to these perspectives, nature is perceived only in the interests of human labour, and human reason is made operational to such a degree that it perceives only 'what it produces itself, according to its own design', as Kant put it.

Ever since Francis Bacon, the relationship between human beings and nature has been continually described as the relationship of a master to a slave.[26] The modern experiment 'history' has largely been built up on this attitude of mind. We need not describe here the appalling consequences – in the form of 'the ecological crisis' – of the dissociation of human history from the nature which is outside human beings and within them. Up to now, the creations of human history have led only to nature's depletion.

If the common catastrophe of human beings and the earth is still to be avertible at all, then it is certainly only synchronizing human history with the history of nature, and if the experiment of modern times is carried out 'in accordance with nature' and not in opposition to nature, or at nature's expense.

In order to arrive at viable symbioses between human society and natural environments, it is essential to 'cool off' human history, and to slow down its one-sided varieties of progress. Its concept of time must be brought into harmony with the laws of life and the rhythms of nature, in the environment and in the bodily nature of human beings themselves. This is especially necessary, since among human beings the progress of one group is always at the cost of other groups. If technological progress is achieved at the expense of nature or the coming generations, this progress is merely a seeming, fictitious progress. We need more systems of equilibrium, in order to keep the advancing processes of history within bounds and to make them endurable. The relationship between progress and equilibrium in the human and natural systems must be brought into a co-ordinated, fluid equilibrium if the cost-utility accounts are to be set up realistically and honestly, and if the sum is to come out right.

[26] Cf. here, with extensive evidence, W. Leiss, The Domination of Nature (New York, 1972); C. Merchant, The Death of Nature. Women, Ecology and the Scientific Revolution (San Francisco, 1980).

In order to determine the necessary *ethical* limitations of human history, it is helpful to make the *natural* limitations of the history of human beings clear to ourselves.

Human history runs its course within the great comprehensive ecosystem 'earth'.[27] The continual and unremitting influx of solar energy, the circulation of air and water, the seasons, the phases of the moon and the regular alternation of day and night constitute the unshakable natural environment for the times, the epochs and the goals of human history. And this comprehensive ecosystem earth, which can be endangered by human history and must therefore be respected, is in its turn a part-system in the ecosystem 'sun'; and so on. Every gaze into the immeasurable spaces of the stellar systems and galaxies cuts human history down to scale, showing it to be a small and limited phenomenon in the evolution of life on this one single planet 'earth'.

But theological insight even more should reduce the earth and the human history that is played out there to their proper proportions, showing their limits, when we think of the heavens and the innumerable spaces of the invisible worlds.

Even human history is not completely delivered over to the arbitrary despotism of present-day human beings. People may be in a position to oppress, exploit and kill other people living at the present day. People may be in a position to burden their children, to ruin the lives of their descendants, and to annihilate the future of coming generations. But they are not able to destroy the life that has already been lived, and the past delight in living of the dead. Apart from the community of hope between the dead and the living, there is also what Whitehead called 'an objective immortality of the dead'. I should like to take up his idea in my own way in our present context by saying that we can be robbed of our future, but not of our past. The dead are safe from us. The

---

[27] J.E. Lovelock, *Gaia* (Oxford & New York, 1979), has shown in his 'Gaia hypothesis' that the planet earth has to be viewed as a unique total organism. *Cf.* also F. Capra, *The Turning Point: Science, Society and the Rising Culture* (New York, 1982). Capra expounds scientifically what Löwith put forward philosophically in the name of a rediscovery of nature; see his critical attitude towards historical existence (Stuttgart, 1960) and towards Christian existence (Stuttgart, 1966). Löwith, like Capra, was influenced by eastern cosmic mysticism.

life which has still to be lived is exposed to danger and annihilation; but the life that has already been lived has been saved from annihilation and is kept safe in eternity from the perils of time.

This means that every gaze into the cosmic world, every glance into the heavenly world and every contemplation of the human past, allows us to perceive the limits of our present history – the limits of its mortal dangers, and the limits of its unique chances.

History, as a general concept, and without the addition of any subject, was and is a fascinating conception of the experiment 'modern times'. It has hence also become the fundamental paradigm of Christian theology in those times. But if we look at the cost and the limits of this experiment, then it is a terrifying concept as well. History became the paradigm of modern theology in the age when the anthropocentric view of the world prevailed: human beings, it was said, are the crown of creation and the centre of the world. Everything was supposed to have been created for human beings and their use. We shall only be able to reduce history to human and natural dimensions if this anthropocentricism is replaced by a new cosmological theocentricism: even without human beings the heavens declare the glory of God. The whole of nature dances in the rhythm of the divine Spirit. Heaven and nature are not there for the sake of human beings; human beings are there for the sake of God's glory, which heaven and earth extol. The more men and women discover the meaning of their lives in joy in existence, instead of in doing and achieving, the better they will be able to keep their economic, social and political history within bounds. 'The experience of history' is annulled and at the same time preserved and embraced in meditation, in contemplation and in the doxology of the Eternal One. The stress of modern history is making people nervous and ill. They can only recover health if they learn serenity in the midst of all their activities.

'The crown of history' is the sabbath. Without the sabbath quiet, history becomes the self-destruction of humanity. Through the sabbath rest, history is sanctified with the divine measure and blessed with the measure of a true humanity.

RESPONSE TO EDWARD SCHILLEBEECKX
AND JÜRGEN MOLTMANN

Gregory Baum

The three principal papers by Hans Küng, David Tracy and
Matthew Lamb have set the stage for an important theological
conversation. They have shown that it is useful to introduce the
idea of paradigm shift into the self-understanding of theology.
This is especially meaningful for Catholic theologians who at one
time believed that theology was *scientia una*. Kuhn's analysis of
the resistance to new paradigms seems to fit the Roman theologians' hostility to the new theologies.

How do the three papers define the new paradigm? If I understand them correctly, they define it in terms of the theologian's
double fidelity: fidelity to the gospel of Jesus Christ and fidelity to
contemporary, critical self-understanding. Küng speaks of 'the
two constants'. Tracy has examined this double fidelity in his
theological treatises. Lamb emphasizes with the others, and more
than they, that the interrelation between these two dimensions
must be mutually critical. The great majority of theologians, it
seems to me, tend to accept this double fidelity, even if they may
not think it necessary to introduce the idea of paradigm shift.

Küng insists that in this double fidelity priority should be
granted to the gospel. In fact, since the modern critical methods
are completely internalized by a theologian, what he or she
experiences is simply the quest for fidelity to the gospel. Honesty
demands that obedience to the gospel be mediated by modern,
critical consciousness. In his paper, Tracy also recognizes that
while the hermeneutical method informs the process in theology,
the interpretation continues to be ruled by the subject-matter: that
is, by the revealed message. Professor Blank has insisted on the
priority of the biblical norm. But since he wrestles in his paper

against the anti-Semitic elements in the New Testament, he also recognizes the mutual critical interrelation between the two poles. His insistence on the priority of Scripture does not place him outside the new paradigm.

The two constants are mutually interrelated in critical fashion. Professor Ricoeur's remarks indicate that the hermeneutical method includes the hermeneutics of suspicion. Fidelity to the Scriptures demands an analytical understanding of the present. Fidelity to the Scriptures demands that it should be read as a message of liberation. Matthew Lamb stresses this point in his paper.

Edward Schillebeeckx's paper, if I understand it correctly, fits perfectly into this common perspective. He recognizes the two poles and their mutual, critical interrelation. With Lamb he puts special emphasis on the role of action in the search for truth. Yet Schillebeeckx does not think that paradigm language is useful. Paradigm language was derived from the history of the sciences, which lies wholly within one cultural period, whereas theology, being much older, also has to take into account more radical cultural transformations from one age to another. Thus Schillebeeckx prefers to deal with the nature of contemporary theology without reference to Kuhn's theory of paradigm shift. Moreover, theology, for Schillebeeckx, is more inclusive than science. He defines theology as 'an hermeneutical enterprise within a practical-critical intension and a criticism of ideology'. This definition makes room for Christian thinkers who are ill at ease at the university. In particular, it acknowledges the concern of Jean-Pierre Jossua who envisages the theology of the future as non-scientific. Schillebeeckx, moreover, adopts the liberationist perspective strongly defended by Lamb. 'Authentic faith in God', he writes, 'only seems to be possible in the context of a praxis of liberation and of solidarity with the needy'.

Whereas there is wide agreement among theologians that doing theology today demands a double fidelity to the Christian message and contemporary critical consciousness, they differ considerably in their understanding of what contemporary critical consciousness implies. For some, the new spirit is summed up by the best of the university tradition: it is basically a development in the order of the intellect. For others the new spirit includes a critical relation to social location and political action. For them, it includes a commitment to social justice, a resistance to domination of any kind. For these latter theologians, theology is therefore quite different from science, as understood by Kuhn.

By way of response, I wish to make a few remarks that emphasize the difference between theology and the sciences. The three fundamental papers of Küng, Tracy and Lamb recognize this dissimilarity very clearly. Küng adds to every thesis articulating a similarity between theology and science a description of how theology differs from the sciences. Still, since most of us are professors at universities, the difference between theology and the sciences deserves emphasis.

1. Of great interest to theologians, I think, is the debate in the social sciences between scientists who insist on the value-free nature of the scientific enterprise and those, usually a minority at the university, who recognize value commitment as a research-guiding principle, and who therefore insist that social science is action-oriented. Psychoanalysis and Marxism are interesting cases. If these two approaches to psychology and sociology respectively are defined in a definitive, closed manner, science is quickly transformed into ideology. But if these two approaches remain open to constant self-criticism, they produce scientific results of great theoretical and practical import. We have here, it seems to me, a certain parallel to Christian theology. Christian theology, defined in a manner that is closed and definitive, easily becomes an ideology, guiding people into rigidity. When this happens, the demand for value-neutrality can be liberating. Despite these special moments, theology must wrestle against the spirit of positivism at the university. When theology remains open to constant self-criticism, it operates out of commitment, brings out the meaning of the gospel, and initiates Christian action in the world. With Lamb and Schillebeeckx I am ready to defend the commitment to social justice, 'the preferential option for the poor' (Puebla, 1979) as a dimension of faith and hence as an integral dimension of theology.

2. It is important to insist that theology, unlike the sciences, may and must learn from the unlearned. Theology is never fully at home at the university. It always depends on the religious experience of the Christian community and the pastoral wisdom of the church's ministry. The theologian teaching at a university must be rooted in the church, must take seriously the reflections of ordinary Christians and their pastors. At this point, even the analogy with committed science such as psychoanalysis and Marxist sociology breaks down. There is a populist dimension in the Christian message that cannot be repressed for long. The truth shall be available to the little ones.

A good example for the influence on theology from the base is the church's recovery of the pacifist tradition. It was the heroic example of the Austrian peasant Jaegerstetter, who refused to bear arms during World War II, and the subsequent witness of Christians in the United States against the Vietnam War and against the nuclear arms race that laid the foundation for a new theology of war and peace, one that became embodied in the recent statement of the American Catholic bishops against nuclear weapons.

Another example is the impact of Third World liberation theology, often formulated as testimony, poetry or sermon, on the theological development in the entire Christian church.

The openness of theology to the non-learned, it seems to me, demands a certain personal style on the part of the theologian. He or she cannot be satisfied with being a professor. In some countries professors are greatly respected, so much so that ordinary people do not engage in conversation with them. Theologians must belong to church groups or other popular organizations in order to remain open to God's voice, to the wisdom from below.

3. Jürgen Moltmann's paper, which I found very difficult, insisted that for Germans history with a capital H has a very special meaning. A theology of history for Germans must deal with a set of questions that may not have the same importance for Christians belonging to other cultures. Theology, if I understand Moltmann correctly, is contextual. This does not mean, of

course, that theology is provincial. Contextual theology retains a dimension of universality. Contextual theology demands the freedom to define in it own terms what this relationship to universality is.

These are considerations of great importance to cultures created through the experience of colonialism. Harold Innis, a well-known Canadian social scientist, distinguished 'metropolis' from 'hinterland', and argued that this distinction, defined first in economic and political terms, had profound cultural and even cognitive consequences. Canada has always been hinterland. First Britain and later the United States were the metropolis. The Canadian economy depended on these centres; Canadian political life was largely shaped by these ties of dependencies. More than that, the intellectual life of Canadians was derivative: Canadians received their ideas from the metropolis. Harold Innis' original contribution was to recognize that none of the social scientific theories devised at the metropolis really fitted the Canadian reality. He asked that Canadians should begin their own, independent research and reflection.

Some Canadian theologians have taken Harold Innis' theory seriously. They wish to create a theology that is appropriately contextual. They do not deny the universal dimension of theology, but they object to definitions of universality made in the metropolis. The demand for universality at the centre is usually the claim that the wisdom of the centre be accepted in the hinterland. An appropriate understanding of universality must be worked out by a process in which all sectors of the Christian world participate, including those at the periphery, those who are usually excluded from the conversation.

4. To emphasize the difference between science and theology, let me raise the question whether it is possible to apply to theologians the distinction made by Antonio Gramsci between traditionalist and organic intellectuals. Most intellectuals, Gramsci argued, belong to the traditional institutions of society, especially the universities. There they serve the cultural tradition. Whether they realize it or not, they quickly become the legitimators of the established order. Even their critical work takes place within the

boundaries defined by the cultural mainstream. The organic intellectual, Gramsci argues, is closely linked to the life of the community. He or she tries to test and clarify the experiences of ordinary people. Organic intellectuals think of themselves as serving the people. They look upon society from the viewpoint of those at the base. They become the promoters of critical thinking.

It seems to me that the preceding remarks 1, 2 and 3 allow me to conclude that theologians may properly be compared to organic intellectuals. While they may belong to the university or ecclesiastical institutions, they are at the same time listening to the reflections and the experiences of ordinary people, doing their theology out of a commitment to the victims of society, and willing to opt for the hinterland against the metropolis. Theologians will have to be at universities, or at least not far away from them, because there alone do they find the instruments of research; but they are also unhappy at the university because they are in solidarity with the ordinary people in whom the Spirit utters divine wisdom. The double fidelity of the new paradigm bears within it explosive power. The mutual interrelation between gospel message and modern critical awareness releases the radical truth of the biblical God, the God of mercy and justice, forever intolerant of oppression.

RESPONSE TO EDWARD SCHILLEBEECKX
AND JÜRGEN MOLTMANN

Bernard McGinn

History is not only a problem for modern theology, but a sign of
linguistic discord, if not division. The issues connected with *die
Geschichte* (especially when 'gross geschrieben') have a
colouration in German that is hard to achieve in English, where
the modest word 'history' has to make do for two German words,
and tends to have less immediate access to metaphysical realms.
There are even some English-language theologians who seem to
think that in order to speak about history in serious fashion they
need to switch into German. Ultimately, though, the problems of
the relation between history and theology are not language-
specific, but are part of the world we live in, at least since the
nineteenth century. The two rich papers we have just heard have
not only highlighted a broad range of the problems of this
relation, but have also suggested some fruitful lines of approach
to the major issues.

At the risk of oversimplification, I would like to suggest that
we think of the issues involved in the relation between history and
theology under three headings: first, the *retrospective* function,
that is, how we make the past, and especially the Christian past,
meaningful and useful for us; second, the *prospective* function, that
is, what attitude we take towards the future; and third, the *critical*
function, that is, what effect does the recognition of historical
existence or historicity, with its flux of meaning and non-closed
character, have upon the truth claim of the Christian religion.

I believe that each of these areas receives attention in the two
papers presented, though with diverse results. Professor
Schillebeeckx offered us a promising hermeneutical model to
explore the *retrospective* function in Christian theology, and has

also provided some powerful reflections on how the paradigm of humanity (is it really a paradigm?) should guide us on how we *prospect* the future. Professor Moltmann concentrated upon the *prospective* function, but also expanded upon a neo–Augustinian model of the interpenetration of the three dimensions of time that has many implications for how theology relates to its past. In what follows, I will highlight what I take to be some major insights of each paper, while raising questions in need of further discussion, especially concerning what I have called the *critical* function in the relation of history and theology.

First, it is worthwhile underlining how useful Schillebeeckx's conception of theology as hermeneutical enterprise is in cutting through many long-standing problems concerning how contemporary theological reflection relates to its past. Schillebeeckx's claim that 'Cultural forms are constitutive mediations of the explicit message of revelation' (p.312) leads him to what I take to be a central insight of his paper, that is, that 'Christian identity of meaning cannot be found on the level of the Bible and the Christian tradition as such . . . this identity of meaning can only be found *on the level of the corresponding relation between the original message (tradition) and the always different situation*' (p.313). The great advantage of this approach is that one no longer looks for the fundamental identity of meaning through relating *terms* (for instance, trying to relate the conclusions of contemporary christologies to the 'two-nature' model of Chalcedon), but rather through the *proportional equality* of relations between various christological paradigms and God's revelation in Jesus.

But this approach seems to present a twofold problem on the *critical* level. First, we might ask how we are to conceive the relation between the original message, the transcendent, or vertical, pole of all temporal expressions of Christian faith and history itself. Is the 'original message' inside or outside history? At times Schillebeeckx speaks of it as ' . . . an event *independent* of men and women and their experiences and history' (p.312), but when he describes it as *tradition* (also p.312), he seems to imply that it exists within history in some way. How are the 'inside' and 'outside' history aspects of any one single event related concretely?

Second, if Christian identity of meaning can never be seen in itself, but only through its diverse cultural manifestations, and if this identity cannot be fixed once and for all, nor its diverse manifestations harmonized on any one level, what kind of claim are we making when we say that Christian identity is *one*, as Schillebeeckx asserts? What is the 'unity in depth' of which he speaks? Given the incredible variety of ways in which Christ and the fundamental Christian message has been conceived, what prevents us from speaking of *plural* Christian identities of meaning? On what basis does Schillebeeckx affirm his unity?

Despite this central difficulty, the advantages of Schillebeeckx's approach are many. First, it avoids simplistic biblicism at the same time that it relativizes the whole 'development of doctrine' issue. Second, it propounds a creative understanding of ideology, the distortions of ideology and the necessity for theology to take an anti-ideological stance; and third, it suggests a concrete prospective for theology centred on human liberation expressed through a praxis of commitment to mysticism and politics. Fr Schillebeeckx has given us not just a paper, but the bare bones of a book, or of a whole theological programme.

Moltmann's paper is equally ambitious, as well as being highly complex. Although its avowed concentration is upon the history of the future, it sketches out the essence of a whole theology of history. Following Augustine, Moltmann affirms that human time is not mere linear succession, but is rather '. . . perceived in the differences of present and future, present and past, and future and past' (p.325). The goal and origin of human history is the eschatological future conceived of as an *adventus* that transcends all conceptions of future as mere experience and that recapitulates all present moments on a new and higher level. On this basis, Moltmann briefly surveys the *retrospective* functions of history in his second part and, in greater detail, lays out the main lines of his *prospective* view of history in the consideration of the future found in Parts 3 through 5.

Given the diverse starting-points, it is instructive to see common elements in the ways in which Moltmann and Schillebeeckx handle what I have called the *retrospective* function of history. Moltmann's critical confrontation of the present past, or tradition, with the past present, leads to a position he terms *relationism*, which bears at least initial analogies with Schillebeeckx's notion of how 'corresponding relations' enable us to appropriate the Christian past without becoming enslaved to it. I have difficulties, however, with exactly what Moltmann means by past present. I take it to be something like what the past was when it was the present, with its own past and still unrealized future. Moltmann seems to suggest that we can summon this past present 'as it really was' to confront tradition (the present past) and thus solve the *aporiai* of modern historicism. But I do not see how we can have any real access to past present, and most theories of history would suggest the same in their opposition to attempts to reconstruct history 'as it actually was'.

Moltmann's views of the *prospective* function of history in current theology seem to me both pregnant and problematic, especially as they impinge upon the *critical* questions of the relation of theology and history. The distinction between the *futurum*, that is, the horizon of the irreversible process by which that which is to come will some day be past, THE FUTURE, that is, the future as *adventus* that comes to confront us with what does not develop out of the present, is the central thesis of his position and it is the basis for the important distinction he draws between *extrapolation* and *anticipation*. On the *critical* level, some questions can be addressed both to Moltmann's notion of THE FUTURE and to the extrapolation/anticipation dialectic.

It is not clear to me what the essence of THE FUTURE may be and upon what grounds it may be affirmed. In what sense can we call THE FUTURE the final event, the ESCHATON in traditional Christian terms, as suggested by Moltmann when he says that in it we 'always align ourselves to what is last and final' (p.333)? If THE FUTURE is the ESCHATON in some real sense, the ground of all hopes and fears, can we provide it with any preliminary or proleptic content – any specification of concrete expectations and disappointments – that in some way might make it the subject of conscious and concrete action and planning? If this is possible, we can also ask what the source of this preliminary content might be. Do we learn about it from Scripture, from current political hopes and fears, from some philosophical analysis of the human condition, or from some combination of these?

My problems about what THE FUTURE really means in practice can be made more specific by a glance at the difficulties involved in the interchange between *futurum* and THE FUTURE in the extrapolation/anticipation dialectic. In spite of Moltmann's insistence that extrapolation and anticipation are joined in a single act (p.333), we may still ask exactly where and how THE FUTURE makes its presence known and how we discriminate between the demands that THE FUTURE makes upon us in relation to those of the *futurum*. For instance, do the major projects with which Moltmann ends his paper belong more to extrapolation or to anticipation? The synchronizing of historical times in the light of the worldwide nuclear threat and the synchronizing of history and nature in relation to the ecological crisis might seem to be reasonable extrapolations from the present sorry state of humanity, but Moltmann seems to hint that they belong more to anticipation than they do to extrapolation. I would like to know on what basis we can ever affirm that any particular hope or fear in the present (even that of nuclear destruction) belongs more to the one or to the other mode of what is to come; that is, to the *futurum* of THE FUTURE.

There are many other issues raised by these two papers that I hope to discuss, especially the contrast between Schillebeeckx's cautions against striving for one paradigm of future theology (pp.316-319) and Moltmann's emphasis on the universal thinking that ought to characterize the future. I do not mean to say that these are necessarily contradictory – they seem to speak to different levels of discourse – but there is much work to be done in relating the present move towards theological pluralism with the world-wide concerns that global issues force upon us.

I will end with a personal suggestion. All theological reflection takes place within the framework of a conversation between past, present and future – and past, present and future theologians. We meet here to conduct a *viva voce* conversation that we hope will advance and enrich theological concerns. As an historical theologian, I would like to insist that we make the dead as much a part of our conversation as the living. It is all too easy to reduce the giants of the past to 'positions' to be applauded or condemned insofar as they serve our own purposes. I think that both of the papers we have just heard urge us not to let our contemporary concerns and prejudices block the dialogue between past and future which it is both our obligation and our opportunity to further and to enrich.

V. THE POLITICAL DIMENSION OF THEOLOGY IN THE NEW PARADIGM

THEOLOGY IN THE NEW PARADIGM: POLITICAL THEOLOGY

Johann Baptist Metz

1. Paradigm change in theology?

1. Let me (incautiously) assume for the moment that there is something like 'progress' in theology. How can this progress be assessed? Perhaps on the basis of paradigm change, in analogy to Kuhn's suggestion? I would hesitate here, and should like to put a number of questions, without aiming at completeness, and without claiming any competence in scientific theory.

What Kuhn understands by progress derives explicitly from an aetiological evolution logic,[1] and is therefore also formulated in neo-Darwinian terms.[2] But is the *logos* of Christian the-ology, with its underlying apocalyptic-eschatological structure, not moulded by a different logic of time, history and development (if indeed we can speak of development here at all)?[3] At all events, for the *logos* of this theology, 'tradition' and 'remembrance', for example, cannot simply be replaced by 'historical reconstruction' on an evolutionistic basis. It is not evident how the evolutionary model could permit a normative use of history, let alone a 'canonical' one.[4]

---

[1] In which – to take up a saying of the 'Darwinian' Nietzsche – evolution aims at nothing except – evolution.

[2] *Cf.* Thomas S. Kuhn, *The Structure of Scientific Revolutions* (Chicago & London, 1962), ch.13. But see also Toulmin's criticism of Lakatos (Popper) taken up by Lamb in his paper. Here the question about time and history could be reconsidered.

[3] On the question about the relation between history and evolution, *cf.* J.B. Metz, *Faith in History and Society*, tr. D.Smith (London & New York, 1980), ch.10.

[4] *Cf.* here Metz, *ibid.* chs.11 & 12.

Is there such a thing as a 'pure' history of theology at all, analogous to the 'pure' history of science and to Kuhn's hermetic scientific community – a history of theology separate from church history, for example, or from political history? Is a new paradigm ever produced internally by theology at all? Is there any such thing as a theological paradigm change independent of reformative processes in the context of the church? Is the history of theological thought not always shaped by the social history of religion and the church?

Who is the conscious subject of theology? What is the place where theology is done? Is this as unequivocally clear for theology as it is when we apply the paradigm theory to scientific history? Does not a change in the subjects of theology and the places where theology is practised perhaps actually belong to the specific theological paradigm change?[5] Finally, are there not always several competing paradigms in theology – constitutionally, and not merely temporarily?[6]

2. I shall therefore use 'paradigm' and 'paradigm change' in theology in a rather broad sense. [7] As *criteria* for a 'new paradigm in theology' I should like tentatively to propose the following:

(*a*) the awareness of crisis and the capacity for dealing with it;

(*b*) the capacity for reduction. I mean this in two ways: first, as a non-regressive reduction of over-complexity and wordiness – language-run-riot (in which the crises of theology are pushed below the surface and covered up);[8] and second, as the non-trivial reduction of doctrine to life, of doxography to biography, because the *logos* of theology always aims at a form of knowledge that is *a form of living.*[9] For the idea of God to which Christian

[5] *Cf.* J.B. Metz, *A New Paradigm of Doing Theology?* (Lima, 1983), *Cf.* also *Concilium* (May, 1978): *Doing Theology in New Places.*

[6] In the light of its content (*cf.* n.9) and in the light of its subjects and the places where it is pursued (the theology of the religious orders, university theology, basis theology, and so on).

[7] Modifications can also be found in contributions by Küng, Tracy and Lamb to the present book.

[8] 'Reduction' as the criterion of a theological paradigm change must not be confused semantically with the same term as it is employed in system theory.

[9] *Cf.* here my attempt to interpret Karl Rahner's theology as a kind of new paradigm: 'Karl Rahner – ein theologisches Leben', in J.B. Metz, *Unterbrechungen*

theology is bound is in itself a practical idea. It continually cuts across the concerns of people who try 'merely to think' it. The histories of new beginnings, conversion, resistance and suffering belong to the very definition of this idea of God. The pure concept 'God' is the contraction, the shorthand, so to speak, of histories, in response to which theology must repeatedly decode its terms.[10]

I should like therefore to name the crises which provide the impulse for a paradigm change in theology (section 2); and shall then try to show why, and in what sense, the 'new' theology which is able to absorb these crises productively and tries to achieve the reductions I have described, is a political theology, or has a political dimension (section 3).

2. The crises

Let me mention three crises which have sparked off new ways of doing theology.[11] They are incidentally so constituted that their productive theological absorption is necessarily *ecumenical* in its very approach, not merely in its result.

(Gütersloh, 1981). I should also like in this connection to point to a paradigm discussion in modern Protestant theology which has meanwhile become a classic: the correspondence between Karl Barth and Adolf von Harnack, which was published sixty years ago. Barth stresses over against Harnack the apocalyptically tense crisis structure of faith, and the proclamation character of theology:

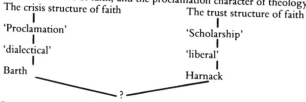

The crisis structure of faith   The trust structure of faith

'Proclamation'   'Scholarship'

'dialectical'   'liberal'

Barth   Harnack

?

[10] In this approach the difference between *logos* and myth, history and histories remains *within* the-ology.

[11] On the following signs of crisis or of the End-time *cf.* among others J. Habermas, *Legitimation Crisis*, tr. T. McCarthy (London, 1976); R Spaemann, 'Die christliche Religion und das Ende des modernen Bewusstseins', *Communio* 8 (1979), pp.251–270; J.B. Metz, *The Emergent Church*, tr. P. Mann (New York & London, 1981); L. Gilkey, 'The new Watershed in Theology', *Soundings* (1981), pp.118–131; also Gilkey's paper in the present volume.

1. *Theology in the face of the modern era*: that is, theology after the end of the religious and metaphysical views of the world – views which still provided the context for Reformation theology.
2. *Theology in the face of Auschwitz*: that is, theology after the end of idealism, or all systems of meaning without conscious subjects.
3. *Theology in the face of a socially divided and culturally polycentric worldwide church*: that is, theology at the end of its cultural monocentricism. In my view this 'end' shelters within itself promising signs of a change.

3. The political dimension of theology in the new paradigm

The 'new' theology which perceives these crises as fundamental crises of theology and which tries to overcome them in productive reduction is a 'political' theology.

1. *Theology after the end of the religious and metaphysical views of the world*

The theological discernment and absorption of this end – that is, the productive grappling with the processes of the Enlightenment – brings to the fore the political dimension of theology under two aspects. Both these aspects have given rise to misunderstanding and semantic confusion in the past, and still do so today. This is because, on the one hand, people have tried to fit this political theology into the already existing divisions of theological labour. This has led to a misreading of its character as *fundamental theology* (see section (*a*) below). On the other hand, another misunderstanding was due to the fact that, after the Enlightment, this political theology was identified with the legitimizing political theology of the pre-Enlightenment era. Its *critical* character was therefore overlooked (see section (*b*) below).

(a) With regard to the first point: the very project of a fundamental theology after the Enlightenment may be termed political theology. The disintegration of the religious and metaphysical world pictures has put an end to the era of theology's cognitive innocence. Theology must now come to terms with the denials of historical innocence through historicism, and with the denials of its social innocence through ideological criticism in both its bourgeois and its Marxist versions. Theology can no longer push the questions invoked here away from its centre into the fringe zones of apologetics. Its very *logos* is affected.

As fundamental theology, it can therefore no longer be content with the usual assignment of historical and social themes in theology to different divisions of labour. As fundamental theology it must be hermeneutics, and its hermeneutics must be political hermeneutics. For it cannot simply leave 'history' to a separate historical theology, as if theology had any foundation without history and without a thinking subject.[13] Nor can it view 'society' as the exclusive domain of social ethics, or the social teachings of the church,[14] as if theology's search for truth and witness to that truth had any foundation completely removed from social concerns and conflicts. Moreover, since the Enlightenment a fundamental theology can no longer simply assume that the relation between theory and practice is, as far as it is concerned, sufficiently settled by way of the customary division of labour between systematic and practical theology. For to assume this would be to conceal from itself the practical foundation of all theological wisdom and the specific form, or

[12] *Cf.* here the project of a practical fundamental theology as practical theology: J.B. Metz, *Faith, op.cit.*, chs.1–4.

[13] *Cf.* here Tracy's paper on hermeneutics in the present volume. Recent discussions about the narrative structure of theology also belong here.

[14] For criticism of this division of labour see now above all W. Kroh, *Kirche im gesellschaftlichen Widerspruch* (Munich, 1982). Here Kroh carries on the first detailed discussion between the new political theology and the traditions of Catholic social teaching.

Gestalt, its theory takes. Fundamental theology, that is to say, must be practical, political hermeneutics.[15] In my view, a fundamental theology of this kind must ultimately again take up the question about the cognitive subjects of theology, and the places where theology is to be done – a question which was supposed to have been dealt with by way of the division of labour in the church.[16]

(*b*) Now of course the disintegration of religious and metaphysical world pictures in the Enlightenment must not be interpreted as if the result were an utterly demythologized and secularized world, with a total divorce between religion and politics.[17] Religion was not completely privatized, and politics was not entirely secularized.[18] Even politically 'enlightened' societies have their political religions, with the help of which they seek to legitimize and stabilize themselves. We are familiar with this political religion in the 'civil religion' of the United States, for example, as well as in what we in Germany call *bürgerliche Religion*. Although linguistically the two phrases 'mean' the same thing (for example, *bürgerliches Recht* = civil law), civil religion and *bürgerliche Religion* can by no means simply be equated, for they derive from very different political cultures.[19] So when in Germany neo-conservatism also recommends the introduction of

[15] H. Peukert, *Science, Action, and Fundamental Theology* (ET Cambridge, Mass., 1984) has developed this approach and carried it further in discussion with contemporary theories of science and action. *Cf.* also Lamb's paper and the work of his own he cites there. From the point of view of liberation theology, of particular importance is the epistemological work by C. Boff & F. Castillo, *Theologie aus der Praxis des Volkes* (Munich & Mainz, 1978). Boff includes criticism of J.B. Metz, J. Moltmann and D. Sölle.

[16] *Cf.* the work cited in n.5.

[17] 'The dialectic of Enlightenment' has already taught us how much the notion of the total demythologization or secularization of the world, and the concept of progress moulded by this idea, became the real myth of early modern times.

[18] For important observations here and on the definition of the tasks of a new political theology see F. Fiorenza, 'Religion und Politik', in *Christlicher Glaube in moderner Gesellschaft* 27 (Freiburg, 1982).

[19] *Cf.* J. Habermas, 'Neokonservative Kulturkritik in den USA und in der Bundesrepublik', *Merkur* (November, 1982).

a 'civil religion',[20], this amounts ultimately to a reproduction of the traditional patterns in which politics is legitimized by religion – in the guise of political theology in its classic form.[21] Of course both political religions, American and German, serve to politicize religion – a politicization which means that religion is assigned a strict social purpose: it is functionalized.

But it is just this politicization of religion which political theology criticizes, and for two reasons. On the one hand, it criticizes it as religion, since political theology contests a religion which acts as legitimation myth and which purchases its discharge from society's criticism of religion through the suspension of its claim to truth. On the other hand, it criticizes the politicization of religion on theological grounds, contesting all theologies which, appealing to their non-political character, become pre-eminently theologies of just this political religion. If we do not want to establish the essence of religion in politics, not even an enlightened politics, we must not suppress theology's political dimension.

Of course this interpretation also provokes questions, and above all this one: if neither civil religion nor its German equivalent is available as the place where, since the Enlightenment, religion and politics can legitimately be reconciled theologically, what then? How then can the universalistic norms of Christianity be brought into harmony with political life at all, since that political life certainly cannot and must not revert to the time before the achievements of the political Enlightenment – the separation of powers, the right to opposition, liberty of opinion, and so forth? Do these universalistic norms make themselves felt when questions about ultimate goals crop up in political life, not merely questions about methods and their application? That is to say, do these norms make their impact when prevailing conditions themselves come

[20] Recently, above all H. Lübbe, following N. Luhmann.

[21] *Cf.* here the critical comments by J. Moltmann, 'Das Gespenst einer Zivilreligion', *Evangelische Kommentare* (March, 1983). I should like to associate myself specifically with his criticism.

under pressure and require legitimation – when a political ethic is required, not merely as an ethic for order but as *an ethic for change*?[22]

2. *Auschwitz – or theology after the end of idealism*

Here Auschwitz stands for the end of the modern era. In this context we have to notice first of all that the catastrophe of Auschwitz takes on paradigmatic character through its very incomparability. It points theology's historical and political conscience away from the singular 'history' to the plural 'histories of suffering', which cannot be idealistically explained, but can only be recollected in the context of a practical intent.[23] But which theology does not live from a catastrophic background, either by turning its back on it – that is, idealistically – or profoundly chafed and disturbed by it?

There is no meaning which one could salvage by turning one's back on Auschwitz, and no truth which one could thereby defend. Theology therefore has to make an about-turn, a turn which will bring us face-to-face with the suffering and the victims. And this theology is political theology. Its hermeneutics is a political hermeneutics, a hermeneutics in the awareness of danger. It criticizes the high degree of apathy in theological idealism, and its defective sensibility for the interruptive character of historical and political catastrophes.

This political theology after Auschwitz is not a theology in terms of a system. It is theology in terms of human subjects, with a practical foundation. It continually introduces into public

[22] See here as long ago as 1969 J.B. Metz in H. Peukert (ed.), *Diskussion zur 'politischen Theologie'* (Munich & Mainz, 1969). At present this question, for example, is discussed under the heading of 'monotheism and politics'.

[23] *Cf.* J.B. Metz, *Faith, op.cit.*, ch.9.

[24] Important elements for a 'hermeneutics in the face of danger' may be found in W. Benjamin's work; *cf.* O. John's pertinent dissertation, ' . . . *und dieser Feind hat zu siegen nicht aufgehört'. Die Bedeutung Walter Benjamins für eine Theologie nach Auschwitz* (Münster, 1983).

awareness 'the struggle for recollection', for the recollecting knowledge which is related to the human subjects concerned. For this theology, the 'system' can no longer be the place of theological truth – not, at least, since the catastrophe of Auschwitz, which no one can ignore without cynicism or can allow to evanesce into an 'objective' system of meaning.

This theology formulates the question about God in its oldest and most controversial form, as the theodicy question, though not in an existentialistic version but in a political one. It begins with the question about the deliverance of those who have suffered unjustly, the victims of our history and the defeated. It continually brings this question anew into the political awareness as indictment, and expounds the concept of a strict universal solidarity, which also includes the dead, as a practical and political idea, on which the fate of human beings as clear and evident subjects depends.

For without this solidarity the life of human beings as subjects tends more and more towards anthropomorphism. The public invitation to apply for the post as successor to the human being as subject has already gone out. The applicant is to have no recollection of past suffering and is to be tormented by no catastrophes. *Time* magazine has already portrayed the successful candidate on its front cover, as the man of the year for 1983: the robot, an intelligence without memory, without feeling and without morals.[25]

3. *Theology at the end of its cultural monocentricism*

Is our paradigm discussion not too Eurocentrically aligned from the outset? I must ask this, because it is only in the light of this question that I can discuss the political dimension of the 'new' theology adequately. It is a fact that the church no longer merely *has* a third world church but *is* a third world church with,

---

[25] *Cf.* here – in connection with the work of Metz and Peukert – M. Lamb, *Solidarity with Victims* (New York, 1982).

historically, West European origins. What does this fact mean for Catholic theology, for example?

On the one hand it means that the social antagonism in the world is moving to the centre of attention in the church and in theology. Conditions which are directly inconsistent with the gospel, such as exploitation and oppression or racism, are becoming challenges to theology. They demand that faith be formulated in categories of resistance and change. Thus theology is impelled to become political by its own *logos*.

On the other hand, in this new situation in which the church finds itself, a process of theological significance is emerging which we should not fail to take into account in our discussion about a paradigm change. The church is on the move from a culturally more or less monocentric European and North American church to one that is world-wide and culturally polycentric. In order at least to indicate the theological import of this transition, I should like[26] hypothetically to divide the history of theology and the church, up to the present day, into three eras: a first relatively brief founding era of Jewish Christianity; a second, very long era, in a more or less homogeneous cultural area – the age of the Gentile Christianity that grew up on hellenistic soil, the West European culture and civilization that was bound up with that and which lasted down to our own day; and a third era, the era of a world-wide cultural polycentrism in the church and theology, which is emerging at the present time. In this era the modern division between the churches, for example, appears mainly as an internal fate affecting European Christendom.[27]

[26] Following a suggestion of Karl Rahner's about the beginnings of a genuinely world-wide church in Vatican II; *cf.* his *Theological Investigations* Vol.20 (London, 1981): 'Concern for the Church'.

[27] Of course, in this hypothesis I have to assume much which I cannot discuss and substantiate here; for example, that there really is such a thing as this cultural polycentricism, and that it has not already been corrupted in germ by the profane Europeanization of the world which we call technology or technological civilization – that is, through the worldwide rule of western rationality, in which far more of the politics, history and anthropology of Europe is concealed than the technocrats of all political colours would have us believe.

Of course the end of cultural monocentricism does not mean disintegration into an arbitrary or random contextual pluralism. Nor does it mean the enthronement of a new, non-European monocentricism in the church and in theology. The church's original western history, which in concrete terms was always also a history of guilt where non-European cultures were concerned, will remain an immanent part of the cultural polycentricism of church and theology. But what is at stake now is mutual inspiration and mutual productive assimilation. This seems to me to be important for our European outlook on the churches and theology of the third world. For I see a reforming impulse coming upon western Christianity from there and, linked with that, the offer of a 'paradigm change' in theology as well. I can do no more than indicate that here, in the context of the political dimension of theology which I have been asked to talk about.[28]

With us this new beginning is associated rather abstractly with concepts such as basis church, liberation theology, and so forth. But here the gospel is related in a highly direct and immediate way to the specific political conditions in which people live. This 'application' generally seems to us too naive, too pre-modern, too simplistic, in view of our own over-complex situation, which has been heightened into extreme abstraction, particularly in the context of all the problems of interpretation in Scripture and tradition which have accumulated in our theology ever since the Enlightenment, and which may be summed up under the catchword of 'hermeneutics'. But if we examine the matter more closely, it becomes evident that in this 'application' we see a new form of theological hermeneutics, which I should like to call a political hermeneutics of danger. The awareness of danger as a basic category of a theological hermeneutics has a sound biblical foundation. The flash of danger lights up the whole biblical landscape; danger, present and impending, runs through all the biblical utterances, especially in the New Testament. As we

---

[28] More detail may be found in my essay 'Aufbruch zur Reformation', *Süddeutsche Zeitung* (April 9-10, 1983). *Cf.* also Metz, 'Toward the Second Reformation', in *The Emergent Church, op.cit.* (*cf.* n.11).

know, the discipleship narratives in the synoptic Gospels are not simply entertaining stories. They are not really even didactic stories. They are stories told in the face of danger: they are dangerous stories. And we have only to read John (15.18f., for instance) or Paul (for example II Cor. 4.8f.): what do we understand about texts like these and their *logos* if, and as long as, the awareness of danger is systematically screened out in our hermeneutics?

Now, this political hermeneutics of danger is certainly reductive – to some degree oversimplifying – and that in the sense of the reductions I named at the beginning as criteria for a paradigm change: practice returns home to pure theory, logic is joined again by mysticism, resistance and suffering once more find their proper place in the theological definition of grace and Spirit. If then there really is 'progress' in theology, and anything like a paradigm change, should we not have to pay particular attention to new impulses like these in the culturally polycentric space for learning offered by the world church and the world-wide Christian faith?[29] Are these things not always bound up with the reformative situations in which Christianity 'returns to its roots'?[30]

---

[29] Of course, this raises the question how Christian universalism can be so understood in the encounter with other religions and cultures that it does not simply, without more ado, 'imperialistically' integrate and subordinate them, but discerns them in their authentic message. I have tried to offer a solution in my reflections on the narrative-practical understanding of Christianity (as distinct from a transcendental-idealistic one) in *Faith*, *op.cit.*, ch.9 (*cf.* n.3). It seems to me that this approach also offers an indication of how the deadlocks (formulated by L. Gilkey in his paper) of a Christian absolutism in the encounter with other religions and cultures could be solved.

[30] Could we not, therefore, after all tentatively include the new paradigm of theology under the heading of 'liberation'? If, for the moment, we start from the assumption that the paradigm that has hitherto moulded modern theology was 'liberty', then the paradigm change in theology would be the change from liberty to liberation. *Cf.* here my reflections in 'Toward the Second Reformation' in *The Emergent Church*, *op.cit.* (see n.11), and the references in n.28. In *The Emergent Church*, in the same chapter, I also discuss the dilemma of Catholic theology in the face of the 'liberty' paradigm.

THE PARADIGM SHIFT IN THEOLOGY

Langdon Gilkey

The motif of the paradigm shift (the 'paradigm' of the paradigm shift?) has proved impressively and surprisingly illuminating in many fields and disciplines other than that of its original habitat, the history of natural science. Thomas Kuhn has contributed to our understanding of past historical developments an element of *discontinuity*, of unexpected and even dramatic mutation, of the qualitative leap into the new (Bergson) in cultural change that seems closer to the actual course of things than the preceding view of a steady, slow accumulation of slight changes leading in one definite direction – much as Marx once shifted our understanding of historical development and possibly Gould will do the same for biological evolution. We are all indebted to this image of a sharp shift of fundamental model, from which model flow the major characteristics of any given historical pattern of thought: its procedures of inquiry, its modes of testing and validation, its most basic forms of theory and the sorts of empirical and practical consequences that result.

As Kuhn's own examples from the development of modern science show, however, this conception of a fundamental paradigm shift in a discipline assumes certain important and essential *continuities* – as did my own examples above from nineteenth-century evolutionary philosophy. For a paradigm in a science even to be able to shift, the continuity of the scientific discipline within which the salto takes place is assumed; and, of course, it is also assumed that a wider culture, at once permissive and supportive of that discipline, remains dominant. Paradigm shifts, therefore, take place within a cultural and historical continuity that itself does not pass away. Our model points to

367

changes *in* a culture's developments, not changes *of* that culture itself, the mutation of the culture into something quite different. Much as the older view of scientific development saw that development as a steady accumulation of cumulative 'advances', the one building on, enlarging and improving the earlier ones, so the new understanding sees this continuity as characterized by sharp shifts of interpretation, method and construction of theory – but nevertheless against the historical background of a continuity within which these shifts can be clearly noted, described, compared. It was, after all, the 'modern scientific community' that experienced or underwent these paradigm shifts; it was the developing scientific culture that turned first to one and then to the other of them, not to mention (of course) the continuity of natural process that was assumed as the relatively stable 'object' which these shifting paradigms successively sought to illuminate. A comparable 'environmental continuity' (of culture and of church) within which significant changes take place, would necessarily be a presupposition for any discussion of paradigm shifts in theology or in theological ethics.

The point of my remarks here is, first, to raise the question whether there might not be other, perhaps more fundamental shifts in historical process than those labelled 'paradigm shifts', shifts on a scale or at a level different from and more fundamental than the paradigm shifts of which we generally speak. And, second, I wish to suggest that two such fundamental 'systems of change' – what I shall call 'continental shifts' or 'epochal shifts' – have been and are taking place around us. To call such continental or epochal shifts 'paradigm shifts' is, I think, misleading: first they do not happen in a discipline, but rather in the entire cultural-historical environment, and therefore are manifest (at least in the long run) in all the disciplines alike. And, second, they result in fundamental changes at the deepest level in the character and quality of life, of 'existence', and so of social structure. As a consequence of those epochal shifts, every aspect of culture, including all its forms of theory, is substantially affected and redirected, often in quite new directions. As a further consequence, the paradigms in all the disciplines shift, and shift in quite new ways, old models now being abandoned as irrelevant and a host of new ones appearing.

Two examples of such epochal or continental shifts in the environment of a discipline or set of disciplines come to mind. One is the development of modern science itself from roughly the fourteenth through the sixteenth and early seventeenth centuries, a development prepared, to be sure, by preceding changes but (like the appearance of Christianity or Islam) ushering in a new historical continuum borne by a quite new community, and so a continuum in which now paradigms can be seen meaningfully to shift. This wider historical change, the development of modern science itself, is the presupposition for Kuhn's analysis of paradigm shifts.

The second is the development, in part caused or certainly fundamentally shaped by the rise of science, of what we call 'modern culture', beginning with the Enlightenment, continuing during the nineteenth and into the early twentieth century. This epoch or continent itself over its course generated innumerable basic paradigms in its wide variety of disciplines: rational and mechanistic; romantic, organic; process, developmental – and so on. It also has helped to encourage a wide variety of different *theological* paradigms. Because of the immense luring and challenging power of this culture, most of these theological paradigms concern the relations of theology to this new 'secular' culture: there were rationalistic, pro-Enlightenment or accommodation paradigms, anti- or transcendent orthodox, reformative or transformational models, progressivist models, dialectical models, and – in our own day – revolutionary. Some of these welcomed the new cultural epoch, some resisted it, some criticized and sought to refashion it – all assumed its powerful, all-engrossing *presence*, and the necessity for a vital theology to be clear and unambiguous about its own relation to this now established culture and about its creative tasks *within* that culture.

For example, to me *both* of the two most pervasive present paradigms in theology represent responses to these two 'epochal' or 'continental' shifts out of which our culture has formed itself:

modern science on the one hand and Enlightenment and post-Enlightenment culture as a whole on the other. First, this is the case with the understanding of theology, in reaction to the development of science, as primarily a cognitive science (*Wissenschaft*) to be understood and developed in its relation to one or another of the major intellectual options of modern intellectual culture: transcendental Thomism, phenomenological and existential philosophy, process philosophy, hermeneutical philosophy, literary criticism, and so on. And, on the other hand, though it might not welcome this interpretation, to me the same is true of *political theology* which interprets theology in the terms of the paradigm of social praxis as understood in the social and critical theories developed in modern socialist culture. This is not to denigrate or trivialize either of these contemporary paradigms. The issues of the cognitive status of religious and theological statements, and that of social justice and liberation, are of course essential to any mode of Christian being, and so are perennial in any historical context. Since the culture that formulated itself around modern science and modern philosophy on the one hand, and modern democratic and socialist theory on the other, remains at present dominant in the West, these paradigms are central to theological expression – and can be expected to continue to develop new and creative paradigms in the decades or so to come.

There are, however – or so it seems to me – important changes appearing within our present post-Enlightenment cultural matrix that represent a more basic shift than this, the sort of continental or epochal shift of which I spoke. Quite possibly (though who knows now?) they are on a scale as massive and transformative as the development itself of the Enlightenment and post-Enlightenment culture of modernity. And just as that massive epochal shift creating our modern disciplines effected an entire series of *new* paradigms, and so of successive paradigm shifts in theology as in other disciplines, so, quite possibly, the present one may be expected to give rise to a quite new sequence of fundamental theological models.

The most important continental or epochal shift I have in mind is represented by the current 'time of troubles' for the Western Enlightenment and post-Enlightenment culture I have just described. Arnold Toynbee labelled 'a time of troubles'[1] a period in the life of a civilization when those institutions, movements and capacities which had been the creative centre of the culture or civilization in question now, under new conditions, reverse their role and generate more problems than they resolve. These institutions serve to threaten rather than to strengthen the continued strength and integrity of the culture in question. There is here, says Toynbee in disagreement with Spengler, no *necessity* of decline or fall; but there is now the new *possibility* of each of these, and there is the possibility of *nemesis* or self-destruction. In any event, there is the new reality, echoed in other such periods (late Hellenistic culture, late mediaeval culture), of the *shrinkage* and the *transformation* of the precedent cultural whole, and subsequent to this, the appearance of these same elements in a quite new synthesis (as in early mediaeval life) – a synthesis whose centres of power and influence may be located quite somewhere else and whose spiritual centre may be dramatically different. Such a process ushered in by a time of troubles would, needless to say, represent the sort of continental or epochal shift to which I have referred. And such a shift, even at its inception or in its early stages, would call for in response an entirely *new* set or sequence of paradigms – as it did in each of the cases cited above – in all the disciplines that remained active and creative. Every age, of course, experiences problems and crises; at certain points in history, however, these seem to mount in intensity, when, as noted, what was once creative and strength-building in the culture now turns and becomes destructive. Old answers now are demonic or irrelevant; new ones perforce appear, and with them the whole range of possible paradigms *itself* shifts.

There are, it seems to me, several important 'signs' that such a time of troubles is upon us in the present post-Enlightenment West. (1) At perhaps the most fundamental level is the incredible shrinkage of the power and influence, in effect the loss of

---

[1] Arnold Toynbee, *A Study of History* (Oxford, 1945), Vol.I, p.53.

dominance, that western culture as a whole has undergone in the past few decades. This is recognized and dismissed (in Europe and America) as the 'shrinkage of Europe's powers', as if the United States had simply replaced a once dominant Europe. This assessment is an optical illusion, I believe; the relations of Europe (1500-1900) to the rest of the world are dramatically different from the relations of America in the latter twentieth century to that world. Only consider that for four hundred years, from the early sixteenth century to the middle twentieth, no non-European power could or did successfully challenge a major European power, and *a fortiori* no extra-European power could challenge all of them together. As a result European powers (and finally in the twentieth century America joined them) were only checked by one another; severally, if they could free themselves from that *intramural* limitation, they could take and rule any plot of land, inhabited or not, small or large, that they wished. The world powers *were* European powers, and only slowly in the twentieth century have any outsiders entered that exclusive club. With such incredible domination making possible the elimination of all non-western rivals, no wonder they thought that history represented progress. The United States has inherited some but by no means all of this dominance. With the (long overdue) break-up of colonial empires in and around 1945, and the failure of the European powers to unite, *most* of the present 'world powers' are in one important sense or another non-western. America remains the sole self-conscious inheritor of that post-Enlightenment European culture, continuing not only its scientific, technological and industrial aspects but also its political, economic and social structures of individualism, of mixed economic capitalism, and of democracy. The rest in one important way or another do not represent that cultural tradition.[2] What is therefore crucial is that, since 1945 and *outside*

---

[2] The situation of the so-called West *vis-à-vis* the Soviet bloc represents a complex set of problems – as Europeans are all too aware. Is that 'culture' a part of the West, to which it seems momentarily opposed, or is it not? Both Yes and No seem to be the answer. In terms of cultural inheritance (point number 2 in the text),

the orbit of this once dominant culture, there have appeared different political, economic and cultural *Gestalten* representing significantly different centres of power, significantly different cultural traditions, and therefore significantly different cultural prospects for the future.

Needless to say, each of these new options, whether one looks east at the Soviet Union and its allies, further eastwards to China and Japan, or to the so-called third world, has (as have also the United States, Canada, Australia, and, say, South Africa) inherited a great deal from this long dominant European culture: science, technology, industrialism; many social ideals ranging from eighteenth-century democracy on to nineteenth- and twentieth-century Marxist communist attitudes – and the universal expectation of a plethora of consumer goods. Nevertheless, each of these other cultural centres has welded this inheritance into a self-consciously and so deliberately different cultural unity from (at least in its *own* understanding) that of the 'West'. As Russia has done something significantly different with science, technology and industrialism than, say, have France, West Germany, England, the Netherlands and the United States, so has Japan; and so, even more, when the forms of their cultures are more stabilized, will China, Iran and the nations of Africa. The political, economic and military domination of the West has, therefore, shrunk immensely in the space of forty years; other centres of political, military and cultural power have arisen, some of them now equal to the West, many more on their way to this point. Most of the West has not realized the full implications of this loss of dominance or thought through its implications for the

inheritance of ideas and especially of fundamental symbols, the answer is certainly Yes: its inheritance is both old and new European, partly Enlightenment, partly Marxism – with a proviso that the concept of Holy Mother Russia is probably its own. On the other hand, in terms of the present point: the military and political dominance of the West, the answer seems clearly to be No. The Soviet bloc at present represents an alternative, and a powerful centre of power to that represented by the nations of NATO, the European economic community and the United States.

future. After four hundred years, it represents a quite new historical epoch for the West, a new, more vulnerable, less central and certainly less directive role in the events of the future.

(2) Perhaps even more fundamental than this relatively 'external' shrinkage is the appearance to the western consciousness – and to that of many outside the West – of the deep *ambiguities* within the creative centre of western civilization. One could of course begin with the excessive individualism and even its tradition of individual rights – especially economic and personal – which have long revealed their potentially destructive as well as their historically creative sides. Perhaps newer and more fundamental (for this includes now the socialist cultures critical of capitalistic individualism) is the awareness of the ambiguity (potentially destructive as well as potentially creative) of the science, technology and industrialism on which basis this culture developed its strength. The world-wide power and domination of the West – as well as many of its creative 'spiritual' accomplishments – found their creative source *here*. Both to itself and to others (eg, Japan after 1857), the West appeared as 'superior' mainly because of these three supremely creative forces, which had therefore quickly occupied the central roles in western culture as a whole.

I need not remind this group that each of these creative forces in our culture: science, technology and an expanding industrialism, now presents to the culture they together established and shaped, not only serious but even lethal, mortal problems or dilemmas. We find this whether we look at the power of our weapons, the dehumanizing effects of a technological and industrial culture, the despoilation of the environment consequent on industrial expansion – or the probable authoritarian results of seeking to resolve these problems. The most creative aspects of western culture as it waxed in strength and influence have, to its surprise, revealed themselves as harbingers of potential nemesis, a prospect literally incredible to the eighteenth- and nineteenth-century founders (from Condorcet, through Comte, Haeckel and Marx to John Dewey) of these cultural powers and emphases. At best, the modern West may resolve these problems located at the centre of its existence by a necessary and radical reconstruction of itself; at worst the ambiguity of these powers: science, technology and industry, will turn more and more destructive. In either case a fundamental change in the structure and the ethos of the culture appears imminent. If anything, therefore, the secular culture is now in more travail; more uncertain, self-doubting, anxious about guilt and its own mortality, than the religious and theological inheritance which only yesterday it so sharply challenged – and this is a totally new situation.

(3) The third sign is the visible weakening of the fundamental symbolic systems constitutive of this Enlightenment and post-Enlightenment culture, those forms of 'religious substance' (as Tillich would say), or perhaps of 'civil religion', that have directed and empowered most of western society since the eighteenth century. Although here and there this symbol system took a theistic form, certainly the central object of its belief was imminent historical development, the myths of historical progress through (note) science, technology, industry, individual rights and democracy – or, in its alternate version, science, technology, industrialism, socialist (communist) ownership, and therefore equality and universal well-being. To each of these 'wings' of most modern post-Enlightenment culture,[3] modern society (in *their* form, to be sure) represents a universal society 'in the making', a society in which the fundamental human problems, namely the deprivation of justice, equality, freedom, peace and general well-being, would gradually cease and become merely technical. Each has represented, therefore, to itself, the

---

[3] Returning to the subject of the above footnote, I have said that in terms of political, military and economic power the Soviet bloc and the West at present represent alternative, frequently antagonistic and certainly significantly different cultural organizations of science, technology and industrialism. In terms of intellectual inheritance, Russia is as much an inheritor of the Enlightenment as the United States probably is; though our ideology is more specifically 'Enlightenment', theirs nineteenth-century socialistic. In this sense the two cultures, like the mediaeval West and the orthodox East, are 'cousins', if hardly 'kissing cousins'; or possibly a better comparison is the Renaissance and post-Renaissance Europe and the Ottoman empire, both inheritors of Hellenism but each fired by a different cultural symbolic system.

beginning of a new sort of society in which history's devastating violence, cruelties, tyrannies and self-destructive conflicts: of nation, race and class, would be slowly eliminated. (Note how much theological reflection has been geared to responding – positively and negatively – to this optimistic vision of history, as it had also to respond to the cognitive claims of the new science out of which the culture developed). This 'salvation history' in its liberal-democratic form influenced and permeated Protestant theology in the nineteenth and early twentieth centuries, forming a new 'Christian' vision of history as progressive and the synthesis recognizable in the 'social gospel' movement. At present its Socialist-Marxist variants have been equally effective in forming the current synthesis of revolutionary action and a vision of history progressing through dialectical conflict to its culmination characteristic of the theologies of liberation and the political theologies of praxis. In any case, the main centre of the fundamental symbolism of Enlightenment and post-Enlightenment culture (its religious substance) was its progressivist vision of history, a progress based on science, technology and industrialism combined with crucial revolutionary or reformist political and social acts (in the past or to come), and so a progress leading – for both its versions – to a brighter future of material, political and human fulfilment.

Our present situation is that in the last half of the twentieth century and on almost every front, this progressivist interpretation of history and of our culture's role in history has proved to be deeply counter-factual and so almost constantly falsified. First, the most advanced cultures of modernity, one after another, have shown themselves capable of depths of destructive evil as profound as any in human history. Second, the dilemmas of a scientific, technological and industrial culture which we discussed above have shown that the accumulation of scientific knowledge, of technological capacity, of social and industrial organization, and even of social ideals, not only does not effect an increment of security and well-being and a consequent eradication of evil and suffering in society; on the contrary, it seems precisely to increase insecurity and suffering. In fact, not merely does it mortally endanger modern society itself: it even threatens, and this *is* new, a continuity of nature and so of life itself. Perhaps most important for a culture whose confidence rested directly in its optimistic vision of the future to come, these dilemmas, and the lethal potentialities for nuclear holocaust or environmental despoilation they represent, have radically revised our vision of the future from a bright one to a very menacing one. Instead of a visibly improved, morally cleansed, even perfected society, the future for ourselves, and especially for our children, while not at all a *necessary* doom, nevertheless contains genuinely macabre potentialities,[4] potentialities which earlier decades would have found utterly incredible, if not neurotic or 'priestly'. In short, the progressivist *mythos*, based on science, technology, industrialism, a correct social ideal, and on the moral progress latc it within all of these, has proved to be incredible in relation to historical experience, even more incredible than theological orthodoxy seemed to the founders of the Enlightenment.

Finally, as with so many symbolic systems associated with established cultures, this set of ideals – whether democratic or socialist – have lost, at least for the present, their luring or their grasping power. Not only are their visions of the future now incredible; even more they appear, to many within them and to most without, to be largely empty, hypocritical and self-serving rationalizations for economic or political privilege, and thus in fact fully as oppressive as they are liberating. The ideals of democracy, of individual rights and of free elections, which during most of the nineteenth century inspired revolutions or reformist movements and new constitutions around the globe, now appear – and with great justification – as rationalizations for economic privilege, admired by and inspiring for only the members of the third world's country clubs and its remaining military and fascist dictators. Correspondingly, the ideals of communism are viewed – and also rightly – in much the same way by oppressed workers in Poland (and probably in Russia as

---

[4] *Cf.* for example, Robert Heilbroner, *An Inquiry into the Human Prospect* (New York, 1974), and Jonathan Schnell, *The Fate of the Earth* (New York, 1982).

well), by Moslems in Afghanistan, and by the long-suffering inhabitants of Laos and Cambodia, merely as obvious rationalizations for political domination and the privileges that go with that domination on the part of the established rulers in the Kremlin or in Hanoi. I gather that the same dissipation of the 'grasping power' of this symbolism has, since the cultural revolution, also widely occurred in China. Ironically enough, the only remaining 'true believers' of these two mythic visions spawned by Enlightenment culture seem to be residents of the prisons of the other: the dissidents in Russia, Poland and China, on the one hand (who frequently utter words straight out of the Enlightenment), and the guerrilla forces in Central and South America genuinely struggling for the oppressed peoples on the other hand. Again, historical realities seem to have made infinitely *dubious* and thus *vulnerable* the deepest 'secular' convictions of modern culture, the 'religious substance' at the centre of modernity itself – as it has also rendered deeply ambiguous the central social and intellectual institutions of that culture. Interestingly enough, current history, perhaps because they no longer rule it, has not so directly assaulted the symbolic interpretations of theology and of the churches.

My own feeling that all of this represents a genuine 'time of troubles' may be an error. But that something has radically changed with regard to the confidence of the culture in its own institutional and spiritual bases: namely in its science, its scientific method, its technology, its industrial plant and its political-economic institutions on the one hand and its visions of itself and of history on the other, of *this* change there can be no doubt. We live in a deeply menaced historical environment, one whose possible future is awesomely terrifying, even unthinkable. This given historical *reality* is diametrically opposed to the shrinking vision of historical reality and of the future on which our civilizations have been based: our present future represents the starkest possible contrast to the 'future' of Enlightenment and post-Enlightenment culture.

This is a vast epochal shift – and it will inevitably change the tasks and the paradigms of theology for many years to come.

Instead of responding to the challenges emanating *from* the culture: its cognitive demands, its pressure towards its own conceptions of justice and its own standards of human *areté* – theology may be called to the quite different task of providing *succour* to the culture in its travail. What that succour may entail is possibly courage, confidence and guidance, and on the symbolic level foundations, basic theological grounding for its norms, and for a new horizon of meaning, as well as criticism of its use of these norms and these meanings. As in all such times, religion, in all its wild and often frightening variety, springs up in old and new forms, in creative and in demonic forms, all about us, setting a whole set of new problems in political, ethical and theological reflection for all of us. To respond creatively and not defensively to a successful, expanding, confident secular culture has been *one* thing and has involved one set of paradigms; to witness to the gospel and its implications in a period of deep cultural anxiety and institutional confusion, of almost irresistible temptations to terrible sin and destruction, even of mortal inter-necine conflict, is quite another, and it will issue accordingly in a quite different set of paradigms. This is the major continental shift I have in mind.

The second continental or epochal shift I have in mind is closely associated with the one just mentioned. We have spoken of the reduction suddenly of modern western culture to *one* of the world's cultures rather than the *telos* and *culmination* of world culture, as it once fondly believed it was. This other 'shift' I shall call the *new form of the encounter of Christianity with other religions,* a mode of encounter one can only name that of 'rough equality'. The encounter of the world's major religions is, of course, not new; it has been frequent and close since at least the seventeenth century, and it steadily increased in extent in the eighteenth, the nineteenth and the early twentieth centuries. These encounters, however, were in a vastly different mode. For Christians of all persuasions they were (without many tremors of doubt) encounters between *the* one true and saving religion and false or near-false religions, or, in a more tolerant though hardly more humble version, in the nineteenth century, between the 'supreme or absolute' religion on the one hand and less advanced, less moral and so 'less pure' forms of faith on the other. It is my guess or 'hunch' that during the latter nineteenth and earlier twentieth centuries this feeling of the superiority of western religions, especially of Christianity, was frequently quite unwillingly, grudgingly and even unconsciously shared by many in other faiths – which is one (though only one) reason why they felt so beleaguered by our aggressive 'Christianity'. In any case, my point is that such a viewpoint is, except in rare cases, now regarded as neither credible nor even defensible – though any theological and/or philosophical implications of this change of attitude are still barely visible.[5]

The reasons for this rather dramatic change in the mode of encounter, from an encounter of a superior with an inferior to an encounter of rough equals, are probably multiple. Since I can sense this shift in my own lifetime (from 1940 when I went to China to 1975 when I went to Kyoto), I have another 'hunch' as to one of its determining causes. This is, I think, closely associated with the reduction and relativization of western culture among the cultures. I do not think this new sense of rough equality among religions comes from any new and sharper *dogmatic* critique of Christianity, for instance, of its christological claims. Intellectual criticism of the dogmatic claim to transcendent absolutism is as old as the Enlightenment, and few surpass

---

[5] I have added 'philosophy' because there is an illusion among the academic community, even (or especially?) among philosophers, that religious doctrines or dogmas are all that are *particular* in intellectual and spiritual life, and that philosophy (because it has no dogmas) represents a universal position – and therefore has none of the problems of the 'encounters of faith' discussed here. This is an illusion. Western philosophy is as *western*, and not Asiatic or Indian, as is Christianity – and perhaps more so. It represents one cultural viewpoint among many, and as a consequence it has the same difficulties transcending that particular cultural viewpoint that a given religion does. In fact, most modern philosophy is at the stage of a somewhat tolerant nineteenth-century Christianity, mildly curious about other forms of 'reason' (eg, Buddhist logic) but utterly confident that western modes of rationality are the most advanced and so superior. It would, therefore, be rare indeed – such is the certainty of most western philosophers that they represent *philosophy* and so universal reason – if *this* discussion ('how do we understand reason now that we recognise the rough equality of cultural philosophies?') came to be carried on under philosophical auspices.

Feuerbach in the sharpness of that criticism. Correspondingly, this critique is as well answered now by theology as it once was. No fundamental rupture in our theological self-interpretation of Christianity has occurred since, say, 1930-40 when – as the easy sense of Christian superiority of the great theologians of that period illustrates – attitudes towards other religions were very different from what they are now.

What has dramatically changed is the relative status of western culture *vis-à-vis* other cultures. The points where, without question, it regarded itself as a superior civilization (one sees these points frequently cited in past apologetic arguments for Christianity – notably my own!): the development of science and technology; the affirmation of individual and social being (leading, as one now hears from Buddhists, to imperialism!); the emphasis on the value of the person and on individual rights; the equality of the sexes(!); the emphasis on personal autonomy especially in marriage; the development of a 'higher personal and social morality notably democracy and humanitarianism; the emphasis on history and progress', and possibly any number more. One aspect of the present problem is that each of these 'clear evidences of superiority', assumed to *be* superior until the 1930s, is now regarded as either of dubious value or of dubious validity. To take just one example: in 1940 the 'western family' (marriage based on a freely-chosen partner and the autonomous family of mother, father and children) was almost universally regarded (as it was by younger Chinese) as the supreme ideal for our species, established by the West and striven for by other 'less developed civilizations'. As I found in Kyoto in 1975, however, these western patterns of family life are looked at as deeply ambiguous, that is, as leading to divorce, as weakening the family bond and as cruel to the elderly – and some solution ('on our own terms') was now being sought. This is, I may add, an argument almost as fully convincing to the listening Westerner as to the Japanese who now makes it. As the cultures have thus become in this sense roughly equal, or are now perceived *on both sides* as equal, so the religions of the cultures are perceived differently than they were. And the arguments that, the cultural fruits of

Christianity being superior, so Christianity itself is clearly superior (an argument only S.K. and Barth might have scorned!), have now long lost their persuasiveness to either partner in the dialogue. Needless to say, losing the humble ally of cultural superiority has not helped to establish the efficacy of the *other* base for superiority, namely, one grounded on a strictly dogmatic basis: 'We are the only faith with divinely revealed truth . . . ' Such dogmatic certitude is now even more difficult than ever. Perhaps most important, one finds in one's self a new psychological (spiritual?) attitude, one of hoping to hear something *from* them. One feels like *listening* for the first time, and possibly (to one's surprise) in the hope that the other may *help* one's own faltering spirituality.

Second, the movement of spiritual power is, at least in the first world, clearly in the other direction; the rising tide of missionary expansion now flows *towards* us and not out from us. People we know, people in our own families, through the mediation of one of these alternative religions, felt this spiritual power – the power of inward and bodily healing, of spiritual unity and identity, of experienced touch with the divine; and many of them have responded to that experience in gratitude and commitment. Under such circumstances one can hardly deny that there is, therefore, truth and grace within these other religious traditions: Zen, certain Hindu groups, Yoga, Sikh Dharma, to name a few.

In short, in our time it is quite impossible to deny the presence of healing grace and healing truth in other religious traditions. This is not to say they have *the* truth or the healing mode of grace, and we do not; to say that would of course mean one has become converted. No, it is a quite new recognition of a certain mode of *relativity* attached to one's own faith, and as a consequence, certain important modes of *dependence* or of *lack* in relation to the other (for instance, in the view of nature or of community); and paradoxically but not strangely, while recognizing this aspect of relativity, one yet retains a kind (*what* kind?) of 'absoluteness' in remaining a believing and committed Christian – as one's partner in the dialogue, recognizing truth and grace within us, retains a quality of absoluteness in remaining a Buddhist. This bizarre situation – of 'relative absoluteness', seemingly with a 'conditioned-unconditioned' – is, I submit, where we are, whether we like it or not. We may not welcome it or even understand it, but we can hardly at this time of day escape from it. For traditional theology it is a very new situation: none of the preceding periods of church history experienced this sort of relation to other religious traditions. Moreover, it contains innumerable theological consequences too obvious to belabour now, consequences only just beginning to be explored. How is one to understand *theologically* this 'relative absoluteness' I have described? What does it do to revelation, to christology, to justification and/or sanctification, to the doctrine of the church, to eschatology and to social praxis? I suggest this too is an epochal or continental shift. It is not a change in paradigm but in the whole cultural and theological environment within which paradigms arise and fall. At least, it is personally and theologically very interesting and sets us some exceedingly exciting theological issues – which one can hardly say about the possible nemesis of peace, even of life itself, that may face us in our secular culture's future.

RESPONSE TO JOHANN BAPTIST METZ
AND LANGDON GILKEY

John Cobb

Langdon Gilkey, as the title of his paper shows, is more concerned to address the theme of the conference than the specific topic of this session. Insofar as he does the latter, it is by showing that global political changes radically alter the context of Christian theology.

I appreciate Gilkey's calling our attention to this wider context and to the fact that the emerging situation requires theological change more radical than that associated with a shift of paradigms in the narrow sense. It would be too easy in this conference to define the elements of consensus we have shared for a generation or more, and to see them as justifying business as usual, especially in the academic community. In fact, we are entering a new situation which will grow out of, but is already shaking the foundations of, the old.

For Gilkey the basic shift is away from the dominance of western culture with its belief in progress and from the assumption of the religious superiority of Christianity associated with that dominance. I agree that these are important, but when the actual changes occurring in these areas are carefully stated, they seem less decisive than some points emphasized by Gilkey and even some he does not mention. To advance the discussion of the new paradigm we need, I will confront Gilkey's formulations critically within a horizon of wide-ranging agreement.

If it were the case that European culture as a whole was no longer a major factor in the world, and that Christian self-understanding had been inextricably bound up with European dominance, then a drastic shift could indeed be affirmed. But Gilkey does not really mean to make such extreme claims. His point is (1) that it is now clear that the appropriation of the science, technology and industry originally developed in European culture does not require the wholesale adoption of that culture, so that the emergence of new centres of world power can have cultural forms quite different from those of Europe, and (2) that the association of Christianity with western culture no longer functions as an apologetic device for gaining its acceptance in those new centres.

Stated in this way his points, while valid and important, do not shake the discipline of theology to the core. Although some Westerners have believed that the great civilizations of the East would have to become completely westernized in spirit and culture to regain economic and political power, this has always been a minority view within those civilizations. They have retained, despite all western challenges, a deep sense of their own cultural superiority. And there have long been western admirers who believed in the possibility of indigenizing science, technology and industry in these societies.

Similarly, although many Christians have relied on western cultural prestige to support missions, and in some parts of the world this has been effective, the situation has been mixed. Early Jesuit missionaries in China were not so chauvinistic about western culture as a whole even when they took advantage of western superiority in particular areas. Major strains of Christian theology (Gilkey mentions S.K. and Barth) sharply distinguished faith and culture. On the other side, the wisdom of the East exercised fascination in nineteenth-century Europe and America and influenced religious developments in separation from much in the cultures of the lands from which it came.

Again, my point is not that the present situation is a mere continuation of the past. It is that a major shift in theology cannot be explained on the basis of these points alone.

A more important change for theology arises from what Gilkey stresses as the loss of cultural self-confidence in the West connected with the assumption of progress. Gilkey knows that this assumption has operated at a much deeper level than the verbal criticisms of the idea and continues to shape theological programmes today. Theology continues to justify itself through correlations with secular disciplines, whereas the deeper abandonment of the sense of cultural progress will make possible and require redefinition of the theological task, perhaps as more generative and less responsive.

Even on this point, however, Gilkey's formulations could be misleading. He invites us to recognize that there are cultural centres independent of the European experience, but on the subject of progress he takes the European experience as normative for all. He knows that in a global perspective a faith in progress, continuous with that of the European past, is more powerful today than ever before, but he flatly denies its validity. I suggest that we might do well to be open to the possibility that China can achieve a less ambiguous form of progress over a sustained period of time.

Loss of faith in progress is rightly connected by Gilkey with our new awareness that continuing the directions taken thus far by the West will led to nuclear holocaust or environmental collapse. To me it seems that this new awareness of the likelihood of an end of history so different from biblical eschatology is the most important really new element in our theological context. Next to it I would place the emergence into positions of intellectual leadership of women who reconsider the Christian tradition (and all civilization) from the perspective of woman's heretofore unarticulated experience, profoundly transforming our perceptions and evaluations.

Gilkey thinks that the dominant style of theology during the days when western culture was confident has been correlating Christianity to aspects of that culture. He locates political theology in that context, thus doubly relativizing it, once to the passing age and secondly, within that age, to one interest alongside others.

I hope Metz will address Gilkey directly on this point. The implication of his paper is that he would argue that the observer role Gilkey takes in his survey of what is going on in the world expresses the situation of the bourgeois individual in the university, and is not really politically neutral. For Metz the lesson of the Enlightenment is that the life of the mind offers no transcendent perspective but is rooted in the historical situation of the subject. Our theology either justifies the *status quo* as in political religion, or criticizes it. Those who live by the memory of the passion of Jesus cannot sanctify the oppression which characterizes history. The denial of progress must not be allowed to make the theologian the observer of the human condition rather than the advocate of God's creatures who are in need.

Metz highlights Auschwitz as one of the major events theologians need to remember. This is commendable. It is too easy for Gentiles to treat the Holocaust as just one more example of man's inhumanity to man – and to women and children – and to begin to speak of rather commonplace instances of Jewish brutality to Arabs with the same word. In the United States also we are realizing how profoundly that memory must alter our theological habits. We have called the Jewish Scriptures the *Old* Testament in contrast to the *New* which is then presumed to supersede it. We have obscured the Jewishness of Jesus even and especially by our historical-critical methods. We have overused and misused the distinction between law and gospel. We have vilified the Pharisees. We have depicted the crucifixion of Jesus as theologically motivated, thereby placing blame on the Jews. Our christologies have implicitly condemned Judaism. Thereby it is not past Christians alone with their overt anti-Jewish teachings, but we ourselves, despite our self-righteous disavowal of prejudice, who remain guilty of Auschwitz and are called, by the memory of Auschwitz, to repentance.

Metz's emphasis here helps us understand what it means to focus on the subject of doing theology. The theology of one who remembers Auschwitz differs from that of one who does not. But here lies for me also a problem in understanding Metz's political theology. Some theologians who remember Auschwitz are moved thereby to support the state of Israel in every effort to ensure that the collective lives of the Jewish people will never again be dependent on the good-will of others. In that case the theologians will support Israel in its aggressive policies to ensure its permanent military security. But others who remember

Auschwitz may resolve instead that never again should Christians stand silently by as a powerless people are oppressed and abused. They may view Israel's treatment of West Bank Arabs as precisely such oppression and abuse, and they may join the hostile criticism of the policies of the Jewish state. Does political theology provide guidance here?

Metz is hardly less impressed than Gilkey by the end of Eurocentrism. But for him this does not lead to interest in other religious traditions. It leads instead to an enthusiastic embracing of the new situation in the Christian church in which the voices of Christians in the third world are heard as equals and partners. Those who have been the objects of European exploitation and concern are now the subject of theology. The Latin American Christians especially speak from a situation of practice which correlates with the danger in which the early disciples lived.

The focus here is on the danger of persecution for Christian faithfulness from political and economic authority. We are all moved and informed by the theology that comes from this Latin American experience, and we await the maturing of Minjung theology in Korea, theological expressions of the post-denominational, post-liberation Protestant church in China, and similar theological developments around the world, alongside the longer tradition of Indian theology.

I hope it does not detract from my warm agreement with Metz on this point if I press the question of his silences. Do we not all live in danger of a nuclear holocaust that could bring an end to history very different from the *eschaton* envisaged in the New Testament? Are we less faithful to the lessons of the Enlightenment if we focus on that danger too? Do not the loss of topsoil in Africa, the deforestation of Southeast Asia, the continuing population explosion in overcrowded India, and the increasing poison in the environment of developed nations pose other dangers which should affect our interpretation of Scripture too? Is not the subordination and exploitation of women by men in all civilizations a situation which also calls on us to ask *who* is doing theology? Should political theology remain silent about *this* oppression?

Finally, I am left uncertain whether Metz is prepared to accept the title of his paper, which suggests that the political is one dimension of theology alongside others, or whether he insists that an adequate paradigm for theology today renders Christian theology in its totality political theology. This question is important in relation to the concerns behind this conference. That the present theological paradigm has a political dimension would be disputed by few who participate in it. But that the one appropriate form of theology today is political theology would be a judgment that would place political theology outside the consensus. This would not necessarily render it wrong. If the new paradigm is understood as that which now provides consensus, Langdon Gilkey seeks another one. I myself believe that the intertwining of the threat of nuclear war, development policies in the third world that require dictatorial governments for the sake of economic exploitation and social dislocation of the poor, and economic policies in the first world that are destroying the life-support system of the planet, constitute a situation so critical that continuation of patterns of theology insensitive to this context is not the kind of thinking to which Christians are now called.

For me that in no way conflicts with interests in new scientific theories and their cosmological implications, dealing with representatives of other religious traditions, listening to the voices of the oppressed, following the disturbing yet promising new insights of feminists, trying to rethink grace, or working on the pastoral responsibilities of the church. On the contrary, it heightens the urgency of these and other tasks. But they all appear in a different light. I hope the truly new paradigm will be illumined by that light.

THE POLITICAL DIMENSION OF A NEW THEOLOGICAL PARADIGM

Claude Geffré

My reflections on the papers of J.B. Metz and Langdon Gilkey centre on three points: first, the notion of historicity proper to theology itself; second, the diagnosis of the world-wide historical crisis we face; and third, politics as a constitutive dimension of the new theological paradigm our historical situation requires.

1. The historicity of theology

I would first like to echo Metz's reserve concerning a comparison of the history of science and the history of theology: it is, in effect, only an analogy with each following its proper logic. In spite of its various 'revolutions', the history of science has been marked by continuous progress. A similar linear interpretation of the history of theology is insufficient, and the same is true of the history of philosophical reason. One must rather consider it as an 'organic totality' whose aspects possess only a relative independence and are mutually reinterpreted when and as they appear. If it is true that a scientific discipline integrates in itself the history which has supported it, it does have to be operative today to refer explicitly to this historical dimension. The historicity of theology is always determined by a double historical reference; on the one hand, its foundation on the original events conveyed by the Scriptures; and on the other hand, its organic link to the tradition from which it issued.

In dynamic vision, just as in science, the *heuristic* value determines the worth of a theological model. According to Kuhn, a model becomes a paradigm when its operational character has been proven. But, even in science, the domination of an absolute model, that is, paradigm, can be such that it becomes a real epistemological obstacle hindering new developments within the scientific system. I think that this danger is even greater in theology, as certain historical blocks of the past have attested.

This is why I question the pure and simple substitution of one theological paradigm for another as the answer to such a challenge, even if I take quite seriously the 'epochal shifts' which Langdon Gilkey believes are discernible in our contemporary historical situation. I would say that, even if one must speak today in terms of a global cultural system, this must make room for local historical experiences of great diversity. I would have several reservations in using the word 'paradigm', as it comports a somewhat imperialistic tone. I would rather speak of a 'structuring horizon' which conditions all modern theology, but which leaves open the possibility of different theological models. Need one recall that, in the end, the evaluation of a theology is a hermeneutical task which consists of 'verifying' whether a particular theology, in response to a historical situation, is supported by the movement of a faith which makes modern believers contemporaries of the original events? Hence, man understands the importance of a critical evaluation of the historical experience of a given era, and this brings me to my second point.

2. The diagnosis of the worldwide historical crisis

What is remarkable in the notion of 'model' is that it represents a phenomenon of co-adaptation between a system of interpretation and a system of action. Before proposing a new theological paradigm, a fair evaluation must be made of the historical situation to which the paradigm proposes to respond.

The two papers we have just heard suggest some extremely valuable elements for further progress in diagnosis of our historical situation. Metz refers to three crises which motivate the elaboration of a new theological paradigm: first, the end of a religious and metaphysical representation of the world, as a consequence of the Enlightenment; second, Auschwitz as a paradigmatic event after which all idealism, that is, any system of thought not taking into account the subjects of history, has become impossible; and third, the end of cultural monocentrism in the West and the move in the church towards polycentrism. Metz makes a political reading of these historical changes and proposes the new paradigm of a 'political theology' as a fundamental practical theology, capable of managing, in the name of the gospel, world-wide conflicts, while at the same time avoiding the ideological function of previous political theologies and the (apparent) neutrality of various professing or doxological theologies.

For his part, Gilkey believes that he is able to distinguish two fundamental or 'epochal shifts' which affect the whole of our cultural and historical environment. First, there is the passage from modernity under the banner of Enlightenment and the myth of progress to a 'time of troubles' underlined by an increasingly menacing future, marked by the perspective of nuclear holocaust, a possible destruction of our environment and the ever-increasing ambiguity of the values of western humanism. In the space of forty years, the political, economic, military and cultural domination of the West has evolved considerably. It is an illusion to think that the USA has supplanted Europe as the creative centre of a dominant civilization. The second 'epochal shift' which all theology must take into account is the end of historical Christianity's absolutism and the new dialogue – on equal terms – with the great religions of the world.

In comparing the two diagnoses of Metz and Gilkey, what strikes me most is their points of convergence and their profound differences. There is a remarkable accord when Metz also speaks of a 'hermeneutics of danger' in the face of an increasingly menacing future, and of a passage from monocentrism to polycentrism. But, at the same time, Gilkey's historical analysis helps us to understand how difficult it is to elaborate a theological paradigm which, on the one hand, proposes to be a post-Enlightenment, post-Auschwitz theology, and on the hand takes the end of the cultural domination of the West seriously. Even if Auschwitz had a universal impact, the historical fate of the peoples of Latin America and Africa is marked by unforgettable memories of other genocides; those of colonization. And who can maintain that the theology of a third-world Church must necessarily answer the challenge of the heritage of Enlightenment, that is to say a non-religious vision of the world? In other words, one might ask if the theological model proposed by Metz is not still somewhat Eurocentric. Furthermore, I notice that Gilkey refrains from proposing a 'political theology' in response to the contemporary challenge.

3. The political dimension of the new theological paradigm

It would seem that all theology of the future must take into account two fundamental historical determinations: on the one hand, the danger threatening the future of humanity, and on the other hand, the end of the absolutism of Christianity. Herein lies an unprecedented situation for theology. The church must witness to the gospel while remaining conscious of its historical responsibility for the survival of humanity and in renouncing its pretension to an absolute exclusivity in the realm of truth. This will involve a revision of entire chapters of theology which has hardly begun.

In the light of these fundamental mutations, need one label the new theological paradigm a 'political theology'? It is one thing to say that the theology of the future will necessarily contain a political dimension, and another to affirm that this theology will be a 'political theology', even if that is to be understood in the historical sense of fundamental theology. If we go all the way with Gilkey's analysis, we can seriously ask whether the 'political theology' is not an historical 'avatar' of the Enlightenment.

According to Gilkey, the great novelty and the major scandal of modern reason, offspring of the Enlightenment, is the failure of the secular religions of progress, history and science. During the

Enlightenment, it was believed that a denial of God was the condition for the construction of the world and the battle against the fatalities of history. Today, one argues that, at least within the three monotheistic religions, it is faith in God which invites the resistance and struggle for liberation and the defence of human rights. I would add that the new theological paradigm must take into greater account what the liberation theologians call the 'historical power of the poor'. Perhaps for the first time the poor are beginning to make themselves heard, and they are saying to the godless men of the first world that God is speaking through them. God is the guarantee of their liberation and not the one who legitimates the power of the State and of money as well as their silent resignation.

This is why I would like to end by underlining the *prophetic* dimension of a new theological model which responds to our 'time of troubles', and which takes into account the end of the cultural and dogmatic imperialism of Christianity.

That will be a theology which announces God as liberator of humanity on earth: that is, a theology for which the cause of God is also the cause for man. That will be a theology for which the church exists not only where the Word of God is announced, nor where the memorial of the Body of Christ is celebrated, but where the humblest of men are united in a fraternity of struggle and suffering. Finally, this will be a theology which witnesses without triumphalism, but with confidence, to the Kingdom yet to come, in spite of the counter-experience of a threatened future.

Ricoeur says that the *metaphor* is to poetic language what the *model* is to scientific language in its relation to reality. I would say that the task of this poetics that is theology is to discover *living metaphors* in harmony with our historical experience. The evangelical notion of 'Kingdom' is one of these. It remind us that only the Kingdom, as the Kingdom of justice and liberty, is absolute. Neither historical Christianity, nor the church, nor Jesus himself, are absolutes. The historical vocation of churches is not the maximum extension of Christianity itself, but rather – in dialogue with other religions and spiritual families – to bear witness to the Kingdom of God anticipated in the paths of history.

VI. PARTICULAR AND GLOBAL ASPECTS OF THE NEW PARADIGM

FEMINIST THEOLOGY IN A NEW PARADIGM

Anne E. Carr

These brief reflections on the provocative papers of Hans Küng, David Tracy, and Matthew Lamb are offered from the perspectives of Christian feminist theology and women's studies in religion. These studies, spurred by the women's movement in society and the church, have brought to light *both* the massive exclusion of women from full participation *and* the active involvement and creativity of women in Christianity. On the one hand, feminist thinkers have shown in historical and theological detail a threefold ideology concerning women in western traditions: women as property, objects, or tools; women as polluting, dangerously sexual, or carnal; women romantically idealized as morally and spiritually superior to men, but childlike and in need of protection in the private realm (Ruether, 1975). On the other hand, feminist scholars have shown that, despite the crippling ideologies which severely limited their autonomy and participation, women have exercised significant leadership in virtually all the Christian traditions and historical periods. Women have claimed a home in a tradition and a theology that has not fully claimed them, but has rather systematically denigrated and excluded them, or denied and impeded their autonomy as human beings and as Christians. Small wonder that some feminist scholars ask whether Christianity is not intrinsically patriarchal, and an unhealthy environment for women, and urge a liberating exodus from its oppressive precincts.

Yet some thoughtful women remain in the churches, where the Christian symbols of God, Christ, the Spirit, grace and the redemptive community continue to be life-giving and transformative, even as they quarrel with 'the fathers and heroes' (Küng) of the theological and ecclesiastical tradition, and even as they insist that the experience of women should be taken into account in the history, theology and practice of Christian life. For women, the old paradigm has indeed already broken down, especially as it is represented in textbooks and histories which record only the theories and the deeds of men, which draw the tradition as a positive development of doctrine, without acknowledging either the oppressive character of biblical religion in its historical and theological journey or the active leadership of women at every stage of that journey.

The two constants of which Küng speaks – the present world as horizon and the Christian message as standard – are affirmed by Christian feminist thinkers, but with some provisions. The present world as horizon must explicitly include those who have been excluded, especially those who are not just one group among many struggling for liberation today, but who are evenly distributed across *all* subordinated groups and across all races and classes. Women represent a unique case. Neither a caste nor a minority, women are more than half the human race. The Christian message is standard as affirmed by women, but only as it is clear that this message is not simply the Bible, whose blame and subjection of women was succinctly appraised by Elizabeth Cady Stanton nearly a hundred years ago as she set out on her bold task of producing a woman's Bible: 'The Bible teaches that woman brought sin and death into the world, that she precipitated the fall of the race, that she was arraigned before the judgment seat of Heaven, tried, condemned and sentenced. Marriage for her was to be a condition of bondage, maternity a period of suffering and anguish, and in silence and subjection, she was to play the role of a dependent on man's bounty for all her material wants, and for all the information she might desire on the vital questions of the hour, she was commanded to ask her husband at home. Here is the Bible position of woman briefly summed up' (*The Woman's Bible*, 1985, 7).

In our day, feminist biblical scholars have offered studies which show that 'de-patriarchalizing' and 'de-ideologizing' are not externally imposed but exposed within the Bible itself as demanded by its literary, historical-critical, and feminist theological interpretation (Tracy). Further, some of these studies have moved beyond the liberal projects of historical criticism by attending to the 'value-conflicts and power-complexes dialectically informing processes of domination and liberation', and the enmeshment of the texts in 'histories of social praxis' (Lamb). The Christian message, the gospel, thus challenges not only later historical and theological construction, but biblical formulations as well.

Tracy's analysis of theology's hermeneutical character accurately reflects the experience of those who affirm the Christian message even as they negate the sexist formulas of the Bible and their effective history in centuries of preaching and theology. As he notes, neither the Christian message nor the present world (contemporary experience) is immediately available; both must be interpreted anew. Neither is one thing in itself. And both are experienced and interpreted in a variety of responsible ways, one of which is the critical correlation of the interpreted experience of women (a pluralism of experiences) with feminist interpretation of the gospel. Thus new interpretation is possible and necessary, and today is risked by women who question the theological tradition. Feminist theology can be described in its moments of protest and critique, historical revisioning, and positive theological construction.

1. *Protest and critique.* Christian feminism is intent, first, to show the systematic distortion within the liberating Christian message in its history. Its critique of ideology exposes the idolatry of a tradition that makes God a male in heaven and thus makes the male a god on earth (M. Daly). That traditional theology, to the world's peril, has legitimated 'macho-masculinity' (D. McGuire); and patterns of domination in relations between God and humankind, Christ and the church, men and women, adults and children, clergy and laity, rich nations and poor, whites and coloured people, humankind and the earth. 'God as dominator' (E. Farley), extended into human relationships, is, from the perspectives of women and other oppressed groups, a distortion

of the God of the Christian message; and is a distortion often found in the major historical paradigms of Christian theology.

In this extension of feminist reflection to other dominations of historical Christianity and contemporary life, Christian feminist theology tries to be internally self-critical (Tracy), and to avoid reversal of dominative patterns. There are other issues to which it relates itself, as it examines the interstructuring of racism, classism, élitism, clericalism, and so on (R. Ruether, 1975). At the same time, it refuses to trivialize the personal and public issue of women, the red thread woven through all these dominating patterns. The 'feminization of poverty' is a recent American example. Whereas feminism itself can become ideological, in its self-critical dimensions it embodies a self-transcendence that is authentically Christian. This is apparent in the effort of Christian feminists really to include other liberation movements to which feminism allies itself. There are close connections (often after some struggle) between feminist ministers and scholars, activists and theologians and, in the Catholic context, between nuns and lay women, in most organizations and conferences. This relates to Küng's point about 'lay approbation' of theology, Lamb's reference to 'popular wisdom' in the Latin American situation, Marty's analysis of the university context of theology, and the question of élitism in church and academy. Feminist theologians are particularly sensitive to the resentment felt among lay people about an academic theology which seems to be addressed *only* to an inner circle of initiates, tends to esotericism, and is unnecessarily abstract and removed from the 'life-worlds of the everyday' (Lamb) and its concrete problems. Some feel that theology is too important to be left to academics.

The 'mutually critical correlation' suggested by Küng as the new paradigm in theology aptly characterizes Christian feminist theology as it participates in, but is also critical of, secular feminism, as it questions society from the perspective of the gospel and feminist theology, and questions theology and church practice from the perspective of feminist theory and practice. As Tracy points out, the concrete subject-matter determines the kind of correlation in any case. Apt, too, is Lamb's description of the dialectical critiques of political and liberation theologies, for questions of value, social and emancipatory concerns, issues of agency and praxis, and ideologies mask the interests of one group as universal, and the uses and effects of images and symbols animate feminist theology. Lamb's point that *any* symbol system or set of ideas may become ideological insofar as it legitimates dominative power is important in regard to religious feminism's struggles with the central symbols of Christianity, especially its male God and male saviour figure. That these symbols have been ideological in their uses and effects in theology and praxis is apparent. That these symbols need not be exclusive and harmful for women, but are open to inclusive interpretation, is affirmed by many contemporary theologies and christologies. Only a transformed Christian praxis will demonstrate their inclusiveness concretely. Meanwhile, as Lamb writes elsewhere, we witness: 'the protest of feminism against the blind rage of sexism which runs like a morally biased fault throughout human history. If the bias runs deep in the caverns of the human psyche, the social distortions and alienations of male-female relationships are all too plain for those with eyes to see . . . Here, as in other forms of bias . . . one is staggered by the overwhelming evidence of anguished human suffering resulting from bias in our historical world. Millions upon millions of women have been battered, dominated, raped, tortured, and destroyed simply because they were women.' (*Solidarity with Victims*, 6–7).

2. *Historical revision.* While sexism is itself a powerful exemplar of dominative power and its victims and is the impetus for feminism's protest and critique, it is equally important to realize that women have been not simply victims but agents in their religious lives; have participated vigorously in every Christian period; have touched the highest reaches of religious self-transcendence; and have produced their own spiritual and theological points of view. As some secular historians have acknowledged the recovery of women's lost, forgotten or suppressed history has provided the most recent redefinition of history itself. To look at familiar historical terrain through the

eyes of women (as the majority of the human race), from the perspective of women's domination or freedom, complicates usual views and reorients historical periods. The goal of integration of women's history into 'history' itself – men's history – stems from an awareness that the historical record is pervaded by patriarchal values and androcentric concerns (war and politics, not child-rearing), and that only the elaboration of women's history will eventually lead to the achievement of a truly universal history.

The implications of women's history for Christian history, a history of ministry and theology which might incorporate the activity and theological vision of women wherever it is found – in popular religion, spirituality, mysticism, preaching, teaching, and the organization and reform of religious groups – are significant. Here, for example, historians of ancient near-eastern religions, the Hebrew Bible, New Testament and early Christianity have already put forward views that challenge the androcentric record. They suggest that gender is relatively unimportant in polytheistic cultures, whereas it is central in monotheistic religions of the Bible (J. Ochshorn); that 'counter-voices' in the Hebrew Bible judge its dominant patriarchal themes, show the equality of female and male in creation and in erotic and mundane relationships, reveal the saturation of Scripture with female imagery (Trible). They show that the ancient goddess was positively appropriated by Jewish and Christian monotheism (R. Ruether, 1983); that the Jesus movement began as a reform within Judaism which embodied an inclusive vision of the Kingdom, goddess language and mythology, and an equal discipleship of men and women (E. Schüssler Fiorenza). Feminist scholars have shown that women exercised leadership as prophets and apostles in the earliest Christian communities, as scholars and foundresses in patristic and mediaeval times, as socially activist organizers in Counter-Reformation circles, and as religious and social reformers in nineteenth-century Europe and America (R. Ruether & E. McLaughlin, 1979). Studies of the mediaeval mystics have brought new attention to theological symbols of 'Jesus as mother' and the 'motherhood of God' (C. Walker Bynum), while traditions of androgynous and spirit christology inclusive of women have been suggested as stretching from the Gnostic gospels through Joachim of Fiore, Jacob Boehme, Emmanuel Swedenborg, to Mother Ann Lee of the Shakers and Horace Buschnell (Ruether, 1983). It is already clear that patterns of female leadership and positive female imagery and symbolism represent a powerful undercurrent to the androcentric mainstream of ecclesiastical and theological history. These provide significant historical precedents for feminist theology in its search for wholeness in the Christian vision (Marty), and a theology that is traditional – responsible to history – as well as contemporary (Küng).

3. *Theological construction.* Beyond protest and criticism, and beyond the revision of history, feminist theology tries to speak of God (Marty) and the meaning of our relationship to God in Christ from the perspective of women's experience in the present world. One example from many in feminist theology may illustrate this constructive work. The radical feminist critique 'Is God male?' (M. Daly) raises the question. In spite of theological denials, it would appear to be so from the persistent use of masculine pronouns for God and the phobic reaction of many Christians when one dares to refer to God as 'she' (Ruether, 1983). Yet it is apparent that 'she' is not only as appropriate as 'he', but is perhaps a necessary usage in our time in order to reorient Christian imagination from the idolatrous tendencies of exclusive masculine God-language and the dominant uses and effects of the father image of the New Testament. There have been suggestions for the use of 'Father and Mother' or reference to God as 'Parent' (L. Gilkey), or for the balancing use of feminine language for the Spirit (the realm) of God (J. Cobb). On the other hand, some feminist scholars have insisted on the need to move away from parental images: these can inculcate a relation of childish rather than adult, religious dependence (Van Herik). Parent-child relationships are not so central in the present since many people are not and do not intend to be parents. Whereas parental images express compassion, acceptance, guidance and discipline, they do

not express the mutuality, maturity, co-operation, responsibility and reciprocity demanded by personal and political experience today (S. McFague).

One Christian reformist theologian who acknowledges the truth of the radical feminist critique of the father-image for God describes the way this dominant metaphor has expanded into *patriarchalism* as a 'metaphysical world-view';, a 'mind-set' that becomes a 'whole way of ordering reality'. In a perceptive discussion, Sallie McFague argues for a metaphorical theology as a 'Protestant' counterpart to 'Catholic' analogical thought, an approach that stresses the 'and it is not' of all analogies of likeness. Indeed, it is the all-too-literal interpretation of a single image that leads much feminist theology to the 'not yet' eschatology of the Bible, or to the tradition of negative theology and the ultimately hidden God of mystery and incomprehensibility. McFague calls for the use of many metaphors and corresponding models for God and for divine-human relationships, since none alone can express their full richness. 'The root metaphor of Christianity is *not* God the father but the kingdom or rule of God, a relationship between the divine and the human that no model can encompass' (146). There is a need for limitation of the father metaphor *and* the use of maternal metaphors *and* many others that are non-familial and non-gender-related.

Noting that our image of God accords with what is most important to us humanly, McFague develops a model of the divine-human relationship from the metaphor of God as 'friend', a suggestion advanced by several writers recently. She offers a variety of biblical foundations, especially Jesus' saying about laying down one's life for one's friends (John 15:13) and his reference to the Son of man as a friend of tax collectors and sinners (Matthew 11:19). In her study, Jesus *is* the parable of God's friendship with us. That friendship is revealed in his parables of the Lost Sheep, the Prodigal Son, the Good Samaritan, and the 'enacted parable' of his table fellowship with sinners (N. Perrin). The Gospels describe Jesus as critical of familial ties and his presence as transforming the lives of his friends. The ideal of friendship, both on the personal level and on that of friendship to the stranger, 'the alien both as individual and as nation or culture', suggests a model 'for the future on our increasingly small and beleaguered planet, where, if people do not become friends, they will not survive' (179–180).

The metaphor of God as friend corresponds to the feminist ideal of 'communal personhood', a relationship among persons, groups, and life-styles that is non-competitive and mutually enhancing, something desperately needed in our imperilled world (Ruether, 1975). It responds to feminist concerns for expressions of divine-human relationship to overcome the images of religious self-denial that have moulded women's experience and engendered deeply internalized patterns of low self-esteem, passivity and irresponsibility, and the search for concepts of 'co-creating, co-shaping, co-stewardship', in which 'relatedness to God is expressed through the never-ending journey towards self-creation within community, and through the creation of ever wider communities, including both other human beings and the world' (J. Plaskow). The theme of God's friendship is intensified in the life and death of Jesus, which reveal a God who suffers for us and invites us into a fellowship of suffering for others. Such a relationship is 'friendship with God: the friend of God does not live any longer "under God" but with and in God' (J. Moltmann). The theme of friendship unites theology with feminist spirituality in its emphasis on women's friendship (sisterhood) or non-competitive, non-hierarchical mutuality: relationship, communion and presence joined with the inexhaustible mystery, never-fully-known otherness of a friend who encourages the passion for freedom, one's own and that of others – in interdependence.

A model of divine-human relationship derived from the metaphor of friendship has to be supplemented with other metaphors and models; it cannot encompass the whole. Feminist theology is just beginning to turn towards more fully systematic concerns. Its efforts hitherto in critique, historical retrieval and construction are marked by attention to the concrete, to experience and the everyday, and to questions of value, praxis, agency, negation and restoration of symbols in their uses and effects. These concerns will persist as it begins to offer new systematic proposals for the whole Christian community and for theology as a whole. This theology will mean that the long-silent majority has found its voice as a rich polyphony not heard before. Long denied in the paradigms of the past, like the voices of other unrecognized groups, feminist theology is indeed a new interpretation.

Bibliography

Bynum, Caroline Walker, *Jesus as Mother: Studies in the Spirituality of the High Middle Ages* (Berkeley, 1982).

Cobb, John B. Jr, *Christ in a Pluralistic Age* (Philadelphia, 1975).

Daly, Mary, *Beyond God the Father: Toward a Philosophy of Women's Liberation* (Boston, 1973).

Farley, Edward, 'God as Dominator and Image Giver: Divine Sovereignty and the New Anthropology', *Journal of Ecumenical Studies* 6:3 (1969), 354-375.

Fiorenza, Elisabeth Schüssler, *In Memory of Her: A Feminist Reconstruction of Christian Origins* (London, New York, 1983).

Gilkey, Langdon, *Message and Existence: An Introduction to Christian Theology* (New York, 1979).

Lamb, Matthew L., *Solidarity with Victims: Toward a Theology of Social Transformation* (New York, 1982).

McFague, Sallie, *Metaphorical Theology: Models of God in Religious Language* (Philadelphia, 1982).

McGuire, Daniel C., 'The Feminization of God and Ethics', *Christianity and Crisis* 42:4 (March 15, 1982) 59-67.

Moltmann, Jürgen, 'The Motherly Father: Is Trinitarian Patripassianism Replacing Theological Patriarchalism?', in *God as Father?* ed. J.B. Metz & E. Schillebeeckx (*Concilium* 143) (Edinburgh & New York, 1981).

Ochshorn, Judith, *The Female Experience and the Nature of the Divine* (Bloomington, 1981).

Plaskow, Judith, *Sex, Sin and Grace: Women's Experience and the*

Theologies of Reinhold Niebuhr and Paul Tillich (Washington, DC, 1980).

Ruether, Rosemary Radford, *New Woman New Earth: Sexist Ideologies and Human Liberation* (New York, 1975).

Id., *Sexism and God-Talk: Toward a Feminist Theology* (Boston, 1983).

Ruether, Rosemary Radford & Eleanor McLaughlin, *Women of Spirit: Female Leadership in the Jewish and Christian Traditions* (New York, 1979).

Stanton, Elizabeth Cady, *The Original Feminist Attack on the Bible: The Woman's Bible* (New York, 1895, rep. New York, 1974).

Trible, Phyllis, *God and the Rhetoric of Sexuality* (Philadelphia, 1978).

Van Herik, Judith, *Freud on Femininity and Faith* (Berkeley, 1982).

THE CONTRIBUTION OF LIBERATION
THEOLOGY TO A NEW PARADIGM*

Leonardo Boff

1. The source of liberation theology: spiritual experience in the encounter with the poor

Liberation theology is rooted in the painful recognition of the misery to which the vast majority of people are subjected. It therefore starts by establishing a brutal fact that cries out to high heaven: the fact that in the Christian region of the globe called Latin America, the great majority of people live and die in inhuman conditions: semi-starvation, infant mortality, endemic disease, low income, unemployment, a lack of social security, hygiene, hospitals, schools, places to live – in fact, in short, that the commodities necessary for a minimum of human dignity are not to be had. Yet this sub-reality of so-called under-development co-exists with another reality among these people: their Christian faith, with its manifold values of hospitality, human warmth, a sense of solidarity, a mighty longing for justice and co-determination and joy in all kinds of celebrations and festivities. Unfortunately this cultural ethic is at present being drained and destroyed by the progress myth to which capitalism, with its élitist consumer thinking, has put its signature.

In the face of this appalling situation, and as awareness of it penetrates them, Christian groups are reacting to rescue the

---

* Leonardo Boff's paper is based on the longer essay, 'Die Anliegen der Befreiungstheologie', which he contributed to *Theologischea Berichte* 8 (Einseideln, Zürich & Cologne, 1979), pp.71-103.

practice of faith in this part of the globe from the cynicism that has traditionally accompanied it in history. Here, in the practice of liberation, two ways of working out the implications of faith have emerged. In one, the aim is to work out theologically the category of sensibility (that is to say, what has been *experienced*); in the other, to work out theologically the category of analysis (that is to say, what has been *thought*). In the first case the starting-point is the ethical sense of outrage; in the second, socio-analytical rationality. These two ways have a common aspect: the first word is always the reality of the misery; theology is never more than the second word. In what I am about say I should like to look briefly at both.

2. The 'sacramental' articulation of liberation theology

Contradictory reality is perceived by an intuitive, 'wisdom' kind of cognition which we might call sacramental. It is perceived in the facts that are its basic definition: the existence of oppression and the urgency of liberation. In faith, many Christians have grasped that this situation runs counter to God's plan in history. Poverty is a social sin which is not God's will. Consequently a change is urgently needed, so that our fellow men and women may be helped and the will of God obeyed.

This perception finds expression in a prophetic indictment and a heartening proclamation of change. These changes give form to the ethical sense of outrage,[1] and throw open a specific understanding of what faith means. We think, for example, of all Jesus' gestures, words and attitudes, which imply a call to

---

[1] *Cf.* M. Merleau-Ponty, *Humanisme et terreur* (Paris, 1956), p.13: 'One becomes a revolutionary, not through scientific study but because of a sense of outrage. Study only comes afterwards, with the purpose of filling up the still empty protest, and making it precise'. See also E. Durkheim, *Le socialisme. Sa définition. Ses débuts. La doctrine saint-simonienne* (Paris, 1928), in which he propounds his well-known thesis that the origin of socialism is to be found in the passion for justice and the deliverance from exploitation.

repentance and conversion, and a change in relationships; his attitude to people on the fringe of Jewish society; his special commitment to the poor; his conflicts with the religious and social conditions of the time; the political element which also belongs to the proclamation of the Kingdom of God; and the motives which took him to his death. All these things take on a special relevance, and ultimately the picture that develops out of them is the image of Jesus the liberator – a picture which differs just as much from an official piety of Christ, the heavenly monarch, as it does from the devotion of the people, with its defeated and suffering Christ.

The subject here is a christology of liberation based on values and themes of change, and on appeals and invitations to liberation. What is required is neither strategy nor tactics; nor are the goals specifically defined. For in a general situation of captivity and repression, it is impossible to proffer a situation analysis in advance, or to discover feasible ways to liberation ahead of the event. On this level praxis has to be pragmatic.

This kind of christology has a certain value because it brings out the indispensable connection between the redeeming event in Jesus Christ and historical liberations. It surmounts a purely inward and privatizing view of the Christian message, and gives it back its inextricable ties with politics. This kind of christology may well be accompanied by an exacting and critical exegesis, by a new interpretation of fundamental christological dogmas, and by an elucidation of the liberating dimensions which belong within all articulations of the Christian faith. But – sensitized by the humiliating situation – in such a way it will react spontaneously out of faith, and will try to direct and live that faith in such a way that it offers support in the work of liberating, economically and politically, the people in society who are humiliated and insulted.

From this angle it is then also possible to criticize the traditional pictures of Christ, because they do not spur anyone on to do something about liberation. On the contrary, some of their elements are used to bolster up a colonialist project of domination. The agonizing and dying Christ of Latin American tradition is what Assmann calls a 'Christ of the internalized impotence of the oppressed'. The Mother of Sorrows, with her pierced heart, personifies the passive submission and subjugation of the woman. Her tears are an expression of the pain that Latin American women endured as the colonizers' greed for power and gold massacred their children. But it is not merely the christology of resignation that is subjected to criticism. Equally under attack is the christology of active domination, with its imperial, monarchical Christ, covered with gold, like the Portuguese or Spanish kings, or with its images of a warlike Christ who knows only victories.

Yet this kind of liberation christology soon runs up against clear limits. Since it does not have any socio-analytical way of looking at reality as its premise, it has very little political power. So it may well happen that the groups holding these views are theologically quite revolutionary in theory, but are in practice conservative, or at most purely progressivist.

Even so, perceptions and commitment of this kind do move people to action. The church has realized that it must not restrict its presence in society merely to the practice of religion (liturgy, spirituality), but that it must also contribute ethical and social initiatives which will foster the whole and integral development of every human being and all human beings. Christian faith as such demands this praxis. Only if it is in-formed by the practice of love (praxis) is it the true faith that brings about salvation. Otherwise it would be empty faith, which does not lead to the Kingdom of God.

Yet since this praxis is not backed up by an analysis of the mechanisms, the effectivity of its involvement is small and incalculable, in spite of the clear basic option. Things cannot go on like this.

To sum up, we may say of this form of liberation theology that it is based on *feeling, reaction* and *action.*

3. Social analysis as the mediating form of liberation theology

This articulation of liberation theology starts from the same spiritual experience with regard to the poor as the sacramental articulation. The ethical outrage that impels it is by no means less. But it communicates its sense of outrage through an analysis of reality designed to expose the mechanisms of this scandalous and wretched state of affairs.

Its main concern is to move the church to a way of action that will help the poor *effectively*. Everything must come to a point in praxis (love). But here the problem arises: which praxis *really* helps, and does not merely *seem* to do so?

In order to see more clearly here, theology sets itself a mediating task in three different fields: social analysis; hermeneutics; and practical pastoral care. In the first (*socioanalytical mediation*) we find the tools to sharpen our discernment of the contradictions in reality, so that naivety, empiricism and moralism can be surmounted, since these only hinder a critical perception. We must then deepen the understanding of our ethical outrage as Christians over the contradictions. Although voices are certainly necessary (since these especially galvanize people into action), reality is not changed by prophetic cries alone, and they do not provide a way of interpreting reality correctly in the light of faith. This is the place of *hermeneutical mediation*. Finally, it is essential to seek practicable and sensible ways of advancing the liberation of the poor within the bounds of the religious, political, military, ideological, economic and all the other forces which simply exist, *de facto*, in the given social organism. This is *practical, pastoral mediation*. Let me now go on to consider in turn these basic ways of mediating liberation theology.

In mediation by way of social analysis (seeing the facts) the point is to grasp reality critically, in order to be able to influence it effectively in the name of our faith. In general, one might say that every theological intervention in the social sector, whether by theologians or by the ecclesiastical hierarchy, presupposes a fundamental sociological theory, which can be either spontaneous or critical. In this sector a more or less pragmatic empiricism (spontaneous and intuitive understanding) represents what Bachelard calls a fundamental 'epistemological hindrance', because as a rule it stabilizes the *status quo*, making it impossible to articulate a liberation theology in a way that accords with the facts. We are therefore faced with the question: what social theory should we employ, in working out a theology of liberation? For factors contribute to the choice of an explanatory theory of society which are not merely objective and rational. They spring also from the fundamental decision of the analyst himself and from his own place in society. Every reflection about human reality takes its bearings from a basic project: that is, from a utopia which a group develops and in which it draws up the blueprint of its future. This utopia is never merely ideological, for it always depends on social and material conditions as well. In principle two types of utopia can be distinguished, with two different kinds of sponsoring groups: one group belonging to the ruling classes, and one belonging to the ruled.

The utopia of the ruling classes means the proclamation of a linear progress without any change in the groupings which lend society its structure. This utopia is based on a firm faith in science and technology, and presupposes an élitist view of society, the achievements of which are ultimately supposed to benefit the masses, little by little. The utopia of the dominated groups, on the other hand, is a society based on equality. It sees the cleavage between the élite and the masses as the greatest hindrance to development; as long as this persists, true progress and social justice will be impossible. The group inspired by this utopia believes with an unshakable faith in the transforming power of the oppressed, who alone can create a society with less injustice and social oppression.

These two basic conceptions influence the kind of analysis chosen. The dominating groups prefer the functionalist method in social studies. Here the ideas of order and equilibrium count above all, and society is understood as an organic whole, with complementary parts. The groups of the people who are dominated, on the other hand, prefer the dialectical method, which centres on the idea of conflict and struggle, and which sees society as a totality that is full of contradictions.

A standpoint which has found expression historically in the liberal tradition views society from above to below; from a standpoint, that is, from which it may quite well appear harmonious. The representatives of the other viewpoint, however, belong to what is historically the revolutionary and Marxist tradition. They see society from below upwards; and from this standpoint it manifests itself as conflict and struggle.

Theology must now emphasize the analysis which best corresponds to the requirements of a faith bound to praxis. Faith therefore determines the choice of the social analysis scheme, and decides in favour of the one that really exposes the mechanisms that cause injustice, that offers the most appropriate means of overcoming this injustice, and that best accords with the ideas of brotherhood and co-determination.

Liberation theology, then, is based on a decision in favour of the dialectical trend in social analysis, and the revolutionary utopia of the dominated. When we talk about liberation, this word therefore expresses a precisely defined option, which is not concerned with progress in either a reformist or a progressivist sense, but whose liberation implies a breach with the present *status quo*. The aim is a liberation that has to do with economic, social, political and ideological structures; and the point is to influence structures and not merely people. The concern is to change the relationships of power between the social groups, so that new structures can come into being which will make more co-determination possible for the people who have hitherto been excluded. Liberation theology takes sides with the oppressed, and believes that it is impelled to do so by faith in the Jesus of history. Abstinence here would mean accepting the situation and, in a subtle way, taking sides with the privileged.

Of course, this option does not exclude the ambiguity which is involved in every liberation process; for not every liberation already means the anticipation and embodiment of the Kingdom of God, and no liberation must be turned into something absolute in itself. Redemption as it is proclaimed by the Christian faith is a comprehensive term. It must not be restricted to economic, political, social and ideological liberation. On the other hand, redemption is not realized without these things too. Christian hope and a proper understanding of eschatology entitle us to maintain that this world is not merely the stage on which the drama of redemption is played out; the world itself is part of the drama. The definitive salvation of the End-time is mediated, anticipated and given concrete form in partial liberations within history, on all levels of reality, though these always remain open for a fulness and comprehensiveness which can be achieved only in the Kingdom of God.

The theory of liberation therefore names three levels on which reality impinges on us, and three corresponding ways of meeting it.

On the *empirical* level, a person is moved by the poverty in which other people are living. He notes the facts in all their infamy, and is appalled. But he cannot get beyond the factual dimension, and does not penetrate to the deeper causes.

This attitude is sometimes even noble – and always full of good will. But the empiricist has a naive awareness, and his help is as a rule purely charitable and ultimately does not take us any further.

Functionalism, in contrast, certainly sees that the facts are bound up with one another, and form a single complex. For functionalism, society is so to speak an organism containing many different functions which must work well together so as to form a social harmony. If disfunctions arise – when the gap between rich and poor is unduly wide, for example – reforms must be set on foot, or the section that is undeveloped, or less well developed than the rest, must be developed, until the social equilibrium has been restored.

The awareness here is certainly critical, for it proceeds from the sense that everything and everybody in society is interrelated. But in spite of that, the real question never gets on to the agenda: why, in the type of society in which we live, are the poor continually becoming poorer and the rich richer, in spite of the considerable economic and industrial boom which we can see everywhere? A critical analysis can prove that development of the capitalist kind comes about at the expense of the people, and generally speaking in opposition to the people. What is called progress favours only certain sections of the population and forces the great majority on to the fringe of events. Because of its development ideology and its credulous faith in progress, functionalism is not able to allow society to function on the basis of humanly admissible conditions which also permit an endurable degree of justice and general participation.

In spite of this, up to a short time ago the large majority of those responsible for the church's pastoral care thought in the categories of this analytical attitude. Full of enthusiasm, they made progress the cry with which they rallied the people. Faith, they said, strengthens the will to development. But in the degree to which those responsible for pastoral care identified themselves with the people and entered into its life, they also discovered that this progress is at the cost of the people, and that they are therefore being increasingly pushed on to the fringes of society. The social system, that is to say, is poisoned – poisoned as a system, not merely in any particular form in which it manifests itself. It is not merely sick. It is doomed.

This insight has recourse to *dialectical structuralism*. It is not content merely to look facts in the face but, by way of precise analyses, exposes the global structure of the system that organizes the society determined by capitalism. According to the encyclical *Populorum Progressio*, it is a system in which 'profit is the real motor of economic progress, competition the supreme law of the economy, ownership of the means of production an absolute right, without any corresponding duties towards society' (No.26). Because of altered historical constellations, capitalism has changed some of the rules of the game, but not the game itself: that is, the system. The main contradiction of this system is that, while everyone contributes to production by means of his or her labour, only a few have power over what is produced, because they are the owners of capital. The others remain 'outside'. Here I use the term 'structuralism' because the analysis aims at the structure which underlies the correlations and cohesions, and the actual facts. Moreover, we have talked about a *dialectical* structuralism, because between the owners of capital and the others, who are owners of working power, there is a difficult interaction, pregnant with conflict, and the interests do not converge. It is the play of these forces that explains the genesis, development and continuance of the type of society we experience.

We call the awareness that identifies itself with this articulation radically critical. It is radical, not because it stirs up emotions and polarizations, but because it penetrates to the roots of the question. The therapy which a radical critical awareness enjoins is not reform of the system but the construction of a society on different foundations. The starting-point should no longer be the capital in the hands of a few, but the work of all. Everyone then has a part in decisions about the means of production, the goods produced and the instruments of power. Liberation theology starts from this radically critical and dialectical structuralist model, as interpretation of reality.

Under-development is the factor linking all the poor countries; and for liberation theology it is of pre-eminent importance that this phenomenon should be interpreted in accordance with the facts. According to this interpretation, under-development is not mainly what the functionalist interpretation of the liberal system would have us believe: a *technical* problem due to the acceleration of a process leading from a traditional and pre-technological society to a modern and technological one. Nor is underdevelopment a mainly *political* problem, so that in order to achieve a homogeneous development, interdependent and unequal countries belonging to the same system would have to enter into closer relations with one another. Under-development is based on a system in which one group of countries keeps another group in a régime of dependency. Here the one group acts as the metropolitan or imperial centre round which satellite or peripheral countries circle, since they are repressively kept in a state of under-development.[2] Under-development and

[2] The bibliography on this subject is enormous. I can do no more than mention a few titles: F.H. Cardoso, *Desarrollo y dependencia: Perspectiva en al análisis*

development are two sides of a coin. The former is the result of the latter. In order that development according to the capitalist pattern may keep up the degree of acceleration and wealth which it has reached in the countries of the centre (the North Atlantic, Europe, Japan, USA), these countries have to keep other countries in their sphere of dependency; and from these other countries everything can be taken and purloined which the countries of the centre require for the wealth they enjoy. This, in the view of liberation theology, is the essential reason for underdevelopment. (There are other reasons as well – biological and health factors, the difference in cultural ethics, and so on. But these are ultimately not decisive.) This dependency determines all the ways in which human life manifests itself: the economic system, the division of labour, politics, culture – indeed even religion. The path which can lead out of the situation, the argument runs, is a process during which the ties of dependency will be severed, and liberation for a self-supporting national project will be begun.

Of course one must be realistic about a theoretical demand of this kind. Severance cannot be achieved through a pure act of will for 'people only make the revolutions which grow up of themselves'.[3] We therefore have to consider what is objectively achievable. The problem is not to become free at all costs; for not every liberation brings liberty. Once achieved, liberation may perhaps lead to independence, but not necessarily to development as well. The Latin American countries could not build up a technology of their own, and no one can develop all by themselves. So we are face to face with a bitter dilemma. 'Either we liberate ourselves without development or we decide for

sociológica: Sociologia del desarrollo 19 (Buenos Aires, 1970); O. Fals-Borda, Ciencia propria y colonialismo intelectual (Mexico City, 1970); T. dos Santos, Dependencia y cambio social (Santiago de Chile, 1970); G. Arroyo, 'Pensamiento latinoamericano sobre subdesarrollo y dependencia externa', Mensaje 1968, pp.516–520; Pedro Negre Rigol, Sociologia do Terceiro Mundo (Petrópolis, 1977).

    [3] J. Comblin, Théologie de la pratique révolutionnaire, Paris, 1974, p.65.

development and subjugate ourselves. A third choice is nothing but a compromise: one restricts development in order to preserve a certain degree of autonomy, or one restricts independence, and certain sectors cannot develop. But this does not take us any further than the simple dependency theory'.[4] It must also be said that in recent years the forces of repression in Latin America seem to have won the game, and to have prevented an organized movement for liberation. This raises the question: does this hopeless situation mean renouncing any thought of liberation? The liberation theologians answer: on a purely theoretical level we must not yield an inch, but must adhere to the negative but correct diagnosis. But as far as praxis is concerned, we must search for ways of initiating a truly liberating *process*, even if the way is long and wearisome. In the present situation there can only be changes *in* the system, so that in the end we do after all arrive at changes *of* the system. This does not at all mean that we have renounced our decision for the liberation intention and for a new kind of society. It is a question of the strategy which – taking the general situation of repression and captivity into account – has to turn this project into fact in the historical conditions of the specific situation.

In this analysis of reality it is not only concerns belonging to the sphere of the social sciences which play a part (sociology, economics and politics). There are also concerns which have to do with the history, civilization and anthropology of the people and are determined by their own folk culture. The great majority of our people has been trampled under foot. In the course of time they have created a culture of silence, and their own ways of giving their life meaning, of being free, and of resistance, even though they have to go on living in captivity. Numerous studies have been made from this perspective for almost the whole of Latin America, studies which investigate popular culture and popular religious feeling and practice as the seedbeds of values as yet untouched by imperialistic ideology. These could act as a dynamic for a true theology of resistance and a liberation process.

[4] *Ibid.*, p.127.

Summing up, this means: anyone who wants to understand the difficulty of development where people are dependent and dominated must not content himself with analyses that are purely sociological or are based on the human sciences. He must view matters in a structural and cultural context. Capitalism, consumerism and systems of dependency and oppression reflect a particular cultural ethic (the meaning of life and death, relationships to other human beings, to commodities, and to the transcendent). This has crystallized into its own historical forms. The modern age has opted for a meaning of life and existence which makes them depend on knowledge and power over everything one comes across – above all, power over the earth, which has to be dominated and exploited, and from which profit must be drawn. This is the cultural ethic on which our western history, as well as Marxism, is based. A revolution which does not change this ethic will provide only a variation on the old theme. It will never bring about a true liberation, at least not the liberation for which serious, reflective groups in Latin America are striving.

5. Hermeneutics as the mediating form of liberation theology

Hermeneutics is the science and technique of interpretation. It is supposed to put us in a position to understand the original meaning of texts (or facts) which are no longer *directly* accessible to us contemporary men and women. Theology continually asks itself: how are we to lay hold of the Word of God – which, after all, has to illuminate all we do – if this Word comes to us in the historical garb of a different mentality, and in different language?

It is only through the mediation of hermeneutics that the theological criteria emerge for our reading, as Christians, of the socio-analytical text (reality): what God has to say to us in the social problems which we previously understood, quite accurately and objectively, by way of scientific reasoning. For this, reason is not enough; faith is required. Through faith – that is to say, through recourse to Scripture and tradition – (the doctrine of the church, *sensus fidelium*, statements on doctrine made by theologians, and so forth) – we perceive in social reality the presence or absence of God. In concrete terms this means: where the social analysis talks about structural poverty, faith talks about structural sin; where the analysis talks about the private accumulation of wealth, faith talks about the sin of selfishness; and so on. In the face of social reality, therefore, theology has a threefold task.

First: theology must assess the quality of the situation in terms of salvation history. It has to judge according to the categories of faith – the Kingdom of God, redemption, forgiveness, grace, sin, righteousness, injustice, love, and so forth – whether the existing model of society accords with God's plan or not. This is the prophetic aspect of theology.

Second: theology must critically think through the tradition of faith anew under the aspect of liberation. It has to ask how far a particular understanding of the Kingdom of God, grace, the church, sin, and human activity in the world leads unawares to the endorsement or legitimation of what ought really to be banished: the gulf between rich and poor. Theology has to be linked, without any kind of double thinking, with the inferences of social analysis, as a theology which really succeeds in interpreting social reality in the light of God's Word.

Third: theology must try to arrive at a theological interpretation of the whole of human praxis – whether it be the praxis of Christians or of non-Christians. It must be permitted to say a word about every kind of praxis, or every way of living together in society. For the Christian faith has to work out a picture of the human being and society, the future and the ultimate definition of history. With this as horizon, Christian thinking is never entirely congruent with any political praxis and can never be reduced to a particular form of society. But the Christian faith helps Christians to decide for this or that model or analysis of reality in the specific conditions of history. Thus liberation theology is convinced that the Christian faith helps to discover the instruments of social analysis which most accurately reveal the mechanisms which are at the root of all the different forms of injustice and violence to which the poor especially are subjected. Moreover, faith helps Christians to support the historical movements which are closest to the ideals of the gospel.

This being so, we have today arrived at the insight that Christian thinking is more nearly congruent with socialist ideas than capital ones. It is not a matter of creating a Christian socialism. It is a matter, rather, of being allowed to say that the concept of socialism – provided that it is really fulfilled and realized – makes it possible for the Christian to live the humanitarian and divine ideal of his or her faith more completely.

Of course, the capitalist system would permit this too (after all, for centuries Christians have lived in capitalist societies), but with many contradictions which could be solved better in a different system, although this too will assuredly not be free of contradictions, even though they may be lesser ones.

6. The practical, pastoral mediation of liberation theology (action)

What has hitherto been worked out in a process of analysis and reflection must now be translated into specific action. Here – avoiding a naive voluntarism – we must proceed from the total interaction of social forces (economic, political, ideological and repressive). It is a question here of pastoral wisdom within whatever scope the objective conditions of reality permit. This has nothing to do with timidity. It is simply a wise estimate of what is possible and achievable. What the church really, specifically means must be translated into the various fields (economic, political and symbolic) that constitute reality; and we have to consider how, out of its own identity as a community of faith, the church can actively contribute to liberation.

An institutionalized community of faith, the church has above all a function as a sign. It certainly plays no determining role in the total social framework, but it nevertheless has an important position, especially in Latin America, where it has significant historical and social weight. Here, with its symbolic function as sign and pointer, its influence must be a liberating one. It must try to see that its word, teaching and its liturgy, what it does in relation to the community, and its interventions with the authorities are efficaciously liberating. For it is undeniable that liberation is one of the dimensions of faith; and this dimension must be untiringly implemented and kept alive.

In addition, the church must enter into conversation with other social groups which are also striving for change in the quality of society. This will make it easier to achieve the necessary impact. For it is not only the church that desires liberation, although – unlike other groups, which restrict themselves to a merely social and historical liberation – the church especially has to maintain the comprehensive viewpoint of a liberation that will be total and all-embracing: the Kingdom of God.

Finally, Christians and possible Christian organizations – without immediately committing the whole officialdom of the church – can and must find a means of action which will not be content to stop short at the symbolic level. On the basis of their Christian faith and conscience, they can also become involved at directly political and infra-structural levels. Here especially the basic communities in the church enjoy relative autonomy, since – because of their grass-roots character – they are directly confronted with liberation problems at the very points where practical solutions are most urgently required.

But our strategic decision in favour of a liberation which really has to do with a new quality in society must be made fully evident, even if the order of things as they have developed in history forces us to resort to purely reformist measures. No one can desire to be free, and to be freed, at all costs. Liberation is the fruit of a process in which all must play their part. It is not the result of a unique act of will. Individual measures are therefore tactical steps. They are not as yet the goal. For that goal is simply and solely liberation itself.

INDIAN PERSPECTIVES IN THE NEW PARADIGMS OF THEOLOGY

Mariasusai Dhavamony

The thought and activity of a given scientific community are dominated by its paradigms. Paradigms are described as 'standard examples of scientific work that embody a set of conceptual, methodological and metaphysical assumptions'.

Briefly, a paradigm is a tradition transmitted through historical examples. Since I choose Hinduism as a background to Indian Christian theology, at the outset I want to make clear that there are differences between paradigms in science and paradigms in religion. Granting that there are similarities between the two, let me note the characteristics of paradigms in the religious tradition that are not applicable to scientific tradition.

First, the influence of interpretation on experience in religion is more problematic. There are some authors[1] who maintain that the differences between various types of religious experience, whether mystical or non-mystical, lie in the way the experience is interpreted rather than in the experience itself. Second, religious experience engages the whole person, his or her reason, feelings

[1] Radhakrishnan for example says, 'If religion is experience, the question arises, what is it that is experienced? No two religious systems seem to agree in their answers to this question. The Hindu philosopher became familiar very early in his career with the variety of the pictures of God which the mystics conjure up. We know today from our study of comparative religion that there are different accounts of the mystical vision . . . Religious experience is not the pure unvarnished presentment of the real in itself, but is the presentment of the real already influenced by the ideas and presuppositions of the perceiving mind'. See his *The Hindu View of Life* (London, 1964), p.19. See ch.1: 'Religious experience, its nature and content'. See also Ninian Smart, 'Interpretation and mystical experience', in *Religious Studies*, Vol.1 (1965), p.75.

and emotions, temperament and life history.[2] True, typical religious experiences can be reproduced in particular scientific communities, but these are more restricted in scope than the particular scientific communities. Religious experience is both non-rational and rational and cannot be totally explained rationally.[3] Third, while interpreting the religious experience, one can read into it more than is warranted or less than what is contained in the experience. Interests and commitments profoundly influence the religious life of individuals and communities more than those of the scientific community. Some interpretations can heighten or lessen worship and other vital aspects of religion. Finally, interpretative beliefs are brought to religious experience as much as they are derived from it.

1. Paradigms in the Hindu religious tradition. What constitutes the essential core of Hinduism? Leading Hindus themselves have answered as follows. Radhakrishnan observes: 'At the outset, one is confronted by the difficulty of defining what Hinduism is. To many it seems to be a name without any content. Is it a museum of beliefs, a medley of rites, or a mere map, a geographical expression? Its content, if it has any, has altered from age to age, from community to community. The ease with which Hinduism has steadily absorbed the customs and ideas of peoples with whom it has come into contact is as great as the difficulty we feel in finding a common feature binding together its different forms. But if there is not a unity of spirit binding its different expressions and linking up the different periods of its history into one organic whole, it will not be possible to account for the achievements of Hinduism.'[4] He finds this unity of spirit not in fixed beliefs or in the celebration of rites, but in a kind of inner experience. He says that intellect is subordinated to intuition, dogma to experience, outer expression to inward realization.[5] Gandhi considers as

---

[2] It is this which distinguishes the specific character of the religious experience, as distinct from purely human experience.

[3] Religion is not a purely rational phenomenon; it contains the sense of the mystery.

[4] See his *The Hindu View of Life, op.cit.,* p.10.

[5] *Ibid.,* pp.10-13.

essentials of the *Sanatana Dharma* belief in the *Vedas*, the *Upanishads*, the *Bhagavad-gītā*, and the *Purānas* (in short, what goes by the name of Hindu Scriptures, belief in *avataras* and rebirth, *varnashrama dharma* (society of castes) in the Vedic sense without discrimination and sense of superiority.[6] K.M. Panikkar thinks that though no definition of Hinduism on the basis of dogmas or beliefs is possible, there is a framework of ideas and doctrines which could be considered as characteristically Hindu. It is within this framework that the different sects and creeds flourish, and they are generally accepted as a common background for all Hindu systems. These ideas and doctrines can be divided broadly into three kinds: ideas about God and human relations with him; ideas about the world; ideas about human life in society.[7] Its attitude towards other religions is one of tolerance, but this tolerance is based on its non-dualist or pan-en-theist presuppositions and on the consequent religious relativism. For instance, even when it attributes validity and legitimacy to Christianity, it holds its own specific nature as Hindu religion, and hence there is no meaning, according to it, in conversion from Hinduism to Christianity, since Hinduism is as good as, if not better than, Christianity.

2. The importance and the role of the community in Hinduism. Many leading Hindus draw a distinction between *Samāj Dharma* (the civic customs of the Hindus) and *Sādhana Dharma* (the Hindu search for salvation: *mukti*). Someone who follows the customs of the caste is considered a Hindu; society's injunctions are external, for they cannot reach down to the level of salvation, which is interior and spiritual. The distinction to a certain extent is valid, though today there is less emphasis on the *Samāj Dharma* and more and more on the *Sādhana Dharma*. Besides, there is no uniform *Samāj Dharma* binding on all Hindus, as the requirements in the case of *brāhmins* are not the same as in that of the *sūdras*. There is also the belief today that Hinduism holds its own *sādhana* as exclusively its own. It is untrue to say that membership

---

[6] M.K. Gandhi, *The Spirit of Hinduism* (New Delhi, 1980), pp.13-20.

[7] K.M. Panikkar, 'Hinduism', in: *Asia Handbook*, ed. Guy Wint (London, 1966), pp.368-74.

in the Hindu community is not based on any profession of a definite creed and that a Hindu is free to believe in what he likes. Although it is true that Hinduism is a religion without any fixed creed and that in it there is no common body of doctrines to which all those who call themselves Hindus are expected to adhere and give common assent, there are some common assumptions which most Hindus at least tacitly accept. These are: the doctrine of rebirth and the law of *karma*; the social structure of the caste system, acceptance of the Hindu Scriptures, and a characteristic outlook on religion as the inner experience of the Absolute.

3. The role of rituals in Hinduism. Ritual has a social function in Hinduism in that the ritual is the embodiment of the faith of the Hindus. It has also an historical function in that it evokes the whole history of Hinduism in its various stages when Hindus visit temples and pilgrim centres. Its symbolic function becomes evident from the fact that rites are performed with the intention of visualizing and presenting the divinity and of participating in it. But rituals according to the Hindu mind have also their limitations and dangers. Ritualism perpetuates only a lower type of religion, appealing to the senses and crudely making 'material' what should be spiritual. Ritualism has a tendency to make religion not only crudely popular, lower, sense-appealing, but mechanical and static. The Hindu religious life consists of worship (ritual), prayer and meditation, which are successive stages in the experience of the divine. The most important thing for a Hindu is to enter into the divine presence and become divine, whether performing ritual, or praying or meditating. It is no exaggeration to say that meditation is the method most commonly used and highly valued among the spiritually intent people of India in their search for religious insight, power and peace.

No organized cult or worship is obligatory on Hindus. They perform these things individually, not congregationally, and of their own free choice. They distinguish between the empirical and the higher (spiritual) type of religion. Rituals and morality belong to the empirical sphere of religion, which is quite legitimate and necessary for people in their stage of development.

But the higher type of religion is the pure, spiritual experience of the divine, of the Absolute. Thus they make a distinction between morality and spirituality, leaving the ritual aspect of religion to morality, and making meditation and mysticism a part of spiritual, higher religion. Ritual and the moral type of religion are regarded as valid in accordance with the type of mind whose religious needs they are supposedly designed to meet. The Hindu would frankly admit that all people are not alike, that they do not all look for the same thing in religion. Therefore each person must be free to find religious satisfaction in his or her own way; and all these many ways eventually result in realizing the divine, the same end for all.[8]

4. The authority of the Hindu Scriptures is decisive in the Hindu belief and way of life. These sacred writings are regarded as conveying unique divine truths which need to be known for salvation. These saving truths are not believed to be humanly made, or even humanly discovered, but divinely inspired. The *Sruti* (the primary revelatory texts) include the four *Samhitās*, the *Brāhmanas*, the *Aranyakas*, the *Upanishads*, and the *Bhagavad-gītā*. The *Smrti* texts (secondary, revelatory texts) are *Sutras*, *Sāstras*, the two epics, and the *Purānas*.

The subject-matter of the whole *Veda* is commonly divided into those which deal with rituals (*karma-kānda*), those which treat of worship and meditation (*upāsana-kānda*), and those which deal with the highest knowledge (*jnāna-kānda*). The Law Books give detailed instructions to all classes of people regarding their duties in life; but these laws have become obsolete and are not followed by modern Hindus. The two epics have their influence in today's Hindu society in as far as they illustrate the Hindu *Dharma* in the character of heroes and superhuman beings portrayed in these epics. The *Bhagavad-gītā* is considered a universal 'gospel' as it gives guidance on all points of spiritual life: *karma, jnāna, bhakti* and *dhyāna*. The aim of the Purānas is to impress on the mind of the people the teachings of the *Veda* and the *Bhagavad-gītā*. Among the *darsanas* (different schools of Hindu theology) *Vedanta*

[8] See D.S. Sarma, *Essence of Hinduism* (Bombay, 1971), pp.20-36.

holds the first place, not only because it is followed by most educated Hindus but because it is thought to be more faithful to the Vedic revelation. The *Veda* is believed to be eternal and non-personal. The knowledge of the Absolute (Brahman) that is derived from it reaches its final realization in the individual spiritual experience after having gone through the various disciplines. Hence the ultimate ground of Hindu religious belief is the spiritual experience of every human being in himself, after he has read and meditated on the sacred texts with the help of the *guru*.

5. Even though Hinduism had no historical founder, there have been historical *gurus*, *acaryas* such as Śankara, Rāmānuja, Mādhva, and the Hindu *bhaktas* of various regions of India, not to speak of the modern leaders such as Ramakrishna, Aurobindo, Gandhi, Radhakrishnan, who have given a special orientation to the Hindu religion and interpreted it in the light of their own religious experience. Their main trends can be divided into two types of the final goal of Hindu religious experience: the absolutist (non-dualist) goal of total identification with the Absolute All-One; and the theist goal of blissful union with a personal God in perfect love.

6. Ways of liberation (*mukti*) are called *yogas* (disciplines), *sādhanas* (practices) and *margas* (courses). Hindus speak of three traditional ways: *karma, jnana,* and *bhakti.* This distinction is never adequate, and in practice the three ways are intermingled. Common Indian tradition finds three main causes for man's bondage. Rebirth is the necessary consequence of our actions; our actions proceed from and are qualified by our desires which have as root our egoism; men are play-things of desires and egoism owing to their ignorance of true reality and hence of the true self. Hence they propose three remedies. As against demeritorious action, the proximate remedy will be to do good and avoid evil; ethical and religious observance is the first step. Very few will hold that this may be itself sufficient to lead to final liberation; but all require it at least in the preparatory stage. As against desire, the remedy is to control and subdue one's passions, aiming at disinterested activity through ascetical practices and/or to purify and

transcend all desires by a single-hearted love of God. Love of God will either imply or easily lead up to true knowledge by the co-naturality of love and the grace of God. As against ignorance, the true knowledge of reality and, in particular, the knowledge of the true Self (thus destroying egoism at its root) is required. The attainment of transcendental knowledge is commonly held to require – with or without the help of grace – a sustained asceticism and a technique of mental concentration (yoga).

By knowledge is understood the mystical apprehension of the true Self. The Hindu doctrines concerning this differ among themselves in proposing this knowledge because of difference of their views on the true nature of the Self and of the quality of their asceticism. The ignorance which binds one to rebirth, according to the *Vedanta*, may be: the ignorance of the true Self's identity with the All-One (Absolutism or non-dualism), or the ignorance of the true Self's true relation to God and lack of knowledge of God (theism).

The way of love (*bhakti*) means a specific religious attitude and sentiment, the essential features of which are faith in, love for, and trustful surrender to, the Deity. It is an effective participation of the soul in the divine; a most intense love for God; a clinging of the heart and mind to God, which follows upon the Lord's greatness. The object of *bhakti* is the Blessed Lord, the Holy God, the Adorable Lord and Master. *Bhakti* is both a means of liberation and its final completion. As the supreme goal, *bhakti* is union and communion with God in the bond of eternal love, implying a deep sense of dependence on and submission to God.[9]

In the theist trends, it is by grace alone that man gains knowledge and is liberated. *Bhakti* is the fruit of divine election. The Lord's grace is healing, illuminating, conforming to divine nature, and uniting with Him. But all this takes place within the system of immanent creation. Though God undoubtedly gives grace freely, this help is never strictly supernatural, for grace restores the soul to its natural divine life. Human beings are divine by nature: this is an oft-repeated principle of Hinduism.

[9] See Mariasusai Dhavamony, *Classical Hinduism* (Rome, 1982): chapters on revelation, salvation, means of salvation, etc.

In regard to the doctrine of grace, the followers of Rāmānuja divided into two schools, northern and southern. They are usually called the ape-way and the cat-way. When a mother ape falls into danger, her young one immediately clings fast to her, and when she makes a leap to safety, the young ape is saved, by the act of the mother, it is true, but in such a way that the young co-operates a little, because it clings to the mother by its own act. But when a danger threatens a cat with her young one, the mother cat takes the young in her mouth. The young one does nothing for its salvation. It remains merely passive. All co-operation is excluded. In sum, the whole difference can be expressed thus:

The northern school: the soul gains God for itself.

The southern school: God gains the soul for himself.

7. The Hindu conception of humanity is religious and is to a certain extent necessary to understand the whole religious quest of Hinduism. A human being in real essence is a purely spiritual self (*atman*). This spiritual reality is either totally identical with the Absolute Being (non-dualist trend), or a mode or attribute of God existing in Him (pan-en-theist trend), or a partly divine being through intrinsic union with God (dualist trend).[10] The spatio-temporal empirical state of existence accrues to humankind through embodiment: that is, a spiritual self becomes imprisoned in a body. The kind of body that a person possesses depends on the kind of action he or she performed during the previous birth. The *karma* law is a universal law of immanent retribution according to which every good act meets with a reward and every evil act with punishment, and thus justice is done either in this life or in the life hereafter; and this goes on in a cycle of rebirths.

8. Hindu theism. The common belief is that God is one, though people give him many names and forms according to their spiritual needs and different degrees of understanding; and that therefore the widest possible toleration is imperative in matters of religious belief and practice. Hinduism has shown in its long history a marked propensity to assimilate rather than exclude various religious currents which once used to be considered alien

---

[10] The technical terms are respectively: *advaita, viśistādvaita, dvaita.*

to its own orthodoxy. The relation between God or the Absolute and human beings is considered to be one of identity or one of union and dependence, deriving from the conception of creation as emanation. For the Hindu it is very difficult to concede that something can come out of nothing. What does not exist cannot evolve into something which exists. What does not exist cannot be produced. Efficient causality always presupposes something to work on. Creation is rather a transition of a being from an unmanifest state to a manifest state through the agency or not of a creator god, who is distinct from it or not.

Paradigms of an Indian Christian theology.

So far I have outlined the characteristic paradigms of the Hindu religious tradition which are needed to formulate the main paradigms of an Indian Christian theology.

1. The ways of thinking of the Indian people have their own peculiarities and theologizing can take place in this climate of thought. It is often said that the ways of thinking of India are represented as 'spiritual, introverted, synthetic, and subjective', while those of the West are represented as 'materialistic, extroverted, analytic, and objective'.[11] This distinction is now being questioned as simplistic; for the cultures of India and of the West are extremely diversified and each one is extremely complex. When we inquire into the meaning of each of these terms, we see that the sense of each is composite and involves a wide range of narrower concepts. However, we have to note that the Indian sages, especially the religious, are more introverted in the sense that they meditate on the inner Self (*ātman*) more than on the outer world; they are more spiritual in the sense that they are more ascetical and disinterested in their search for the Absolute; more subjective in the sense of the realization of the spiritual subject in human beings; and more synthetic in the sense that they seek to experience the unity of all beings in the Absolute and of the All-One in the plurality of beings.

[11] On this point, see Hajme Nakamura, *Ways of Thinking of Eastern Peoples* (Honolulu, 1964), pp.3 ff.

2. The experience of the uniqueness of Christian faith, of the uniqueness of Jesus Christ as Saviour of humankind, has to be realized in the Indian view of religious experience. In India the prevalent Hindu attitude is that all religions are the same, implying that they are one in their essential content, although each expresses this content in its own particular idiom which is largely due to accidents of historical and geographical circumstances. Or they give another reason to show that all religions are the same; namely, that they all have the same aim in as far as they all are expressions of the human quest for the eternal. There is also the belief in India that Hinduism in its essential content is the one true religion, universal and eternal (*sanātana dharma*), valid for all times and for all cultures, which lies behind all particular cults and creeds. Hence it is an important task of Indian Christian theology to face this problem of religious relativism and find the true way of understanding and interpreting the uniqueness and transcendence of the Christian faith.

3. Another significant characteristic of Indian religious experience is its insistence on intuition and on the 'psychologically mediated' quality of religious experience. Radhakrishnan can be cited as representing this way of thinking: 'While fixed intellectual beliefs mark off one religion from another, Hinduism sets itself no such limits. Intellect is subordinated to intuition, dogma to experience, outer expression to inward realization. Religion is not the acceptance of academic abstractions or the celebration of ceremonies, but a kind of life or experience'.[12]

We see that the Indian view of religious faith and of experience is purely spiritualist. There is always behind this kind of thinking the notion that what is pure, authentic, genuine in religion is what is purely spiritual, and what is material or phenomenal or empirical or historical is secondary, transient and ephemeral. Asian Christian theology has to take into consideration the priority of the spiritual in experience without denying or belittling or devaluating the empirical, temporal, historical.

---

[12] See his *The Hindu View of Life*, *op.cit.*, p.13.

4. Indian cultural traditions with their symbolic, narrative and mystical background may understand the Christian Bible more penetratingly and more adequately than cultures which are secular and conceptual. A spiritual introverted, synthetic and subjective outlook (in the good sense) may give a deeper understanding of the Bible than an outlook that is 'materialistic, extroverted, analytic, and objective'.

We may derive certain methodological principles from the Indian way of reading the Bible by examining how leading Hindus themselves understand the sacred writings of a religion. The classic example is Gandhi's outline of the essentials of the correct interpretation of the scriptures of different religions: 'A prayerful study and experience are essential for a correct interpretation of the scriptures. The injunction that a *shudra* may not study the scriptures is not entirely without meaning. A *shudra* means a spiritually uncultured, ignorant man. He is more likely than not to misinterpret the *Vedas* and other scriptures. Every one cannot solve an algebraical equation. Some preliminary study is a *sine qua non*. How ill would the grand truth "I am Brahman" lie in the mouth of a man steeped in sin. To what ignoble purpose would he turn it! What a distortion it would suffer at his hands! A man therefore who would interpret the scriptures must have the spiritual discipline. He must practise the *yamas* and *niyamas* – the essential guides of conduct. A superficial practice thereof is useless. The *Shastras* have enjoined the necessity of a *guru*. But a *guru* being rare in these days, a study of modern books inculcating *bhakti* has been suggested by the sages. Those who are lacking in *bhakti*, lacking in faith, are ill qualified to interpret the scriptures. The learned may draw an elaborately learned interpretation out of them, but that will not be the true interpretation. Only the experienced will arrive at the true interpretation of the scriptures. But even for the inexperienced, there are certain canons. That interpretation is not true which conflicts with Truth. To one who doubts even Truth, the scriptures have no meaning . . . Another canon of interpretation is to scan not the letter, but to examine the spirit'. [13]

[13] Mahatma Gandhi, *The teaching of the Gita* (Bombay, 1971), pp.13-14.

This is not to suggest that we have to follow the principles of interpretation of sacred scriptures as outlined by the Hindu authors, but that we have to examine them and evaluate them in as far as they contain valid elements that can indicate an Indian way of understanding the sacred writings.

The Indian modes of systematic thinking on what is contained in sacred writing may be divided into three types: that which recognizes only perception and inference; that which recognizes insight or intuition in addition to perception and inference; and that which substitutes revelation for intuition. These are considered essential means of arriving at valid knowledge. Indian systems call them *parmānas: pratyaksa, anumāna,* and *śabda.* Scriptural knowledge (*śruti*) is derived from divine testimony (*śabda*), and has to be interiorized through intuitive experience (*anubhava*), and in this way of grasping the scriptural truth Hindus commonly agree. Here again the Indian theologian has to reflect and evaluate such modes of interpreting the sacred writings.

5. We may distinguish these major realities of the Indian subcontinent in regard to historical and socio-cultural tradition. First, in India we find some of the great religions of the world: Hinduism, Islam, Jainism, Sikhism, Christianity, and so on. In this context a theological understanding of world religions and of the uniqueness and transcendence of Christianity is important. Inter-religious dialogue and the theological understanding of that dialogue are equally important.

Second, India is a country of strong interplay of ancient cultures with immense scope for the enrichment of spiritual and moral values. The relationship between Christian faith and Indian religious tradition has to be conceived on the model of incarnation; and the process of expressing this faith in terms of culture is 'inculturation'. This is the global process of interaction between the Christian message and cultures, with all the outcomes for cultures and/or for the Christian message.

Third, India is a country subject to poverty and exploitation, injustice due to caste, communalism and other social discriminations. In this context Christian thinkers are called upon to give a theological understanding of liberation and progress. Liberation theology in India is different from that of Latin America. India is predominantly a non-Christian country, less influenced by Marxist ideologies and methods and less subject to totalitarian and oppressive régimes than Latin America. India is affected by peculiar social factors such as caste and communally divided loyalties; beliefs such as rebirth and the law of *karma*. An Indian theology of liberation has to take these factors and problems into account.

Conclusion

I have indicated some of the paradigms of the Hindu religious tradition and of the Indian Christian theology to be developed in that context. This attempt is neither complete nor thorough, for every paradigm pointed out above is rich and deep enough for a full-scale treatment. Indian theology itself is in its initial stage, and so far there has not been any notable attempt at building it. To make a good beginning is half-done, as the saying goes, and I hope that Indian theology will be taken as a serious concern of the church in India.

VII. RETROSPECTS AND PROSPECTS

A NEW BASIC MODEL FOR THEOLOGY: DIVERGENCIES AND CONVERGENCIES

Hans Küng

Do we need something like a new paradigm, or basic model, for theology today? Does anything of the kind already exist? This was the question from which we started out at our international symposium, and it was discussed from the standpoints of the most varied theological schools, countries and continents, and from all the possible aspects suggested by theology's present situation.

In spite of all the different theories, methods, structures, even in spite of different theologies – are there any constants running right through such a 'new paradigm' which all Christian theologies must assume as premise if they wish to offer a scientifically responsible and justifiable account of the Christian faith today?

This symposium was no small venture. What can always happen at a scientific or scholarly congress strikes very much deeper at theological conferences, where the highly personal faith of a man or woman is always involved. Here there can be serious differences and controversies – so serious that in earlier times they were even capable of splitting churches. We certainly live in more peaceful times, ecumenically minded as we are. Of course there were controversies at this symposium, but the atmosphere made it plain that they were controversies between colleagues, even friends. This was the more remarkable because here the most widely differing theological schools, trends and theologies were represented here. No one – least of all the *Concilium* theologians – was striving for a uniform, standardized, theology of the kind embodied, for example, by neo-scholastic theology before the Second Vatican Council, which belonged within the framework of the mediaeval-Counter Reformation Roman Catholic paradigm. Our goal is a plural theology, open to learn and ready to discuss; one which – rooted in the Christian tradition – can provide an answer to the challenges of our time.

I. Paradigm and paradigm change

Readers will have to judge for themselves how far individual authors entered into the problems involved in the paradigm theory, and how far they skirted round them. Not all the theologians concerned realized before the symposium what an adventure they were letting themselves in for; and of course it was noticeable from the papers whether these had been preceded by intensive ponderings about Kuhn's theory – whether, that is, an author had really submitted himself or herself to the paradigm theory, or was expressing his or her own theology. However that might be, the papers were at all events informative and stimulating.

It was undoubtedly a disadvantage that Thomas Kuhn himself, who had been invited, was prevented by circumstances from being present at the symposium. As a result, the philosophical 'opposition' to the paradigm concept was well represented, but we lacked the professional 'defence' (on the basis of scientific theory) which Kuhn could have provided on his own behalf.

For it was to be expected that the concept of the paradigm would be controversial – among theologians, for whom it was largely new, but also among philosophers. In the discussion the most acute critic of Kuhn's paradigm theory, the philosopher Stephen Toulmin, made no secret of his scepticism about the term 'paradigm'. Yet it became clear how much *links* Kuhn and Toulmin, in spite of their different methodological procedure (in Toulmin a more piecemeal technique, going into the details of terms and judgments and their development; in Kuhn, interested as he is in the total constellation of beliefs, values and techniques, a more sweeping 'paradigmatic' approach). We may view the link between the two in its negative aspect, as the rejection of anti-historical logical empiricism, with its formalistic approach (which we still come across in Popper, as an inheritance from the Vienna school), where interest is confined to the change of terms, and to the logical connections in the advancement of knowledge and science. Or we may see it positively, as an affirmation of the unity of the theory, history and sociology of science. In this sense it is an observation of the intellectual development of scientific theories in the context of the social-historical development of scientific schools, professions and institutions. The discussion showed clearly that if the concept of the paradigm is taken over into theology in a differentiated way, substantial differences about the concept shrink to a minimum – practically to the question whether the *term* 'paradigm' in this sense is a happy coinage or not. (Toulmin's parting shot was: 'Between you and myself is only *one word*, nothing else!')

The subject which concerned us all is too important to be reduced to the question of a word. Yet a word is needed. Hardly any suggestion for replacing the word 'paradigm' (basic model) was any more convincing, not even Claude Geffré's proposed 'structural horizon'. On the contrary: it was possible to establish that, ultimately speaking, the term seemed to be usable, though it was increasingly clarified, so that the initial scepticism diminished as more material for clarifying the thing itself was put forward. What really is at issue is the far-reaching, profound alterations in the history of theology and the church. Here it emerged that for these epochal shifts – what Langdon Gilkey called 'continental shifts' – hardly any better expression can be found than that of the change from which a new 'paradigm' then emerges (for the hellenistic-Byzantine imperial church, for the Latin-western papal church, for the Reformation, for the modern era or the Enlightenment, for the post-Enlightenment or post-modern era).

Of course the premise is that this term should preserve its breadth and elasticity on the one hand and, on the other, the firmness and precision that clearly emerges from the preparatory papers. If the paradigm is used for all manner of things, the concept becomes threadbare. Not *everything* can be a paradigm. No; not every theory, not every method, not every hermeneutics, not every theology is already a paradigm. The preparatory papers followed the definition which Kuhn used to delineate his term, and made it clear that a paradigm in the precise sense is 'an entire constellation of beliefs, values and techniques, and so on, shared by the members of a given community'.

It was important that no objections were made to two postulates: first, the fact of *epochal shifts*, which determine the history of theology, the church and the world in general; and second, the proposed *periodization*, which after all largely takes account of the periodization of world, church and theology with which we are familiar, even though we based our reflections only on the history of Christendom hitherto (ignoring other cultural areas and religions), and were indeed bound to do so (as Jürgen Moltmann made clear).

In the course of the discussion there was often talk about the *crises* in theology and church which led to a paradigm change (for example, the replacement of Jewish-Christianity by hellenistic Christianity, which J.B. Metz stressed, or the crisis in the early Middle Ages and the East-West schism, or the repeatedly cited two great crises of the Reformation and the early modern era). But in this account I shall confine myself to the factors *in our crisis today* which may serve to bring out the contours of a new paradigm (a post-Enlightenment or post-modern paradigm), for which we have as yet discovered no keyword. Of course, more might be said about the mechanisms which thereby come into play, and the contributory scientific and non-scientific factors; about the necessity of conversion in the transition to a new paradigm; and about the uncertain outcome should there be a dispute about different paradigms.

What is at least certain is this: neither an individual theologian nor theology as a whole can simply *create* a paradigm. A paradigm grows up in an exceptional complex of varying social, political, ecclesial and theological factors, and matures slowly. This highly complex process does not always have to take as dramatic a course as in Luther's case, but it certainly includes not merely gradual but also drastic changes – in fact paradigmatic ones – and during this process an individual theologian will sooner or later find himself confronted with the question whether his or her own paradigm of theology still corresponds to the paradigm of the time. He will have to choose the paradigm with which he wants to work. Sometime or other he will have to choose, and reveal his loyalties, his ties and his concerns.

II. Aspects running through the discussion

Before I mention the individual factors in the crisis, let me establish a few fundamental points which our discussion brought to the fore.

1. The particular community (Kuhn) in which the theological paradigm change takes place is *the community of theologians* (scholars or non-scholars, theologians at a university or in a basic community, professional writers or laity). The community belongs within the context of *the community of believers* (that is to say, the church, in the broadest sense of the term), and has as its background *the community of humanity in general* (that is, human society).

2. *The paradigm of theology* is to be seen in the context of *the paradigm of the church*, and against the background of the paradigmatic transformation of *society in general*. That is to say, the histories of theology, church and world must be analysed in conjunction with one another and – as was repeatedly stressed (especially by Boff, Dussel and Metz) – not from a Eurocentric standpoint.

3. *The thinking subjects* of theology, and *the places* where theology is pursued, can therefore change. This was frequently brought out (Baum, Boff, Greinacher, Jossua, Metz). The place where people do theology is not necessarily a university. It can also be a basic community. And it can be pursued not only by academics (let alone male academics) but also by women and non-academics.

4. *Theology* cannot simply take over a paradigm from *the natural sciences*, or abstract from science the raw material from which to construct a new theological paradigm (as Aquinas did with

Aristotelian physics, or Protestant theology with Descartes and Newton). But theology must not, like neo-scholastic theologians or Protestant fundamentalists, ignore the results of science either. The dialogue between science and theology has to be a dialogue between equals (Toulmin). On the one hand, this will make clear the limitations of science (seen in an extreme form in behaviourism and psychoanalysis). But on the other hand the 'topical significance' of scientific ideas and methods of analysis (which must be investigated in a patient 'piecemeal' examination) will also be made fruitful for theology.

5. The philosophical discussion about the paradigm-change theory compels theology for its part to clarify *the relationship between rationality and irrationality*, and to do so strictly in accordance with theological and non-theological factors. According to Bubner, this means considering especially:

 (a) *the relation between reality and language*, empirical experience and theory, facts and perception;

 (b) the problem of *periodization* by way of paradigms: it is only through the new that 'the normal' becomes old; the old, the new, and the threshold of a new epoch emerge over against each other and together with one another. Divisions of time cannot be made by time itself, or from a supra-historical standpoint outside time. They always have to be made immanently and relatively:

 (c) the problem of *the dialectic of knowledge and history*: the internal history of theological scholarship and the conditions that provides its external framework cannot be separated but must be seen in conjunction with one another. Theology cannot be explained by social factors, nor can we simply abstract from these. It is true of theology as of other disciplines that no theory is ultimately the master of its conditions; yet, within the framework of this dialectic of knowledge and history, it is all the same, no longer completely at the mercy of these conditions.

6. *The criteria* for a new paradigm would be a subject for further discussion in the future. For theology, one important

specification of the criteria found in Kuhn is the capacity for being aware of crises and for coping with them (Metz). Crises are interruptions of accustomed complexes of living and thinking, so that the world of theology and church is not the same before and afterwards. Karl Josef Kuschel has referred to these epochal crises, which are so characteristic of our time. He also sketched the dimensions of a post-modern paradigm of theology and the church. Here I can only underline what was said and develop it from different viewpoints. David Tracy and Matthew Lamb refer to other aspects and authors. The papers and responses show the many differences and divergencies, both in points of detail and as a whole. A consensus, which is what I am mainly concerned with here, was to be found at least in the analyses of the present crisis.

III. What characterizes today's crisis?

1. *The end* (after World War II) of 400 years *of western* political and military, economic and cultural *hegemony* (first European, then American); and the development of other political and military, economic and cultural centres of power (Gilkey); *polycentricism* (Metz).
2. A profound *ambiguity* in science, technology and industrialization, which are the basic forces of our civilization in West and East – ambiguity, because these forces are potentially both creative and destructive. Technological and industrial culture is marked by latent and fatal potentialities for destruction: destruction of the environment, and possibly the destruction of humanity, through nuclear overkill (Blank, Cobb, Gilkey, Metz, Moltmann, Schillebeeckx).
3. *Social antagonism* – exploitation and repression, racism and sexism. Apart from cultural polycentricism, this is the central challenge to theology, church and society in our century (Boff, Carr, Cobb, Gilkey, Metz, Moltmann).
4. An evident *shaking of the foundations in the symbols* underlying modern culture, which is dominated by the myth of progress

in all fields – scientific, technological and industrial, as well as political and social. An optimistic modern view of history (supported by progressive theologies and ideologies of both liberal – democratic and socialist – Marxist provenance) was followed by a widespread pessimistic lack of orientation, by hopelessness and fear of the future (Gilkey and others). This is certainly characteristic of modern affluent industrial societies. It does not apply to all countries in the third world (Cobb).

5. Signs of crisis and developments that are especially momentous for theology, in the framework of the modern paradigm, can be deduced from the changed, and now precarious, position of *the book*, the role of *the university*, and *theology* as one of the human sciences. It can also be seen from the position of *the Christian church* (Marty). The book, academic theology and the churches are all endangered by opposing pressures: by hyper-modern differentiation and specialization, by individualism and pluralism, as well as by an anti-modern, reactionary de-differentiation and drive to uniformity both by 'the hunger for totality' and totalitarian tendencies of secular and religious provenance. Today many impulses for academic theology, which can often be so sterile, come from outside (Baum, Jossua, Schüssler-Fiorenza). Fiorenza).

6. The loss of political and military, economic and cultural hegemony is accompanied by *an undermining of Christianity's dominance* as the 'one true', 'absolute' religion, 'outside which there is no salvation'. For the first time we see the encounter between Christianity and other religions on the basis of 'rough equality' (Gilkey's phrase; see also Cobb). From this there follows:

7. *A loss of credibility* among Christians and secular post-Christians whenever Christianity is still viewed from the outset as a 'higher civilization' (because it allegedly promotes the development of science, technology and industry, or brings in its train individual freedoms, equality for women, and family stability). Instead there is a serious preparedness on the Christian side today really to listen to other religions, and to learn from them (Cobb, Dhavamony, Gilkey).

8. *Historical catastrophes* (two world wars, then Auschwitz, Hiroshima and the Gulag Archipelago, but also the periodically recurring mass hunger in the third world) have made us conscious that today it is impossible to fabricate idealistic theological constructions of history any more. Theology has to be practised in the face of these concrete, plural histories of human suffering (Metz). These histories especially make an 'option for the poor' (Boff) an urgent necessity, though the poor are not merely the materially needy but those who suffer in body and mind (Marty).

9. Among the multiple histories of suffering is the suffering of millions of women who, over centuries of patriarchal supremacy, have been dominated, battered, raped, tortured and destroyed. Women's new awareness of their identity, equality and dignity has brought home to us, almost more than any other development in our century, the degree to which we are involved in a revolutionary shift from an old paradigm to a new one. For this new female consciousness, the old paradigm has broken down, even though it is still passed on in the textbooks of 'classic' theology, church history and canon law (Carr, Schüssler-Fiorenza).

IV. Fundamental dimensions of the new paradigm

Some factors which have to be thought about and taken into account in all the different sectors and themes of theology and the Church are:

1. The biblical dimension

(*a*) The problem of *continuity* in a paradigm change demands particular reflection in Christian theology, for even in a new paradigm it is *the old gospel*, and no other, that has to be newly interpreted for our time (Schillebeeckx). The significance of this single constant (Christian tradition, the gospel, faith in God in Jesus Christ) is the one thing that must always persist and prevail throughout all the paradigm changes in theology and the church (Jüngel). This was repeatedly stressed on all sides.

(b) *Testimony to the gospel* and its implications is especially necessary *in 'a time of troubles'*, which – no longer threatened by secular faith in progress – is menaced by fear of the future, the shaking of institutions, and the possibility of deadly conflicts of all kinds (Jüngel, Gilkey).

(c) The importance and necessity of *the methods of historical criticism* for a 'contemporary' interpretation of Scripture and the texts of the Christian tradition was clearly affirmed (Blank, Ogden, Kannengiesser). The role of Scripture in the new paradigm remains a criteriologically liberating one; ever since the Enlightenment, biblical hermeneutics has had to go hand in hand with historical criticism, even though today's hermeneutical tools (eg, structural text analysis) may have become more sophisticated. No one wanted a reversion to an anti-Enlightenment, fundamentalistically rigid, or a post-Enlightenment, dogmatically reduced, biblical hermeneutics (in the style of the recent German (Catholic) adult catechism, for example).

(d) The gospel of the God who reveals himself in Jesus Christ can no longer be proclaimed today without awareness of the problems involved in a patriarchal symbolic language. What is theologically relevant about Jesus Christ as the Son of God is not that he was a man but that he was a human being. But God himself should no longer be thought of and preached in exclusively male metaphors, as father, ruler and judge. He should be thought about and proclaimed inclusively, so that the experiences of *femininity and motherliness* are included (Carr).

2. The historical dimension

(a) In a post-Enlightenment, post-modern theological paradigm, *time* must be understood *historically*, not simply in a linear sense. The dimensions of time, past, present and future, are to be seen, not as linear succession, but in their dialectical interlacing as a network of time (Moltmann).

(b) In a new paradigm, *historical criticism* retains its function; it must criticize and relationalize the absolute claims made by rigid dogmas and institutions.

It must not, however, lead to an absolutization of the present, and to an absolutism of the human subject, and hence to a general relativism. That is the danger of liberal historicism.

On the contrary, historical criticism must also remember that its own present and the subjective standpoint are also relative. A general relativism then gives way to relationalism, in the form of a general web of interconnections and relationships (Moltmann).

(c) *History and nature* must not be torn apart into a view of nature without history, and history without nature (Moltmann).

The relationship between *human beings and nature* must not be regarded and practised as if it were the relationship between master and slave (the usual attitude in modern science, technology and industrialization). Human history must rather be synchronized with the history of nature, so that we may arrive at a new, viable symbiosis of human society and the natural environment.

(d) In a shared world and a shared world history, the subject of which is humanity as a whole, there will only be a common future or none. World peace has become the condition for the survival of humanity. The new paradigm must consequently be a '*paradigm of humanity*' in the face of indescribable inhumanity. That is to say, humanity must permeate it and be its imprint, though this humanity certainly finds its proper justification and foundation only in *the humanity of God*, revealed in *Jesus Christ*.

(e) Hitherto, the history of this humanity of ours has been written largely by men as a history of men. The history of women – the greater part of humanity – has often been ignored and to some extent suppressed. Women are rightly demanding *the integration of women's history* in history itself – both the history of women's suppression and the history of their activity and creativity in society, state and church throughout the centuries (Carr).

3. The ecumenical dimension

1. In the face of the multifarious political, economic and military threats to our one world and the common future of humanity, *the transition from particularist to universal thinking*, and from *'controversial' theology to 'ecumenical' theology* is an imperative requirement. Denominational Christian traditions must not be given eternal permanence, but must be accepted for what they contribute to an ecumenical community of all Christians. An ecumenical style of thinking is needed, in which what is particular and denominational is not seen as the realization of the whole, but may be understood as part of a comprehensive Christian truth. This inner-Christian *oikoumene* can for its part be the model for a future *oikoumene* of religions and cultures (Moltmann).

2. *The multiplicity of religions* and the problem of religious relativism means that we have to find the right way to understand and interpret *the uniqueness of the Christian faith* (Dhavamony). We have to arrive at a 'relative absoluteness' which has countless consequences for the understanding of revelation, christology, justification, church, eschatology and social practice (Gilkey).

3. *The Indian* (or Chinese or Japanese or African or Latin American) *'way of reading the Bible'* is not merely legitimate. It is necessary. This is the only way in which we can be enriched by the spiritual, moral and aesthetic values of other religions and cultures (Dhavamony).

4. The ecumenical dimension of the new paradigm includes, not only an *oikoumene* between churches, religions and cultures, but also an *oikoumene between the sexes* (Carr). 'In Christ' it is not only the difference between masters and slaves, Greeks and barbarians that is ended. The division between men and women is ended also. In a new paradigm of theology and the church, a further cementing of the inferior position of women, and in particular a continued refusal to ordain them in the church, would be positively absurd (Carr).

4. The political dimension

1. The new paradigm of theology has *a fundamentally political dimension*. The relationship between theory and practice in theology should no longer be determined by a division of labour between practical theology and social ethics (even Christian social doctrine) on the one hand, and systematic theology and dogmatics (even the doctrine of the church) on the other. All theology must learn to think practically and politically. We therefore need a *practical, political hermeneutics* which is critical of all attempts to politicize religion as a way of legitimating and stabilizing particular relationships of domination and power (Metz).

2. It was and is undisputed that theology in the new paradigm has essentially a political dimension. What was a matter of *controversy* was whether European – let alone West German – political theology, or even the liberation theology of Latin America, could provide the new universal paradigm. It was questioned whether any single theology can make this total claim, especially when it is a matter of theologies which otherwise distrust all universal 'imperialistic' claims to validity.

3. I myself should like in retrospect to put on record the point of view which found expression in all the preparatory papers, *a number of different theologies* are possible within the one post-Enlightenment, post-modern paradigm, or basic model. Different theological trends, schools and locations compete for the best way of shaping the paradigm, its presuppositions and consequences. A hermeneutical and a political theology, a process theology, and all the different expressions and trends of liberation theology (feminist, black or third world) can co-exist and compete within the bounds of a contemporary post-Enlightenment, post-modern paradigm of a Christian (ecumenical) theology. At all events, the new paradigm needs the world-wide political perspective and this means that the different continents (not merely Latin America) and religions (not merely Christianity) must all be taken into account.

It is important that we theologians of a new paradigm – confronted as we are with firmly-rooted, tenacious and long-lived traditionalistic paradigms – do not lose sight of what binds us together. All mutual theological provocation and confrontation, justified and necessary though it is, should not lead to self-aggrandisement, support of particularist concerns, isolation and separation. It should rather encourage reciprocal and spiritual interpenetration, mutual enrichment, and transformation on all sides so as to unite all who are concerned for the all-embracing liberation of human beings in a post-colonialist, post-patriarchal – in short, post-modern – paradigm embodying what Schillebeeckx aptly called 'the cry for the humane'.

This conference was merely a beginning. Work within the framework of Christian theology must go on. It has to become more precise, more concrete, and more fully enriched by facts and material. The paradigm theory is no more than a hermeneutical framework. Only when it is implemented materially and historically, and when its analysis of the present becomes efficacious, will it reveal its illuminating power. This is certainly not true of Christianity alone. It is quite conceivable that the paradigm-change analysis could be applied to other religions – to Judaism, Islam, Buddhism, Hinduism and the Chinese religions. Here too a beginning has been made. A similar symposium was held in January 1984 in the University of Hawaii in Honolulu, the main subject being 'Paradigm changes in Buddhism and Christianity'. This conference, presided over by Professor David Chappell, was inspired by our Tübingen symposium. It still has to be assessed. But I am convinced that its results, like those of our symposium, will be influential for some time to come.

PARADIGMS AS IMPERATIVES TOWARDS CRITICAL COLLABORATION

Matthew L. Lamb

Hans Küng in his summation asked whether it is possible today, in spite of all our differences and divergences, to reach a basic hermeneutical consensus in Christian theologies on international and ecumenical foundations. David Tracy's summation indicated how any adequate response to such a question demands attention to the concrete contexts of our efforts at articulating new paradigms. From the perspectives of my preparatory study, as well as the discussions and debates at this symposium, I believe that it is vitally important to continue the communicative praxis of dialogue and debate, not *in spite of* all our differences and divergences, but precisely *because of* them. The very concrete dialectics of the efforts at communicative action within this symposium indicates how any quest for new paradigms is not so much indicative of past or present achievements, as an imperative towards ever more serious and committed critical collaboration.

The question mark which has hovered over this enterprise from its inception -'A new paradigm in theology?' - has not been removed but intensified by our agreements and disagreements. As Paul Ricoeur reminded us, the dialectics of question and answer is not a logic of complacency, but calls for a logic of commitment to address theoretically and practically the very difficult issues challenging us today. Some of those issues were raised in the introductory remarks of Jerald Brauer, Hans Küng, Jürgen Moltmann and Norbert Greinacher. Others have been raised by other papers and presentations throughout this symposium. The value-conflicts and power-complexes which distort reason and religion, the world and the Christian message, into ideologies of domination, can only be recognized and overcome if we take seriously the questions and criticisms posed by the victims of domination.

If Heidegger could remark that 'the question is the piety of thinking', then the presentations and interventions from our colleagues engaged in political, liberation, feminist, black and third world theologies have very forcefully called our attention to how the question mark hovering over this symposium must never be a mark of a liberal take-it-or-leave-it attitude. Rather, it must remain for all of us a mark of serious commitment to sublate the many alienations and systematically distorted communications resulting from class oppressions, patriarchy, racism, pollution (a consequence of technocentrism) and militarism.

The concrete dialectics of communicative action in history, society and church have been raised forthrightly in the presentations and discussions here. We can reach a genuine hermeneutical consensus only if we make our own the critical perspectives offered by the voices of the victims. Johann Baptist Metz spoke of the hermeneutics of danger informing the apostolic witness of the New Testament, which Leonardo Boff's presentation dramatized. Indeed, as Enrique Dussel reminded us, our sisters and brothers in many third world countries are doing theology under the shadows of 'a hermeneutics of death'. By calling our attention to how women, and children dependent upon women, are so often the primary victims of domination, Ann Carr, Elizabeth Schlüssler-Fiorenza, Mary Collins and other feminist theologians have stressed how any new paradigm for theology requires profound intellectual, moral and religious transformations of the personal and institutional ways in which theology is done. Certainly, the fact that more women are now engaged in theological research and teaching than ever before in history is a sign of hope and transformation. It is also a sign of contradiction insofar as the subjects and institutions of theology are distorted by patriarchy. Mariasusai Dhavamony and John Cobb have emphasized the need to accept fully the challenging questions arising from the ongoing dialogues of the world religions.

A central aspect of the contemporary, as distinct from the modern, situation is precisely the manifold efforts on the part of many religious and theological communities to develop dialectical criteria to discern ideological distortions in the traditions of religion and reason. Paradigms are not conceptual entities floating in some Platonic heaven. They are, as Küng has continually reminded us, entire constellations of beliefs, values and practices shared by a given community. Theology is now being done in new ways by communities of worship and praxis among the poor, women, non-European races, environmentalists and pacifists. These voices of witness and critical reflection have not been heard in much modern Christian theological discourse. By and large they call for a deeper and more genuinely communal appropriation of the gospel message and traditions. As Edward Schillebeeckx, Gregory Baum and others have indicated, the intellectual and religious praxis of these basic Christian communities critically discerns the systemic presence of sin and injustice within the personal and social mediations of *both* our religious traditions *and* our contemporary world. The need for dialectical methods to critique ideological distortions in the personal and social mediations of faith and reason is neither a total repudiation of faith and reason (hence the continuity of tradition in the new paradigms), nor a blanket acceptance of all the personal and social mediations of faith and reason (hence the discontinuities in how faith and reason are expressed in different paradigms).

The *international* dimensions of the process by which ideological distortions are discerned will require, as Boff and Dussel have stressed, a serious, sustained critique of present economic and political imperialisms whereby late capitalist and state socialist superpowers exploit whole peoples and countries as marginalized or peripheral colonies. This symposium, for example, should clearly go on record as repudiating the dominative tendency of treating theologies elaborated in solidarity with the victims of imperialism, of patriarchy, of racism, or of technocentrism as though they were only partial or particular aspects of dominant first world or western theologies.

The *ecumenical* dimensions of discerning ideological distortions will require serious and sustained criticisms of all sacralist uses of religious symbol-systems and institutions to foster and legitimate dominative power. Only recently has there emerged a dialogue of world religions in contrast to the wars of religion which for so many centuries have distorted (and in some places still distort) faith as a tool of domination and violent oppression. We Christians have much to repent and confess. For centuries the cross was betrayed by the sword as Christian beliefs, values and practices were distorted into tools fostering and legitimating first the Holy Roman Empire and then sovereign nation-states. The *oikoumene* which new paradigms in theology promote must be based, not on such domination, but on the inclusive wisdom and love to which Dhavamony and Carr have referred. The universality of faith, as a knowledge born of love, is not a universality imposed dominatively from the top down. Rather, it is a universality emerging from the genuine praxis of Christian beliefs and values within local communities. In this perspective, the church is not an imperial monarchy, nor an agnostic anarchy, but a sacramental communion of communities.

Such new paradigms in theology do not arise in a trouble-free and placid discussion. They are formed in the 'time of troubles', to which Langdon Gilkey has referred, challenging the practices of faith and those of reason. Until the modern period, the cultural and social matrices in which theological paradigms were elaborated tended to identify the expressions of religious faith with a genuine knowledge which could be opposed to ideology or heresy in a more or less objectivistic manner. Pre-modern theological disputes, as Charles Kannengiesser and Stephan Pfürtner have indicated, centred on conflicting understandings of faith and the diverse ecclesial communities in which those paradigms arose. To the extent that such faith expressions and ecclesial institutions became involved in the European wars of religion and attendant sacralisms (Catholicism supporting a Holy Roman Empire, Protestantism supporting emergent nation-states), the Enlightenment shifted from a sacralist faith-ideology dichotomy to an increasingly secularist science-ideology dichotomy. Religious faiths in general were suspect as ideological distortions or superstitions, and the truth claims of those faiths were either to be relativized (historicism) or to be falsified (Marxism) by the advance of modern science and technology. Brian Gerrish, Bernard McGinn and Martin Marty have shown some of the implications of this modern shift in regard to historicism. Nicholas Lash, Edward Schillebeeckx and Jürgen Moltmann have extended these implications into the area of ideology-critique and Marxism.

The new paradigms emerging in our times, however, can no longer avoid a critique of modern science and technology as themselves just as susceptible of ideological distortion in the service of domination as the expressions of faith. The horrors of our so-called progressive and enlightened twentieth century expose the myth of 'progress through technology'. In no other century have so many human beings been killed by their fellows. Auschwitz, Hiroshima, the Gulag – and their many other analogues – are not merely temporary aberrations within modern secularism. Rather, they are exaggerations of the latent powers in science and technology to destroy life and freedom when such science and technology are informed with the dominative injustices of classism, sexism, racism, technocentrism or militarism.

In our post-modern contemporary situation, appeals to reason or science as against religion and faith ring hollow. In the light of possible nuclear warfare, appeals to progress through science and technology sound like the clang of a tolling funeral bell. Hence there is need for what in my preparatory paper I termed a 'double dialectic'. Political and liberation theologies emphasize the need to criticize dialectically both sacralism and secularism. The tragic transition of modernity was the transition from sacralism (in which religious symbol and social systems legitimated domination) to secularism (in which scientific symbol and social systems legitimate domination). This double dialectic repudiates neither faith nor science; instead it goes to the heart of our post-modern situation by criticising the forms of domination which ideologically distort faith and science.

New paradigms, therefore, will radically challenge the economic, political and cultural domination by late capitalists and state socialist superpowers. The creative centres of the modern age have become, to borrow Toynbee's phrase, the merely dominative and repressive centres of power as force. If the new paradigms in theology are to collaborate in bringing about more just world orders, then there must be what Baum, Gilkey, Greinacher and Moltmann called clear commitments to solidarity with the emerging new creative centres among the victims of modern domination. Metz termed this solidarity a messianic coalition among those struggling for more just and humane societies, churches and worlds. John Coleman and other feminists have indicated how a major issue in these struggles is how precisely we can transform our dominative institutions in non-dominative, non-violent ways. Jürgen Habermas remarked on the difference between the ecological crises and the increasing possibilities of nuclear warfare. Nuclear militarism challenges us to recover and create new modes of conflict-resolution, with attention to specifically moral and humanly political forms of diplomacy – otherwise there may be no more eyes or teeth left.

The temporal and historical dimensions of these tasks within new theological paradigms, as the contributions of Eberhard Jüngel, Schubert Ogden and Claude Geffré indicate, demand both narrative sensitivity and ever greater and more extensive interdisciplinary collaboration between theology and contemporary science and scholarship. To understand and transform the concrete situations locally and globally demands a praxis informed by the most demanding theories, that is, theories heuristically attuned to the praxis of reason as raising ever further relevant questions.

The philosophers or theorists of science – Bubner, Habermas, Ricoeur and Toulmin – were united in their recommendations that we should not get bogged down in the theoretical controversies surrounding Kuhn's, or others', use of the term paradigm. Jossua and Coleman, among others, have seconded their recommendation. Margaret Masterson found that Kuhn himself, in his original study, used the term paradigm in at least twenty-two different ways (*cf.* her 'The Nature of a Paradigm' in Lakatos & Musgrave, eds., *Criticism and the Growth of Knowledge* (Cambridge, 1970)). I am confident that a study of the many uses accorded the term in this symposium will establish that, at least in this regard, we have been faithful to Kuhn's own performance or praxis of paradigm analysis. Yet, as Habermas and Toulmin made clear – and as the use made of the term in the planning of this symposium confirms – the real significance of paradigm analysis has been its rhetorical dismantling of the primacy of subjectless and ahistorical theories in the analysis of science. The continuing discussions and debates among the philosophers of science emphasize how, as the works of Helmut Peukert and Richard Bernstein have demonstrated, there is an important shift from theories of science to theories of action and communicative praxis. No longer can theorists of science avoid the hermeneutical and dialectical issues involved in the concrete historical and social contexts within which science is practised. The praxis of scientists, with their disciplines and professions, their institutions and texts, their paradigmata and topoi (Toulmin), shift our attention from a primacy of theory to a primacy of praxis.

I believe that the discussions and debates at this symposium have tended to validate the conclusions of the review I offered in my preparatory paper. Post-empiricist philosophies of science tend to exclude the possibility of arriving at a complete and coherent articulation of 'the new paradigm', as though it could be a monistic metatheoretical absolute, deductively or inductively articulating rationality fully. Also excluded is the adequacy of inferring from this radical incompleteness that 'the new paradigm' heads toward the incoherence of an arational or irrational relativism or anarchism. Such an inference is premised on a similarly mistaken assumption that, if rationality exists, it must be capable of complete and coherent metatheoretical articulation.

Instead, the discussions and debates in this symposium have indicated how attention to the praxis of theorizing within communities engaged in empirical, hermeneutical and dialectical inquiries enable us to articulate coherently – yet always incompletely – heuristic relationships within and among these communities of inquiry. The praxis of collaboration in the new paradigms hermeneutically and dialectically relates scientific communities to the many other communities of inquiry (political, aesthetic, moral and religious) which constitute humankind's ongoing efforts to realize reason in history and society.

The prospect of achieving cognitive consensus might well be distant. Nevertheless, a dialectical understanding of the new paradigms as imperatives towards communicative and effective collaboration impels us to continue. Our consensus of commitments to the ongoing transformation of our churches and of the contemporary world situation reveals something important. It shows how the new paradigms in theology fulfil their role as theoretical and practical counterparts of the 'already but not yet' imperatives of Jesus's preaching and practice of the reign of God.

SOME CONCLUDING REFLECTIONS ON THE CONFERENCE: UNITY AMIDST DIVERSITY AND CONFLICT?

David Tracy

All I can hope to do in these brief concluding comments is to provide a few reflections on a few issues emerging from this conference on 'a new paradigm in theology?' I shall concentrate on the possible unity emerging from the fruitful diversities and even conflict of theologies within the conference itself. Even if my reflections proved persuasive, they would not, of course, resolve the major substantive differences at stake. But they would suggest how much differences can be discussed by all who implicitly or explicitly share a modern (or post-modern?) understanding of Christian theology: that is, all the participants in this conference.

1. A shared paradigm among differences and conflicts?

In spite of a wide and growing plurality of particular models for theology, there does seem to be a shared general model for theological reflection in our period. In its simplest form, this model may be called a revised correlational model for theology. More exactly, theology in our period has many particular material models. The particularity of each is largely determined by the particular set of material questions and discernments of our contemporary situation which demand a theological response, and by the equally particular interpretations of certain symbols, doctrines, images and narratives, and so on, chosen from the Christian tradition to respond to those questions. And yet, amidst what William James named 'this blooming, buzzing confusion' and, as is also clear, the conflicts within the plurality of particular

461

models for theology, this conference seems to afford a general, heuristic model for theological reflection which informs discussion and argument over more particular models.

Let me recall the most important characteristics of that general model. First, a definition: theology as hermeneutical can be described as the attempt to develop mutually critical correlations (Tillich, Schillebeeckx, Ricoeur, and so on) in theory and praxis between an interpretation of the Christian tradition and an interpretation of the contemporary situation. In one sense, this hermeneutical formulation is simply a rendering explicit and deliberate of the fact which unites all forms of theology: that every Christian theology *is* interpretation of Christianity. Precisely as *interpretation* of the tradition there can be no naive claims to immediacy nor to certainty. There can and must be claims, however, to a genuine mediated and situated understanding of the tradition itself. As Christian interpreters of the Christian tradition, we recognize that the history of the effects of that tradition are present to and in all theologians both consciously and, more importantly, unconsciously. Theologians have the task, therefore, of rendering as explicit as possible an interpretation of the central Christian message for a concrete situation, and of showing why others should, in principle, agree with that interpretation.

As soon as any theologian interprets the tradition, he or she can also recognize that it is *we* ourselves who are doing the interpreting. It is, in sum, concrete human beings in concrete personal, social, cultural, political circumstances who are asking questions – some ancient, some unnervingly new – of the tradition. Insofar as we are interpreting the Christian tradition seriously – that is, theologically – we acknowledge its claim to our full attention, its claim to challenge not only our present answers but even our present questions. Insofar as *we* are *interpreting* that tradition seriously, we also recognize that we are not subject-less, context-less, history-less interpreters. We are first ourselves in these particular, concrete, personal, social, cultural, political circumstances. We try to grope our way to an understanding of those circumstances. We try to discern the signs of our times –

indeed, especially those signs of radical interruption (Metz, Gilkey, Cobb, Baum, Schüssler-Fiorenza, Boff, Dussel, Moltmann).

Unlike the later Hegel, none of believes that *we* possess an 'absolute knowledge' in regard to this process of discernment of either our historical situation or the tradition. Like Hegel and unlike the neo-scholastics, we do believe that even reason has a history (Gerrish, Toulmin, Habermas, Küng, Lash, Jüngel, Coleman, Geffré, Jossua), that the 'not-yet', the negative, is part of tradition and situation alike and all our discernments of each. We believe that we pursue not certainty but understanding, and do so with the knowledge that our interpretations too will prove inadequate. For all is interpretation.

The groping, tentative, often conflictual and interruptive character of any of our individual interpretations of tradition and situation in this conference is not, therefore, a weakness but a strength. It is, more exactly, the only strength available to us: the need to interpret the plural and ambiguous tradition for an ever-changing pluralistic and ambiguous situation, the need to give up the quest for an illusory ahistorical certainty and live the quest for a situated understanding of the Christian tradition in a particular place at a particular time.

The hermeneutical model suggested above is nothing other than the attempt to render explicit this inevitable process of contemporary theological interpretation. The model's central claim is that it is not imposed on the process of interpretation but is an explication of the several and related dimensions of the process of interpretation itself (Carr, Ogden, Jeanrond, Jüngel, Geffré, Ricoeur). To understand theology, therefore, as the attempt to develop mutually critical correlations in both theory and praxis between an interpretation of the Christian tradition and an interpretation of the contemporary situation, is simply to render explicit some principal needs for all contemporary theological interpretation. If the model succeeds it does provide a general heuristic model – no more, no less. That model, as heuristic and general, can guide discussions and assessments of concrete programmes of particular differing, arguing, conflicting theologies. The model can never *replace* those particular material theologies, any more than the general and abstract can replace the concrete.

To recognize, with A.N. Whitehead, the dangers of the 'fallacy of misplaced concreteness', is at the same time to acknowledge, again with Whitehead, the value of the abstract. Any good abstraction can always provide an enrichment of an understanding of some crucial aspect of the actual task at stake. To abstract a general, heuristic model that can be shared by *all* contemporary theologians who have embraced a situated historical, practical understanding and have abandoned the illusion of a context-less certainty, is to aid all theologians to interpret and thereby to converse and argue over their differing interpretations.

Our contemporary theological concerns involve not merely historical consciousness (Troeltsch, Lonergan), and radical historicity (Heidegger, Gadamer), but the interruptions of concrete historical event in our time (liberation, feminist, political and ecological theologies). Amidst even these necessary interruptions and inevitable conflicts we can still converse and argue our individual points as a conflicting but genuine community of inquiry and praxis. As John Courtney Murray justly observed, it takes a great deal of agreement in any community to allow for genuine disagreements. If we focus only on the disagreements we seldom, if ever, realize how much agreement there must be in order that we all know that, on this particular question or interpretation, we genuinely disagree.

If theology is to remain a communal discipline where all theologians can know where they differ from one another and why they disagree, there will be sufficient agreement on the nature of the theology itself to allow those differences to become fruitful and those disagreements to be discussable by the whole theological community. For this very reason, the sessions of this conference provide a useful test-case of the question of theological reflection today. For, as suggested above, there is *no* one formulation of the theological question in our period which unites all in this assembly. There is no single material answer on any of the particular questions addressed *within* each session which remains unchallenged by the other respondents to the same issue.

What, then, is an observer of all the sessions to think? Some may suggest that the conference is an excellent illustration of the 'chaos' of contemporary theology. Neo-scholastics and all traditionists and fundamentalists would surely make this charge before returning to their untroubled and ahistorical fortresses. Others may suggest that the conference demonstrates an unintended example of that kind of lazy, restless 'pluralism' which simply cloaks real differences by blessing all difference: the kind of pluralism which is driven not by the pursuit of situated practical understanding, but by an unconscious indifference to truth and argument, a kind of pluralism which quickly degenerates into a 'repressive tolerance' (Marcuse).

My basis suggestion throughout these brief reflections is that neither chaos nor 'repressive tolerance' adequately express the kind of pluralistic theological reflection represented by the conference, and by the hermeneutical model which I have suggested functions in the conference papers and in the assembly-wide discussion of those papers. My suggestion is, rather, that any observer can note that, sometimes through the differences and conflicts and sometimes in spite of them, different theological proposals suggest that a general hermeneutical model of theological reflection is present – and present as shared. There is a sufficiently shared element to allow any observer to know that theology is a discipline with communal, that is, shared, disciplinary ideals. Each theological speaker has engaged in the kind of contemporary situated theological interpretation outlined above. Some (Boff, Collins, Lash, Küng, Metz, Lamb, Carr, Gilkey) – to all our gain – have made that situated understanding explicit.

Each theologian, precisely by abandoning pretensions to ahistorical certainty and by embracing situated interpretations as understanding, works implicitly or explicitly with some kind of general model like that suggested above. This means that, as a contemporary theologian, each theologian is a concretely-situated interpreter of the tradition for a concrete situation. Each theologian, precisely as interpreter, must interpret the tradition for and in a concrete situation. Insofar as he or she does that, as theologians they will interpret tradition *and* contemporary situation. They interpret the situation, as Christian theologians, by attempting to provide Christian construals of that situation. These discernments, in turn, lead them to interpret the tradition itself anew (and *vice versa*). They interpret the tradition both to retrieve often forgotten, even repressed, disclosive and transformative aspects of tradition and to criticize and even suspect other aspects of the tradition (for instance, the mystico-political symbols of liberation, emancipation and redemption). They also interpret the tradition with not only a hermeneutics of retrieval, but a hermeneutics of critique and suspicion. They do so by recognizing, for example, the privatizing elements in the tradition; by criticizing the fatal silence on nature in much western, including contemporary, theology (Cobb, Toulmin); and by rendering explicit both any repressed systematic distortions in the tradition (sexism, racism, classism, anti-Semitism, élitism, and so on).

Insofar as theologians engage in hermeneutics of both retrieval and critique-suspicion of the tradition *and* the situation, they also *implicitly* correlate the results of all these interpretations. Those correlations will inevitably prove to be, moreover, correlations in both praxis and theory. The correlation will ordinarily prove 'mutually critical' – a phrase introduced to remind theologians that prior to the actual analysis there is no way of predicting what concrete kind of correlation is needed in this particular instance. In some cases, there will be a *confrontation* between the Christian tradition and the contemporary situation. In other cases, mutually critical *analogies* (as similarities-in-difference) may prove what is needed. In rarer cases, an effective *identity* of meaning may obtain.

In sum, a revised correlational method is simply a rendering explicit of what happens in every concretely situated theological act of interpretation. The revisionary character of the present model is revisionary by spelling out more explicitly three factors which earlier 'liberal' models of correlation tended to ignore. First, 'correlation' is a logical category which suggests a whole spectrum of possible responses, either identity (*no* difference) or analogy (similarities-in-difference) or even confrontation (mutually exclusive differences). Unlike some earlier liberal models of correlation, there is no built-in 'prejudice' towards harmonization in the contemporary correlational model. Second, this same principle is further clarified by the phrase 'mutually critical'. Here again, it is not the case, as in some earlier formulations of a correlational model, that there are 'questions' from one 'source' (the situation) and answers from another (the tradition). Rather, in every concrete case of theological interpretation there is a need to allow for the kind of interaction that occurs in all true interpretation as genuine conversation. *The need* for real interaction between text and interpreter, and thereby between tradition and situation, is emphasized by this phrase 'mutually critical'. Third, the additional phrase 'in theory and in praxis' is also intended to remind concretely-situated interpreters that every act of theological interpretation is situated in a particular practical situation, and that every correlation in theory is also a correlation in praxis with a practical intent. In any attempt at genuine theological correlation, praxis too should be made as explicit as possible (in social, cultural, political and religious terms).

To summarize: the revised method of correlation, thus interpreted, is simply one way to explicate the shared and thereby communal character implicit in all contemporary theological interpretation. Inasmuch as that method does its task of explication well, it aids the wider conversation, that is, the community of inquiry called theology. There exists sufficient agreement on what the contemporary theologian is doing when he or she provides a situated theological interpretation of the tradition to assure that disagreements will prove genuine disagreements within a real community of disciplined inquiry. The revised correlational method always remains only a general heuristic method to guide, but never to replace, the results of any concrete theological interpretation of the meaning and truth of a concrete symbol in a concrete situation. The general method guides as helpful abstractions always do. Any method that has not fallen into the temptation to become one more 'methodologism' remains a helpful and necessary abstraction. 'Methodologism' is merely the latest outburst of the quest for ahistorical certainty, and the most recent expression of the fallacy of misplaced concreteness.

This general hermeneutical model is a method used implicitly and sometimes explicitly in all contemporary, situated theology-as-interpretation. That method would become a methodologism only if it exceeded its heuristic status and tried to replace particular theological interpretations. Yet recalling that method of correlation helps the entire theological community to allow for a responsible pluralism or polycentrism; that is, an arguing and often conflictual set of sometimes complementary differences, and sometimes mutually exclusive disagreements within a shared context of basic, heuristic, methodical agreements on how to proceed in analysis, interpretation, discussion, argument and conflict itself.

The general and abstract, and the methodical guide heuristically but do not rule. Only the concrete rules; and the concrete is always a particular interpretation of a particular symbol for a particular practical situation.

2. Prospective: the priority of the future

For a Christian consciousness, origin is not end. And even 'end' is not a strict *futurum* but finally an *adventum* (Moltmann), the genuinely new as threat and promise from God, the genuinely new in the situation we are called to discern, even the new in the tradition we are called to retrieve anew. Any attempt to suggest future reality from a Christian theological perspective, therefore, is not merely a prediction based on the origin of an already existing form – even so sprawling, plural, conflictual and tentative a form as the several kinds of proposals and interpretations represented in the conference as a whole. With a quiet despair bordering on fatalism, even theologians, even, indeed, progressive theologians, sometimes say that even the future is not what it used to be.

But it never was. The Christian revolution of consciousness is a revolution which cannot stop and cannot presume to know with certainty either future or present or, as we saw above, even the past. The presentness of the past is present for a Christian consciousness as the presence of memories ever in need of retrieval to unleash their subversive power anew. The presentness of the present is present through the ever-shifting moments of attention and discernment, interest in ever-new questions, constantly emerging new signs to discern and new demands for action and thought alike. The presentness of the future is present as both *adventum* and *futurum* through the promises and threats of the Christian Gospel; where that future reign of God proclaimed by Jesus enters history ever anew to upset all calculations; and where the always-already-not-yet event of Jesus Christ keeps coming as *adventum*. It comes thus in ever new forms to unleash new demands for fresh interpretation and concrete actions, in situations where the future must have priority for a Christian consciousness.

Any 'prospective', therefore, for the kind of theological concerns and methods represented by the conference so far, can at best provide some 'hints and guesses' for the kind of theological work needed in the future. A retrospective, in and of itself, is not a prospective. Yet this much does seem suggested by this brief retrospective: the pluralism-polycentrism within Christian theology will increase. The demands of facing massive global suffering in all its forms, as well as serious inter-religious dialogue, will also increase within Christian theological consciousness. The past suggests that the different kinds of difficult questions released in all theology by the concerns expressed in the conference will arise again in even more pointed and intense forms. If these questions are to be asked as new ones by a theological community, something like the revised correlational method suggested above will need further revisions, reflection and discussion.

As a Christian theological community, in different communities and cultures (Collins), we are just beginning to find ways to articulate the rich aspects of our own inner-Christian ecumenical and thereby pluralistic, polycentric reality. We are just beginning to formulate a duly theological hermeneutics which can retrieve the subversive memories of the tradition and criticize and interrogate the actualities of error and systemic distortion in the tradition and situation. We are just beginning to find ways to allow the different concrete personal, social, cultural and political contexts which impinge upon all our work to enter fully into theological reflection itself. That will help us to hear one another again. We are just beginning to allow the mystico-political reality of Christian faith to enter into a conversation serious enough to allow for mutual transformation with the other classic religions (Dhavamony, Cobb) and classic secular, scientific and humanistic and post-humanistic world-views (Toulmin, Habermas). We are just beginning. We are, by any reasonable account, not-yet there.

And as the entry of the crucial adverb 'not-yet' indicates, the sense of the priority of the future over both the present and the past must come to dominate all Christian theological reflection. That is as it should be. It is clearly not the time for the theological community to rest in the present, or to bask in a sense of false self-congratulations on the past. The sense of all that is not-yet is too strong to allow for any such premature and finally immature closure. The signs of the times are once again upon us. These signs are signs of the priority of the future; of possibilities we have not yet dared to imagine; of promises and threats like nuclear holocaust, massive global suffering and oppression, endemic sexism, racism, and ecological disaster we have not yet fully faced; of the full actuality of the always-already-not-yet event of Jesus Christ in our midst.

Origin is not end. Retrospective is not prospective. To propose that what we can most expect is the unexpected is not utopian but cold reality. That much, at least, the honest, troubled strivings and conflicts expressed in the different and often conflicting interpretations in this conference can teach us. We find ourselves open to the future as the unexpected with neither certainty nor security, but with that *docta ignorantia* granted us by the always-already-not-yet event of Jesus Christ.

THE ECUMENICAL SERVICE

SERMON ON THE TEXT MATTHEW 8.20

Walter Jens

'Foxes have holes and birds of the air have nests; but the Son of man has nowhere to lay his head'

(Matt. 8.20).

I am imagining a craftsman somewhere in South Korea, a thoughtful man, arrested for some political offence, who, while he is in prison, reads the New Testament for the first time, line for line, chapter for chapter – provender for long days and longer nights. I am imagining too a woman in Tanzania, advanced in years, who once learnt to read with the help of the Gospels. Finally, I have in my mind's eye a young Sri Lankan Marxist, an unorthodox advocate of socialism – enlisted under Trotsky's banner, not Stalin's – who comes across a little-known but important work of Christian Marxist provenance, which starts him off on an attentive study of the New Testament. The book that so inspires him is Rosa Luxemburg's treatise on 'Church and Socialism', written in 1905 under the pseudonym Chmura ('Cloud'). Stimulated, then, by Chmura, the rosy cloud – meditations about the difference between religion and dogma, biblical humility and what it has to say about equality and brotherhood and ecclesiastical hierarchy – the Trotskyist reads with the same open-mindedness and the same critical, voracious eagerness as the Korean craftsman and the old woman in Tanzania, who by way of the Bible learnt to read: reads the Bible untouched by all the deciphering skills of the theologians – reads it like a story real enough to be possible.

What, I ask myself, will they think, these three readers, for whom the story of the marriage in Cana and the vision of doubting Thomas are spell-binding reading, a 'once upon a time' destitute of all solemn exhortation, because resurrection and a catch of fish, flight and miracle, *a* fig tree and *the* cross, jostle one another on one and the same level; because the dove from heaven is presented with the same prosaic matter-of-factness as the ox in the stall or the bread which – again – can be at once everyday food and sacred provender, crust and wafer.

How homely and how bursting with reality it all seems, they will think, the three of them, and will be able to imagine it all – the desert and the temple, the gnats and the fishing-nets, as clearly as if Jerusalem were not far from Seoul, or in the middle of Africa, or in Sri Lanka: a farmer's similes, fishermen's tales, the catch questions so loved by the intellectuals, the word-twisters of the schools and the party headquarters – all true to life, and translatable from then to now without the slightest trouble.

Sublimity next to the simplest pointer, devout precepts side by side with market gossip, the unassuming, physically concrete smuggled into hymnic spirituality: 'Hallowed be thy name. Thy kingdom come. Thy will be done, on earth as it is in heaven. Forgive us our debts as we have forgiven our debtors. And lead us not into temptation'. 'Strange', they will think, the three of them, who are reading the Gospel for the first time, full of astonishment and pleasurable expectation, with a fresh eye and a healthy pinch of scepticism, 'Strange how consistently here the man praying passes from the holy name to the heavenly kingdom, from God's will to guilt and deliverance, the interplay of heaven and earth, temptation and preservation – and then, quite suddenly, right in the middle: the needs of the body; the need to be satisfied through bread, a reminder of the food which every man and woman needs between morning and evening'. A breath of the down-to-earth in the very middle of talk about the things of the spirit: *give us this day our daily bread*. If they were theologians, the three of them, they would be astonished, in expounding Matthew 5, verses 9 to 13, to find that it is the very central verse whose request is the most modest of all: bread for the day. The material thing are given just that importance which is defined in exemplary fashion in the most spiritually audacious writing known to German literature, Schiller's *Aesthetic Letters*, where he writes: 'A man is little enough

when he has eaten his fill; but eat his fill he must, if his better
nature is to rouse to life'.

Nail and thistle, the soil and the pitcher, the fodder rack and the
rusty hasps: it is the smallest things of all – our three will be
thinking – the quite-evidently-real, which lend the biblical stories
their conviction and make Jesus of Nazareth – this man described
in such concrete individuality – the one whose shadow falls on all
succeeding ages. If he were described as a more 'universal' figure,
as more 'timeless', more 'ubiquitous', that shadow would long
since have lost its contours and its colour, and thereby its own
unique profile, the profile which – quiet though its colours are –
lets him survive where the elevated and the universal pale into
nothingness.

What a strange person, they will say, the three of them: up in
the heavens and down in the dust, close to the clouds but close too
to the lowest things on earth, remote from us, yet as near as a
second skin, born poor, dying in wretchedness, hunted from
childhood up – a man whose peculiarity is evident enough if we
realize all the things he didn't have: the right to be born in his
parents' home, to grow up among friends, to feel at one with
relatives and neighbours, to enjoy market chat and gossip at the
well; marriage and a trade; to grow old among children and
grandchildren; and to die like Abraham, 'old and full of years'.
Jesus the carpenter and teacher of the people, described in Old
Testament style: a resurrected Joseph, perhaps, who, having gone
down to the pit, only endures the descent into hell metaphorically
and, after a short night, is permitted to see a long light.

And now, instead of that, the manger as cradle and the gibbet as
deathbed; instead of that, the road and not the Herodian palace;
instead of that, the common people, the women who were his
hangers-on, the sinners and the semi-crooks, a court more fitted
for Don Quixote and Sancho Panza than for Arthur's knights, the
pure and the polished, in the aura of the Grail. Here there is
boozing and whoring and racketeering. Here people foregather in
darkness, not in light. Here every step is spied on by informants,
Roman and Jewish squealers. Here it's bad luck for the person
whom the great despise and the little people too – for someone at

whom the city people turn up their noses (with Herod Jesus may get by as a clown, at most) and whom the villagers, his own people, would really have liked to make short work of: 'And they rose up and put him out of the city, and led him to the brow of the hill on which their city was built, that they might throw him down headlong'.

Jesus of Nazareth, the three would say (knowing as little about Augustine as about Luther and Bultmann, but knowing all about what it is to be overcome by what one reads – reading in the style of Barlach's monk: engrossed, part of what he reads, spellbound by the present event) . . . Jesus of Nazareth, a son of the night, brother of the stars, not of the sun, was one of us: extolling the weary and heavy laden, because it was to the weary and heavy laden that he belonged; calling blessed the suffering, the persecuted, the peacemakers and the merciful, because he himself belonged on the side of the suffering and persecuted, the peacemakers and the merciful. Consoling the frightened because he was frightened himself. Always alone – forsaken by friends, always in the desert and not in the towns; Jesus the abandoned: while he suffered and lamented and in the end shrieked aloud with pain, round about him they slept and lied and under the heavens held their tongues.

Jesus the miserable: a man who envied the beasts, the foxes and birds, the one who was hunted by the bloodhounds but also by the wildest rumours, and who had to 'get rid of the crowds' in order to pray.

Jesus the guilty one: how many children had to die, our three readers will say, so that one chosen one should survive (and survive to be crucified!). How many people, drawn into the ruinous vortex of this one man, have cursed him, the guiltless one who made himself guilty: the parents, forced to look on as their children were butchered, no less than the raised Lazarus, who perhaps cursed Jesus (our three may think) because he knew how terrible it is to go down to the pit, and that for a second time – thanks to the miracle man: the end of it all, a daily nightmare of death.

Lazarus as Jesus' impeacher – how differently the well-thumbed stories look if we read them from an alien perspective, with the fresh eye of our three characters – if the guilty, suffering, solitary, hunted, threatened and tortured Jesus comes into view: a man who snaps at the rest, 'I implore you not to tell anyone else the miracles I have done'. Someone who falls back defeated when he meets with hostility, as he does in his father's town; someone who weeps and falls dumb – fewer and fewer words and then, at the end, only the cry and the silence.

Jesus the brother, in a world in which Gethsemane and Golgotha are as present as Maidanek and Treblinka – present in the Argentinian death zones, the torture chambers in El Salvador and the labour camps of the Soviet Union. Jesus in the striped jacket, the J on the shabby cloth, Jesus the Jew-boy, fetched home to the reality of the twentieth century. This is not Dostoevsky's parable of the Grand Inquisitor: this Jesus is not hunted out, hunted into freedom. This Jesus would be pushed on to the front of the stage, first to the stone quarry, then into the gas chambers, wrapped round by the incense clouds of cyanide. 'Yes, that's what he looks like, our neighbour', the three readers will say: 'just like this, in a world where there are fewer and fewer people who do *not* experience torture and violent death, the garotting and the final liquidation, as a daily threat.'

And now I ask myself: what are they going to think, the three of them, in South Korea, Tanzania and Sri Lanka, when we tell them that the name of this silenced Jesus with the yellow badge (for he was indeed a Jew, the very personification of abandonment) . . . what will they say, when they hear that the name of this brother and victim is pushed forward today to bolster up power, defend horrors, glorify authority, magnify success, decry fear, disregard poverty? And that his name is made a pretext for these things among his own people, those who call themselves his followers? Jesus of Nazareth, abandoned to ridicule! The powerless one derided in a church of power! The man who overturned the tables of the money-changers, jeered at in a congregation that knows all about the sharemarket and the stock exchange! The advocate of peace booed off the stage by a swarm of clerics, many of whom who – faced by the despairing who ask: 'And if I wanted Jesus to tell me "should I drop the bomb?", what would he say?' – respond with a fatherly nod and an *absolvo te, mi fili*.

Love of our enemies distorted to hate of the wicked, the Sermon on the Mount translated into a balance sheet, the common servants of all split up into the superintendents and the deacons, the popes and the bishops, the curates and the prelates, and a throng of the hoi polloi; authoritarian structures developed out of democratic blueprints; the triumphalism of the victor replacing the sufferings of one who was defeated; an existence made up of honours and high places (the Lord Bishop in the front row, next to the mayor) exchanged for Jesus' role of 'the last' – the last of all, sitting on the stool of repentance, in the dark.

And what is the point of it all? our three readers will ask. Why this domesticization of the poor and fallible Jesus by the representatives of power? Why this separation of Jesus the pleb from his own people? Why is the non-violent one given a place beside the possessors of the instruments of violence? Why is this child of the night made to stand in the sun of prosperity, pomp and success? Why, finally, the million reiterations of Peter's betrayal 'I do not know the man' on the part of the official churches, at a moment when in Latin America martyrs are every minute suffering Jesus' *mors turpissima*?

But I am sure that the three readers will know the answer. They will know why Jesus of Nazareth, abandoned by his own people from that time on, is still hanging on the cross. We find the most human idea that was ever thought unendurable, for that very reason: we cannot endure it because – reversing the traditional system of values – it says that it is only nearness to the cross, only the idea of suffering, and the capacity for suffering *with*, that have anything to tell us about the rank of a human being – the closeness to the night and the desert, to loneliness and despair. It says that for Christians 'defeat' stands for 'dignity', 'powerlessness' is the guarantee of authenticity, 'temptation' apparently the *sine qua non* of faith; that to serve others means much, and to let ourselves be served means less than nothing.

This negation of the puritan system of values is the greatness of Jesus' great reversal. It is a negation that makes a mockery of success in the sense of 'you are what you have', and shows up the complacency of Christian politicians for what it is: diabolical. Where the first have not become the last, Jesus the brother is still outside the door.

And it is just this that 'the first' are very well aware of, our three readers will conclude. That is why they are afraid of the Nazarene. And because they are afraid of him – him, the Son of man, who is the *alter ego* of millions of tortured people – they turn him into their accomplice, make the maltreated Jesus (and with him the suffering Father) participate in their victories on the battlefield or the field of diplomacy; while by way of the Christ of the church's Councils – that second figure of the Trinity, about whom one can talk so urbanely and so knowledgeably – they push the Man of Sorrows out of sight. 'Dogmas', says Karl Marti, 'imprison him; power stretches him on the cross; definitions nail him down; churches raise him high.'

But our three readers will not lift their eyes to the victorious banner of the church. They know where to look for the resting-place of one who called the foxes blessed because they have holes, and birds because they have nests. That resting-place is not in the heights. It is in the midst of us. In dust, blood and wretchedness, Jesus of Nazareth, with the crown of thistles, the red paper cloak and the yellow star marked J, takes on the majesty of the beggar whom the mighty fear because he, who is without a home, is for that very reason omnipresent. He is the brother who holds, not the sword of justice, but the broken mirror, the glass that reflects us and – clouded and dusty as it is – becomes our judgment: *But the Son of man has nowhere to lay his head.*

INDEX OF NAMES